D0930060

'7 6

B

I SANG THE
UNSINGABLE

BETHANY BEARDSLEE
WITH MINNA ZALLMAN PROCTOR

I SANG THE
UNSINGABLE

MY LIFE IN TWENTIETH-CENTURY MUSIC

UNIVERSITY OF ROCHESTER PRESS

The University of Rochester Press gratefully acknowledges generous support
from the Howard Hanson Institute for American Music at the Eastman School
of Music at the University of Rochester and the John Daverio Endowment of the
American Musicological Society, funded in part by the National Endowment for
the Humanities and the Andrew W. Mellon Foundation.

Copyright © 2017 by Bethany Beardslee and Minna Zallman Proctor

First published 2017

University of Rochester Press
668 Mt. Hope Avenue, Rochester, NY 14620, USA
www.urpress.com
and Boydell & Brewer Limited
PO Box 9, Woodbridge, Suffolk IP12 3DF, UK
www.boydellandbrewer.com

ISBN-13: 978-1-58046-900-5

*This work is a memoir. The experiences and conversations recounted here are the
result of the author's recollection and are rendered as a subjective accounting of
events that occurred in her life. Her perceptions and opinions are entirely her own
and do not represent those of the publisher or sponsors.*

Library of Congress Cataloging-in-Publication Data

Names: Beardslee, Bethany, author. | Proctor, Minna, author.
Title: I sang the unsingable : my life in twentieth-century music / Bethany
    Beardslee with Minna Zallman Proctor.
Description: Rochester : University of Rochester Press, 2017. | Includes
    bibliographical references and index.
Identifiers: LCCN 2017026561 | ISBN 9781580469005 (hardcover : alk. paper)
Subjects: LCSH: Beardslee, Bethany. | Sopranos (Singers)—United States—
    Biography.
Classification: LCC ML420.B213 A3 2017 | DDC 782.42168092 [B] —dc23 LC
    record available at https://lccn.loc.gov/2017026561

This publication is printed on acid-free paper.
Printed in the United States of America.

To all "girl singers," past, present, and future,
for keeping alive the music of their time.

CONTENTS

ACKNOWLEDGMENTS

This book would not have been possible without my goddaughter, Minna. A thousand thanks and my deepest gratitude. I also would like to thank Faith Compo, who listened to my early attempts and gave me her insights on the book's early beginnings. I wish to thank Robin Cherry, who interviewed me and researched those very beginnings. Unless otherwise indicated, all photographs are from my personal collection. The European American Music Distributors Company kindly granted permission to reprint here extracts from Webern's *Five Canons*, Schoenberg's Three Songs, and Schoenberg's *Erwartung*.

I guess none of the events would have happened if Jacques Monod had not appeared that May night in 1950, and to him I wish to extend heartfelt thanks.

—BB

To be honest, I never believed that my life would lead me into a world of contemporary classical music. I never imagined that I would marry a composer, then another composer. That Milton Babbitt would compose Philomel for me. That I would premiere music by Stravinsky, and would stand in Carnegie Hall one day and sing orchestral songs by Anton Webern. As a child growing up in Lansing, Michigan, I played tennis, dreamed of movie stars, and danced to Glenn Miller. I may or may not have had the career I was supposed to have, sung the music I was supposed to have sung, or the music I dreamed of singing, but I think I was destined to sing.

PART ONE

CHILDHOOD
(1925–50)

Figure 1. Nanette Montier and me at Duck Lake, ca. 1928.

CHAPTER ONE

CHRISTMAS 1925

For so much of my career I sang music that people described as diffi- cult, experimental, even unsingable. And though I didn't start out life with a knack for the unconventional, I learned to understand it, interpret it, and eventually love it. My life story, however, starts—as so many lives do—conventionally. How else would it start for the "girl singer" from East Lansing? I was born on Christmas Day, 1925, the first baby in the brand- new Sparrow Hospital of Lansing, Michigan. It was an auspicious enough distinction that my picture was published in the newspaper. The nurses told my mother that I must be named Bethany; I was a Christmas baby, after all. I've long thought that being born on a joyous holiday filled with music was a good omen, and when people hear that my birthday lands on Christmas, it somehow always makes them smile.

My mother was already forty when I was born, and since my older brother Perry, born two and half years earlier, was handicapped because of complications during delivery, she was rather anxious about having an- other baby. I arrived safely, and my older sister, Helen, was delighted at last to have a sister after three brothers. She made Bill, Walter, and Perry all troop down to the hospital to meet their new sister with her. My father, Walter Beardslee, went on a spree and bought my mother a beautiful dia- mond ring as a present.

Lansing was a typical midwestern town, graced by one special feature: It was the state capital. Our capitol building, like so many at that time, was a replica of the Capitol building in Washington, DC, but with a beauti- ful park extending around it, and it symbolized Lansing's prominence.

Otherwise, Lansing was an industrial town, home of the car industry, primarily Oldsmobile and Fisher Body. The headquarters of Ford Motors and General Motors were in Detroit, about fifty miles southeast. In those days, it was the burgeoning car industry that made Michigan such a prosperous state.

In those flush, pre-Depression years, my father had joined some other families from Albion and Lansing to purchase a cluster of cottages at Duck Lake, a small lake less than an hour south of Lansing. I remember those early summers at Duck Lake. In fact, probably my earliest memory was the sound of lapping waves on the shore of the lake.

Every summer, the very same day that school recessed, Mom packed the Hupmobile with enough groceries for a week, plus our luggage filled with summer clothes, and off we went. There were eight of us in all: my parents, my three brothers, Bill, Walter, Perry, my sister Helen, me the baby, and Laddie, our German shepherd. Our Hupmobile sedan, the coach to Duck Lake, was a grand, luxurious car. It had four doors and was completely handmade. The windows had curtains with pull-down cords embellished with tassels. The seats were upholstered in crushed velvet. The roof and sides were also soft velvet, like the seats. Spare tires were mounted in the front fenders, and of course there was a huge running board by which to get in and out of the car. There was a square trunk attached at the back for luggage. It was a shiny black with chrome trimming everywhere. My father kept it spotless.

Father always drove, as women seldom were allowed to drive back then. When we arrived we were greeted by the Stablers, Blacks, Montiers, and Burtons—all the families with cottages near us.

The cottages at Duck Lake were modest and close together, hugging the shore. Ours was a white clapboard cottage with window boxes that Mom filled with colorful pink petunias facing the morning sun. Downstairs was a living room with a large stone fireplace. Off it was a screen porch with a big swing. The kitchen was to the left of the front door and the dining room to the right. The upstairs sleeping quarters consisted of one large open space for my brothers and sister, fashioned with three-quarter wood dividers. I was in a small crib with my parents, who had a proper enclosed bedroom, also on the second floor. In Bill's section, there was a huge poster of Lindbergh's flight over the Atlantic in 1927. The screened-in porch downstairs holds the deepest memory for me: the lapping of the lake, its patter lulling me to sleep.

Those were bucolic days of swimming, tennis, and being pulled in a red wagon by my brother Walter, or playing with Nanette Montier, who

Figure 2. The house at Duck Lake. *Left to right:* Clyde Burton, Helen, Bill, Mother, and Father.

was also three. Every house had its own dock. We favored birch canoes and flat bottom rowboats for fishing—Duck Lake, after all, was only a mile across.

Helen was a wonderful swimmer. She could swim across the lake and back with Bill following closely in a canoe to watch over her—which he did, I'm sure, at Mom's insistence. Perry was watched over by Laddie. Laddie was a beautiful German shepherd, buff colored, with a white chest with a slight sprinkling of black on his back. (He was hired out to the movies once for *Strongheart*—about a movie dog like Rin Tin Tin.) If Perry waded out too far, near the sudden drop-off that was fifty feet from the shore, Laddie would swim out and pull him back, tugging his one-piece bathing suit until Perry was safe on shore.

My brother Bill, competitive and handsome, was older than me by sixteen years and in love with Jane Stabler, whom we all assumed he would marry. My beautiful sister, Helen, was nine years older and seemed always to have been in love with her high school sweetheart, John Maynard, of a wealthy Lansing family: His father was the manager of the Lansing J. C. Penney. My brother Walter, named after my father, was my hero because of his gentle, kind nature. He was the middle child—ten years old when I was three—too young to be with Helen and Bill's friends and too old for Perry and me. Perry was named for Commodore Perry. It is an interesting

Figure 3. Me at Duck Lake. Our cottage is on the left.

bit of Beardslee family lore that our distant relation Admiral Beardslee accompanied Commodore Matthew C. Perry in his forays into Japan in the 1850s. Admiral Beardslee returned to Japan years later and had a monument erected for Commodore Perry.

I can vaguely remember the dance hall where my oldest brother Bill, Jane Stabler, and my sister Helen would go dancing. At night it seemed almost magical, all aglow with old-fashioned Japanese lanterns, everyone doing the foxtrot and all the popular dance trends of the twenties.

There were no stores nearby at the lake, so we'd make do with the groceries that Mom had packed for most of the week. Joe Poor, the iceman, would arrive in the morning with a huge block of ice slung over his shoulder and gently deposit it into our wooden metal-lined icebox, where it would last two days at most. Then Mr. Darrow might drop by, leaving pike and sunfish from his morning catch. Mom immediately cleaned the fish to be ready for dinner that night. At last, on Friday night, Dad would arrive from Lansing with the Hupmobile loaded with a new supply of groceries.

Walter has told me that these were great times for our family, those long days of carefree, happy living. When Labor Day weekend arrived, we sadly packed up our things and said goodbye to our summer paradise. For me, however, it was short lived. I was only three when Dad sold the cottage in 1928.

It was the Roaring Twenties, and my father played the stock market like everyone else. He'd done well, and one day came home and said, "Ella, I bought you a house!" It was on East St. Joseph Street, or as we all called it East St. Joe Street, in an upscale neighborhood of tree-lined streets and stately homes. The house was a beautiful Greek revival with a wide front porch flanked by four towering white Doric columns and was built around 1860 for John Kerr, a newspaperman and former mayor. It was one of the first fine residences in Lansing. The neighborhood is now called Old Lansing, but back then it was a proper family neighborhood. Ransom E. Olds Anderson of the Oldsmobile dynasty lived two blocks from us. Malcolm X lived on the other side of town, on West St. Joe Street in the African American neighborhood near the auto factories. The Martindales lived around the corner, and Charlie Martindale and Walter were close friends. The Pletzers lived next door and the Morans just down the block. I went to the Cherry Street School, a few blocks from where we lived, from kindergarten to third grade.

Dad was a homebody, and he really *curated* our house. With his brother Jay, who was an interior decorator, he chose everything with great attention—from the imported French wallpaper in the front hall to the furniture. We had a huge, deep-blue jacquard davenport, Chippendale dining-room furniture, and two beautiful sideboards for my mother's candelabra, silver, and good china. Mom insisted we have a baby grand piano, which stood in a corner of our living room. Pianos were household items in those days. Helen took lessons on it, but I was so young then that jumping on the davenport and doing headstands seemed far more important.

Lansing was in an agricultural area in the state of Michigan. Every day at noon, WKAR (the college radio station) would play John Philip Sousa marches and report on the weather and other agricultural data for the farmers. My father, being born on a farm, was always interested in the farmers' report. We had no record player, and so the whole family would listen to the radio together in the evenings before and after supper. *Tom Mix, The Lone Ranger, Inner Sanctum*, and the *National Farm and Home Hour* were favorites. Saturday afternoons my mother listened to the Metropolitan Opera, and Sunday night was the *Voice of Firestone*. There was classical music occasionally on the radio but not often.

Sitting in his chair, smoking a pipe, and reading the *Lansing State Journal*, our one local newspaper, was my father's idea of true contentment. He made wonderful fires during the winter and I was happy to sprawl out on the living-room floor and read the comics. My favorites were *Prince Valiant, Dagwood and Blondie, Dick Tracy, Mutt and Jeff*. I would cozy up

Figure 4. The house at 213 East St. Joseph Street, Lansing. Photograph by David Caterino, August 31, 1985. Courtesy of the Caterino Real Estate Collection, Forest Parke Library and Archives, Capital Area District Libraries.

to Laddie on our oriental rug near the warmth of the fire. Laddie originally was Bill's dog, but he became mine when Bill left for Annapolis. Laddie even walked me to school—my constant companion.

My parents shared a love of gardening, and our house was surrounded by beautiful gardens. There was a rock garden next to the house and two long gardens bordering each side of the back lawn next to the barn. We had a grape arbor with swings at each end, and a large screened porch with a canvas glider where I rocked myself to sleep on hot summer afternoons. The house on 213 East St. Joe was our castle.

My mother, Ella Simpson, was a true Victorian in every sense of the word. She was born in 1885 and died in 1985. There were six children. Her father, William Simpson, had been the district court judge in Au Sable, Michigan and had also been quite successful in the lumber business. Mom said their home was the first one in Au Sable to have electric lights. The home was well-to-do, with servants, music, and genteel manners.

On Sundays, this Victorian family would traditionally gather around the piano in the music room to sing. Both my mother's father and her brother Robert had beautiful tenor voices, and all of the girls knew how to play the piano. Although Aunty Inez, the oldest, usually was the pianist, Aunty Irene, the youngest, was the most musical. Later Irene would earn her living playing piano for silent films in the days before talkies—until she got married. She never had lessons and played by ear. But because the Simpsons fell on hard times after Grandpa Simpson went deaf and had to step down from the bench, Irene wasn't able to go to college as her older sisters had. My mother and Aunty Inez went to Oberlin College for two years to study music, mainly voice and piano. In those days just after the turn of the century, two years was considered sufficient college education for a young lady.

My father, on the other hand, was a self-made man. His parents were farmers who came from Pontiac, Michigan. He never went to college and, as the oldest of four, began working as a window dresser at Arbaugh's department store in Lansing as soon as he left high school. He went on to work in the advertising department of Arbaugh's—before he had made enough playing the stock market to stop working. That was all before the crash, of course.

Figure 5. My mother with her mother, ca. 1901.

Even though we all inherited his blond hair and blue, blue eyes, I never knew Grandpa Elmer Beardslee. I didn't know my Great-grandfather Walters either, but my grandmother Margaret Walters Beardslee was a remarkable figure—a modern woman, well ahead of her time. Her family, the Walterses, had a large farm and were well-to-do. There is still a Walters Lake in Pontiac today. Grandma Beardslee always managed her own affairs and had a reassuring manner: "Don't worry, you can count on me." She definitely wore the pants in her marriage. Her love was baking, and on her visits she made us delicious sugar cookies the size of a large silver dollar. Grandma Beardslee wore her long hair in a bun and never took off her corset—she didn't feel she was properly dressed without it. She was practical and thrifty, and always had a large black purse near by, which as a little girl

Figure 6. Grandma Beardslee at the farm with her big black purse.

I assumed held all her worldly treasures. She was not a churchgoer but had an amazing, silent nature, and I don't think she ever cried or got upset even during the difficult times of the Great Depression. Through the years she skillfully sold off farmland from her holdings to help her children. She quietly helped put one grandchild, my cousin Evans Noyes, through medical school. Like many Victorians, after her husband died, Grandma Beardslee went to live with her daughter, my aunt Katherine, and her husband, Uncle Charles Noyes. She lived with them until she died, for in those days that was normal. A nursing home was unimaginable for my grandparents. They expected to be cared for by their children.

I loved visiting my cousin Evans Noyes in nearby Owosso, Michigan. Aunty Katherine was extremely beautiful, and Uncle Charles Noyes liked taking family pictures. I presume there wouldn't be any pictures at all if he hadn't been around. This Christmas photo at our home in Lansing is one of my favorites. I'm holding my two Raggedy Ann Dolls. You can see how our house filled up with relatives for the holidays.

My uncle Jay, Dad's brother, lived in Detroit and was, as I mentioned, an interior decorator who worked for Woods Ltd., a well-known English interior-decorating firm. Many of the clients, Henry Ford among them, were from Grosse Pointe. So Dad had Uncle Jay's expertise to draw on. They were both born with impeccable taste. Uncle Jay and Aunt Verna would drive up from Detroit to visit on weekends with Lady, their pure white German shepherd dog. I hated Lady. She never got along with Laddie, and she would growl whenever children were around. When I was little, I often

Figure 7. Christmas at 213 East St. Joe, ca. 1930. *Standing from top left:* Uncle Carl, Mom, Helen, Grandma Beardslee, Aunt Katherine, Father; *seated:* Uncle Jay and Aunt Verna with their dog, Lady; *the children:* Perry, Cousin Evans, me, Walter, and Bill, with our dog, Laddie.

wondered why Aunt Verna didn't have children. She was very pretty and clothes conscious, but never lifted a finger to help Mom on those weekend visits. They bought a new car every year. I guess they could live in "Detroit auto style," not having five children to feed, like my father.

I never heard Mom swear. She abhorred crudeness but loved to whistle when puttering around the house. This was a sign she was in a good mood. Her idea of escape was reading, and she always seemed to have her nose in a book. My mother would rather read than cook—and often did. I can still hear my father at the table asking every night, "Ella, where is the salt?!" because she was too distracted by the story she'd just read or the book she wanted to get back to, to remember to put out the salt. That said, we always ate with a complete table setting: damask tablecloths, folded damask napkins, and lovely china. Appearances and a genteel lifestyle were important to her. She emphasized correct table manners and politeness with us—they were character forming. Mother didn't *put on* airs; she *was* airs.

Whether my parents were passionately in love at one time, I'll never know. I always remember my parents as rather old. That may be why I have no memories of them embracing like newlyweds and never saw my father horsing around with my brothers. Mom relied on the security that my father would always take care of her. And yet, I have the feeling it was my mother who held my father together emotionally. He had the imagination and creative instinct, and she was practical and down-to-earth. Dad was highly emotional and would tear up when he heard me sing. Mother's feelings for my father were marked by loyalty, devotion to her children, and support for him during trying times. A Victorian woman did as she was told. Dad always wore business suits and would kiss Mother politely on the cheek when he left for work.

CHAPTER TWO

THE GREAT
DEPRESSION

I was only four when the stock market crashed in October 1929. A great deal of *my* childhood was circumscribed by the Great Depression. Father lost everything—a considerable fortune. He had refused to get out of the market even when my mother, who was paying attention to news from across the country that there was trouble in the economy, pleaded with him. My father felt it was his patriotic duty to stay in the market. "I won't betray my country," he said. Instead he cashed in a $250,000 life insurance policy (a considerable amount in those days) and held on as long as he could, which was far too long. He held out until everything was gone.

Those years left a mark on me. My parents seemed to suddenly grow still older in my eyes. Mother stopped wearing beautiful clothes and always had a concerned look on her face—no doubt she had reason to worry, about Perry and about my father. It was the beginning of hard times for us, and my father's fuse was very short. Dad yelled a lot, and I became expert at not hearing him. I remember my mother giving him the silent treatment when he got angry. Her ladylike poise meant that she wouldn't *stoop* to arguing. I would do anything to escape my father's wrath. Only four years old, I spent a lot of time across the street at Ronny Aiken's house, where it was quiet and serene. I'd run over there all by myself whenever I heard Father start yelling. Ronny lived with his grandmother, who we called "Gaumps." I loved her and loved it there. Gaumps's kitchen was full of laughter and cookies with milk. That little-girl behavior of not hearing, or simply leaving, became part of my personality. Even now, I'll walk away from arguments, just stop listening. I simply hated confrontation.

Figure 8. My father, ca. 1900.

I was too young, of course, to understand Dad's stress and the fact that we might be forced to sell our beautiful, big home. When I think now, ninety years later, about his yelling, I realize it probably would have been unmanly for a man to cry about our state of affairs. So he yelled. But my mother just seemed to ride through it all. I have always been frugal with money because of these early memories. The impressions they left seem impossible to erase.

I couldn't possibly have understood all of the pressures on my father. He didn't just take care of us but also helped support his brother Carl. Uncle Carl lived in Lansing, too, had a family to take care of, and was chronically unemployed. He could not hold a job and seemed simply to be unlucky in everything he tried, even trucking. Once he drove a truck of grapefruits from Florida to Michigan, and they rotted along the way— doubtless this was before they had refrigerated trucks. Uncle Carl was a melancholy man and always in need of Dad's help. I don't think he ever smiled. He wore his apologetic sadness on his face all the time. Life for him was a shackle to be endured. Meanwhile, Dad had to feed his large family and not lose our home.

The Great Depression hit Lansing especially hard. So many autoworkers were laid off. We had breadlines like any other city. However, our family was lucky in some ways. My brother Bill had just graduated from Annapolis with an engineering degree. An engineer from Annapolis must have been an attractive prospect for an employer even in those extreme times. Bill found a position at Oldsmobile right after graduation and began contributing to the family. My father, too, returned to his old job at Arbaugh's Department Store. Frank Arbaugh was one of Dad's old friends. Dad's salary was reduced from what it had been but he was thankful to have a job. My father did the layouts for Arbaugh's ads, which then ran in the *Lansing State Journal*. My father was a perfectionist and did meticulous, time-consuming work. His script, done freehand, would shame a teacher of the Palmer Method (the way we were taught penmanship in those days)—it was so beautiful. He designed the weekly sale ads, pasting pictures of the merchandise and words to the templates.

Arbaugh's was the largest department store in Lansing at the time, and I thought it was magnificent. It had a mezzanine, an elevator with wooden paneling, and pneumatic tubes that whisked away your money (cash, of course—there were no credit cards back then) up to the accounting department. Your change came speeding back through the tubes along with a receipt. All of the clerks wore white paper wrist cuffs in handling merchandise. Arbaugh's was only a few blocks from where we lived. Sometimes when I visited Dad at his office on my way home from school, I would find Laddie under his desk. It was apparently common to see Laddie walk into the store, take the elevator directly up to Dad's office on the third floor, and wait there until it was time to go home.

If you've gone through the Great Depression, it changes you. It makes you frugal, so fearful of being poor that you get angry with people who waste money. In a way though, I think there is nothing worse than being "proudly poor." My mother was proud. She snubbed the lower classes and didn't want to be made to feel as if she were part of them. But although we lived in this beautiful house, we were as poor as church mice.

Throughout the Depression, my mother continued to set the table with damask tablecloths and napkins. Our best china came out for Sunday dinner. My mother was holding on to the illusion of those better days, those glorious days, trying to keep the family's spirits positive. And yet the memories are painful.

I remember taking canned goods for the poor to the movie theater downtown when I was six or seven. If you brought food, you got free admission to watch cartoons—the Katzenjammer Kids, Popeye, Mickey Mouse, and so on. Movies became a haven, a flight from hard times. Life was wondrous in the world of make-believe, and Hollywood was an escape for everyone—until you emerged from the theater into the harsh light of day and the reality it illuminated.

There is an old photo of me from when I was about nine years old. I'm looking down and have a sad expression. My hair is Dutch-boy bobbed, not particularly flattering, and I'm wearing one of my sister's smocked dresses. I often study it and think, "I wonder what she's thinking?" She's me. That little girl from long ago had no idea what life had in store for her. What was on her mind that day? What made her sad? There are more old school photos where I stand with my head tilted, and though the other children are smiling, I'm not. I wore my sister's hand-me-downs—a blue sweater and plaid skirt I wore so many times to school that eventually they could have walked to school beside me. Coming home for lunch was pretty much the same as wearing old clothes: my mother's homemade vegetable soup, day in and day out. Actually, Mother's soup was extremely nutritious, but boring every day.

There were good memories too, of course. I recall specific moments. My father's homemade vanilla ice cream. Grandma Beardslee's delicious sugar cookies, which we stole from the pantry. The laziness of Sunday after

Figure 9. In the garden at East St. Joe Street, ca. 1934.

noons. Relatives visiting in their Sunday best, and Mom's burned pot roast. The shape my father's body made when he bent over to tend the length of flower gardens behind our stately home. Lying as a child in the smell of warm, newly mown grass. Lemonade on hot summer afternoons, served by mother on our side porch with its wicker furniture and the canvas glider where I rocked myself. Listening to the comforting murmur of my parents' voices coming from downstairs as I fell asleep. The smell of my father when I would sit in his lap as a small child, as he read the evening paper and smoked his pipe. My mother's insistence on good manners, her love of reading, and her whistling while doing her housework. Reading the comics by the fire with Laddie beside me. My father doing the dishes with my mother after supper and then cleaning off the stove with the perfection he put into everything. Mom's delicious canned fruits, the fabulous ice cream sodas at Rexall's drug store downtown, and huge choices of penny candy at Sam's neighborhood grocery, just a block from where we lived.

Dad loved Sunday drives in our Hupmobile, and he loved scouting properties. I can still hear him: "Now look at that house, Ella—I think it has real possibilities." Of course, from my mother's perspective, he was talking about a rundown shack. But she would smile and nod. My father never tired of looking at property—a pleasure I seem to have inherited. Perry and I were always in the back seat enjoying these Hupmobile rides, knowing that Dad would eventually pull into the A&W Root Beer stand on Washington Avenue and St. Joe Street. There we had a large delicious glass mug of root beer with the foam high and running over the top.

I remember one afternoon in particular: my father took me to see *Gone with the Wind*. I must have been fourteen years old. He knew that it was an important historical film about the Civil War and the effect it had on the South. Afterward, we had dinner in a Chinese restaurant, and he told me how our Grandpa Simpson had fought in the Civil War as a young man. I felt very grown up having Father all to myself.

My mother was a devout Episcopalian. All of us had to go to church, no matter how loudly we objected. Father stayed home with Perry and always forgot to turn off Sunday's dinner—meaning pot roast. Thus, many a burned pot roast!

Until much later, when I began to sing in the church choir, going to church was a bore and filled my childish imagination with all the sins I had committed during the week—stealing cookies from the pantry, taking pennies from my mother's kitchen change to go buy penny candy at Sam's grocery store. I was a sensitive child and believed everything the minister said about moral behavior.

CHAPTER THREE

EAST LANSING

In the end, we did lose our beautiful home on 213 East St. Joe Street the year I turned ten. I never learned the particulars, but I suspect it was a foreclosure. The family moved to East Lansing, a small middle-class suburb, scarcely three miles from Lansing and closer to my mother's sister Irene and Uncle Wesley Ceeley. East Lansing centered around the Michigan State College of Applied Science and Agriculture, as it was known in those days. Now it is Michigan State University. Mother, of course, was delighted, as she wanted all of us to have a college education. We rented a small house on Michigan Avenue that we called the "house with the eyebrows," because of the black, curved upper trim framing the front windows. Despite the cramped bedrooms, and the fact that I had to share a bed with my sister, there were things that I came to love about living there. One of those things was Mother's enclosed porch off the living room. It was sunlit and filled with houseplants. For me, it felt like a secret garden.

We stayed in that house for only two years before moving to the second of what would be a succession of five homes. It was in that second house on Christmas morning, 1938, my thirteenth birthday, that my father gave me a beautiful blue Columbia bicycle. As was his way, my father had chosen for me the finest bicycle made, complete with every bell and whistle. It had chrome fenders, a streamlined front horn light, an instrument panel that told the speed, coaster brakes, a luggage rack, and stringed webbing around the back wheel so your skirt would not get tangled. I can still see that bike and remember the feeling of being overwhelmed that Christmas morning. I had never had a lot of toys and knew my father had made a real sacrifice to give me that bike. Yes, my best present ever and a major life event I've never forgotten. I kept that bike for a very long time. It became my transport to school and later to college.

We'd congregate on our bikes in the middle of the street to decide what to do. There were hardly any cars, so we owned the neighborhood sidewalks and streets, entirely unconcerned about bumping into anything but each other! My new bike was my status symbol, and I kept it immaculate.

By the time we were in the second house, I'd turned into a real tomboy. We rode our families' discarded Christmas trees like horses. Wearing an old cape around my shoulders, I pretended to be Errol Flynn in *Robin Hood*. We could look behind and see the tracks that our tree-horses left in the snow. We'd charge at each other, brandishing make-believe cardboard swords. We dared each other to jump off the second-floor porch of my house into a huge bush. Betty Hilding was my best tomboy friend. Al Larkin, who lived next door, was the organizer of games and my hero. His younger sister Cynthia was such a crybaby, but we had to put up with her for Al's sake. Burt and Kenny Edelson and the Theroux children were also part of the gang for everything from football to throwing snowballs and building forts.

I played a mean game of marbles, and I took excellent care of my colorful glass marble collection, including two aggies (shooters). I kept them in a cloth bag tied with a string. We'd clear a spot of ground and dig out a hole in the center with the heels of our shoes. We'd line the marbles around the hole and then bring the aggies into action. I'd spin marbles into the hole with an unerring eye and thumb.

I kept a scrapbook with cutouts of all my favorite movie stars. I was in love with Robin Hood (Errol Flynn) and Marie Antoinette (Norma Shearer) and all her beautiful dresses and hairdos. Those were the days of movie heroes and starlit heroines. One of our gang, Gloria Loudenslager, subscribed to *Photoplay* and *Modern Screen*, and she always passed them on to the rest of us when she was done reading. We'd all gather on Gloria's front steps for long summer afternoons, mooning over our favorite movie stars, charting our Hollywood careers and our leading men.

That summer we had to put Laddie to sleep. Laddie was not only an exceptional dog and family member since before I was born, but he'd always been Perry's protector. He'd been shot several years earlier after chasing a neighbor's cat (though we never really found out the specifics). The bullet lodged so close to his heart that the veterinarian had to leave an opening in his chest to drain the wound. As he aged and got more arthritic, he was in constant pain. "It was the merciful thing to do," said Mother. I wept, and after that Mother refused to get another pet.

It was 1939, and our country was slowly recovering from the Depression. Father had a new job as manager of the Merchant's Association in Lansing. I am not sure what he did exactly, but the job suited him. Many business-men knew Daddy, and he was well liked. After all, he had been in the retail business over twenty-five years. During the same period, we moved *again*, back to Michigan Avenue. By this time Mother was so tired of moving, she just couldn't face it and took to her bed. So the rest of us, especially my sister Helen, did all the packing and unpacking.

The house on Michigan Avenue was close to a town park where I played tennis all summer long with broken-down tennis racquets and balls that had seen better days. My best friend that summer was Pat Hayes, whose father ran a business that involved S&H Green Stamps, which you collected at the register when you bought groceries or gas-oline to redeem for merchandise. It was a new selling gimmick that merchants were using to promote their goods. You could exchange the little books filled with stamps for any kind of housewares or appliances. I think Mother actually used them to get some glassware and pots and pans for the kitchen.

Winters, I ice-skated, pretending to be the Olympic figure skater and movie star Sonja Henie. In those days skating ponds were iced-over fields the town opened to the public. They were full of potholes, and you took many a spill. There was usually a small shack with benches where you could warm yourself around a kerosene stove. I would skate until dark. Then I took up roller-skating and learned all the various skate dances. Mother put a stop to it because she didn't want me going to the roller rink and associat-ing with the riffraff. Yet she never came down to the rink herself to see that there was nothing to make such a fuss about!

Helen was going to be married. She was engaged to her high-school sweet-heart, John Maynard, and the wedding was planned for right after she graduated from Michigan State. The new house on Michigan Avenue had a large porch with a table piled high with wedding gifts. Mother and Helen totally immersed themselves in the preparations. Dad didn't involve him-self at all, but I assume he paid for the whole affair. I had always idolized Helen and was so proud to be in her wedding procession wearing my first long gown, not as a bridesmaid, but the next step down—whatever that is. When I saw my sister come down the aisle of our church I couldn't believe anyone could be so beautiful. Then the new bride and groom left for Dartmouth, New Hampshire where John was finishing his final year at Dartmouth College.

Figure 10. My sister Helen.

Throughout my childhood, my sister, nine years older, inhabited a world apart from mine. Her friends were from wealthy families, and she had always traveled in that milieu. Unconsciously, as a little girl, I saw through her a world I could never be part of. It was my mother and Helen's world, and I didn't feel as if I belonged. That transparent barrier became part of my inner self—an interior sense of how you move through the world that is a reflection of early life experiences and clings to you forever.

It was in that house on Michigan Avenue where I became entranced by the beauty of classical music. We had a roomer that year who had a record player. He'd play Tchaikovsky and Berlioz, but there was one album in particular that he just played over and over again—side 1, flip, side 2, flip back to 1—Rimsky-Korsakov's *Scheherazade* and the *Great Russian Easter Overture*. Every time I heard that music start up, I'd creep up to his door and sit quietly on the floor in the hallway to listen. I simply loved the orchestral sounds. Strangely enough, I had no idea what I was listening to and wouldn't learn those titles until much later.

Of course, I also loved the big bands. My favorite was Glenn Miller, and then there were Tommy Dorsey, Duke Ellington, and Benny Goodman. I adored the Modernaires and Ella Fitzgerald. Not only did Ella have an irresistible rhythm but there was a happiness in her voice—even when she was singing a sad ballad. She just never sounded sad! This was my American culture. I was brought up on the popular music that was playing on the radio and jukeboxes—the music I shared with my high school friends. We sang the songs and danced to the music. We wore saddle shoes, short skirts, and cardigans with dickies, and we jitterbugged.

My brother Walt was a wonderful dancer. I would watch him glide smoothly over the dance floor with my cousin Connie Ceeley—also a beautiful dancer. Certain boys were always in demand if they knew "the steps."

By the time I was going to high school, we'd moved yet again, to a Spanish-style house on Grand River Avenue. Poor Mother—she'd really had it with all the moving! But on Grand River Avenue, I had my own bedroom for the first time. And this house had an upstairs terrace where I could sit in our old canvas glider from East St. Joe Street and read. That summer I read Romain Rolland's *Jean-Christophe*, and then I read *Anna Karenina*—I was hooked on the classics. But I was also, alas, an adolescent, which meant I read countless pasty romance novels, too.

Our family was shrinking. Bill and Helen were both married, and now it was just my parents, Walter, Perry, and me. Walter had just started Michigan State College and was working at the college power plant to earn spending money. I was babysitting to earn my saddle-shoe money. By then, I simply took it for granted that I would always wear hand-me-downs from my sister and then, later when I was in college, from Cousin Nancy Ceeley.

In tenth grade, Margo Greene became my favorite friend and confidante. She was an only child being raised by her mother, who worked at the State Capitol Building in Lansing. Margo and I spent a lot of time together talking endlessly about our hopes, aspirations, and, naturally, about the opposite sex. We passed notes during study hour—a hefty correspondence about the boys we liked. I was in love with Tommy King, a senior who played basketball, as well as "Rabbitt" Reisser, also a basketball player. Our romances were all conducted on a purely imaginative plane. I was dreadfully shy and Margo was even more shy. Really, she was *my* support system, as she never admitted to her own crushes. And I was really beginning to bloom. I fussed over my hair, wore lipstick, and would contrive to shyly pass whichever "boyfriend" I'd set my sights on in the hall at school. Between classes I'd always dash into the girls' restroom to check my face. That was critical. You never knew when you might run into *him*. Doesn't that all sound familiar! I was a healthy American teenager.

I wasn't a provincial girl, though. I knew there was a world outside of Lansing. My favorite class senior year was civics with Mr. Draper. We'd read the local paper and discuss all the news of the day. We'd parse the editorials and ended up having some lively debates in class—often about the war, now that the United States had gotten involved, and how it touched our lives. For example, East Lansing High School was a public school, and because of war shortages, unable to go through with plans to get a new football field.

At the time, I'd also started taking piano lessons with the unfortunate Mrs. Scholl, East Lansing's local piano teacher. Mrs. Scholl quickly recognized how inept I was at the piano and would spend my lessons filing her nails, and then collect her money. Those were painful hours for me and they must have been deadly boring for her.

Our chorus teacher, Miss Weissinger, was the first person ever to recognize that I could sing. My senior year in high school she gave me the lead in the school operetta *The Count and the Co-ed* (a deviation from her usual Gilbert and Sullivan repertoire). Connie Hutty usually got all the solos and leads, so getting the lead that year also marked an important conquest for me!

My leading man was Johnny Hays, who was one of the funniest, most brilliant, and original guys in our class. Johnny would have gone on to be successful in anything he tried, but he was killed in the war on D-Day. He was our first classmate to die, and it was an unspeakable loss.

Something very important happened the day after the performance of *The Count and the Co-ed*. All of a sudden people—even boys—were stopping me in the hallway, coming up and talking to me and complimenting my singing. I felt special and started thinking that maybe I had a talent. More important, the fact that I could sing gave me some kind of currency that I hadn't had before. I had spent high school in the background, looking on with envy at the girls with steady boyfriends. All of a sudden, I was *popular*. And if singing was the key, I thought to myself, so be it.

Margo and I stayed friends as I started branching out, but drifted apart when I got adopted by a new group. In those days we called it a "clique," and the word didn't have negative connotations. There were six of us: Sally Clark, Betty Lou Ruhling, Glennis Grimes, Katherine McCartney, Peggy Frimodig, and me. Many a Friday night was spent partying at Sally Clark's. Partying meant dancing in the living room to records, sipping soft drinks and eating potato chips. My adolescence knew no drugs, no alcohol; instead, we had lots of camaraderie and fun with our boyfriends. I guess there were those who drank beer and smoked but we avoided those kids because they were "fast." Then one night at a sleepover, Betty Lou told me about intercourse. Mother had never spoken about such things to me. I was *horrified*.

In high school I blamed my parents for never allowing me to bring my friends home—it seemed like such an important component of a teenager's popularity. But because of Perry, we had a closed household. I like to think that it would have been different today, but back then I was sometimes embarrassed about Perry's condition when a boyfriend would pick me up for a dance and meet him. I was probably far more aware of it than anyone else.

Dances were held in the gymnasium. The parents—never my parents—would sit in chairs along the wall while we danced on the gym floor. The band played on a raised stage. We wore long dresses and corsages. We'd dance to the music of Dusty Rhodes or Bud Bell's bands, and then we would go for hamburgers at Wimpy's afterward—where it was perfectly normal for a crowd of teenagers in long dresses and suits to troop in for hamburgers and milkshakes. You'd walk to the dance and back home with your date.

My first serious boyfriend was Robert Stack (*not* the movie star). It was the spring before graduation. Bob Stack was handsome and just about as shy as me. I was always very aware of him, because he lived across the hall from the Huttys in their apartment building. Connie Hutty and I would often get together and sing duets while her mother (who was a professional pianist at Michigan State for the man who would soon become my first voice teacher) accompanied us. Bob would sometimes come over to listen, but I never guessed he was interested in me. Finally (it took him a *long* time to ask me out) we figured out we liked each other and began to "date." Talk about two naïve young lovers. He never even kissed me, but when he held me close while dancing I belonged to him. He was *my* beau.

I graduated from high school in the spring of 1942. I was only sixteen. The country was at war. Just six months earlier, on December 7, 1941, the Japanese had bombed Pearl Harbor. The next day President Roosevelt gave his famous speech calling it "a day that will live in infamy," and the United States entered World War II. President Roosevelt interned all of the Japanese in prison camps in the US interior until the end of the war. He was afraid of the possibility of spies, although it is a well-known fact that none of these Japanese, most of them US citizens, were spies. Our midwestern small-town newspaper was definitely biased and left out the worst details, the concentration camps, and other atrocities. But we listened to the radio every night, and Father religiously turned on Edward R. Murrow where we heard reports on the bombings in London. I remember so well Murrow's voice saying, "This is London calling."

My brother Walter was drafted that same spring and went to Burma (now Myanmar), where he was a mechanic for the new P61 Black Widow fighter planes serving under the command of General Joseph Stilwell. Stilwell, who was in charge of the China-India-Burma Theater, was known as "Vinegar Joe" for his caustic personality. Stilwell was fighting to keep the Burma Road from Japanese control because it was the only route available for transporting supplies from the United States that came in through the port of Rangoon (now Yangon).

Our senior prom, back in East Lansing, was a night I shall never forget. After the dance, many of us went down to the Lansing train station to say goodbye to our classmates who'd been called up for duty: Bob Muncie, Dick Cruise, Bill Carlyon, and one other, whose name escapes me. Why do I remember this night so keenly? Walter in Burma and now my classmates leaving—the war, which before had seemed so far away, was becoming very real. I knew Bob Stack would be drafted soon. And when he did leave, Bob gave me a gold bracelet with pink stones that I kept for years and sent me a photo of himself standing next to a motorcycle in his army garb. We lost touch, but he came back safely from the war. Bob is still alive, still handsome, and living in Escanaba, Michigan. You never forget your first puppy love.

That summer after high-school graduation, my father was selling war bonds, and I tried packing K-rations on an assembly line. K-rations were boxes containing a soldier's breakfast, lunch, and dinner. I was standing between two older women who were working at an extraordinary pace. I tried to keep up with them so that the line wouldn't be interrupted. I felt like Charlie Chaplin in the movie *Modern Times*! How anyone could do the same gestures over and over again was unbelievable! I lasted all of one week. I abandoned my K-ration job and unexpectedly found a chance to spend precious time with my father. His long-time secretary Sadie, whom he'd brought with him from Arbaugh's to his new job at the Merchant's Association, had quit, and he made me his part-time secretary while he was looking for a replacement. Each morning we would drive down together to Lansing and stop off at the Home Dairy for breakfast, then go on to his office. I felt very close to my father in those summer months and proud to be part of his daily routine. I did a little bit of typing, answered the phone, and enjoyed an unfamiliar feeling of importance. Mother would pack a sandwich lunch for me, egg salad or tuna fish, every day, and Dad would go out to lunch with one of his merchant friends.

After my parents' dear friends, the Burtons, died, Dad decided to purchase their home on University Drive. This was (*thank goodness!*) the last of our moves, and it was just right for us at the time. It had four bedrooms; we kept the extra one for a visiting grandmother. Mother had a rose garden that pleased her, and Dad had a new Buick. I lived at home and as usual babysat for pin money. Perry was finishing up high school in Lansing, where he was in a special class. Perry had many friends, and when he received his diploma at graduation, they all cheered. Perry, despite his handicap, was a very popular fellow.

World War II was in full swing. And ironically the war put the country back on its feet and out of the Great Depression. Everyone was needed, and everyone was finally working. Young men were drafted, and factories were buzzing with wartime manufacturing.

CHAPTER FOUR

COLLEGE YEARS

I enrolled as a freshman at Michigan State in the fall of 1942 at the age of sixteen. My tuition was $42.75 a term, or $128.25 a year. I think I must be exceptionally concerned with money—perhaps even more than the average Depression-era baby—because I remember the precise amount, down to the cent, of my tuition. Except for Bill, who went to Annapolis, Helen, Walter, and I all went to Michigan State. In my day, it was a small college of ten thousand students and extremely beautiful, with lush lawns, extensive gardens and greenhouses, a singing carillon housed in Beaumont Tower, a pine forest, a library, dormitories and class buildings. Campus was an easy bike ride from our house.

My freshman year at Michigan State, I was not thinking of majoring in music and took a general liberal arts course. I remember playing a lot of bridge in an ongoing bridge game held in the Union Building, the social hangout for students. I joined the staff of the college yearbook and was photo editor, which meant lining up class pictures. It was a hell of a job, and I resigned after only one term. I considered majoring in science, probably because I was taking a great course in physiology. I also took history and Spanish. I did take voice lessons as an elective, but that was only for fun.

My first voice lessons were with a boastful bass-baritone, Fred Patton, who'd had a career in oratorio and a bit of opera. He was a wonderful teacher for a beginner; he just let me go. He assigned second-rate American art songs such as "Ah! Love, But a Day" by Amy Cheney Beach, or "If I Could Tell You" by Idabelle Firestone, and of course the Italian Anthology, where every beginning singer first encounters the Italian language. When he felt I had mastered a song, he'd doodle a diploma, or a picture that somehow related to the song, or other such nonsense on my sheet music. His comments to me consisted of "Annie"—that was his nickname for me—"let it out. Let it out!" Which I assumed meant that he wanted me to sing louder. He only knew operatic singing of the Wagnerian bluster.

He had a huge ego and was a happy man who dressed smartly and was always on stage. His speaking voice was loud, and though I never heard him sing, I'm certain it, too, was huge. He was a lot of fun and had a beautiful daughter, Jesse Patton, who became a successful New York fashion model. And although Mr. Patton must have thought I had a singing voice because he did encourage me to major in music, he never really showed me how to sing. I'm sure that with his huge bass-baritone sound, he thought I would never be loud enough. But in some important way, he gave me exactly what I needed at the time—the *joy* of singing.

This joy took me out of myself—it was a kind of transport, or ecstasy, that I eventually would come to refer to as "the other one." Who was the "other Bethany" I was coming to discover? She was, to put it simply, someone who loved these physical sounds coming from her body. And little Bethany, with her pin money, tuna fish sandwiches, and hand-me-down dresses, got pushed aside, at least for a moment, when I was singing.

I confess that at this age I was only thinking of meeting the man of my dreams and getting married like my sister Helen, whom I idolized. But working with Fred Patton was a turning point. You see how life's biggest decisions are sometimes made as if by accident? I had absolutely no knowledge of classical music, but just because I loved singing, I naively decided to become a music major.

Entering the world of classical music was an awakening. All of a sudden—and until the day I graduated from college—the music department became my world. I would leave for school first thing in the morning and not come back home until dinnertime. My first year, I remember spending a lot of time just listening to the masterworks, thrilling to the new flights of emotion I would find, sitting alone in the student listening rooms. Of course, after that followed what would be years of keyboard harmony, music theory, harmonizing figured bass, advanced harmony with Dr. Owen Reed, and species counterpoint. It was god-awful. I relied heavily on my pianist boyfriend, Philip Evans, to come to my aid for these subjects. Piano lessons were, as usual, impossible, as my fingers flopped around the keyboard with the endless repetitions. I was only ever able to conquer the first few pages of a given piece. It sounds from all this as if I had no business being a music major, but I was stubborn and competitive, and I had discovered classical music.

Figure 11. Portrait of me by a college friend.

There were so many opportunities to hear music in those days. Big acts came in from the big managers in New York to play community concerts in the large concert hall downtown. Michigan State also hosted major artists in the field house. It was there that I heard: Rachmaninoff play the piano; the young Vladimir Horowitz, who played *The Stars and Stripes Forever* as an encore (we were blown away); Lily Pons, in a glamorous gown, singing the "Bell Song" from *Lakmé*, or other opera arias—she was a high coloratura and that was her recital repertoire. I barely heard the music itself; I only saw a beautiful woman in a gorgeous gown singing trills and high notes, looking like she was what music consisted of. Both the musician and the opera star in her thrilled me.

We also had more intimate performances of chamber music in our small recital hall at the music department. It only sat about three hundred people. (I had my graduation recital there.) It was where I heard performers chosen by the faculty, for instance the Budapest String Quartet, or Artur Schnabel playing Beethoven sonatas. Here, Lotte Lehmann sang the complete *Winterreise*, accompanied by Paul Ulanowsky. On stage, she looked like a casually attired hausfrau, totally immersed in Schubert's music. After Lehmann's recital, all of us voice majors had our photo taken with her, and she stopped to talk to us.

It seems ludicrous, perhaps, but we were *required* to go to the concerts by visiting artists. We had cards that were punched for each performance we attended, and you were reprimanded if you didn't go to enough concerts—the faculty felt it was a valuable learning experience.

Dr. William Kimmel, who taught music history, was my absolute favorite professor. He was also the choir director at my mother's Episcopal church in Lansing, where I sang. I can still remember our college *a cappella* choir warming up on the "Et incarnatus est" from Bach's B-minor Mass with Dr. Kimmel, and that high pianissimo, ethereal entrance the sopranos have toward the middle of the piece. Often a group of us—Norma Lou Gregg (my competition), Bob Huber, Clifford Claycombe, and I—would go over to Harbourn's (our favorite coffee shop) for lunch, and Dr. Kimmel would hold court. He talked about everything, philosophy and aesthetics, as well as music.

Dr. Kimmel was homosexual and kept it a secret. But when they did find out, Michigan State fired him. There was still a great deal of hostile discrimination in the forties. He moved to New York City and taught at Hunter College until he died. Years later, Dr. Kimmel came backstage to congratulate me after a performance of *Pierrot lunaire* that I sang at Hunter with Pierre Boulez. I threw my arms around him and said, "Oh, Dr. Kimmel! How wonderful to see you." It was the first time I'd seen him since college. He never truly had any inkling of how important he was to me in those days long ago. And there he was, congratulating *me*.

We had no opera theater at Michigan State, so my college years were spent learning the art-song literature, piano music, chamber music, symphonies, and oratorios. Opera was a foreign territory, although I knew of its existence, but that was not what my vocal studies were focused on. I loved a course on Wagner's leitmotifs that I took with Dr. J. Murray Barbour, and I knew one or two arias and a scene from *Faust*, which Suzanne Pfitzner taught during my senior year. Suzy Pfitzner was one of our voice teachers and an oddity in the department. She wore the most eccentric clothes—haute couture left over from the twenties. It was something to see her swishing down the hall, in her long dresses, dramatic scarves, and jewelry. I'm sure she wore the same clothes that she had brought over from Europe. She just never took to American style—the sweaters, short skirts, and saddle shoes we all wore.

My life came to revolve around learning, singing, and hearing music. Sometimes Dr. Kimmell and Dr. Gomer Llewellyn Jones—a faculty composer and musicologist from Wales—would bring their respective church choirs together—the Episcopal church, where I sang, and the Presbyterian church on the other corner of the same block in Lansing. We would do all of the major oratorios by Bach, the Brahms *German Requiem*, and Handel's *Messiah*. Before I knew it, I had sung in the choruses of many major oratorios. Music surrounded me seven days a week.

On Tuesday nights I often went over to the Lucases to sing lieder. I had met Dr. Lucas, who taught in the horticulture department, at my summer job in the college nurseries my senior year. He and his wife were German Jews who came to Michigan before the war. He was an accomplished botanist, which was one of the primary specializations of the university. Every week I would go to their house and read through lieder with Dr. Lucas at the piano. Later his wife, Margaret (they had no children), would bring out a delicious *kuchen* and some tea. Our Tuesday-night readings of German songs must have reminded them of their life in Europe, where gathering together and playing lieder for one's pleasure was a tradition going back to Schubert's *Liederabends*. I'll always remember that gentle couple. When I stepped into their home, I felt like I'd walked into the *fin-de-siècle* Vienna of Stefan Zweig, Mahler, and Schoenberg. How happy I was to become part of their world; how happy they were to see me at their door.

When I was at Michigan State College the music department was filled with French and German émigrés, mostly Jewish, who'd come over from Europe in the late thirties: Maurice Dumesnil, a pianist known for his interpretation of Debussy (he wrote two books on the subject), came from France. Alexander Schuster was a cellist and conductor who'd come from Germany. His brother, Joseph, also a cellist, was the principal cellist for the New York Philharmonic. Ernst Wolff was our harpsichordist from Germany. The Italian master of the euphonium, Leonard Falcone, was our band director. Also there were Dr. Jones and Dr. Kimmel.

Probably our most famous faculty member was the pianist Frank Mannheimer. Although he was born in Dayton, Ohio, he had performed extensively in Europe and America and considered England to be his home. When the war broke out, he could no longer return there and took a position at Michigan State. He taught the Matthay piano technique and was noted for his annual summer piano institute in Duluth, Minnesota. We were very fortunate to get him. Not only did he have the best students but pianists from all over the world would come to the institute to study with him.

The rest of the faculty, such as the composer H. Owen Reed, and music theorist Paul Harder, were from the Eastman School. Dr. Barbour, my acoustics teacher, wrote the seminal book on acoustics, *Tuning and Temperament*. By an accident of fate and war, it was perhaps the greatest department the university has ever had.

The musical landscape of the United States in those years was profoundly formed by the migrations of the war. In Europe, modernism had been divisive and often elitist, but in exile it came to represent something richer, almost ethical, a united political front. According to Ehrhard Bahr in his book *Weimar on the Pacific*, "It became evident to the Weimar exiles that modernism had to develop an art that made no compromises yet was still able to reach society." And it was

> in this domain that one can see what Schoenberg had in common with Bertolt Brecht, Alfred Döblin, Thomas Mann, and Franz Werfel, even if they had differing opinions about the forms of aesthetic experimentation or the means of reaching an audience. The task of reaching out to an audience without making compromises was easier in the 1940s than it had been during the 1920s as the modernist exiles now had a political agenda in common, regardless of whether they were conservative or radical: the defeat of German Fascism in Europe.[1]

A mass exodus of Jewish and non-Jewish intellectuals, artists, and scientists came over from Europe in the years from 1933 to 1949. Although the musicians who ended up at my department were from somewhat conservative artistic backgrounds, it was quite different on the West Coast, where modernism prevailed. Writers, filmmakers, architects—Thomas Mann, Franz Werfel, Bertolt Brecht, Fritz Lang, and Richard Neutra—went to California for the climate and stimulated an unparalleled wave of wartime creativity. The direction of classical music was being challenged in Los Angeles by Arnold Schoenberg, Theodor Adorno, Ernst Křenek, Ernst Toch, and Hans Eisler. It was being challenged on the East Coast by Béla Bartók, Stefan Wolpe, Julius Schloss, and Erich Itor Kahn. This gale force of musical influence, in particular Schoenberg's new twelve-tone method, would come, in no small part, to define my own career.

CHAPTER FIVE

LESSONS WITH
J. HERBERT SWANSON

After my freshman year, Mr. Patton retired, and my new voice teacher at Michigan State College was J. Herbert Swanson. Mr. Swanson was the total opposite of Mr. Patton; his ego was subdued, he had a polite manner, and wasn't all about being loud on stage. Mr. Swanson was a real voice teacher. He had a light baritone voice and had studied in New York City with the Italian tenor Bernardo De Muro, who taught the Italian method, what you would call "bel canto" for want of a better term. The voice was placed forward, with emphasis on deep breathing and using the front of the face for resonance. A high palate gave warmth to your sound, and I developed a silvery timbre to my singing. My voice was a light lyric coloratura and I eventually developed a three-octave range. I would warm up with an exercise on the syllable *nee*, using the *N* to make sure the vowel *ee* was held high against the back molars by the tongue and bounced into the resonators. Then I would slowly blend it through all the vowels, keeping my palate high. Over my course of study with Mr. Swanson, this well-placed, silvery quality became my sound. Long after I'd stopped being his student it never changed—although it became warmer and darker in my forties. I think of Mr. Swanson as the teacher who gave me *my* sound.

My speaking voice had a girlish quality (it still does), and I was blessed with a natural singing voice, good tonal memory, and good relative pitch. Throughout my career I never worried about my voice. I didn't wrap scarves around my neck or gargle honey. I could always just jump out of bed, and my voice was ready to go! I took my voice for granted and expected it to be ready to do as I commanded. However, I wasn't a fool and always wore a headscarf in winter and rainy weather.

Mr. Swanson had a wonderful ear and caught any imperfections in the *passaggio*, which is the most difficult part of the voice to develop. It's where you shift gears from the lower range into your higher range, and it must be done smoothly, so the singing is seamless as you ascend a scale. Naturally I loved descending scales, since my high range was where I was comfortable, and hated working ascending scales, which he made me do over and over again.

Mr. Swanson was an intellectual about singing, and the wonderful thing about him was his love of the art song. His knowledge of the art-song literature was huge, and my perception expanded *exponentially* under his tutelage. I read through Schubert, Schumann, Brahms, Debussy, Fauré, and other wonderful composers with student pianists and Dr. Lucas. I fell entirely in love with art song. By the time I graduated, I wanted to be a bona fide recitalist.

My junior year, I went to Chicago with Aunt Irene to participate in a singing contest held at a radio station. We stayed at the Palmer House, one of the fanciest hotels in Chicago. I sang some light operetta from Deanna Durbin's or Jeanette MacDonald's repertoire—the sort of music that I thought would impress them—and I won. My prize was a ballpoint pen. It was one of the first ballpoint pens patented in the United States and probably considered to be a terrific prize. All I remember was that the damn thing leaked ink all over my hands. But who cared? Being with Aunty Irene was fun in spades. I think in many ways we were two of a kind.

I was already becoming very competitive. I wanted the solos. My main rival was Norma Lou Gregg, a coloratura, who also had a pretty voice and was very smart. Singing gave me a lot of confidence. Being pretty and an irrepressible coquette, I had boyfriends for movies, dancing, and playing the piano while I sang. There was one with a car and one who played trumpet in a jazz band. I'm not going into details, but I kept my wits about me during college. I knew I wanted to be a professional musician and that's where my attentions were focused. I wasn't going to be distracted or anchored down by marriage. I had seen enough of that at home.

CHAPTER SIX

FATHER

On a cold wintry evening in 1944 my father was taking Grandmother Beardslee back to Detroit where my uncle Jay lived. When a tire went flat, Dad got out and fixed it himself. It was a cold night. He shouldn't have been out in the cold; he was still recovering from recent extensive dental work. When he returned from Detroit, he came down with what we thought was the flu. When he started coughing up blood, Dad was taken by ambulance to the hospital. It turned out that he didn't have the flu, but monocytic leukemia, a cancer of the white blood cells. On the doctors' advice, Mother immediately had him transferred to a hospital in Ann Arbor that had better facilities and doctors than the one in Lansing. She moved into a rooming house in Ann Arbor, so she could go to the hospital every day to be with Daddy. My sister came as often as possible: Mother couldn't be at home, and someone had to help with Perry, since I had my studies. Daddy needed frequent blood transfusions, and many of my student friends from the music department drove up to Ann Arbor and contributed to my father's blood bank—a kindness I will never forget. My father passed away that spring, in April of 1945.

The one thing I had longed for was the chance to have *adult* conversations with my father. Maybe I was hoping it would cancel out the fear of his yelling I had as a child. (But that never happened.) I wanted, at the time, to know this shy man with his appreciation of beauty—the artistic nature I saw in his exquisite penmanship. His devotion to my mother and his family, I took for granted. I thought I didn't know his desires, and what he was really like. I loved my father, and wanted to exchange thoughts and develop a relationship with him. My father wasn't open

Figure 12. My father and me in front of my parents' first house on Lenaway Street.

like that. I knew he favored me. I was always just his youngest. He called me Dolly from the day I was born, and now he was gone.

Walter got leave to return home from Burma because of Dad's illness, but just missed seeing him before he died. That summer of 1945, peace was declared, and the war was finally over, so Walter did not have to go back. He immediately took advantage of the GI Bill to finish his final years at Michigan State. The beauty of living in East Lansing was that Helen, Walter, and I could all get an education while living at home with Mother. It was wonderful having Walter around. We formed a close relationship, for I was no longer just the kid sister. He loved my singing and often came to concerts with me. He met a beautiful girl, Elaine Lantta, who was one of his college classmates. They fell in love and married after they'd graduated. Walter wanted to continue graduate work in political science at the University of North Carolina, so they moved to Chapel Hill. Kind and gentle Walter. Many years later, my mother told me that Walter said, "Mom, if anything happens to me, put my soldier's pay toward Bethany's education and make sure she finishes college."

After Daddy died, the first thing Mother did was to pay off the mortgage on her house to be free and clear. She sold our car, since she didn't know how to drive. Dad's salary was gone, and she only had a small life insurance policy, social security, and some help from my brother Bill. Nineteen forty-five was the first year that the government really paid out checks, though social security had been voted in during FDR's administration ten years earlier. Mother was proud and did not want any more financial assistance, and she began to take in roomers for income. I was in my senior year. Our roomers were students from the music department, so there were constant sounds of music in our "conservatory" house. The piano worked overtime. Either Mother was playing for me, or a roomer (pianist) was playing for us after dinner. My mother loved music. Often when I came home from my lesson, I would sit on the radiator in the kitchen and share my news of how Mr. Swanson was developing my technique or about the songs he had assigned or what choral work we were singing with Dr. Kimmel. Mom's meat-loaf dinners were a great tribute to many of our young aspiring musicians.

I graduated in June 1946, and I didn't know what to do. I had lived at home throughout my college years. Money was still so tight after Dad died, so I decided to stay another year at Michigan State and work on my master's degree in music. It was a lovely year: I got the lead in a musical comedy, *What Goes Up*, put on by a student group, and Bob Huber, who went on to be a rather successful stage director, directed the production. I felt like Mary Martin.

That summer before graduate school, I also had my own half-hour program on the college radio station, WKAR. Bob was the announcer, and Mary Goodell was my pianist. Mary had played for all my lessons with Mr. Swanson as well as my graduation recital. Mary could sight read anything at the drop of a hat; she was my mainstay through all my college years. She was such a developed pianist that she never went to conservatory—she went right into being a private student with the famous Schoenbergian pianist, Eduard Steuermann, in New York. In later years she became head of the Hoff-Barthelson Music School in Scarsdale, New York.

All summer I would run over to the radio station straight from the nursery where I worked planting and weeding in the college gardens, arriving for my program in shorts with a bandana around my head, looking dirty and mussed, but—as always—I was ready to sing. I was late all the time, and Bob would have to ad lib on the air until I got there. It made him furious. Mary and I thought it hilarious. Fortunately, Bob had a crush on me, and thank goodness (given my disheveled state) it was radio and not TV.

The year of graduate school passed quickly. I felt adrift. Walter was married and in North Carolina. It was just me, Mother, and Perry left in the house. I was twenty-two years old. It was time for me to leave too, time for me to make it on my own.

CHAPTER SEVEN

NEW YORK, HERE I COME

My mother's sister, Irene, had a fantastic personality. She would have made a wonderful comic actress in the movies. She loved to have a good time, eat candy, and read movie books and pulp fiction. She had a trumpet of a speaking voice and it seemed to follow that she adored tenors. She wasn't as pretty as my mother nor as proud or inherently strong, and wasn't in the least cultivated—in the sense that she always pronounced any foreign name in music totally wrong, which would irritate me to no end, especially as I got older and better educated and turned into more of a brat about these things.

When I was little, I was always delighted to go over to Aunt Irene's house. Irene played the piano better than either of her sisters and could play any pop song by ear. She really should have studied classical piano and should have had a bright career, as she was likely the most innately musical of the family. Her home had a large record collection, mostly of arias by her darlings, Mario Lanza and Jussi Björling, and piano concerti by Rachmaninoff, a name she really butchered. Her daughter Nancy was a fairly good pianist; I would often sit on the piano bench next to her and listen. I must have been only thirteen, but I remember her practicing *Clair de lune* of Debussy.

It makes perfect sense that Aunty Irene was the one paying particularly close attention to my musical path. Early on, she saw my talent clear as day and eventually took it upon herself to do something about it. When I think

Figure 13. My mother and Aunt Irene with our Hupmobile in the background.

about the beginning of my career, it really does seem simple: One day just after that final year at Michigan State, Aunty Irene said, "Ella, I think we should take Bethany to New York and let her sing for Bernardo De Muro on Mr. Swanson's recommendation."

Aunty Irene's husband, Wesley, had died suddenly of a heart attack while shoveling snow the year before. Out of the blue she was a rich widow, and she took advantage of it. Irene had always been a treat to be with, but now she had a special knack for important indulgences. A fabulous trip to New York City was just the sort of idea she would come up with. She booked us a room at the Waldorf Astoria, an appointment with the great tenor Bernardo De Muro, and an audition at Juilliard, and off we went. We were going to see *everything* in New York City, because traveling with Aunty Irene was fun, and also take care of the serious business of launching my career as a famous singer.

Bernardo De Muro, of course, had trained Mr. Swanson, my voice teacher at Michigan State, in *bel canto*. It was only through Mr. Swanson that I was able to get in to see De Muro at all. He lived in a sumptuous apartment in the East 50s, and I remember the heavy oak furniture, oriental rugs, and beautiful piano. He also had his own professional studio pianist on hand for my audition. The singer himself was quite small and very Italian. I thought he looked like a bald Beniamino Gigli.

I had prepared "Caro nome" from *Rigoletto* and some Schubert songs to perform for him. He probably didn't need to hear all that music sung all the way through, but I suspect he wanted to be as polite as possible as a favor to his former pupil. He listened and then declared, in very poor English: "It eez a verreey pretteey voice, butta not for zee ohperah."

I never forgot that moment. I guess Mr. Patton, with his "Annie, let it out!" would have said the same thing.

While we were in New York, I also auditioned for Juilliard, which despite its importance in my life, I remember peculiarly enough as a nonevent, a bland classroom and some faculty members. I probably wore the same best dark blue polyester suit I always wore. I sang "Caro nome" again and "Depuis le jour" from Charpentier's *Louise*. There were no pronouncements made after I sang. I left the audition without any better sense at all of my future as a singer—though I knew by then I was *not* going to be an opera singer.

I think Aunty Irene was disappointed as we headed back to Michigan. As for me, I didn't care about "zee ohperah." There was no opera theater at

Figure 14. Me in my blue suit in front of the old Juilliard.

Michigan State, so it was unknown territory—it just didn't matter. In fact, I'd taken a course in Wagner with Dr. Barbour in my senior year. I thought Wagner's music long and the plots stupid, a bunch of gods prancing about and singing endless long passages of music about their problems. It wasn't where my musical heart dwelled. I loved art song and its poetry. But Aunty Irene worshiped the opera, the showiness, her tenors. She had wanted opera for me.

To our surprise, Juilliard called and offered me a full scholarship. And in a moment, all was fine with Aunty Irene again.

Phil Evans, my buddy from the music department, had also been offered a piano scholarship to Juilliard, and so we planned to travel together with his parents to New York in their family car. I keenly remember the day we left East Lansing, my mother standing on the curb waving tearfully as we drove off.

The skyline was something to behold as we closed in on New York City from New Jersey. I was excited. We drove through the Lincoln Tunnel up the West Side Highway to International House on Claremont Avenue, just across the street from Juilliard, where my mother had booked a room for me. I said goodbye to the Evanses and started to feel frightened only in the moment their car pulled away. I turned away from them and walked up the steps to check in. That night in my room, I cried. I missed home. I was all alone, thinking everything had been a terrible mistake.

How was I to know that I would spend the next ten years of my life in New York City? How was I to know how dramatically and quickly my life was about to change?

PART TWO

THE MONOD ERA (1948–55)

Figure 15. Me in 1948.

CHAPTER EIGHT

JUILLIARD

When I woke up the next morning, hungry from having skipped dinner the night before, I was put out with myself for all the childish bawling. I walked outside and down Riverside Drive. The sun was out, and the day glittered with brisk, autumn air. At that moment I felt happy, and the city was enchanting. On the corner of 116th Street and Riverside Drive, I came across a sign advertising a room for rent. When I rang the bell to inquire about the room, the landlady, a Mrs. Furlanich, responded that it was small and I might not like it, but for seven dollars a week, I didn't even stop to consider downsides. I took it on the spot and moved in the very same day. One suitcase, packed with sheet music—a score of *La bohème* (a Christmas present from my brother Walter), two volumes of Schubert's songs—and my best hand-me-downs. Good thing I traveled lightly. It was indeed a very small room, the very modest maid's room of an Upper West Side classic six. Along one wall, there was room enough for a wardrobe, a bureau, and a sink. When you turned away from the sink, you bumped into the single bed. Right in the middle there was a window looking out over an airshaft. It was brutally hot in New York City that year, and there wasn't any air conditioning, so I lodged my mattress half out the window to get some fresh air. I was desperate. It's a miracle I didn't fall out the window.

The apartment as a whole, on the other hand, was quite spacious, and Mrs. Furlanich rented rooms to four of us. She favored one roommate in particular, David Poleri, who was a young tenor with the New York City Opera—and would sometimes even make dinner for him. I could often hear him singing full voice in the shower next to my room. His was really the first decent professional voice that I'd ever heard not in a concert. He had a gorgeous sound, quite like Mario Lanza. Aunty Irene would have approved.

He also had quite a reputation as a difficult character and famously walked off stage in the middle of the last act of *Carmen* in Chicago not too many years after that, telling the conductor, "Finish it yourself!"—though I don't have a recollection of him being especially eccentric, just loud and full of himself. But I probably assumed that's how all professional opera singers acted! He was killed in his heyday in a freak accident with his wife when the helicopter they'd chartered to tour Hawaii crashed into the side of a volcano.

Let me tell you about *my* Juilliard. In 1947, Juilliard was located in a large grey concrete building at the corner of Claremont Avenue and 122nd Street, where the Manhattan School of Music is now. There was a beautiful foyer on the first floor with marble tiles, a large oriental rug, and a chandelier. Besides that, there were two concert halls (one large and one small) and the school's administrative offices. Upstairs were studios, classrooms and, toward the back of the building, the practice rooms. On the top floor were rehearsal rooms for the large orchestra, opera theater, and chorus. The cafeteria, student lockers, and diction classrooms were in the basement. The music building back at Michigan State had been brand new but small. There was an old Victorian mansion behind the music building where we would practice and rehearse. Its beautiful practice rooms were all wood, especially the choral room. You felt like Kirsten Flagstad when you were singing. We used to throw open the windows so that everybody could hear us. Juilliard was a much larger building in the city, and it had this huge entrance. You felt like a professional singer the moment you walked in, but you didn't feel like a big singer because you'd practice in these little rooms without the wood.

I loved the neighborhood. Walking over to Riverside Park, I'd hear pianists, violinists, and singers practicing. Music just seemed to pour out of open windows. Heading up Claremont Avenue from *ma petite chambre* on Riverside Drive to Juilliard was always a joy. Columbia University was nearby as well as the beautiful Riverside Church, International House, and Union Theological Seminary. Being surrounded by academia and music made me feel right at home. I was content and independent, and felt as if I'd started taking charge of my life.

After I got to know my classmates a little, and found new people to room with, I ventured away from my first tiny room in Mrs. Furlanich's apartment. I moved into an apartment on 122nd Street with a mezzo-soprano, until she stopped paying the rent and got us into a real pickle that my brother Bill had to bail us out of. In my second year, Tina Castagneri (another mezzo-soprano, who later married the composer Lou Calabro) and I moved into a big, dark green room in an apartment on 112th Street and Broadway. We were renting from two strange Jewish sisters who lived there and kept their father holed up in the tiny maid's room off the kitchen. We stayed in that crazy green room until I met Jacques Monod.

Mother had promised me twenty-five dollars a week to help me out. Frankly, how she managed to find the money I'll never know, but those checks arrived like clockwork in the mail every Monday. On my twenty-five dollars, I budgeted seven dollars a week for rent, and the rest went mostly for food. You could get a cup of soup and a sandwich in Juilliard's cafeteria for twenty-five cents. A spaghetti dinner at Tops, where a lot of students who were on budgets would eat, was only a dollar. Five cents went for the subway and three cents for a postage stamp to keep Mother abreast of things. I borrowed all my scores from the vast library at Juilliard. In the hallways, my classmate Charles Bressler used to quip when he saw me heading in his direction, loaded down with music, "Here comes Beardslee with half the library under her arms!"

I was assigned to study voice with Catherine Aspinall, who had studied with Queena Mario, a famous Italian coloratura, who in turn had studied with Marcella Sembrich, one of the first great Metropolitan Opera stars from the 1880s. Once again, I would be studying the Italian method. Miss Aspinall was a handsome woman and took pride in her appearance. She seemed to have a new dress every time I turned around. Miss Aspinall worshiped the music of Mozart and Handel, and she summarily pushed my art-song repertoire aside. She loved the purity of long line singing found in those two composers' works. She also loved the oratorio repertoire, so I worked on that alongside whatever music I was learning for Opera Theater. She had a flighty way about her, and her speaking voice was always rimmed with laughter. Her sound when she sang—which was often, because she demonstrated a great deal—was beautiful, a testament to her solid training with Queena Mario.

I was fortunate to have David Garvey as my accompanist. He'd sit outside our practice room, going over scores, while Miss Aspinall ran us through some exercises. Then she'd summon him in to play. He was an excellent pianist and went on to be Leontyne Price's exclusive pianist throughout her long career.

Miss Aspinall was a good teacher because she left me alone. Because of my training with Mr. Swanson, my voice was already well placed, so with Miss Aspinall, I worked mostly on repertoire and on breath support. Our lessons were only thirty minutes long—quite a bit shorter than my leisurely hours spent with Mr. Swanson, during which we had time to let conversation roam from technical points to his knowledge of lieder.

Sometimes I would have a makeup lesson at her charming apartment on West 10th Street in the West Village. I remember thinking to myself, "When I get to be a famous singer, I want an elegant apartment, just like this!" She was independent, powerful, and beautiful. Being around her, it was easy to think that I'd be just like her. I would never get married, I'd be powerful, and I would live in Greenwich Village.

The president of Juilliard at the time was the composer William Schuman. He had introduced a new pedagogy for music theory called "Literature and Materials." It was a departure from the old system that had vexed me at Michigan State; but theory was theory no matter what or how they taught it, and I suffered miserably through all of it. Anything intellectual about how music was constructed was a bothersome thorn in my side.

My enthusiasms were as consistent as my dissatisfactions. My favorite class, naturally, was Sergius Kagen's repertoire course, for which we concentrated on the major song cycles, and many of which I already knew from my thorough preparation at Michigan State. We were each assigned several songs a week, and then we had to perform in class, with Mr. Kagen accompanying us on the piano. The performance was the best part, because he was such a wonderful musician. Though I distinctly remember one poor girl who was so shy, we could scarcely hear her sing. Mr. Kagen would goad her, "Please, don't die on me, Miss Roitinger. Don't die on me!" It became a recurring joke among us.

Meanwhile, the dread that I wouldn't have enough money clung to me like my own shadow, and I realized I needed some kind of supplement to Mother's checks. In those days, in order to hire yourself out as a singer, you first had to find a management agency—which was hardly the complicated matter it is now. I found Inge Wank's number in the yellow pages and signed on with her. Getting an agent for singing gigs was quite straightforward—as long as you sight-read music, you could hire out for work—and there were a lot of jobs for young singers. Inge found me two jobs, one at a temple in Orange, New Jersey, and the second with a double quartet at St. Nicholas Collegiate Church on Fifth Avenue—another extraordinary building that met the wrecker's ball shortly after I started singing there.

There was a postwar building craze in Manhattan, and buildings were going down and coming up everywhere. My fellow singers in the double quartet at St. Nicholas were wonderful and included the soprano Sarah Carter, the alto Alice Howland, and the bass Cleve Genzlinger.

But my real extra income came by way of NBC and the Toscanini Television Concerts, which came about through Robert Shaw, the choral director at Juilliard. His professional touring group, the Robert Shaw Chorale / Collegiate Chorale, was hired by NBC to perform in the Television Concerts series, broadcast out of a small auditorium (Studio 8H) in Rockefeller Center, featuring the great conductor Arturo Toscanini. When Shaw needed extra singers to supplement his regular group, he'd call on a few of us Juilliard students. This was a marvelous confluence for me: Not only did I have lavishly paid part-time work for which I was able to buy new clothes but I had several opportunities early on in my career to sing under Toscanini.

    Shaw had an interesting way of placing us. I had a baritone on one side of me, and an alto on the other—whereas conventionally, I would have been in the soprano section. I think Shaw felt he achieved a homogenous sound by arranging his singers in this manner—that our voices would come at you as one big sound. He may have been the first to experiment with this setup. I tell you one thing though: You had better know how to sing isolated like that, because there was no one standing next to you to help you with your part.

    What I remember liking most about the job was going downtown— away from the Juilliard campus—to Rockefeller Center. I felt very important riding the elevator to my grown-up rehearsals with Toscanini. Quite possibly, I was still so naïve about the opera world that I didn't know to distinguish Toscanini from any other conductor. If I had studied at Indiana State University, where they had a huge opera theater program, and I had been selected to sing with Arturo Toscanini, Herva Nelli, Jan Peerce, or Nicola Moscona—I would have been positively overjoyed. But I was an art-song singer, and I was probably a little overly blasé about the situation. *My* idols were Lotte Lehmann and Elisabeth Schumann.

    Between 1948 and 1950, I sang in the chorus for Beethoven's Symphony No. 9, Brahms's *Gesang der Parzen*, and Verdi's *Requiem* and *Aida*. During the broadcast of *Aida*, Toscanini put me and three other sopranos in an enclosed box on stage to simulate the effect of singing from offstage. There was a glass window through which we could see Toscanini conducting, but was it ever hot and sweaty in that box!

Teresa Stich-Randall, who was singing the role of High Priestess, was stuck in the box with us. I loved her voice. She was still just a young girl then, and I think Toscanini had discovered her. She left immediately afterward for Europe, where she had a major career. In many ways she was more European than American; she even won the title of Kammersängerin from the Austrians in 1962.

We actually performed the Verdi *Requiem* in Carnegie Hall, instead of at NBC. I remember so clearly that in the "Libera me" section of that performance, Herva Nelli, who was one of Toscanini's preferred soloists, started going off pitch—right in the part where she's singing alone over the chorus. Toscanini kept waving at her to stop, but she knew it was broadcast television and just plowed forward, dragging the chorus along with her as her voice got flatter and flatter. The next day we all had to go back to Carnegie Hall to re-do that part for the RCA Victor recording. So even if the broadcast version was muddled, the one that you hear on the box set is perfect. Toscanini was a big fan of Herva Nelli's voice and chose her again as Aida. He even left his baton to her when he died.

As exceptional an experience as it was to sing under Toscanini and participate in some of his last performances (he was in his eighties), I'm not convinced this contract work for NBC was his very best. His famous temper was perhaps less fiery than it had been earlier in his career—which was good—but his tempi were often rushed. And the sound engineers always had quite a time with him, because he couldn't keep himself from singing along as he was conducting and the microphones in recording sessions pick up *everything*. In 2012, David Denby wrote: "Arturo Toscanini screaming '*più forte!*' at the NBC Symphony in his live recording from Carnegie Hall of the Verdi Requiem is almost terrifying—the enraged old man wanted the audience to feel the power of the 'day of Judgment' section of the piece. Any modern recording executive would have taken the scream out or made the ensemble do the section over. But the scream is imperishable."[2]

His son Walter could often be found lurking backstage with a ready supply of Life Savers to feed his father—an attempt to get Toscanini to keep his mouth shut while the microphones were on. I do think he must have been magnificent when he was conducting in Italy before the war. But what we have for posterity are these performances, which were on TV and made into albums. When I look at those broadcasts today, with the dramatic close-ups of Toscanini's fierce, strong features, I can't help myself from thinking, *There's that mole on his cheek*. I couldn't possibly forget that mole, or his beautiful white hair and intense black eyes.

I did start expanding my horizons to include opera repertoire. I enrolled in Opera Theater and went on to sing in two operas at Juilliard: Mozart's *Figaro*, in which I sang Susanna; and Benjamin Britten's *Beggar's Opera*. The opera theater crew in those days was avant-garde. They even mounted a production of Luigi Dallapiccola's opera *Il prigioniero* that may well have been an American premiere. Frederic Cohen was the opera stage director, and his wife, Elsa Kahl, taught body movement. They were both German émigrés formerly connected with the famous Black Mountain College. Frederick Kiesler, another émigré, was the set designer and created for Juilliard usable set designs with what he called his biomorphic furniture: All the pieces were blue and abstract and could be completely modified at will. Kiesler had been friendly with many of the major figures of the European avant-garde, including the architect Adolf Loos. The opera theater's orchestra conductor was Frederic Waldman, and our rehearsal pianist was Morton Siegel. Morty was brilliant. I nursed a huge crush on him that came to nothing, because he was pining after the soprano Evelyn Aring.

If you graduated from Juilliard in the 1950s and had a decent sound, chances were at least 60 percent that you could go on to earn a living as a singer . . . especially in Europe. The years I was there, from the fall of 1947 to 1950, Juilliard produced the most wonderful group of singers, a number of whom went on to have major careers.

My classmates included Leontyne Price, who was one of the first African Americans to have a huge public career in New York and Europe. Price had private patronage to come to Juilliard and already was a kind of diva when she arrived—Paul Robeson had put on a benefit concert to raise funds to send her to New York City. Russell Oberlin was another classmate, who, along with Charles Bressler and Betty Wilson (both also at Juilliard), went on to become a founding member of the New York Pro Musica under the direction of Noah Greenberg—part of the early music revival movement that became influential in the next two decades. The heavy, square-framed Gladys Kuchta, who looked middle-aged even when she was young, won many of the leads in Opera Theater (the director Frederic Cohen simply loved her voice) and went on to have a formidable career in Germany, singing Verdi and Wagner with the Deutsche Oper. Lenora Lafayette, a talented African American singer from the South, had as beautiful a sound as Leontyne Price. She was at Juilliard for only a year before being grabbed up by a European impresario. She went on to have an important opera career and was the first African American to sing at London's Royal Opera House.

Later on, Shirley Verrett and Evelyn Lear had successful careers first in Europe and then at the Met. In those days, young American hopefuls had to work in Europe first and come back to the Met, because the European artists controlled the rosters at the major American opera houses. There were Robert Shaw's soloists: Florence Vogelson, who had a gorgeous voice and a big range; and the contralto Florence Kopleff. Florence Kopleff was terribly in love with Bob Shaw; she followed him down to Atlanta when he moved there—even though he was married. She was devoted and resigned herself to being an old maid, working near Shaw, rather than having the major career I think she could have had—all because she couldn't have the love of her life. There was Martha Flowers, who sang in *Porgy and Bess*, and Bonnie Parcell, Louise Natale, Corinne Swall, Marianne Weltmann, Evelyn Aring, and me—to name just a few of the extraordinary singers in this group. I certainly didn't feel like a big fish in the midst of all of those large soprano voices—but we all did just seem to come together in those vibrant years at Juilliard.

Those were just the singers. Apart from my fellow Michigan State alum and former boyfriend, Phil Evans, I also remember the pianist Paul Jacobs, who, like me, went on to have a significant career in contemporary music. Paul and my first husband, Jacques Monod, would have furious debates in the Juilliard cafeteria: Schoenberg versus Stravinsky. There were wonderful conductors, Samuel Krachmalnick and Paul Vermel among them. Before Jacques, I dated the conductor Maurice Bonney, an intense, square-jawed man who was always trying to throw me down onto my narrow bed in my tiny room. Bonney is credited with founding (or at least reviving) the symphony orchestras of Albuquerque, New Mexico, and then Anchorage, Alaska, of all places.

It was simply a wonderful time for classical music in New York. Juilliard had a free-ticket box just inside the side entrance door for concerts downtown at Carnegie Recital Hall and Town Hall. I took advantage of those tickets whenever I could. The concert halls frequently gave away tickets when they wanted to fill out the audience for an emerging performer. A number of important performers had their debuts under the beneficent curating of Norman Seaman, who made these concerts happen. At those concerts, I'd collect brochures for the upcoming appearances of renowned performers that I wanted to save up to see. I heard Jennie Tourel, Maggie Teyte, Uta Graf, and Lotte Lehmann at Town Hall. "Someday I will sing on that stage," I thought to myself, as I watched and heard these wonderful artists.

If you were lucky, you could get a student pass to the old Metropolitan Opera on 39th Street and sit high in the balcony, where they had desks for students who could listen and study the score. This was where I heard Renata Tebaldi in *La traviata*. Tebaldi was sensational. I happened to be with a classmate, Marianne Weltmann, that evening, and the two of us walked practically all the way back to the Upper West Side talking about Tebaldi, her sound, how she had impressed us, and Verdi's music. We hardly noticed the seventy blocks we had covered.

Fans of divas demanded high drama. In those days, when both singers were at the height of their careers, there were the Renata Tebaldi lovers and the Maria Callas lovers. Gunther Schuller, who played French horn in the orchestra at the Met during those seasons, dismissed the rivalry between these two remarkable sopranos as theatrical pyrotechnics for the newspapers. Their differences, he aptly explained, had more significantly to do with their formation. Tebaldi had studied with Carmen Melis and cultivated *verismo*, a high naturalism that suited characters such as Mimi. Callas, on the other hand, studied the more traditional *bel canto* under Elvira de Hidalgo, with an emphasis on artful technique—what Gunther described as "*bel canto* with its pure lines but also its technical agility, the ornamental roulades, trills, virtuoso scales."[3]

By the time I saw Callas, in 1956—the season of her Met debut—in *Lucia di Lammermoor*, she'd just lost fifty pounds in six months and her voice surprised me by how distant it was. I was accustomed to her recorded sound, and what I heard in the big hall was nothing like the recordings. I think her best work must have been what I heard on those recordings with the Italian conductor Tullio Serafin at La Scala. The New York reviews equivocated about her frail top notes and unparalleled dramatic interpretation—which I don't remember at all. My focus was on her sound, which was so much less than what I expected. I wondered at the time whether losing all that weight had made her sound smaller or whether she was simply past her prime. I do wish that I could have seen her in *Tosca*, and at least gotten a chance to appreciate her in a real dramatic role.

I like Gunther's perspective here on what made Callas unique, because it has to do with her musicianship and supports my conviction that understanding a piece musically is key to a great performance:

> Most informed people know that Callas not only had a remarkable voice (replete with a stunning coloratura technique), but that she was also arguably the greatest dramatic actor on the operatic stage. What is less appreciated, but to which I can personally attest, was the way those two aspects of her art arose out of her instinctual feeling for music, in whatever style

she was singing. In other words, her much-admired acting was developed from or through the music and out of her deep understanding of it.[4]

In my school days, I was getting a proper introduction to the opera in New York City. Ljuba Welitsch singing *Salome* with Fritz Reiner conducting was stunning. Her laser-beam voice cut through the loud Strauss orchestra. And another singer I loved was Eleanor Steber singing Mozart. What a joy hearing this great singer spinning out Mozart's vocal line.

I idolized Elisabeth Schumann, the original Sophie of *Der Rosenkavalier*. I loved the purity of her sound and her beautiful use of *portamento* for Strauss. It was always in good taste and never overindulgent. I tried to copy her singing line, intently studying the rise and fall of her phrasing when she sang Schubert's lieder. Great singers can teach you so much.

Postwar New York was bursting with creative energy. It seemed in particular as if musical theater was eager to make up for lost time—and everything else that had been stifled in the grim years of war. On Broadway, the titans Richard Rodgers and Oscar Hammerstein II were mounting one production after the other. Some of the musicals of the time included *Annie Get Your Gun*, *Kiss Me, Kate*, *South Pacific*, *Guys and Dolls*, *The King and I*, *Damn Yankees*, *Peter Pan*, and *My Fair Lady*. I always thought that in another version of my life, I would be singing in *South Pacific* instead of Mary Martin. I think that would have been a blast. Off Broadway in the Cherry Lane Theater, Kurt Weill's *Threepenny Opera* was playing, starring his wife, Lotte Lenya. These musicals ran for years and were revived on stage and in film in the decades to follow. The abstract expressionists—Willem de Kooning, Jackson Pollock, Mark Rothko—were changing how people consumed art. In those years, Arthur Miller's *Death of a Salesman* was running, along with Eugene O'Neill's *Long Day's Journey into Night*, Paddy Chayefsky's *Middle of the Night*, Tennessee Williams's *Cat on a Hot Tin Roof* and *A Streetcar Named Desire*—the list goes on.

Riches everywhere! And yet truthfully, Broadway was beyond my pocketbook. Movies, however, and poetry readings and concerts (with student discounts) were affordable. A number of radio stations had programming devoted to contemporary and classical music—such as WQXR, WNYC, WOR, and WBAI, to name a few. New York City had an impressive *four* newspapers covering musical events, and Section Two of the Sunday *New York Times* was entirely devoted to classical music! Talk about bygone days. At least four halls put on concerts besides Carnegie Hall and Town

Hall. Betty Ussachevsky, the wife of the composer Vladimir Ussachevsky, ran the poetry readings at the 92nd Street Y, where one could go to hear Dylan Thomas, W. H. Auden, William Carlos Williams, Marianne Moore, and countless others read their poetry. The Thalia Theater, on West 95th Street, and the Paris Theatre, tucked in near the Plaza Hotel on Central Park, showed the foreign films that went on to influence an entire generation of American directors: *Le diable au corps* with Gérard Philipe, *Les enfants du paradis* with Jean-Louis Barrault, and Jean Cocteau's *La belle et la bête.* New York in the fifties and sixties was a cultural cornucopia. And I was in the middle of it all.

We were happy. I have the impression now that there just weren't as many people in New York back then, that life for young students was simpler and full of fun. Artists were everywhere, rents were cheap, and most of us lived *in* Manhattan. There was more than enough work for everyone. And unlike young musicians today, we just assumed we were needed. I was already singing professionally while I was still at Juilliard. My performances were reviewed in the newspaper! I can't stress this enough—we were all working and performing in those days. It wasn't just some dumb luck.

That said, I did have lucky breaks. I was at Juilliard at a propitious time. William Schuman, the new president of Juilliard, was a composer (unlike his predecessor Ernest Hutcheson, who considered Juilliard predominantly a conservatory for a select number of gifted performers), and was very invested in new music and performance. In the spring of 1950 I was Jean Morel's soloist for Mahler's Fourth Symphony. Morel, the principal conductor of the Juilliard Orchestra, was extremely tall and handsome, and conducted French music superbly. He was an influential teacher—James Levine and Leonard Slatkin studied with him. Under his stewardship at Juilliard, the orchestra was built to a very high standard. After the war, President Schuman was instrumental in arranging a tour for Morel and the orchestra to Japan.

A high point for me came after a 1950 League of Composers concert at Carnegie Recital Hall, when I received my first major New York review from Virgil Thomson, along with a picture, in the *New York Herald Tribune.* This was in fact quite a coup for a young singer—still a student, no less. About my performance, Thomson wrote: "Perfect in French, perfect in English, and perfect also in her German (heard at a recent Alban Berg concert) this singer actually lets you know what a piece is about and what the notes of it are. She sings the words and sings them on pitch. If she will correct a slight tendency to croon, she can be a great singer of songs."[5] Virgil

Thomson was known to be unforgiving in his reviews of famous musicians, and here he was giving me technical critiques! I think of that last line and marvel at how enduring its effect would be, how prescient his recommendations were. I didn't know it back then, but maybe Virgil Thomson did: I was going to become a singer of contemporary art songs. But a newspaper review, no matter how impressive, wasn't the catalyzing influence. There was a much more ferocious storm that was standing in the wings, ready to sweep me into its electrical, tempestuous, and all-consuming vortex.

CHAPTER NINE

THE MONOD ERA, 1949

Ben Weber was a portly, sweet, and rather shy composer who lived in a ground floor apartment of an old brick townhouse in Greenwich Village. He had a lovely garden right off his living room, and one could imagine Ben spending long afternoons in his garden thinking about the music he was writing. Whenever I was in that garden it was for one of his fabulous dinner parties, which were sought after because Ben was such a marvelous cook.

I first met Ben at Juilliard when he chose me to sing one of his new pieces, *Concert Aria after Solomon* for voice and chamber orchestra. I didn't know his work, but I was interested in art song—and new music or old music, I wanted to sing! We quickly grew fond of each other. He wrote beautifully for voice and I wonder whether that was because he himself would have loved to become a singer (a tenor, as he once confessed to me). Ben was gay and loved to do wonderful impressions of famous divas "doing their thing." More soberly, Ben made his living as a music copyist. This was still long before the era of computer engraving.

I premiered Ben's *Concert Aria* at his Composers Forum Concert in December 1949. The Composer's Forum concert series, first launched in 1935 under Franklin D. Roosevelt's WPA program for the arts, featured two new composers for an entire half of a single program and included an open discussion and question period with the composers at the end. I have always liked this concept, especially for contemporary music.

I would sing Ben's *Concert Aria* again in spring of 1950 as part of the Alice M. Ditson Festival in the McMillin Academic Theatre (now Miller Theatre) at Columbia University. Alice Ditson, the widow of the music publisher Charles Ditson, had made a bequest to Columbia to support contemporary American composers.

There was a young Frenchman, Jacques Monod, in the audience at McMillin Theatre that night, May 5, 1950, and if Jacques hadn't heard me sing, I'm sure my career—and life—would have moved in an entirely different direction. But he heard me and then came backstage after the concert to congratulate me. He was twenty-three and spoke only French, so I barely understood a word of what he was saying. That left me to focus on how handsome and foreign he was, his energy and charisma. He looked like Gérard Philipe, the French movie star I had just seen in *Le diable aux corps* at the Paris Theatre. He asked me out for a drink and I, managing to intuit the invitation through the foreign language, accepted. I asked him to wait while I changed out of my "uniform" (my terminology for my singing dresses) and into street clothes.

Over coffee, Jacques explained that he had come to New York with the Parisian composer and conductor René Leibowitz, who was recording for the new label Dial Records. They were preparing Alban Berg's *Kammerkonzert* for piano, violin and thirteen wind instruments, and Arnold Schoenberg's *Ode to Napoleon*. I'd taken only two years of high-school French and deciphered this much information with great difficulty. How I longed for subtitles that night! In rapid-fire French, he went on and on about Arnold Schoenberg, Alban Berg, and someone called Anton Webern. He also spoke of making me a great singer of contemporary music—he'd been entirely convinced by my performance that night. I had no idea *who* these people were he was talking about. I'm sure that Sergius Kagen had never made a single mention of the Second Viennese School in our repertoire class. As to whether I wanted to become a great singer of contemporary music, well, that seemed entirely beside the point. I was out on a date in New York City with a handsome, exciting Frenchman who admired my singing.

The very next day, Jacques came to see me again, and the day after that, and after that. He was a very insistent person and determined to be around me. It was as if Jacques had come to some kind of decision—end of story. I assumed most Frenchmen did not waste time in what we Americans call courting. Ours was a whirlwind affair. From one moment to the next I was utterly in the thrall of this dynamic man. And that, in a nutshell, reader, is actually how I began my career as a singer of contemporary music.

In no time at all, we began to live together and rented a large room on Riverside Drive and West 110th Street. When I wrote my weekly letters to my mother, I left this detail out. She was still sending me an allowance, and Jacques was being subsidized by the French francs his mother tucked into her letters. Our parents were completely in the dark about our living together.

The room was in a strange building, which was something like a cross between an apartment building and a boarding house. Our floor had a community kitchen plus a very large bath that served four large bedrooms looking out over Riverside Drive. There was a businessman at the end of the hall whom we rarely even saw. There was a couple on one side of us—he was a bus driver and his wife was in a wheelchair. On the other side lived a single woman who gave us no end of grief when we rehearsed the Alban Berg and Anton Webern songs. Our rented upright piano faced her wall, and she'd bang on it if we were still rehearsing after dinner when she was just home from work. Jacques often banged angrily in response. He could not tolerate interruption.

Living with Jacques wasn't easy at first, as I often did not understand him and he continued to only speak French. I tried to make do. His English at last began improving when he became fascinated by the Korean War. The war had him always reading the newspapers, trying to understand battlefield maneuverings and what was happening politically.

Jacques was desperate to stay in the United States. I eventually learned that he was specifically desperate to get away from his domineering family and be on his own. In order to remain in New York, Jacques obtained a student visa and entered Juilliard. He'd already had rigorous training at the Paris Conservatory and had studied composition with Olivier Messiaen and then later with René Leibowitz. At Juilliard he was assigned to work with the Dutch composer Bernard Wagenaar. According to Jacques, their lessons were merely "polite chitchat." Wagenaar was well aware of Jacques's musical sophistication and was complicit in Jacques's conviction that his study at Juilliard was a mere formality—a way of staying in New York City.

Jacques had had years of solfège training, reaching his *première médaille*, which was the highest honor. He also acquired absolute pitch under Noël Gallon's rigorous instruction.

Jacques started studying with René Leibowitz after graduating from the Paris Conservatory. Leibowitz was a Polish Jew who had survived the

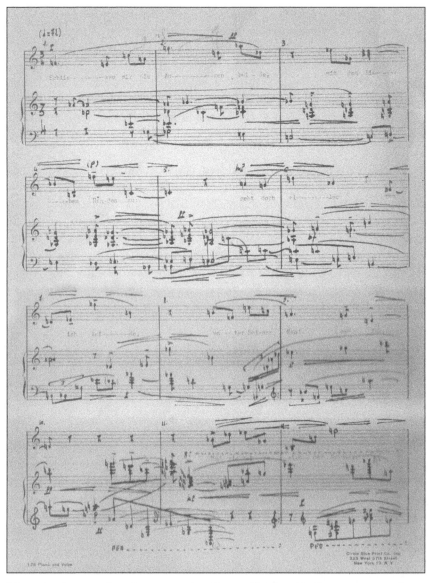

Figure 16. A page of my Berg score, hand copied by René Leibowitz.

war years in Paris. Before the war, he had studied composition and orchestration with Maurice Ravel and was introduced to Arnold Schoenberg by the German composer Erich Itor Kahn. Leibowitz went on to study with Anton Webern. After the war, Leibowitz was the only one in Paris with whom young composition students could study Schoenberg's new twelve-tone method. Messiaen really had little interest in the twelve-tone method, so many young composition students—Jacques himself, André Casanova, Antoine Duhamel, Serge Nigg, Michel Philippot, and, briefly, Pierre Boulez—retreated to Leibowitz. René also had a rare library of scores of music from the Second Viennese School (many of the plates had been hidden during the war), some of which he'd copied out himself by hand. I learned Webern's *Three Songs*, op. 25, and the beautiful twelve-tone version of Berg's "Schliesse mir die Augen beide" off manuscripts René had copied himself.

This was the legacy that Jacques had come from. It was so different from my own education and, for me, meeting Jacques meant crossing into a whole new musical environment. I was smitten; I would have followed Jacques anywhere. If he'd declared our mission to be Gregorian chant revival, I would have stood proudly right alongside him.

As I mentioned earlier, my enormous debt to Ben Weber cannot be overstated. Not only did he bring Jacques Monod into my life, but it was through Ben that I met the remarkable composer and intellect Milton Babbitt, who would become a central figure in my musical career.

Jacques and I had been invited one evening to Ben Weber's for a dinner celebration. Ben had prepared a wonderful meal and was in especially good spirits that night, for the Ditson Fund had just given him a grant to record the *Concert Aria after Solomon* for the American Recording Society. I was rather pleased, too, for it would be my first commercial recording. From the living room door of Ben's charming apartment into the rear garden you could see the last strains of evening twilight when we arrived. Sitting in a chair with one leg draped over the arm and smoking a cigarette was the other guest for the evening, Mr. Milton Babbitt. He was thin and slightly bald and had remarkable blue eyes and a gorgeous speaking voice. Milton's smile was warm, and right away he impressed me as charming, cultivated, and very intelligent. He was articulate in a way I'd never heard before, nor since. He spoke in complete sentences, organizing his words into paragraphs and perfectly formed thoughts. Over that first dinner, I found that he would often seize on a comment someone made and, without hesitation, vastly expand upon it. He seemed to know everything

Figure 17. Milton around the time when I first met him. Courtesy of Betty Ann Duggan.

about anything. His conversation ranged from pop songs to Broadway to Schoenberg. He was a very sociable character.

Jacques sat, uncharacteristically quiet. He was awestruck.

Milton was telling us about a musical that he and Richard Koch, along with Richard Child, had just finished, called *Fabulous Voyage*, based on Homer's *Odyssey*. Originally, it was to have been a vehicle for Mary Martin, but the producers had declared it too elegant and clever for Broadway. They suggested it would be the kind of show to mount in London. I, for one, have always fantasized about a parallel existence in which I have Mary Martin's career. But that night, in the company of those men, I had no interest in being anyone except me.

We didn't get back to Riverside Drive until late. But I remember feeling, shall we say, *momentous*. It was as if over the course of the evening, something had turned over, and I had been drawn in, definitively, to the wondrous world of composers.

CHAPTER TEN

WORK WITH JACQUES

Jacques was a great one for organizing and also convincing players to participate in his projects. Over his first school year, he put on two very important, unprecedented, concerts at Juilliard: two programs from the Second Viennese School. On December 18, 1950, we mounted an all–Alban Berg program. Beveridge Webster, from the piano faculty, played the Berg Sonata, op. 1. I sang three groups of Berg's songs—the *Seven Early Songs*; Four Songs, op. 2; and three unedited songs.

I remember well how I prepared for that big concert. At the time, I had a temple job in East Orange, New Jersey, and would take my pitch pipe and song scores with me on the bus on the way to work. I'd sit in the back of the bus where no one could hear me singing and humming softly to myself. One day, Abe Berman, the cantor at the temple, overheard me working away on the twelve-tone version of Berg's "Schliesse mir die Augen beide" and remarked, "Bethany, where are you finding those wonderful pitches? That piece is remarkable!"

I can still hear Berg's arching, beautiful vocal line today. I wonder what the cantor's reaction would have been if he'd heard the piano part that accompanied that voice line—he would have liked it even more.

Learning Berg's *Seven Early Songs* was fairly easy, as they were tonal. Berg had regarded these songs as student compositions, worked on during his apprenticeship with Schoenberg. And yet it was the very first piece that Jacques taught me. If the music wasn't new enough, working with Jacques was certainly a new chapter in my education. The score in my library today is crossed with his insistent markings over the few bars I struggled with. There were certain lines that he wanted me to emphasize with rubato, even

Figure 18. Jacques, me, Donald Nold, Morty Siegel, Evelyn Aring, and Corinne Swall outside Juilliard.

though I had never done rubato in such a tight ensemble—just voice and piano. Idiosyncratically, given the improvisational quality of the technique, Jacques wanted a planned, organized rubato.

Berg's Four Songs, op. 2 were another story entirely. For one thing, the voice line is enmeshed in a rich, highly atonal piano part. The poetry—by Friedrich Hebbel and Alfred Mombert—was very dramatic. I worked hard to learn and then memorize these songs. And yet I went on to program them again many times over the course of my career.

The last work on our all-Berg program was the *Lyric Suite*, played by the still newly formed Juilliard Quartet. I have often wondered how Jacques was able to pull all of these forces together. Whom did he confer with in the Juilliard administration—Lucy Rowan Mann, the concert director? Or Mark Schubart, William Schuman's assistant and a composer in his own right? In any case, the all-Berg program was one of those miracles Jacques made happen by force of will.

The Juilliard Quartet, started in those years with the encouragement of William Schuman, took an immediate interest in performing new music. (Schuman actually founded the Juilliard Quartet in 1946, with the idea that the resident quartet could play the music of new composers.) The first members were Robert Mann, first violin; Robert Koff, second violin; Raphael Hillyer, viola; and Arthur Winograd, cello. They were all quite young. That season they also played all of the Bartók quartets at New York Times Hall, and then the complete Schoenberg quartets with the wonderful soprano Uta Graf at the Museum of Modern Art.

We would sometimes cross Claremont Avenue from Juilliard to an apartment building where one of the quartet members lived (I can't remember which one) and listen to them rehearse. I remember how enthusiastic everyone was over Ralph Shapey, the composer of one of the new quartets they were rehearsing. Ralph was a pupil of Stefan Wolpe, another émigré from Europe teaching in New York, and Ralph's music showed real talent. In person, I found Ralph to be feisty and a bit crude. He demonstrated very little tolerance for what he termed "second-rate contemporary music" and aired his opinions freely—never watching his language or caring about how people responded to him. Ralph was very short and had a wild mess of hair and a commanding way about him. In the early sixties, later in our friendship, Ralph would write two outstanding pieces for me, *Incantations* and *Dimensions*.

The following spring, on May 14, 1951, Jacques organized an all–Anton Webern program. As far as I know, these were the first all-Berg and all-Webern programs at Juilliard and perhaps in New York. Again, the Juilliard Quartet joined, and honored, us with a performance of Webern's *Five Movements*, op. 5.

Webern's music was a test for me. The *Drei Volkstexte*, op. 17, and the *Five Canons*, op. 16, were real killers. I think that in certain respects the Webern *Canons* were my rite of passage into the world of new music. Let me show you an example from Webern's op. 16. This is the fifth canon. Any singer can see what I mean about the difficulty.

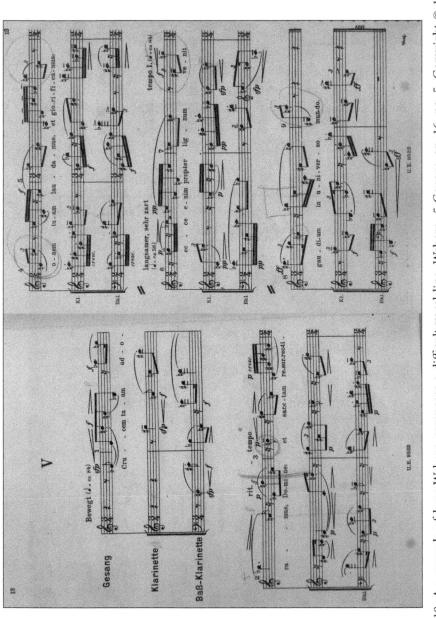

Figure 19. An example of how Webern composes a difficult vocal line. Webern, 5 *Canons*, op. 16, no. 5. Copyright © 1924 by Universal Edition Vienna. Copyright © renewed. All rights reserved. Used by permission of European American Music Distributors Company, US and Canadian agent for Universal Edition Vienna.

I later found out through Hans Moldenhauer, who wrote the defini-
tive biography of Webern, that I had performed the world premieres of
Webern's opp. 16, 17, and 25.

Now, years later, I look at my old Webern scores and can't remember a single note—the augmented fourths, sevenths, and wide intervals jumping all
over the vocal line—whereas a Brahms song, or one of Babbitt's vocal lines,
are etched into my memory forever. Why can I remember a Babbitt vocal
line and not the Webern, which I studied so intensely? I am convinced it's
because Milton's vocal lines contain a preponderance of thirds, fourths,
fifths, octaves—all the intervals inherent in tonal music.

Jacques had initially come over to the United States with René Leibowitz to
record for Dial Records. René's affiliation with Ross Russell, the producer
of Dial Records, meant that Jacques and I were swept up into the recording project. We had to seize the opportunity while René was still in the
country, which I don't think was longer than six months. Ross Russell, who
owned a record store in Los Angeles, had only recently founded Dial. At
inception, the company's sole purpose was to record Charlie Parker, who
was on the West Coast. Although Dial originally specialized in jazz, it went
on to become one of the first US record companies in the 1950s to create
a catalog of only contemporary music—and Leibowitz conducted many of
the pieces. For the life of me I don't know if Ross Russell thought he was
being opportunistic, or whether he was just being egged on by René. But
the Dial catalog went on to include Schoenberg, Webern, Berg, Bartók,
Stravinsky, Messiaen, Gösta Nystroem, and even John Cage. In February
we recorded the *Seven Early Songs*, three unedited songs by Alban Berg,
and Anton Webern's Four Songs, op. 12.

On the same album, Jacques recorded the Webern *Piano Variations*,
op. 27. Played correctly, the Webern *Variations* often involve crossed
hands. This is difficult maneuvering, but necessary. I listened to Jacques
work for hours on the *Variations*. He was able to achieve Webern's dynamics while keeping a legato line. This *legatissimo*, or connection, between the
wide intervals of Webern's music is extremely important. And yet the dynamics can't fall by the wayside—not in the least. The piano is by nature a
percussive instrument, meaning the sound decays almost immediately, so
this *legatissimo* and the dynamics were not easy to achieve together. Both
elements working together make a tremendous difference to how a listener
experiences Webern's music. For me, Jacques's recording remains the de-
finitive performance of this work.

So, here I am, coming from the Midwest with its devout churchgoing and its Protestant work ethic. All of a sudden I'm dropped into the lap of highly sophisticated musicians, I have a Marxist-communist boyfriend and friends who are politically liberal, interested in new ideas, and some living quite openly, unmarried and sexually free. A turnabout to be sure.

I had a new repertoire, and I was changing as a person, too. East Lansing seemed to be light years away. I had experienced so much in such a short time in New York City. My hometown looked provincial and small, especially when I brought Jacques to East Lansing that summer to meet Mother and Aunty Irene. I don't have to tell you that these two midwestern sisters found him to be *unusual*. It all started out as a terribly awkward visit. Jacques's English was still primitive at that point, and they just didn't quite know how to react to him and his heavy accent. Neither of them spoke a lick of French. But Jacques could be very charming when he needed to be, and with me as interpreter, they eventually grew to like him. We gave a recital for the Music Department at Michigan State—all my old teachers! Even though we performed classical repertoire, I could feel how much I'd grown since I had left for Juilliard, and I had no desire to return to East Lansing.

About this time, Jacques composed *Four Songs for Voice and Clarinet*. Believe it or not, I performed them with the young Meyer Kupferman. He was a freelance clarinetist at the time but later became a famous composer and taught for years at Sarah Lawrence College. He composed highly original twelve-tone music: large orchestral, extremely dissonant works, with a complex use of many series in its texture. In those days I thought of Meyer as part of the gang, a good friend of the oboist Josef Marx. Josef was in the process of launching a music-publishing business that specialized in early music, such as Guillaume de Machaut and Giovanni da Palestrina. I never cared for Josef's oboe sound. I sang Paul Hindemith's *Die Serenaden* with him, which has a whole section for just voice and oboe. Well, I thought, that was dreadful. His playing was thin and reedy. "From the French school" is the way I always thought of it, though Gunther Schuller writes in his memoir, *A Life in Pursuit of Music and Beauty*, that Joe's unpopular sound was mostly influenced by his teacher in London, Léon Goossens.[6] So I guess in the end, his playing was . . . from the English school. Geography aside, the sound was god-awful. But he was a first-rate musician, could play anything that was put in front of him, and perhaps most notably, got involved in publishing early music decades before early music came back into vogue.

The most beautiful piece of music by Jacques that I ever sang was his *Passacaille* for voice and seven instruments. I loved the instrumentation, the long vocal lines, and the way it complemented my voice. Only a Frenchman could have written that piece.

What was exciting at the time was that I was beginning to perform with other freelance players in the city. I sang the Webern *Canons* with Luigi Cancellieri on clarinet and Sidney Keil on bass clarinet. Luigi was one of Gunther's boys from the Metropolitan Opera Orchestra. Then I performed more of Ben Weber's music, *Songs for Voice and Cello*, op. 15, with Seymour Barab, a fine cellist. Like George Perle and Ben Weber, Seymour had come to New York from Chicago, where they had all been involved in the new music scene. Seymour went on to become a fine composer specializing in children's opera. Freelance musicians like Luigi, Sidney, and Seymour were to become my heroes—often *unsung* heroes. Not only did I depend on them but they played difficult music with me and were paid barely enough for all of their hard work.

I was caught up in the newness of all this music, and I was a curious musician. Yet there was a part of me that didn't really care what I was singing. I was madly in love and, under Jacques's tutelage, I had suddenly mastered a great deal of difficult music—without even really noticing. In fact, I thought at the time that Jacques was crazy to have dedicated himself to this twelve-tone music! But Jacques was on a mission, and I had become an integral part of it.

You must remember that up until then my ear had been grounded in tonal music. Ultimately, all music, no matter what its compositional style, *is* tonal. Consider Webern, who composed with wide skips for the voice. I had never sung anything like it. Webern's vocal lines were hard to learn, but I found the secret to singing them: The challenge is to make them sound like music. I know that statement sounds ridiculous, but for me that's what singing new music has always been about. You see, I think of it as "getting into the composer's head." Now, with Webern, I had to take his phrases and through repetition after repetition find the important pitches that gave a tonal sense to the phrase. I'd maintain all this through a legato line. Somehow my ear found its way.

This ability to make tonal sense of any musical phrase in a new work was something I found intuitively. If I couldn't figure out the tonal sense of what I was singing, it just wouldn't feel like music.

Finding that tonal sense involves hearing how pitch raises and lowers itself in the context of the music. Relative pitch forces you to hear that way. I can hear how pitches lean into one another or away from each other. With Webern's wide intervallic lines, it was particularly hard to hear, because the relationships between the wide intervals are not so apparent. But if you reduced them to a small cluster, you would find that many of them were just chromatic half steps. In the final analysis, I tonalized everything I sang in one way or another, and once I'd done that I could sing any composer's work. All music is tonal, and that conviction became an invaluable component to my ability in the years to come to learn and interpret the challenging music I would build my career on.

Staking the same ground from a composer's perspective in his memoir *Knowing When to Stop*, Ned Rorem wrote:

> I've always assumed that the whole of music—indeed, the whole of the universe—was tonal and that assertions to the contrary protesteth too much. All music, including Boulez and Babbitt, is tonal to my ear, and I'm convinced (but can't prove) that everyone, including Babbitt and Boulez, hears music tonally. Should a score appear wildly complicated, I listen simply by imposing a subliminal pedal-point beneath the wildness, and the complicated filigree falls into place. By tonal I mean, of course, derived from the overtone series, a cosmological given.[7]

When I wasn't working with Jacques, I never used the piano, since I was the worst of worst pianists. So it was almost by accident that I always learned a new score *a cappella*—a system I stuck with through most of my career.

There were many advantages to working this way. First, I could hear my voice with no extraneous noises. Second, I'd feel my body and find technical solutions to problematic leaps within a phrase. Last, I was developing "pitch memory," a term I use for reinforcing relative pitch. For instance, if someone were to play a whole step difference in the beginning measure of a Webern song and I began to sing, my ear would instantly recognize that something was wrong.

A practice session with Jacques lasted two hours. Years later, Jacques would tell the *New York Times* that experience had taught him you need at least one hour of rehearsal for every minute of music. We'd begin after I had, more or less, learned my vocal line for whatever piece we were working on. Jacques was insistent about dynamics and precise rhythm when we rehearsed. Constant repetition built my strength, breath support, and dynamic control. We often worked with a metronome, something I had not done before as a singer. Jacques would never accept less than perfect and the end result was that we were always overrehearsed.

Jacques hated performing. His face would take on a gray pallor right before we went on stage, which I assumed was a *crise de nerfs*. I, on the other hand, loved singing before an audience and stepped onstage without a second thought. But the fact was that we were always so overrehearsed that I never would have had any reason to feel nervous and was always very confident. I could have sung the recital standing on my head.

CHAPTER ELEVEN

FAREWELL, JUILLIARD

Nineteen fifty-one was our last year at Juilliard. I never would finish my diploma requirements. Miss Aspinall gave her usual spring recital of her students. It constituted a final assessment for the year. I sang twelve-tone songs by Leibowitz and Webern, and Jacques accompanied me. After I finished, the voice faculty began arguing because it wasn't the usual repertoire. They couldn't come to a consensus on how to grade me. Miss Aspinall later told me that Mack Harrell, who was also on the voice faculty and had just that season sung *Wozzeck* under Dimitri Mitropoulos, finally stood up and challenged any of the faculty to try singing what I had just sung. Yes, I passed.

When I'd appear at my lessons with my new music scores after meeting Jacques, Miss Aspinall would throw up her hands and say, "My dear, you should be singing Handel, not this music!" It was a reaction I would come to get used to in those early years. Singers specializing in new music, especially twelve-tone music, were almost nonexistent.

There was an exception in Eva Gauthier, one of the first singers to put Gershwin on her art-song programs. She came from Canada and specialized in French repertoire. Gauthier spent several years in Paris and had known Ravel. She was famous for her French and American art-song recitals. Then she went to Java with her husband, an importer, and learned and sang Javanese music while she was there. She particularly liked to wear Javanese silk dresses when she sang. Gauthier favored tonal composers, although she did perform the speaker's part in Stravinsky's *Perséphone* in New York City. She actually showed up at one of our new music concerts in the early 1950s—a tiny woman well into her eighties.

Another exception was Alice Esty, a wealthy woman in her own right who had commissioned music from a number of French composers, especially from the group known as Les Six (Georges Auric, Arthur Honneger, Darius Milhaud, Francis Poulenc, Louis Durey, and Germaine Tailleferre). She also commissioned Americans, including our own Ben Weber and Ned Rorem. Esty was an actress of sorts and studied with Lee Strasberg and Harold Clurman. Really, she was more of an art patron than a performer and when she did sing something new, it was invariably tonal songs.

Janet Fairbanks was a singer who performed new songs by American composers on her annual programs. Again, it was mostly tonal music, and she was somewhat limited vocally. She died young at forty-four in 1947— before I even knew about new music.

Jennie Tourel, on the other hand, was a wonderful recitalist. She performed annually at Town Hall, where I heard her sing a new song cycle by Paul Hindemith, *Das Marienleben* (The Life of Mary). The recital was around Christmastime, and I distinctly remember she sang the whole cycle holding a white fur muff in both hands in front of her velvet gown. She was accompanied that night by Erich Itor Kahn, who was not just her partner but also a fine composer. Like Lotte Lehmann, though, she was more of a traditional art-song singer.

Helen Boatwright recorded one large collection of Charles Ives songs with John Kirkpatrick, thus introducing this repertoire to recitalists. Nell Tangeman, who had a beautiful voice, never made it to the big time but she sang American art songs, especially those of Ned Rorem. One of Rorem's favorite singers and champions of his music at the time was Phyllis Curtin. There were these flashes of attention to new music, but as far as I know, no one else in New York was singing *serial* music.

My Juilliard years were coming to an end. In late June 1951, Jacques returned to France and waited for me to join him there. I spent the month of July with my brother Bill, who lived near Albany and worked as the manager of factory automation for General Electric. It was quite an important field in the 1950s, and he was able to arrange a summer job for me at GE so that I could earn spending money for Paris. Bill and his colleagues had invented the automatic stick shift and were influential in the design and building of the Lockheed Constellation, the largest passenger airplane introduced yet.

I had a short visit with my mother before setting sail. My next-door neighbor, Betty Stone, got married that summer. Betty had been a piano major at Michigan State and a good friend. Guy Hill, whom I'd been dating

Figure 20. A bridesmaid back in Lansing soon after I'd met Jacques. Forbearing Guy is on the far right.

before leaving for Juilliard, was in the groom's party, and I was a bridesmaid. Mother had always hoped that I'd marry Guy because he came from a wealthy East Lansing family and was finishing law school. The night of the wedding I drank too much gin-soaked fruit punch and got horribly drunk. Poor Guy had to drive me home and I made him pull over halfway so that I could vomit on the side of the road. I was so sick and I just kept saying, "Jacques . . . Jacques . . . ." Guy had no idea what I was talking about!

In mid-August I sailed out of Montréal by way of the St. Lawrence River on a student ship called the *Volendam*, which I think must have been used as a troop carrier during the war. By marvelous coincidence, it turned out that the boat was filled with young Fulbright students on their way to Europe. We all had a wonderful time together, despite the dreadful food. By the time we docked in Southampton two weeks later, we felt like family, embracing before we all went off on our separate ways. I will never forget the dessert. It was exactly the same thing every single night: ice cream, flavored like powdery vanilla, chocolate, and strawberry, molded into a perfect, inedible square.

Jacques and I met up in Amsterdam, which was still devastated by the war, like so much of Europe. After our extended separation, we spent two wonderful days together in Amsterdam *not* sightseeing. And that was what it was like for little old East Lansing me to see Europe for the first time: It was utterly romantic. All I remember is being so happy to see Jacques, and the inside of a Dutch boarding house.

Mother proudly announced our engagement in the *Lansing State Journal*, unaware, of course, that we had been living "in sin" for a whole year. It wasn't as if we had formally gotten engaged. My family just took it on faith when I made plans to go visit Jacques and meet the Monod family that we *were* engaged.

CHAPTER TWELVE

PARIS AND THE MONOD FAMILY

I loved Paris, with its Napoleonic architecture and beautiful boulevards. But who, I'd like to know, doesn't love Paris? Even Hitler wasn't allowed to touch Paris during the war. It was, nonetheless, a somber city when I arrived. I could still feel the war's effects reflected on people's faces. Paris was subdued by its long recovery from the German occupation, and the insult of the division of Europe after the war. When I returned to Paris years later in 1978 and then again in 1993, I found each time a completely different city, a tourist paradise: the bridges gilded anew, sparkling fountains, expensive shops, and light-hearted, chic Parisians.

The next five months I spent with Jacques's family: getting married, exploring Paris, and learning the peculiarities of my new in-laws. The Monods lived in Asnières, a suburb of Paris. They were an old, established French Huguenot family. Dr. Monod was a respected surgeon. Among Jacques's many notable relatives were a Nobel laureate in medicine (another Jacques Monod) and the great film director Jean-Luc Godard (a distant cousin).

Out of necessity my French improved. The Monods introduced me to home-cooked French cuisine. In my life, I had never tasted such wonderful food—never eaten rabbit, tasted French bread, or drunk *vin ordinaire* at every meal. The table wine was delivered to the house (just as milk was back home in the States) in wine bottles with no labels. Wine was just another food to the French.

The only woman in the Monod house I felt the least bit comfortable with was Marie, the chambermaid, who corrected my French, always

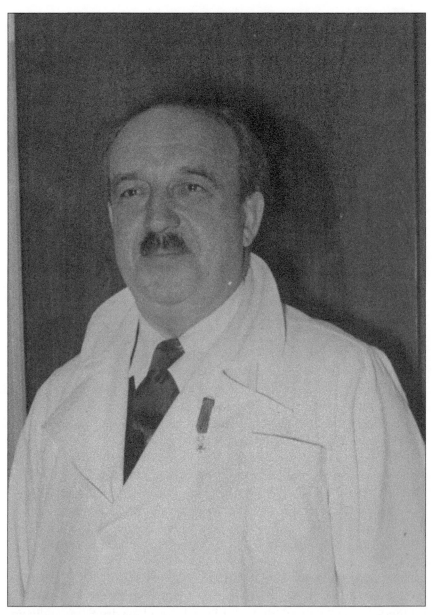

Figure 21. Doctor Monod.

smiled, and admired my American clothes. I tried to be my best with Madame Monod *chez elle*, but was always ill at ease. My trousseau, consisting of pretty summer frocks, couldn't have been a more awkward wardrobe choice. Mrs. Monod always wore a tight, severe black skirt with white silk blouses, black shoes and stockings, and a brooch at her neck. I can't imagine her opinion of my colorful cottons—I even had spaghetti straps on one dress! Although she could be very pleasant, she was unpredictable. If I had one word to describe her, I'd choose *austere*. The cook, Zélie, seemed to be her closest confidante, and they were on a first-name basis. Other than that, Madame Monod was dedicated to her son. She had *willed* Jacques through years of music study and obviously intended for him to become a great musician.

Dr. Monod, on the other hand, was devoted to his work and light-hearted. He had an agreeable nature and I grew very fond of him. He often teased me about our "American pasteurized food," and he was so right. (I had been definitively won over by French bread, homemade *confiture*, and Zélie's cooking.) He was very interested in early Roman statuary and had quite an amazing collection on display in the otherwise petit-bourgeois living room. I noted how he held his hands in a cupped manner at the table—the protective, careful gesture of a surgeon.

I heard many tales at the dinner table about the war years. The Monods, in particular, had adventures to share. Dr. Monod had sheltered his mentor and teacher, a brilliant Jewish surgeon, throughout the war at the Rothschild Hospital where Monod was chief surgeon. Shortly after the fall of Paris, Madame Monod fled with the children on a long trek to Ouzouer-le-Marché, where the Monods had their country home. They thought they would be safer there. Meanwhile, Jacques stayed in Paris to pursue his studies. He worked for the French underground (the *maquis*) and became a Marxist. Jacques once told me, "The only happy and exciting time of my life was the day when Paris was liberated and we [the communists] thought we might assume political control in France." He also told me a story of carrying a gun in his school briefcase to be delivered to the Resistance, and of how he was stopped at a checkpoint when he left the subway. The German soldier even opened his briefcase, but fortunately the gun was buried under the huge pile of music scores and remained undetected. Jacques must have been terrified.

Jacques was the oldest of four. He had two brothers, Daniel and Philippe, and a sister, Lily. Daniel was no longer living at home, so I never had a chance to meet him. My French was still not fluent, yet I could tell

Figure 22. Sightseeing in the Loire Valley with Doctor Monod, Philippe, Mme. Monod, me, and Jacques, in front of Chambord, still empty after the war.

that the family was going out of its way to be considerate of me and show its best side. I think they gradually grew to like me—much as my mother and Aunt Irene figured out after a time how to like Jacques. I feel as if I can place the moment of acceptance to a weekend at their country home in Ouzouer-le-Marché. We'd drive out every Friday, passing through Chartres with its beautiful cathedral. Everything was more relaxed than in Asnières. Meals were less formal, and I actually rode a horse for the first time. Walking through the village, I'd be amused to see women peeking through lace-curtained windows at the American girl in her summer cottons. We took sightseeing excursions through the chateau country of the Loire Valley. Some young cousins came to visit and of course laughed at my clumsy French. I just laughed along with them. We'd all figured out how to be together, and I must have been feeling more at ease if I could laugh at my own French!

Jacques and I often went into Paris to visit René Leibowitz. We would leave Asnières early in the morning, catch the train to the Gare St. Lazare, and go straight to René's at 17 quai Voltaire. The old building had a lovely court-yard you passed through from the street to get to the walk-ups. It happened to be the same building where the composer-critic Virgil Thomson kept an apartment. Later, Rudolf Nureyev lived out his last years in a luxurious apartment on quai Voltaire. It was a perfect location, right on the Seine in the center of Paris.

René was a tall, lanky man with stooped shoulders who spoke beautiful English with hardly a trace of an accent. We loved being with him, and away from the restrictive atmosphere of Asniéres—his relaxed way, his warm hospitality, and the interesting conversation. René had written one of the first books about the twelve-tone method, *Schoenberg et son école: l'étape contemporaine du langage musical.* He was considered somewhat lightweight by music theorists, but it was René who was responsible for the historic Dial recordings. In his later years he would become a conductor of consequence in Europe and England.

I befriended René's young American mistress, Ellen Adler, the daughter of Stella Adler, who ran the Actor's Studio back in New York. I don't know how they met, but I believe it was at Salzburg, where René conducted the music festival. She did the vocal recitation on Schoenberg's *Ode to Napoleon* with René for Dial Records—a recording that turned out to be the source of much friction between Schoenberg and Dial's founder, Ross Russell—but I didn't know about that at the time. I was just happy to have an American friend. In his writings about Paris, Ned Rorem described Ellen Adler as having a "dizzying black tiger beauty," but I remember in particular being amused at Ellen's idea of housekeeping: You threw a dinner party by candlelight in order to hide all the dust balls, and you filled the apartment with as many flowers you could buy on any corner in Paris. Ellen was fun, *just* what I needed, and it was such a relief to have someone to speak English with! She was also a friend of the painter Fay Lansner and Nina Bauman, who had been in Paris right before me. Nina married Alvin Bauman, a composer and a close friend of Milton. Jacques and I socialized often with the Lansners and the Baumans once we got back to New York.

Meanwhile, Madame Monod took over the planning of our approaching wedding. I was asked to sign a document called "*separation bien*," which I didn't question and naively didn't identify as a prenuptial agreement. It was of no interest to me. She outfitted me in a made-to-order white brocade wedding dress, graced with the usual veil. The reception and honeymoon were to take place at the elegant Hotel George V in Paris. Several of my American friends—Seymour and Miriam Shifrin, Iona Sutton and her husband—happened to be in Paris at the time. I had sung Seymour's music

Figure 23. Jacques and me on our wedding day.

that season in New York and asked him to give me away at our wedding—
just like me to have a composer give me away! The rest of the guests consisted of a large ensemble of Monod relatives and colleagues of Dr. Monod.

Everything was so unreal. I truly was a stranger in a strange land. I felt
as if I were watching myself in some movie, as if I were someone I didn't
know. It was similar to the feeling that I got when I performed—when I
was able to step out of the regular me that I knew so well and watch the
other, showier me be remarkable on a stage, or at my Parisian wedding.
Not surprisingly, Jacques was totally indifferent to the whole event and just
wanted to get back to America and away from his family as soon as possible. There were moments for me of feeling lonely and wishing my family
were with me to share such an important occasion. I could only take comfort in my closeness to Jacques when we were alone together.

The reception was a strange affair. I knew none of Jacques's relatives, who
were stiffly seated and staring with wan expressions at us. I danced with Dr.
Monod, who seemed to enjoy himself. But the aunts glowered away in their
austere, long black dresses, holdovers from prewar sensibilities. Jacques described them as his "tubercular Valkyries," a comment I've never forgotten
in all these years. It was just another reminder of Jacques's whole attitude
about his family and their bourgeois ways.

I regret that Mother did not attend our wedding. She had never traveled abroad, spoke no French, and was extremely shy about anything
foreign. I'm sure this accounted for her hesitancy about coming. For my
mother, it would have been like going to Mars, and she wouldn't have liked
it, so it was just as well, I suppose, that she didn't come. And yet, what a
missed opportunity! I fantasized how my mother and, especially, Aunty
Irene would have loved Paris—the three of us, with me as guide. Looking
back, I feel very sorry that my mother was forever the martyr and seemed
to have every virtue under the sun, while her children were off enjoying
things—such as Paris—that she would never see.

Madame Monod had made arrangements for us to honeymoon for a
week at the hotel George V in Paris after the wedding. Then we headed
back to Asnières. I was now a French bride.

That fall, while still in France, we learned of Arnold Schoenberg's death
on the radio. I knew Jacques was upset, as he had always wanted to meet
Schoenberg and looked forward to an occasion when we returned to the
States. But from my perspective, Schoenberg was the villain behind all
this twelve-tone music. I was still feeling confused at the time and hadn't

entirely accepted this new style of music. In context, it wasn't new so much as unfamiliar, and I simply hadn't heard enough yet to be comfortable with it. I was dutiful, though, and followed the direction that Jacques set for us, adhering to my husband's musical interests. I was a new wife, a new singer, and still a very young woman. I had a lot of growing up to do in the world of music.

CHAPTER THIRTEEN

HOME AGAIN

It was so nice to be back in New York at last, speaking my own language—which didn't mean that I was entirely back to my old self. I returned from my Paris sojourn with a new, unexpected set of problems: I couldn't face American bread, Wonder Bread especially. It was awful! And because we were on a tight budget, Jacques had to make due with packaged Brie—don't even mention other so-called cheeses. I can still see Jacques sitting at the table in front of a plate of crackers, peeling the tin foil off a triangular piece of Kraft Brie. I had at last fully come to understand his boisterous complaints about our crappy, processed American food. There is so much more international food and more sophisticated tastes today in New York City.

We came home by boat in December and settled into a cheap apartment on East 7th Street, between Avenues C and D. We had a barrel of wedding gifts, our usual rented upright piano, and an adopted cat we found on the street and named Isaac. I loved our neighborhood. At the time, our East 7th Street neighborhood was mostly Orthodox Jewish. Little boys with yarmulkes and side curls played in the streets. Elders strolled past, with their long black coats, beards, and stovepipe hats. There were open markets to buy your fresh vegetables every day except on Fridays and Saturdays, and a hardware store where you could find anything. This was my Sholem Aleichem world.

During that period, Jacques fell in love with cowboy movies—all action and not that much dialogue. So after morning practice, we'd head to the neighborhood movie house, where admission was only ten cents. My mother had stopped sending money after I got married, so until I found part-time singing work, Madame Monod was our financial mainstay. Her letters to Jacques were stuffed with fistfuls of French francs and arrived regularly. Where she found the money was a mystery to me. She might have been shaving it off her housekeeping allowance. There was no doubt that Jacques was her favorite son, her gifted firstborn.

Jacques and I started spending time with Milton and Sylvia Babbitt after we came back to the city. They were a very social couple in the early years of their marriage, which meant that friends were always flocking in and out of their East 19th Street apartment. The composer Al Bauman and his wife Nina would come through, as well as the *New York Herald Tribune* music critic and composer Arthur Berger and his wife Esther, Seymour and Miriam Shifrin, and other composers. It felt to me like we were there all the time. The first really decent publicity shots we have of the two of us were taken in the Babbitts' living room, sitting at Milton's piano.

In those days, Milton smoked Picayunes, a very strong southern cigarette, and Jacques smoked French Gauloises. Sylvia Babbitt and I made a habit of just moving into the kitchen to talk. If there's one thing I hate, it's smokers! There was nothing for it. It was the 1950s, and people smoked.

Being married to a composer of serious music is not easy. Especially when you're the one who has to take care of every detail of daily life that doesn't include composing music. Sylvia virtually gave herself over to Milton's needs. She was his chauffeur, concert companion, mother to their daughter Betty Ann, keeper of the household expenses—taxes, bills—and answerer of the telephone. Of course, all of her tending gave Milton the time he needed to compose.

In certain respects, Sylvia was also my social bridge to Milton. When I wasn't onstage singing his music in those early years, I tended to shrink in Milton's presence, always worried I would say something wrong. Sylvia would run interference. She was always calling us to deliver a message from Milton, or she'd bring a message back to Milton about some concert or social event to which the four of us were planning to share a cab. We all depended on Sylvia to keep us operational. For, in his own way, Milton too was keeping me close, even if our relationship was perennially mediated. In the end, and with an eye to the future, Milton knew that I could sing his difficult music—sing it well and often. And sing it I did.

In a short time, Sylvia also became my dearest friend. We used to go shopping at Ohrbach's and S. Klein—department stores right around the corner from our apartments. We loved to shop, and she was really a great one for finding a bargain.

Sylvia was always impeccably groomed. I never saw her without make-up. (I often wondered if it was Milton who insisted on such decorum or

Figure 24. Jacques's and my first publicity photo as a duo, taken at the Babbitts'.

whether she came by it naturally.) She was a funny gal, too: She sang pop music and had a real feel for it. She kept an eye on her figure and would come down on me right away if I gained too much weight.

Sylvia never complained. Her face to the world had a sense of humor and a refusal to let anything get her down. In later years, when she was in a nursing home after she'd suffered a series of heart attacks, I went with Milton to visit her. There she was, propped up in bed, her funny old self—enjoying soap operas all day on the TV and being waited on for once. Milton made it his business to be with her almost on a daily basis, which showed their abiding loyalty for each other. I sometimes wondered if Sylvia would have liked to have had more than one child, or if she already, in a way, had two. She was without doubt the caretaker in the family.

When the Babbitts were young, they were always socializing. When he got older, Milton barely saw anyone save at concerts or receptions in Princeton or New York. Privacy became more and more critical to Milton with the years, and Sylvia saw to it that he got it. I don't think anyone could have served Milton's needs the way Sylvia always did. Not only was she a remarkable person, but she was in her own way responsible for Milton's extraordinary output.

Looking back, I've realized that *fate* placed me around the corner from the Babbitts for those first ten years I was in New York City. It was a sign that Milton would go on to be such a huge influence on my singing career, though I certainly didn't know it at the time. It was Silvia who found us the apartment on East 17th Street, a stone's throw away from their apartment, but even Silvia couldn't predict the future or engineer fate. These years were the beginning of a close, lifelong friendship with the man who went on to compose some of the most complex music that I would ever sing.

In 1951, Milton dedicated his new song cycle, *Du*, to Jacques and me. *Du* was set to a cycle of seven poems by the German poet August Stramm. Milton had composed the piece that autumn while we were in France. Our feeble, rented upright piano was really passable only for practice—but now we had to use it to prepare a score in which all durations of pitch, dynamics, and rhythm were precisely notated and customized to dramatize Stramm's abrupt poetic expression ("Dein Schreiten bebt" ran the first, short line of "Wiedersehen"). In other words, every musical event was accounted for by the composer. It had an ethos of sheer comprehensiveness that I think defines Milton's music, and preparing it was the greatest challenge that Jacques and I had faced up to then.

I set about learning my pitches and what I thought to be the rhythm of my vocal line—at least I thought I'd learned it. Was I ever wrong! The next stage of preparation was the grueling ensemble work. Milton's rhythm is such that I felt like I would never be able to synchronize with the piano. We'd work with a metronome. Jacques would halve the tempo to start with, and incrementally speed it up one notch at a time. We worked especially hard on the rhythm of the second song in the cycle, which was marked 120 to the quarter note—a very hard, fast tempo. As always, our practice involved repeating and repeating until Jacques felt we had gotten it perfect. Starting at 60 to the quarter note, we'd get it right at last, and then he would move that metronome up another notch, slowly, slowly, one notch at a time . . . until we achieved Milton's tempo marking. In retrospect, I don't think I realized that this was also exactly how Jacques practiced the piano—it was the way he was taught to practice—and I was just "singing along with Mitch." On the other hand, you needed to put in exactly that kind of work on a score like *Du*. In the process, I learned a very effective system for handling complex rhythms.

Jacques taught me the repertoire that would define my career, and he taught me how to work hard. Effective or not, he called all the shots, the tempi, the interpretations, the programming, how we rehearsed. Jacques suffered terrible anxiety, and he absolutely *had* to prepare until there was no risk whatsoever of error in performance. I didn't have to keep everything in control like that in order to perform, but when I sang with him, I did. I worked within his box.

We always worked in the morning. If I took a time out to do some housework before practice, Jacques would stop me and say, "That's enough. Let's get to work." Jacques was definitely the boss. I wonder now whether I was so afraid of confrontation with him (or was it my father?) that I just let him determine everything. Those work sessions were so tedious, and the work arduous. But I didn't like to argue, I was in love, and I admired Jacques. It was as simple as that. And so we rehearsed and rehearsed until I felt I would scream if I heard another "*encore une fois!*"

It was restrictive. Great performances *don't* come from overrehearsing. Great performances come from the acoustics of the building, the instruments, the way you feel on a given night, how your body feels, and perhaps the love you have for that particular piece. A lot of ingredients come together to make a great performance—you just can't get it from overrehearsing.

When I was on stage performing, even overrehearsed, I still sang with a strong sense of myself. Jacques didn't muffle me on stage, because he couldn't. The Bethany that emerged in concert was a force. Onstage, I couldn't be just a robot that Jacques used to help him learn his part!

Perhaps just as important, Jacques and I always performed from memory. We repeated the material so many times that memorizing it was a simple matter. Knowing the music that way liberates you from the score and adds an extra dimension to your performance. It's basically a kind of utter freedom. Having said that, I should probably also say that I never felt hindered when I did perform with a score, which I did often when I was preparing a work that didn't involve Jacques. It was entirely different, for example, to prepare instrumental pieces—for which I was left to my own devices, and always sang from the score.

Although in retrospect I can see that my greatest musical interpretations could never have emerged in the hesitant, perfectionist environment that Jacques depended on, I learned a great deal in those years. I learned difficult music. I learned how to overprepare. I learned how exquisite Jacques's playing was. These were also the years in which I taught myself how to interpret and express music that was in many respects incomprehensible to me at the time; I taught myself how to work difficult vocal lines and intervals. Eventually I was able to learn music this same way by myself.

Once we learned *Du*, we went on to perform it many times from memory—which, it turns out, is the only way you can really perform Milton's music. Webern seemed easy compared with *Du*. You can't ever bluff a good composer with a so-so performance. When Milton heard *Du* for the first time on our rented upright on East 7th Street, a big smile appeared on his face. He must have been pleased with what we had accomplished after all those hours of work. Jacques's feat of wrenching the music out of that rented piano was in itself monumental. Milton was well aware of the challenges his music presented to performers, and he truly appreciated our efforts. He heard *everything*, and we knew we had to be perfect for him.

Jacques was fond of cats and particularly adored his plump, ten-year-old Siamese Bouboul, who was back in France. Bouboul was treated with the respect due royalty in the Monod household. Bouboul had the grand honor of being allowed to lie on the radiator, snuggled into Jacques's cashmere scarf, while Jacques practiced. One day our East 7th Street cat, Isaac, disappeared. We'd found him on the street, and had never gotten him fixed. He was always running after female cats, and we could often hear the horrible serenade of cat courting coming in through the window. When he didn't come home, we assumed he'd decided to return to his old ways. After Isaac, we never had another pet together.

We ended up staying just a year at East 7th Street. Then one day Sylvia called to tell us that her friend Betty Grayson was giving up a beautiful six-room apartment on 315 East 17th Street facing Stuyvesant Park because she was headed to the new state of Israel to live on a kibbutz. The apartment was in a large brownstone on a block made up of brownstones between First and Second Avenues. Her third-floor walkup was huge. It had large windows, an oversize living room, and a small guest bedroom, both looking out over the park. It even had a study, a small dining room, and a kitchen with pantry. The back hall led to an oversize master bedroom, and then *another* small bedroom. The toilet was separate from the bathroom, European style. There were marble fireplaces in the living room and master bedroom. In the morning, the apartment would flood with sunlight. And just three houses down was Dvořák's brownstone home, where he composed the *New World Symphony*. We were ready to move in! Betty left some of her furniture, which was a godsend, since Jacques and I couldn't have furnished more than two rooms of that massive apartment. The rent was $150 a month, a bit of a stretch for us, and yet we signed the lease totally unconcerned about an amount we really couldn't afford.

Our landlord, Dr. Gottesman, lived on the first floor and had his office on the ground floor. The second floor had two smaller apartments: A painter lived in one, a business couple in the other. The third floor belonged to us. Our top-floor neighbor, Mr. Elliot, took in stray cats and must have had more than a dozen. He was the ASPCA of the neighborhood.

We worked like beavers painting and fixing the apartment up when we first moved in. One morning Jacques was putting polyurethane on the floors and brushed himself into a corner. He was trapped. We had a good laugh over that.

Inevitably, we were always late with our rent. When we'd dash down the stairs to the ground-floor exit, Dr. Gottesman would be there, standing in his doorway—sometimes still in his pajamas—demanding his overdue rent. But we would just fly past, giving Dr. Gottesman a smile and a lame excuse. Dodging the landlord was a constant nightmare for me, but Jacques never seemed concerned.

Jacques had written a piece for string quartet and voice right after we returned from France that I never had a chance to perform. As I recall, he wrote it very quickly, and I have no idea what happened to the score. But after that he went into a hiatus and didn't compose a note for a very long time. He claimed he needed to rethink his ideas. I suspect what happened to Jacques was a consequence of Milton's powerful influence and the effects

Figure 25. Peeking through the divider to the living room from the kitchen at East 17th Street.

of their long discussions about music in the living room while Sylvia and I hid from cigarette smoke in the kitchen. *Du* was a turning point for Jacques. After all, we had just learned it, and Jacques must have been curious about its compositional nature. I've often thought that *Du* will someday be to music historians what Kandinsky's *Composition VIII* is to art historians. Milton was taking Schoenberg's method further.

Even while taking a break from composing, my husband was clearly anxious to get back into the New York musical scene. Ever since Juilliard, Milton had been the center of that scene. Milton knew everyone and everything going on in New York. Jacques settled us into our new apartment and then got busy trying to launch Monod projects. He was on the telephone all the time. Sometimes our phone bill was almost as large as our rent.

Meanwhile I had found a part-time secretarial job in the afternoons at the prestigious New York Junior League to add to the church singing because we needed the additional income.

My church job was now at the Church of St. Luke in the Fields in Greenwich Village. We worked under the wonderful organist Clifford Clark. It was a small, select, and paid choir. The music we sang—from Gregorian chant to Bach and Mozart—was first-rate. Clifford had good musical taste and kept a lovely apartment on the church grounds, all of which were contained in a whole block of Hudson Street. Riding in the crosstown bus to choir rehearsal on Thursday nights, I would pass the Cherry Lane Theatre when it was on Christopher Street. Lotte Lenya was then singing in Kurt Weill's *Threepenny Opera*. If you want to learn German diction, listen to Lenya singing Kurt Weill! Every time I passed the theater, I thought, "Bethany, you've got to go and see her. She is a legend." But I never did. It seemed like I was always either too busy or just plain broke.

CHAPTER FOURTEEN

NEW MUSIC IN
NEW YORK CITY

I n the fifties, there were several established groups in New York City that held regular concerts for new music. The International Society for Contemporary Music (ISCM), the League of Composers, and the American Composers Forum were the three groups that operated uptown, with performances at Carnegie Recital Hall, the Donnell Library, McMillin Theatre, and the 92nd Street Y. With Milton's support and his persuasive personality, Jacques took over as program director of the New York chapter of the ISCM. In retrospect, probably no one wanted the job. It meant that Jacques spent all his time on the phone, arranging programs, talking to composers, and finding players for the coming season. There were decisions to be made about what works to program, rehearsal locations, and hardest of all, the scheduling of rehearsals to coincide with everyone's free time. All of this was to be negotiated on the very slim budget allotted to the performers. Roger Sessions was president of the board. Money came from private donors as well as foundation grants and subscription sales.

At the same time, Gunther Schuller and his friend, the composer Maxwell Powers, started a series at the Greenwich Village Music House. The series was made up of programs with early music on the first half and contemporary music on the second. I sang on several of these programs. The series only lasted a few seasons, but Gunther would turn out to be an invaluable connection for Jacques. He was able to help Jacques find excellent players for the ISCM concerts—many recruited from the Metropolitan Opera orchestra, where Gunther was playing horn in those days.

Gunther was personable. He knew how to make you feel comfortable, which is a special kind of grace. He was a serious composer and in years to come had an amazing career as a conductor, writer, and teacher. He was also prodigious, the kind of guy who only ever needed four hours of sleep and seemed to have dozens of projects in the works at any given time—including running his own publishing and recording companies. He was constantly involved in the contemporary music scene and also allied himself to the jazz world. Gunther and I became good friends, especially in later years when we were both serving on the board of Pro Musicis. He would often ask for my recommendations on which singers to nominate for its award.

There was yet another group in New York during those heady years, the League of Composers. They were the more conservative faction. The group was run by Claire Reese and Aaron Copland. Copland was already a powerful figure in American music by the early 1950s. Along with Virgil Thomson, Ned Rorem, and Elliott Carter, he had studied with Nadia Boulanger in Paris. She was a strict pedagogue who taught all aspects of tonal music—harmony, species counterpoint, Bach counterpoint, and fugue. In particular, Boulanger was reputed to give rigorous critical responses on her students' work. She lived into her nineties and built up a huge roster of students.

Downtown, the fantastic dancer Merce Cunningham, the pianist David Tudor, and the composer John Cage were experimenting with (for want of a better word) *experimental* music. In my circle, which was the Uptown Group, these experiments were not taken seriously. For many of us, Cage was a figure of fun. Really, their collaborations had so much originality and played with such unusual ideas—whether one could appreciate them musically or not was another matter—that they gained popularity. To some extent, a whole audience of enthusiasts grew up with Cage's abstract music via Cunningham's productions.

At the time, we regarded Cage as harmless: one who was seeking newness and notoriety at the expense of the art form. We did not consider, perhaps, that the experiments would have repercussions and would effectively change the order of things for future composers. Whereas Brahms had grown up in a composer's world that made sense—the common-practice tradition—the sensibility for fragmentation was cultivated and became part of the texture of musical influence in the 1950s. In other words, Western developmental music, from Bach to Brahms, was challenged. In retrospect, the twentieth century, and all of the music that touched me, was a passage of sorts from the nineteenth to the twenty-first century. The mid-century was perfectly poised to be an exceptional time in music. As the composer Roger Sessions suggested in 1944, the war brought unique sensibilities together:

> In 1933 Schoenberg came to the United States and ten years later became an American citizen. In the country to which he came, musical activity is intense on many levels, and despite many necessary reservations the development within the last generation has been phenomenal. Musical education has penetrated everywhere; both the general level and the quality of instruction available on the highest level of all have risen to a degree amazing to all who confronted the musical conditions of thirty-five years ago. American composers of serious intent have begun to appear in considerable numbers, and to achieve an influence and recognition undreamed by their predecessors; moreover, they have become aware of themselves, of their inner and outer problems, and better equipped to face these. Above all it has become evident that musical talent, the raw material from which musical culture grows, is strikingly abundant.[8]

Today we have an explosion of influences, a wild cross-fertilization—pop music, ethnic music, serious music. The territory for new composers is vast. I can't see from here where it's all going to take us. But in my estimation, much of the music written today, with few exceptions, is not of the quality of the 1950s and 1960s. Perhaps the vastness of these influences, coupled with a kind of popular-culture professionalization, has led to a discernible "dumbing down" of the art form.

In those early years of my career, we developed close friendships with New York composers, many of whom went on to define "modern music" in the next quarter century. In addition to the Babbitts, there was French-speaking Marc Wilkinson. Marc often came over for dinner. His mother was French, and he was a bit of a Francophile. He turned out to be a great help to Jacques. After Marc left New York in 1956 to settle in London, he became a renowned composer of theater and television music. I sang a beautiful early piece by Marc, *Chants dédiés*, on one of Gunther's Greenwich House programs.

We also saw the lovable Seymour Shifrin and his wife, Miriam. Seymour was one of the nicest persons I've ever known. His gentle nature reminded me of my brother Walter. It was Seymour who gave me away at my Paris wedding. They were part of the McMillin crowd in those early days and close to the Babbitts. Seymour left New York to teach at UC Berkeley and then Brandeis in the 1960s, where he remained until he died. He composed well-crafted twelve-tone music. I sang two of his early songs in the 1950s, and in the years that followed I heard many performances of his music. Today, his work is seldom played—like that of so many of the fine composers I knew in those New York days.

We spent many evenings with Al and Nina Bauman. Jacques and Nina knew each other from his Leibowitz days in Paris, and I instantly took a liking to her. She was petite, vivacious, and bubbly. Al and Nina were both deep into Wilhelm Reich, all the rage back then. I remember one night I had an awful cold and was worried because I had a concert coming up. The Baumans put me into an orgone box, promising that thirty minutes would cure me. It was dark in there, and I sweated profusely, but it didn't cure my cold. A shot of whiskey might have been a much better solution.

We did so many concerts uptown at McMillin that Milton, Jacques, Silvia, and I made a tradition of walking down Broadway to a small bar, the Gold Rail, for a beer afterward. Sometimes we were joined by other members of the McMillin crowd, like the Shifrins or the Bergers. At the end of the evening we'd all hop in a taxi back downtown to the East Village. Those are memories that I cherish, the wonderful conversation and camaraderie. I loved my life as a young singer.

Meanwhile, outside the city, we were often invited to perform at Princeton University because of Milton. The Music Department at that time was housed in Clio Hall, a small Grecian-looking temple on campus. These were my first impressions of the university that later became a major part in my life. Picture an office where Roger Sessions, the elder statesman, would be talking to Milton, who was always smoking his Picayunes and *always* had one leg draped over a chair arm. Ed Cone, Arthur Mendel, and then Earl Kim would arrive, one after the other. Eventually the musicologist Oliver Strunk would stroll in, too. Then we'd go to the Balt for lunch—always Milton, Jacques, me, and whichever composition student wanted to tag along. It was a golden age for composers at Princeton: Alden Ashforth, Philip Batstone, Benjamin Boretz, Bill Carlin, Johnny Eaton, David Hamilton, John Harbison, Michael Kassler, Paul Lansky, Fred Lerdahl, David Lewin, Lewis Lockwood, Donald Martino, Malcolm Peyton, James K. Randall, Charles Rosen, Michael Steinberg, Henry Weinberg, Peter Westergaard, and my future husband, Godfrey Winham, to mention just a few.

As for Jacques, he was all regime. We'd practice in the morning until I left for my afternoon job at the New York Junior League. I have no idea why

I wasn't summarily fired. I always arrived late, going on fumes from an exhausting morning rehearsal. But my boss and the gang at the office had read some of my reviews and decided to be fans, which somehow translated into being tolerant of my tardiness—though if I had gotten fired, I might have been a little bit grateful to have one less job. It seemed like I could never sit down, kick off my shoes, and relax after dinner. There was no time. We were living practically hand to mouth. Reading the *New York Times* or the *Herald Tribune* on the subway on the way to work was my one moment of escape.

And there was a great deal going on in the world to keep up with. Dwight D. Eisenhower was elected in 1952, renewing our hopes for ending the war in Korea. In *Life* magazine, I saw pictures of the new young Queen Elizabeth's coronation. She was so beautiful, though I'm sure she was also quite overwhelmed by the duties before her. Occasionally we even went to a movie.

That year I learned more new music. Most of what Jacques and I memorized in that period, we would perform over and over and over again in our recitals. I memorized songs by Webern, Michel Philippot, Schoenberg, Roger Sessions, Seymour Shifrin, and Alvin Bauman, as well as more of Milton's work. Jacques would, of course, always conduct the ensemble pieces on the ISCM programs. Works by Berg, Webern, and Schoenberg in particular became absolutely central to our performances. In later years, without Jacques, I incorporated much of this same repertoire into my programs.

I wasn't just a recitalist; I was the "Girl Singer from East Lansing," as Milton used to call me, who took on the canon that constituted music of that moment. I was performing the newest techniques and ideas of music composition in the legacy of Schoenberg.

Jacques had taken charge of the ISCM and was entirely running the series. He was determined and charming, and the board trusted him. This position finally landed Jacques squarely in the middle of the new music scene and was a perfect platform from which to champion the Second Viennese School. In the programming, he gave preference to premieres of twelve-tone music. In the first season of ISCM, he didn't explore *any* other music—all those many gifted American composers who weren't dodecaphonists. It would be a year before I got a chance to sing Aaron Copland. I've never sung Irving Fine. And I didn't get to sing the work of wonderful composers such as Israel Citkowitz, Samuel Barber, and Theodore Chanler until the 1970s. But Jacques was strategic. By working so exclusively in this musical vein, he was forging a singular professional niche for us. He also, I should be clear, loved this music and believed in Schoenberg's new system.

You didn't want to cross Jacques, for he would never forget it. He was very paranoid about people in general, and fiercely loyal to his friends. The former trait became self-destructive. He was highly opinionated and uncompromising, and couldn't accommodate himself to another person's point of view—qualities that did not bode well for our marriage. It also made things more difficult for him along the way professionally.

In later years, everyone was always after Jacques to conduct. I keep coming back to the conviction that Jacques should have had the career that Pierre Boulez had. But Boulez was willing to compromise where Jacques wasn't. Jacques, for example, insisted his players rehearse with the same intensity he brought to the rehearsals that he and I did alone. I'm sure that Boulez had a similar desire for rigorous preparation—especially where his own work was concerned—but he was also more practical. Not even the best conductors get as many rehearsals as they would like. You can't push people that hard. It's too expensive, and freelance musicians don't have that kind of time. Jacques demanded hard work from everyone, maintained high expectations, and studied his scores. When he was given the time he wanted, he produced extraordinary performances.

I was twenty-seven years old and starting to wonder what all of this new music was going to get me—except a reputation as an oddball. The fees were miserable. I felt isolated and was starting to long to do recitals of classical music. That was not to be! Paradoxically, though, I was happy, for I had married a composer-performer and now I seemed to hold the unique position of "Girl Singer" among brilliant composers in New York and Princeton. I know it sounds like a contradiction, but there were two sides to me: One side wanted to explore new music, and the other clung to my love of classical art song.

CHAPTER FIFTEEN

" A L L   T H E
R I G H T   P E O P L E "

J acques stayed on as the dictator of ISCM from 1952 through the early part of 1955. He had full control of programming, chose the composers, and organized rehearsals. It was a job that suited his artistic and controlling personality. No one else, as I've said, really wanted that job—it was practically volunteer work. But Jacques wasn't one to miss an opportunity; he was starting to leverage his reputation as a new music impresario to garner favors.

Here are some of the freelance musicians I had the privilege of working with: James Politis, Murray Panitz, and Robert di Domenica, flute; William Arrowsmith, Henry Schuman, and Josef Marx, oboe; Luigi Cancellieri, Jack Kreiselman, Irving Neidich, Art Bloom, and Alan Blaustein, clarinet; Sidney Keil, bass clarinet, John Barrows and Gunther Schuller, French horn. There were many wonderful string players, such as Isidore Cohen (violin), Seymour Barab (cello), the violinist Abram Loft of the Fine Arts Quartet, and members of the New Music String Quartet. Among the pianists were Robert Helps, Lalan Parrott, Russell Sherman, and Jack Maxim. When I walked into a first rehearsal and saw any one of these players, I'd know I was in good hands.

The composer Vladimir Ussachevsky was our recording engineer. Vladimir was a big, very handsome Russian who worked alongside Milton for years at the Columbia-Princeton Electronic Music Studio. When the studio was being installed at 125th Street, the tapes that Vladimir had been keeping of our ISCM concerts were lost in the move—thrown out, I presume. It was a mystery that was never solved and is a tragedy. To think that all of those wonderful performances are gone forever.

In the 1953 season of ISCM concerts, Jacques broadened the repertoire. In addition to Babbitt, Carter, Sessions, Shifrin, Schoenberg, Berg, Philippot, Hindemith, and Webern, we also played Andre Casanova, Chou Wen-chung, Aaron Copland, Peter Racine Fricker, Earl Kim, Dika Newlin, Priaulx Rainier, Leonard Rosenman, Julius Schloss, Gunther Schuller, Leopold Spinner, Egon Wellesz, and Stefan Wolpe. It was a blend of older, well-known composers and younger talents. Jacques's selections were mostly atonal or twelve-tone, with just a little tonal music thrown into the mix.

I never got a chance to know many of these composers. I never met Michel Phillipot when we were in Paris, although Jacques was his champion for years. Even today he regards Phillipot as one of the finest composers in France. Leopold Spinner's music was similar to Webern's and could be mistaken for it if you looked at his manuscripts—I sang often from manuscripts at the time. Julius Schloss was another Schoenberg student who escaped from the Nazis by way of China to New York.

In 1954, ISCM produced works by Hans Erich Apostel, Edward T. Cone, Luigi Dallapiccola, Miriam Gideon, Robert Helps, Erich Itor Kahn, René Leibowitz, Keith Robinson, Arnold Schoenberg, Ralph Shapey, Igor Stravinsky, Ben Weber, Marc Wilkinson, and Alexander Zemlinsky.

In addition to Miriam Gideon, a few other women composers were active in the New York scene in the 1950s: Ruth Crawford Seeger (Pete Seeger's stepmother), Peggy Glanville-Hicks, Vivian Fine, and Louise Talma. To me, the two standouts were Vivian Fine and Miriam Gideon. Miriam was a student of Roger Sessions and adamant in interviews that she thought of herself as an American composer and not a "woman composer"—at least not until the feminist movement of the 1960s made that something that needed to be considered. I wish I'd had a chance to sing a Miriam Gideon score, but it never happened. Vivian Fine wrote *A Guide to the Life Expectancy of a Rose*, which I sang and Jacques conducted at the Martha Graham Studio. Vivian's first-rate music was my only experience with a female composer's work until many years later.

When I reflect today on how I felt about the music I was singing, I feel compelled to explain that the task of learning and performing was always about moving from one piece to the next without too much consideration of whether I liked something or not. There were exceptions. Sometimes I loved a new piece: *Die Serenaden* of Paul Hindemith or *The Leaden Echo and the Golden Echo* by Egon Wellesz, for example. (And it might be worth pointing out that those were both tonal works.) The appreciation that I have today for so much of this repertoire came with time and familiarity. That said, over all those years, I was clear on the conviction that I was singing music of high quality. Maybe my memory has endowed some of the music with a bit of fairy dust, but I don't think so!

For three years straight, we were always learning new music, especially, it seemed, Schoenberg. We worked to death three very hard songs by Schoenberg (op. 48) on poetry by Jacob Haringer, which we sang for the first time in the second concert of the 1953 season, along with the Hindemith and Wellesz that I mention above. The third Schoenberg song, "Mädchenlied," was a killer. Schoenberg tends to mark some of his music with impossible tempi. "Mädchenlied" was marked 198 to the eighth note. Even with Jacques's militant metronome, we just could not get it up to Schoenberg's tempo—and I defy anyone to try it. Luckily Schoenberg did take care to describe the pace as "Leicht, nicht hastig" (light, not hasty) and *that* was how we performed it. According to Schoenberg's American publisher, Boelke-Bomart, the three songs were written during the winter of 1933, during Hitler's rise to power. It was also the same year that Schoenberg fled Berlin for America and consequently a dark period in his life. Schoenberg had completely obliterated his memory of having written the songs in this set. When they reemerged, thanks to the attention of a few close friends, Schoenberg just gave them the next open opus number; hence, they are op. 48. We gave eight performances of the songs, and I grew to like them quite a bit.

Boelke-Bomart had been founded by the music engraver Walter Boelke with the idea of creating a modernist publishing house—in the tradition of Schoenberg. Walter was a great ally of Jacques in that period. They met in 1952 at a launch party for one of the Schoenberg Boelke-Bomart publications, and Jacques immediately became Boelke's consultant. Jacques and I used to visit Walter and his wife Margot in Hillsdale, New York, in the summer. Boelke's social network comprised all the Communists living in Long Island who hadn't been blacklisted. The Boelkes had a wonderful house and many fascinating friends and visitors—including Monica Mann (Thomas Mann's daughter and a friend of Margot's). It was great fun to go out there—not a piano in sight—to relax, eat wonderful food, escape the hot city, and meet all of those extraordinary characters. And of course it made Jacques so happy to be in his Marxist element.

Figure 26. Here is a page from my *Mädchenlied* score. You can see from Jacques's notes littering the page how emphatic and rigorous a coach he could be. Schoenberg, *3 Songs*, op. 48, after poems by Jakob Haringer. Copyright © 1952 by Boelke-Bomart. Copyright © renewed. Copyright © 2012 assigned to Schott Music. All rights reserved. Used in the world excluding the US by permission of European American Music Distributors Company, agent for Schott Music. Used in the US by permission of Belmont Music Publishers, Los Angeles.

Figure 27. In one of my B. Altman discount wedding dresses. The picture appeared on the jacket of the *Altenberg Lieder* recording. Photograph by Fred Plaut.

During this period, we were living on such a modest income that I had to be inventive when it came to my performance outfits; the only really decent gown I owned was my wedding dress. So I had a brilliant idea. I would buy marked-down wedding dresses from B. Altman's and pair them with different-colored stoles. I could buy a new dress for only ten dollars, because once a wedding dress had even the tiniest bit of dust on the hem, they couldn't sell it at full price anymore. To me, B. Altman's was the Rolls-Royce of department stores. It was a huge, old neighborhood store with an elegant, stately charm. When you walked in off the street, the quiet was astonishing. The grandness and space created an otherworldly effect that just seemed to absorb the noise of the streets and the shoppers.

I went along happily with my wedding-dress costume solution until one day Sylvia suddenly exclaimed, "That's enough, Bethany! I never want to see you in white again!" So I hit the thrift stores instead. My favorite was Encore, which was located in the East 60s near the New York Junior League office. Encore was where the wealthy East Side clientele left their evening gowns on consignment, and it was a treasure chest of all the famous designers. Some gowns had been worn only once or twice. The prices were steeper than the B. Altman discount rack, but well worth it.

In a buffoonish 1969 review of several New York City concerts, the *New York* magazine critic Alan Rich included a footnote *defining* what he meant when he said "the hall was packed with all the Right People":

> *Right People: major composers—Copland, Carter, Cage, Sessions, Babbitt, Feldman—at a concert of new music; Rubinstein or Serkin at a piano recital; leading singers from the Met or City Opera at vocal events. Five points extra Bernstein (at anything), Virgil Thomson (at anything not Thomson or French) or Peter Mennin; two extra for Julius Rudel or Mayor Lindsay (if he stays until the end); one for Zinka Milanov. Rubinstein went to the opening-night "Manon" and stayed until the end: ten points.[9]

That was, of course, a full decade later than the period I've been describing, but new music royalty was already in early evidence when I would give an ICSM concert. Here is a picture of the audience that I saw from the stage. They were mostly composers and always sat in the same seats. Carlos Salzedo and Edgard Varèse would sit together, speaking French (Salzedo was an elegant harpist who always kissed your hand when congratulating you. Varèse was a burly lion of a man with unruly, snow-white hair who *never* came backstage); Stefan Wolpe and his wife Irma, whom I didn't meet until years later; Milton and Sylvia Babbitt; Helen and Elliott Carter; Wallingford Riegger, a loner; the feisty Ralph Shapey and his wife, the painter Vera Klement; Louis Stanley and his wife (Stanley was working on a biography of Dimitri Mitropoulos, the music director of the New York Philharmonic at the time); Seymour and Miriam Shifrin; Otto Luening and Jack Beeson, both on Columbia's faculty, would often show up; Marc Wilkinson; Alvin and Nina Bauman; majestic Miriam Gideon and her husband; and probably other composers I can't recall now. There were many young student composers, mostly from Columbia University, plus a small devoted public, cultural New Yorkers curious about new music.

From my vantage point on stage, these composers were the first generation whose music I sang. In the sixties and seventies, it would be their students whose music I sang. And those second-generation composers are the teachers of today's new composers. I retired in 1984, though, so my perspective as a performer only takes us that far, and almost all of the first generation has died. Elliott Carter passed away in November 2012 at the age of 103.

Singers can always see their audience and it was curious how many always sat in the same spot in the hall. Perhaps that is why I can still see so clearly a certain coterie of "old faithfuls" in my memory.

Perhaps the greatest triumph of the ISCM during the Monod era was the all-Webern concert on December 28, 1952. The concert took place at the 92 Street Y on Lexington Avenue and 92nd Street. Kaufmann Concert Hall had much better acoustics than McMillin, which had been built as a lecture hall. The hall was beautifully suited to chamber music. It also served double duty as a stage for the great poetry readings that Betty Ussachevsky held there, and where I'd heard Dylan Thomas, W. H. Auden, and Marianne Moore.

This program was more extensive than the one we gave at Juilliard in 1951, just a year and a half earlier, with the Juilliard String Quartet. That concert was less formal, and we approached it playfully. It was something that we did as part of Juilliard, and it wasn't advertised or reviewed. This second one included more pieces. It was advertised, and most of the New York public that followed new music was there.

We also had the help of the New Music String Quartet, as well as Sidney Keil on bass clarinet and Luigi Cancellieri on clarinet. (They had played the Webern *Canons* for us at the Juilliard concert.) The New Music String Quartet, like the Juilliard Quartet, was one of the best string quartets for new music at that time in the city. They were all remarkable musicians, who unfortunately played together for only a short time. It was an honor to work with them: Broadus Erle, first violin, who went on to join the Yale faculty; Claus Adam, cello, who soon after became part of the Juilliard String Quartet; Matthew Raimondi, second violin, founder of the Composers String Quartet; and Walter Trampler, viola, who played for years with the Chamber Music Society of Lincoln Center.

Webern's music had become stylish with the avant-garde after the war. I think its charm lies in its brevity, open texture, and delicacy. Webern loved particularly the range of *pianissimo*—***ppp*** to ***p***. His music was ideally suited to my lyric voice. And since Webern's pieces are so short, we were able to do nine of them on one program.

The concert was a success, and we had great reviews from the *New York Times* and *New York Herald Tribune*. The critic Arthur Berger wrote in the *Herald Tribune*, "It is only through performances of last night's caliber that we may come to appreciate Webern's music, for its spare constellations of notes are almost all about color, subtle variations of loudness, and delicate balancing of tones widely removed in pitch." Berger remarked that an all-Webern program was an unprecedented and significant choice, and he was especially generous to our performances:

> More than a small part of the credit for this goes to the performers for their intimate knowledge and understanding of the music and the great pains that had obviously gone into mastering its enormous difficulties. Jacques Monod who appeared both as conductor and as piano accompanist is clearly one of the best musicians around, and he brought staggering discipline and shading to his executions. Accompanying Bethany Beardslee in two groups of songs without the aid of printed music was a sheer tour de force. The young soprano for her part maneuvered the relentless vocal skips as if they were no more challenging than scale-wise passages, and her light voice is extraordinarily suitable to the skips and gives a curve to their ostensible angularity.[10]

Arthur Berger was an excellent reviewer, and excellent reviewers are few and far between. He listened with particular acuity because he was a composer, and his complete review of the evening captures what made that concert so important among the many that Jacques mounted. Berger left reviewing shortly afterward to become teacher of composition at Brandeis University, where he remained the rest of his life.

Igor Stravinsky and Robert Craft attended the concert that night, according to Milton. They sat way down front. Craft had met Stravinsky in 1948 and introduced him to Webern's music, which Stravinsky grew to love. In a published interview with Craft, Stravinsky said, "Webern is for me the *juste de la musique*."[11] His interest in Webern is probably the reason that Stravinsky finally came to experiment (not entirely successfully) with serialism in his later years, after Schoenberg had died. I have often wondered if Stravinsky would have tried twelve-tone when the master was alive? I doubt it. Composers have huge egos.

CHAPTER SIXTEEN

THE DUO

Recital Tours for the Association of
American Colleges and Universities

A s I have said, Jacques insisted that both of us perform from memory when we did recitals, and he billed us as a duo. I don't think he wanted to be upstaged for even a minute; it would have damaged his ego. While we were as busy as ever, mounting ISCM concerts in New York City, Jacques came up with the naïve idea that every college in the United States was just dying to hear the music of the Second Viennese School. After all, he thought, we had developed a huge repertoire. Why shouldn't we generate some income from it? So he got in touch with Mrs. Norwood Baker, who ran the arts program wing of the Association of American Colleges. The program had been designed to send artists in residence for two-day visits to small liberal arts college campuses around the country. The fees were modest; we earned between $350 and $400 for both of us, expenses included. And since neither of us knew how to drive, we traveled by bus or train.

Some of the more progressive schools requested a completely contemporary music program, but for the most part, the touring concert was half classical and half new music. We'd perform a Brahms group, a beautiful song cycle by C. P. E. Bach, and a group of Purcell or Haydn songs. The great relief of our arduous barnstorming America with the Second Viennese School tour was that I was finally able to sing classical repertoire! After intermission, it was nothing but new music. I am sure that the students and the majority of the faculty had never heard this repertoire. We'd host a workshop on the following day so that the students could ask

Figure 28. Publicity photo with Jacques taken in the Babbitts' apartment.

questions about the music. They would usually sit there mute, cowed by the material, until a faculty member broke the ice. Music students in those days had never heard of the Second Viennese School. I sympathized with them, for neither had I until I met Jacques!

Our first tour was in 1953. We traveled from Fargo, North Dakota, down to Alabama and Florida. In Miami I had the taste of fresh fruit served in a wonderful salad. I had never tasted citrus newly picked off trees. What a difference. Discoveries like those were rewarding, but I will also *never* forget the grueling nineteen-hour bus trip back to New York from Florida.

We were preparing for a second tour for the Association of American Colleges and Universities, when while rehearsing one day with my workaholic husband, I sneezed. I felt a small pop in my lower back. Such a small event, but it developed into chronic pain. It got so bad that I had to stand up in the bus all the way from Westminster, Maryland, back to New York. Sylvia sent me to her doctor, an internist. When he pressed his thumb hard into the sore spot, the pain was excruciating. The doctor advised me to wear a support, a corset of sorts. I suffered from lower back pain for years after that. It never affected my singing, but it made all that bus travel even more dreadful. I'm sure it was a psychosomatic response to how hard Jacques drove me.

Our second tour in 1954 hit small colleges like Beloit, Dartmouth, St. John's, Western Maryland (recently renamed McDaniel College), Drew University, and the University of Louisville. With the exception of Beloit College in Wisconsin, all of the schools were on the East Coast, which made traveling easier. In Louisville we met the composer George Perle, who was a big fan of Alban Berg's music. George had studied privately with Ernst Křenek. George and Jacques hit it off immediately. After the concert, I had to sit and listen to the two of them talk shop for what seemed like hours. I was in a bad mood, very hungry after singing, and had to wait and wait until dinner was finally served by our hostess, who was a dear friend of George's. To be fair, she hadn't known we were coming. George had issued the invitation spontaneously. That said: Never keep a singer waiting while a steak thaws. Especially a singer who has just sung a recital of difficult repertoire and needs a relaxing glass of wine and a good meal.

I believe song recitals are a high form of chamber music. By performing from memory, in particular, Jacques and I achieved a real ensemble and perhaps raised the performance standard of playing such difficult music. You'll see it in all chamber music performed from memory—with that kind of ensemble work, having memorized the music tightens the unity of the music. You're able to join as one into the music. Part of that is visual. If you don't have to look at the score, you can look at each other—especially in a string quartet. Of course, a singer and a pianist don't watch each other in the same way, because singers are generally facing the audience, and yet the sense of security is very strong. You know, for example, that if you do a rubato or decide to phrase something slightly differently, the pianist will move right along with you. Because you both know the music so well, it's easier to glide. If I were to come in at the wrong time, Jacques would be able to jump into the right spot with me and never have to worry about finding his place in the score. But I never did miss an entrance, and I never got to test that fail-safe—the clear result of our spectacular overpreparation.

We rehearsed meticulously—even the familiar old classical literature. Jacques was uncompromising and a perfectionist—a difficult position to take in this world. He reminds me now of the late conductor Carlos Kleiber, who was also never satisfied and for that reason gradually isolated himself from the conducting world. Like Kleiber, Jacques would eventually leave performing and concentrate on teaching and composing. When he was asked in later years to conduct, he would refuse, unless it was a project that interested him. He always said yes to performing Schoenberg, though, especially if he could finagle unlimited rehearsal time.

Many years later, according to the composer Tom James, Jacques was asked by the New York Philharmonic to step in and conduct a Babbitt piece that Leonard Bernstein refused to tackle. Jacques's response to the compliment was to request eight rehearsals. He was offered two hours instead and refused the job. Jacques would never let himself be complicit in an inadequate preparation.

It was different for me. When I was on stage singing I left little, dutiful Bethany backstage. I became *Bethany*, my crazy, true self. With Jacques, I was so overrehearsed that I could have almost, in a flash, stood to the side and just watched this woman sing. She was the "other one," lifted completely out of herself, and carried away by the music. Who was this person gliding on wings of song? She was me—but what about afterward, offstage? Where did she go? Many performers have a separate persona they inhabit in their private lives. Perhaps the transcendence I experienced on stage was talent, which is indefinable and so different from one person to the next. I know that for me it was embodied in the act of singing, and only then.

CHAPTER SEVENTEEN

FIFTY-NINE NEW
PIECES OF MUSIC

Early on, Jacques got it into his head that I should study with Louise Zemlinsky, the wife of the famous composer Alexander Zemlinsky. In 1953, I finally agreed—although I certainly didn't share his opinion that I needed a teacher at this point. And even if I did, Mrs. Zemlinsky wouldn't have been my first choice. She had had only a short career in opera before fleeing Europe with her husband and settling in New York. Her husband died shortly after their arrival, and Mrs. Zemlinksy settled into her official position as a Viennese widow.

Her studio was on Riverside Drive, and I did love walking down the long hall of her apartment and seeing all the photographs of Zemlinsky, Schoenberg, Webern, and Berg hanging on the walls. I remember a photograph of Berg and Webern standing together in a field—perhaps during the period when they were both studying with Schoenberg: Berg, tall, with a poetic face, dark wavy hair, and sensuous mouth; Webern next to him, so much shorter, with his steel-rimmed glasses and bird beak of a nose—he could have been mistaken for a bank teller. And as I looked at that picture I would think of their music. Berg's rich, romantic texture, and Webern's open, pointillist style. It's funny how their music almost matched their physical appearances.

Mrs. Zemlinsky was a health-food addict and one of the first people to tell me about the benefits of eating yogurt and whole grains. Her usefulness to me as a singing teacher was, however, predictably dubious. My lessons consisted of holding my hands on my chest and making single sounds, which she corrected. I got fed up and left, telling Jacques we had better ways of spending our money.

Because of my strong technical training with J. Herbert Swanson and the confidence I had in how he'd taught me, I felt that I couldn't learn anything from Mrs. Zemlinsky. She never explained anything. She wasn't a real teacher, and I'm not sure she had a concept of how the voice was produced. I say that, and yet she must have been an intelligent teacher for some, because of her reputation. But I didn't want a teacher, and there was nothing that I was hoping to get from her. Mrs. Zemlinsky, however, remained in touch with Jacques and was quite devoted to him, always addressing him as Dr. Monod. In turn, he advised her on the handling of her husband's musical estate. That was perhaps Jacques's ulterior motive for talking me into studying with her.

Later, after Jacques and I broke up, Claus and Eleanor Adam convinced me at a cocktail party that I should go study with Eleanor's mother, Helen Bentz. I think that she *did* help me. I'd always had such a light voice, but she coached me to make a bigger sound. I was perhaps assuming that my sound would just grow naturally from all of the singing I was doing—the voice is a muscle, after all. But Mrs. Bentz made me sing with an even sense of wideness, which opened up my sound more. It was an open-throat technique. Mr. Swanson had always taught me to sing to the point, and that was the focus of the sound. He wanted a voice to have lots of center. Mrs. Bentz took that idea and expanded it for me. She was very physical and made me hear my sound down to my toes. We did massive yawning gestures. She had me open my sound up high and then do a rolling descent in triplets—up and down in a big sweep. She had me use more breath and move the sound horizontally out from the center. It was an amazing way to develop the highly focused sounds that I'd learned in the Italian technique. Working with her gave me an openness that I didn't have before.

Living in New York in the fifties had one big advantage. Many things were cheap, and admission to art museums was free. I would meet up for lunch with my friend, Fay Lansner (who knew Ellen Adler in Paris). She was a stunning, dark beauty, and I very much admired her painting. We'd eat in the small cafeteria of the Museum of Modern Art near the sculpture garden. I loved to visit the magnificent statue of Balzac by Rodin and the beautiful nude women by Aristide Maillol that graced the garden. After seeing the permanent collection (there were far fewer special exhibitions in those days), we would have lunch and talk about art and the pros and cons of marriage—the usual girl talk.

Except for the French francs sent from time to time by Madame Monod, I was solidly the breadwinner in our marriage. There were weekly paychecks from my part-time job, plus monthly fees from church and temple. Our touring and New York concert appearances just didn't make up the difference. At least I could fall back on my typing skills, but Jacques had never worked. Music was all he knew. This kind of life was never going to raise us out of living day to day on a shoestring. Our existence was exciting but taxing. My commitment was based on admiration of my husband and the belief that we were making an important contribution to the music of our time. Looking back, I guess it was really youthful enthusiasm and the energy that goes with it.

In the *New York Times* we read that Joseph Stalin and Serge Prokofiev had both died on the same day—March 5, 1953. How strange that a tyrant and a wonderful Russian composer would be going together—in different directions, as far as I was concerned. Nikita Krushchev became Russia's premier after that, and we all nursed hopes that the Cold War might come to an end.

For the occasion of Schoenberg's eightieth birthday, Jacques organized several all-Schoenberg concerts. One of those concerts was at Drew University in Madison, New Jersey, where the remarkable composer Dika Newlin taught. Dika was a child prodigy from my own hometown, East Lansing, and went to UCLA to study with Schoenberg when she was only sixteen. Dika was a character. She wasn't very pretty, but she was terribly funny. In her later years, she got into being a punk-rock performer. It's hard to imagine, but if anyone could engineer a transformation like that, it would be Dika.

Dika admired Jacques and had invited us several times to perform at Drew. For Schoenberg's eightieth birthday, Dika and Jacques decided to mount two programs of solo piano works and the songs. For the first program we performed: Three Piano Pieces, op. 11; Four Songs, op. 2; Six Little Piano Pieces, op. 19; Six Songs, op. 3; Two Songs, op. 14; and Two Piano Pieces, op. 33. The second program included: Five Piano Pieces, op. 23; Three Songs, op. 48; Piano Suite, op. 25; and finally another group of early songs, Eight Songs, op. 6. I don't know why, but for this concert Jacques played the early songs (op. 3 and op. 6) from score. I imagine he didn't feel challenged by this early period of tonal Schoenberg and didn't feel the need to prepare the life out of them. Schoenberg's early songs are in the Wagnerian tradition and not suitable for me—they're much better for a heavy voice. But they were easy enough to learn, and I whipped them off.

On February 15, 1954, Jacques and I presented the first of what was planned to be two duo recitals under the auspices of the ISCM at the 92nd Street Y's Kaufmann Concert Hall. This time, he played everything from memory. We opened the program with Six Songs, op. 3 of Schoenberg. These were followed by Five Songs, op. 4 of Webern; three unedited songs by Alban Berg; and Three Songs, op. 23 by Anton Webern. Following intermission we performed Four Songs, op. 2 by Schoenberg; Two Songs, op. 14 by Schoenberg; Four Songs, op. 12 by Anton Webern; *The Widow's Lament in Springtime*, a gorgeous single song on a William Carlos Williams poem by Milton Babbitt; *Du* by Babbitt; and finally Four Songs, op. 2 by Alban Berg. These significant concerts were the artistic culmination of our work together. It was a culmination and a kind of tipping point. The first program was never reviewed, and I think Jacques was terribly discouraged by that.

In preparing for the second concert, we were simply derailed by the fact that Milton's *Vision and Prayer*, which was slated to be the program's centerpiece, wasn't finished in time. Milton had originally conceived of the piece—destined to become one of his most important contributions to electronic music—for voice and piano, but the early work never really came to fruition. In addition to all of that, Jacques was growing far more interested in conducting and ever less interested in playing piano. The Duo was beginning to pull apart. We never held the second concert.

Meanwhile, I was twenty-nine, and I had learned a repertoire that encompassed the complete songs of Berg, Webern, and all of Schoenberg—with the exception of his groundbreaking song cycle *Das Buch der hängenden Gärten*. In the five years that I was married to Jacques, I learned fifty-nine pieces of new music, most of it from memory. It is an unbelievable amount of music and a daunting repertoire, but it was the herculean effort that gave my musical career its raison d'être.

CHAPTER EIGHTEEN

1955 AND PIERROT LUNAIRE

A Tumultuous Year

Nineteen fifty-five was the year I ended my relationship with Jacques, learned *Pierrot lunaire*, and met Godfrey Winham, who would become my second husband.

To prepare Schoenberg's *Pierrot lunaire*, Jacques insisted I learn to sing the pitches first and then break the vocal line down into "pitch-contoured speech"—that precise coinage came later, from Godfrey. "Pitch-contoured," as opposed to "semi-spoken," means that you can feel the rise and fall of the voice line's phrases. Semi-spoken would be a much more leveled sound.

I was furious! I had heard Erika Stiedry-Wagner's recording of the piece with Schoenberg conducting. She definitely spoke it more than sang it, and I didn't understand why I couldn't do the same. I didn't understand why I had to learn the pitches in order to perform a spoken part. *Pierrot* had twenty-one sections and ran a full thirty-plus minutes. Jacques, contrarian or perfectionist, made me learn to sing it before he'd allow me to speak it.

In addition to learning *Pierrot*, I had started doing a lot of secretarial work for Jacques as well my part-time work at the Junior League. By the fall of 1954 our marriage was wearing thin. I'm sure that most of my anger with Jacques came out of being exhausted and frustrated over having to learn yet another big work.

In fact, Schoenberg very specifically wanted the pitch-contoured interpretation—which he called *Sprechstimme*—because it would give a tremendous dramatic variety to the little clown, Pierrot. It was a new kind of vocal technique that he was determined to have incorporated into the music. Although he supervised the Columbia Records recording that Erika Stiedry-Wagner had made, he had been famously disappointed. Stiedry-Wagner didn't have the right vocal equipment for the part—she was an actress. That early recording had come about because the conductor Fritz Stiedry was a close friend of Schoenberg's and wanted Schoenberg to cast his wife as the speaker. But Schoenberg had written the piece for the actress and cabaret singer Albertine Zehme, who'd originally commissioned it and premiered it in Berlin. It was a part for a singer who could act and never was intended for an actress.

Jacques was absolutely correct in his interpretation. In his direction to me, he was only following the composer's own notes. In the foreword to *Pierrot lunaire*, Schoenberg had attempted to clarify what he meant by *Sprechstimme*: "The indicated rhythms should be adhered to, but . . . whereas in ordinary singing a constant pitch is maintained through a note, here the singer immediately abandons it by falling or rising. The goal is certainly not at all a realistic, natural speech . . . but it should not call singing to mind either."[12] Schoenberg's note may not have been entirely clear in its intended results and has been much debated ever since. In fact, Pierre Boulez later wrote: "The question arises whether it is actually possible to speak according to a notation devised for singing."[13]

Under Jacques's direction, I learned the pitches of *Pierrot*. Now I am glad I did. *Sprechstimme* is a fascinating technique. You can hear the canons between voice and instruments in no. 17 ("Parodie"), and the wonderful duet in no. 7 ("Der kranke Mond") between speaker and flute, which comes the closest to a sung line. You can hear the colors and range in the movement from whisper to loud, intense speech. There's a way you can glide intoning phrases—half intoning and half speaking, and drop your voice to subterranean depths as in no. 8 ("Nacht," Passacaglia), where the notes themselves would be impossible to hear if spoken, especially the sung pitch on the word *verschwiegen*. The *Sprechstimme* technique drew from me dramatic colors I didn't know existed in my voice. And the instrumental combination was just right: piano, violin/viola, clarinet/bass clarinet, cello, and flute/piccolo, with several of the players switching between instruments. Five players was a perfect combination—one that didn't overpower me.

I sang *Pierrot* throughout my career. Jacques's influence was unmistakable—for years after that first performance. When Jacques and I reunited the original gang (except for the flutist) in 1967 for a performance of

Pierrot at Sanders Theatre at Harvard, the review in the *Harvard Crimson* paid tribute (perhaps unwittingly) to all of that original painstaking work:

> Set to rather morbid poetry by Albert Giraud, [*Pierrot*] exerted a curious kind of fascination on the audience—except those Philistines who apparently could not take it and left in the middle. The work's success owes in no small part to the performers, particularly conductor Jacques-Louis Monod, who made eminent sense out of music that is all too easily incomprehensible, and "narrator" Bethany Beardslee whose negotiation of all the weirdities of Schoenberg's technique of *Sprechstimme* must have been one of the most chilling and *engagé* of all time. She seemed remarkably at ease in this unlikely blend of speech, intonation and song, and hers is the supreme achievement of having made dramatic and musical sense out of a style that is usually presented as a musical oddity.[14]

I would like to add that there is an enormous repertoire of contemporary vocal chamber works, many of which grew conceptually from *Pierrot lunaire.* When it comes to difficult twentieth-century music, it is far easier for a composer to have a smaller instrumental piece played than to mount an orchestral performance or an opera. Thus, this five-piece chamber group with voice became an important model, not only for contemporary composers, like Phil Batstone with his *Mother Goose Primer,* but also for early new music composers—Stravinsky with his *Poémes de la lyrique japonaise,* for example, or Ravel with his *Trois poèmes de Stéphane Mallarmé* and his *Chansons madécasses.* Many new music organizations developed around the grouping of the five-part *Pierrot* ensemble—the Fires of London (originally the Pierrot Players), the Da Capo Players, and the New York New Music Ensemble.

Our first performance of *Pierrot* took place on February 25, 1955, at the Contemporary Music Festival held at the University of Illinois in Urbana. That night, with Jacques conducting, I also sang Hindemith's *Serenaden,* and a new work by the Princeton graduate student Stanley Seeger, *La femme à l'ombrelle* for voice and instruments. We also did two recitals of lieder of the Second Viennese School during the festival.

Stravinsky labeled *Pierrot lunaire* the "solar plexus as well as the mind of modern music."[15] As stars align, while we were in Urbana, Jacques and I met his son Soulima Stravinsky, who taught piano at the university, and Soulima's charming wife, Françoise. We spent a lovely evening at their tasteful home, with its distinctly Continental atmosphere. Soulima, Stravinsky's youngest, looked so much like his father, with his slicked-back hair and similar facial features, that it was almost eerie. He told us how his father would have him try out the rough drafts of his piano concerti measure by measure. In gratitude for Soulima's patient assistance, his father had dedicated a number of pieces to him. Jacques and Soulima spent the evening speaking French together, while Françoise showed me around their beautiful home. Meeting and being able to spend time with two such cultivated people was, for me, the highlight of our stay in Urbana, which as far as I was concerned was otherwise just a flat, midwestern town.

Back to the salt mines: I was fed up with Jacques's authoritarian ways, and felt, quite simply, overworked! Between secretarial work for him and my part-time job, my burden had become really excessive. And then he and William Bayard Carlin, a graduate student from Princeton, decided to start the "Composers Catalog." It would be another new Monod Project, the straw to break the camel's back.

The Composers Catalog was a crazy scheme to collect all the manuscripts of a number of unpublished contemporary composers. The plan was to house them, receive orders for copies, and distribute them. We'd take the onion skin sheets to Independent Music, an offset printer in the city, where a copy was generated, and have them sent from there to the customer. Again, these were the days before computer-engraved scores. Major scores were hand-engraved for the big publishing houses, like Schirmer, C. F. Peters, Universal, or Boosey & Hawkes. We were concerned about the composers who didn't have the support of big publishers. We wanted to build a massive library of unpublished scores. We even set out to contact composers about the idea, and the initial response was very enthusiastic. We never collected any scores, although we printed up a catalog. It had a lovely cover by Sylvia Shapey.

I don't remember whether the catalog ever got mailed out to the colleges and performers we were hoping to attract as customers. The whole plan turned out to be unsustainable, despite all the work we put into it. With his steady stream of new ideas and headstrong notion that the world was at his beck and call, Jacques was simply unmanageable.

On my end, I was having an ever more difficult time trying to contain my own feelings of discontent. My anger finally exploded that spring, and we started arguing all the time. I couldn't tolerate how bossy he was, or how profane his swearing. He was always cussing in French, and overusing "*Je m'en fous!*" or "*Tais-toi!*" He thought I couldn't understand his horrid French slang. But I'd gotten hip to it all and also knew how much he used me during our practice sessions to learn his own part. Years later, Jacques

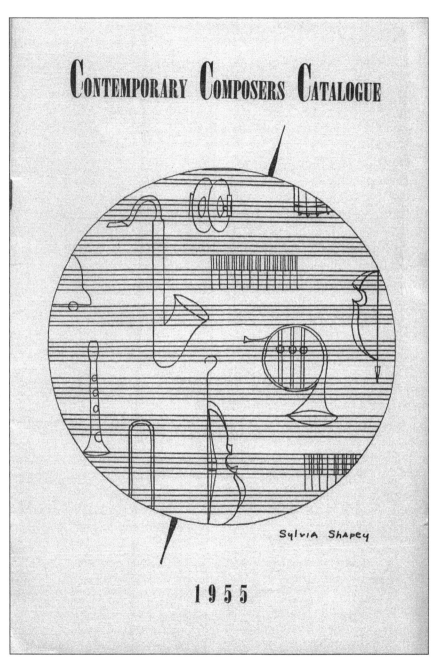

Figure 29. The ill-fated Composers Catalogue cover designed by Sylvia Shapey.

admitted to me how much he'd hated playing the piano. And I have to think that that is why he swore so much. He may well have been angriest at his piano—and at himself.

Our first years together had been wonderful, mostly because we had a powerful sexual chemistry. But after so many exhausting hours of rehearsal, even sex became intolerable. Finally all I wanted was to be out of the relationship.

The final straw for us was my affair with Bill Carlin, the co-editor of the catalog, in the spring of 1955. Bill was attractive and understanding. I needed that, so I was drawn to him. For Jacques it was the "ultimate betrayal." He was an incredibly proud man, and yet he was the one responsible for bringing Bill into our lives.

In the middle of this mayhem, Madame Monod arrived. She had planned her visit much earlier, and it was just bad luck that she landed in this landslide. Needless to say, she was puzzled. Jacques must have confided to her at the start that he was planning on leaving. She asked me why, and I told her that we were incompatible. I can't imagine how Jacques explained it to her; it was private between them. Jacques had always had a tortured relationship with his mother. She was domineering, and I'm sure this had a profoundly complicated effect on his relationships with women. After she went back to France, Jacques left. Then he came back a week later, probably because he was broke. His return didn't help matters.

After yet another argument I packed my clothes and left. I spent two weeks with my pastor, Father Leech, and his wife, Ruthy, at the rectory of St. Luke in the Fields, where I had my church job. A lot of things were closing in on me. It was more than I could toss off when I was performing—which at least would have been a kind of escape. I was broke, so I had to go back to the apartment. When I returned, Jacques was apologetic about the fight. But my feelings toward Jacques had changed, and he knew it.

The tension between us was unbearable. We couldn't stay together in the apartment, no matter how broke we both were. And finally Jacques left for good.

Of course, I was anxious about my mother. We'd never had a divorce in the family. But when I told her what was happening between me and Jacques, she didn't bat an eyelash. She just said, "Okay, darling. I'm behind you." She was my biggest fan and kept all of the reviews that I proudly sent her. I wanted her to know with conviction that I was a success and that everything was going to be okay. I knew goddamn well that I could take care of myself. I had a career. I could earn money. I had a great apartment. I was independent and not the least bit frightened of being alone.

Yet there I was, alone, in the big apartment on East 17th Street. I wondered at first whether to look for smaller quarters. It felt like the old days when I first arrived in New York; I was independent and free to make my own decisions. To my surprise, I found I had many friends. Bill Carlin remained a good friend. Milton and Sylvia were always nearby, and I began to frequently see Henry and Diane Weinberg (before Henry came out as gay), Fay and Kermit Lansner, and other friends Jacques and I had cultivated. I still had income from my job at the Junior League plus my singing engagements. I had a terrific apartment and decided to do what my mother had done—take in a roomer. I let out the two back bedrooms to an actress and a photographer, to help pay the rent, and moved into the front bedroom. I had my own entrance; the roomers used the back-hall entrance. I was by nature careful with money, and it seemed all of a sudden I had enough to pay my bills. Gone were those ghastly telephone bills. This short time period was a godsend. I didn't have a new difficult piece of music to learn and was able to just enjoy being with friends. I was overcome with sudden and complete tranquility. Some of that sense of well-being, it should be said, may have come from the new relationship I'd started with a young English composer who was studying with Milton at Princeton—Godfrey Winham.

CHAPTER NINETEEN

CAMERA CONCERTS WITH STANLEY SEEGER

Between these dramatic interludes, the leaving and reconciling, I managed to notice that Jacques had become more focused on conducting. I'd come home from work and find him conducting through scores, singing them to solfège syllables. While we were having problems, Jacques had gone out and found himself an "angel"—which is to say that he'd convinced Stanley Seeger, whose music we'd performed that season (1955) in Urbana, to back a new Monod scheme.

Jacques's patron, Stanley Seeger, came from a wealthy lumber and oil family, had studied composition with the Italian composer Luigi Dallapiccola, and was a graduate student at Princeton when we met him. He was loaded and gay, and he always had a refrigerator filled with Champagne whenever we went to see him in his New York pied-à-terre. Remember, I had just sung Stanley's *La femme a l'ombrelle* in Urbana. Hot on the heels of our success there, Jacques, in his usual charming way, persuaded Stanley to mount a series of concerts at Town Hall under the title Camera Concerts. The idea appealed to Stanley.

The first Camera Concert took place that fall, on November 30, 1955, in New York's Town Hall. Jacques needed me to perform *Pierrot*. In preparation for the event, Stanley took me to the couturier Martha West and outfitted me in a sumptuous gown of black tulle. In the 1950s, evening dresses were ankle length with huge, bouffant skirts. I counted six different skirts over a stiff crinoline. Stanley decided I should wear a crown that resembled a wreath of diamondlike stars. It was the first concert gown bought just for me that wasn't from a thrift shop. Even my shoes were black silk, with rhinestone heels. I think the idea was to make me look like a commedia dell'arte Columbine. But I felt like a storybook princess.

I will never forget that evening. Because Stanley had such vast resources, he was able to publicize the concert highly, and it seemed like everyone was there. Jacques had chosen a beautiful program. Edgard Varèse's *Déserts* was on the early part of the program, and *Pierrot* followed intermission. *Déserts*, as you may know, is a work for woodwind, brass, and percussion, with interpolations of organized, giant *SOUND* on tape, stereophonically transmitted on two channels. It was a noisy piece, with recordings of industrial, urban America. Electronic music was in its infancy at the time. Varèse insisted on the volume being turned up to its maximum, so that the sound practically shattered the rafters of Town Hall. No one had ever heard anything like it. All the way back in the dressing room where the players were warming up, we could hear *Déserts* thundering away. I thought to myself, *Pierrot* is going to sound like a tin whistle performed by little Mary Moonlight after that cacophony. Despite it all, we gave a great *Pierrot*. Of course we did—we were totally overrehearsed. I sang entirely from memory. Robert Helps played piano, Isidore Cohen was on violin, with Charles McCracken on cello, James Politis on flute, and Jack Kreiselmann on clarinet. Jacques conducted. They were great players, and it was a big night for everyone. After the performance, I was called back on stage for several bows and handed an amazing bouquet of birds-of-paradise. Stanley, bless him, had thought of everything. The saturated orange of the bouquet was a striking contrast against my black tulle gown! Even after all these performances, I wasn't at all used to receiving flowers.

But Jacques had figured out a way to betray me even in the midst of that glorious night. He'd included a biographical note in the program for the tenor Rawn Spearman, who sang a short Stravinsky piece, *In Memoriam Dylan Thomas*, and of course Jacques had his own biographical note, too. But there wasn't a word about me. I was simply billed as the "speaker" in *Pierrot*. I don't know whether Jacques did it deliberately, or if it was just another example of his taking me for granted. In other words, even if it wasn't deliberate, it was malicious.

Jacques gave one more Camera Concert the following spring, on May 7, 1956, introducing the wonderful Hungarian-Italian singer Magda László to New York. Of course there was a spectacular picture of Magda in the program. Magda was a wonderful singer who had sung a lot of Luigi

Dallapiccola's music in Europe. That night she sang Dallapiccola's *An Mathilde*, for voice with instrumental ensemble. Jacques did all the conducting. The program also featured Aaron Copland's *Music for the Theatre*, the Handel-Schoenberg Concerto for String Quartet and Orchestra with the Juilliard Quartet, and Webern's *Variations for Orchestra*, op. 30. Again, a perfect program, as were all of his carefully curated programs.

So, with Seeger's money, Jacques was trying to establish himself as a conductor. However, his angel seemed to lose interest quickly. I never knew the details, but life seemed to have taken a dramatic and bitter turn for Jacques. He stayed in New York to do one last concert: Eight days later he conducted on a concert sponsored by Bethsabée de Rothschild, where I also sang. (Bethsabée later took the name Batsheva after moving to Israel, but I always knew her as Bethsabée.) The program featured Monteverdi's *Orfeo* and a new work by the composer Vivian Fine. Jacques conducted the whole program and then immediately left the United States.

PART THREE

GODFREY
(1956–62)

Figure 30. From a series of pictures of me and Godfrey just after we met.

CHAPTER TWENTY

A SEASON OF CHANGE

Summer 1956

J acques was gone. He mounted and conducted that last concert at Bethsabée's, then left for South America. After that he went on to Germany to study conducting.

During this turbulent period, I went to visit my mother in Lansing. After I came back, I decided to go out to Amagansett, Long Island, with my friend Fay Lansner. Fay had rented a cottage and knew many other painters who trekked out to what was the wilderness of the Hamptons in those days. Painters liked the ocean, the light, the dunes, and the accompanying isolation. Jackson Pollock and Lee Krasner lived nearby. We even ran into Jackson one summer in the local grocery store—he was drunk, which Fay told me was common. Those were his final days, though I hardly knew it at the time. Later that same summer, he died in a drunken car crash.

Fay and I walked on the beach, relaxed, and talked. I told her all about everything that had happened, and confided in her about Godfrey Winham. I took in a healthy dose of quiet and lovely sunsets. It wasn't a long escape from the city and my eventful life, but I remember it as a joyful time.

Shortly after I returned from Fay's, Glenn Gould called and asked me to perform Schoenberg's *Ode to Napoleon* at the Stratford Summer Festival in Ontario, Canada.

In Schoenberg's setting, Lord Byron's diatribe against Napoleon is actually written for a male speaker (not a singer), string quartet, and piano. But Glenn may have been distracted from Schoenberg's vision. He had gotten it into his head that he wanted to play and conduct. It was the first time he was going to try to conduct from the piano. Glenn was still quite young at that point, only twenty-four, but even at that age, he was already retreating from performing. By 1964 he had stopped entirely—less than a decade after his wonderful Town Hall debut.

Before rehearsal we met at a coffee shop in Stratford to talk about the score. Even though it was July, Glenn appeared wearing a heavy winter coat, a hat and gloves. He was quite a hypochondriac and did not like people to touch him. I had heard he was eccentric and was prepared for his quirks.

Glenn was so private that people often assumed he was asexual or gay. He was neither. In fact, in later years, he had a long love affair with Cornelia Foss, the wife of the conductor Lukas Foss. I would come to know Lukas well—especially during the period when Cornelia moved to Ontario to be with Glenn.

Meanwhile, Glenn was curious about me, and especially how I'd gotten interested in Schoenberg. He wanted to hear about the early concerts Jacques and I had done. He was also interested in what was going on in new music in New York. He'd done a bit of composing himself and written a string quartet. We talked about contemporary composers, mostly the ones he favored. He did most of the talking.

During rehearsals of the *Ode*, the quartet and I found Glenn very difficult to work with. He was an extraordinary pianist, but he had strange musical ideas that he imposed on the performance. He didn't always seem to feel beholden to a composer's intent, or if he did, he went about realizing it differently than anyone else. I was, and am, a huge fan of his 1955 recording of Bach's "Goldberg" Variations. But our performance together was a shambles as far as I was concerned. In addition to the problem of Glenn's conducting while playing, the *Ode* simply is not written for the female voice, something I didn't realize until I tried to perform it. My friend Ellen Adler had recorded the piece for Dial Records with René Leibowitz conducting and Jacques on piano, so I knew it had been done by a woman. I just didn't know what a mistake it was, and I don't think Glenn did either.

I learned much later, however, about a 1951 letter from Schoenberg to Ross Russell, who ran Dial Records, in which Schoenberg threatened to ruin Dial for issuing Ellen Adler and René Leibowitz's performance of *Ode to Napoleon*. The actual letter has disappeared, but the Schoenberg archives have a copy of Schoenberg's dictation of the letter into a tape recorder. Not all of the words can be distinguished because of his heavy accent, but this much we have: "In spite of my protest," dictated Schoenberg, "you have published Leibowitz's performance of my 'Ode to Napoleon' with a woman's voice, which I find terrible. . . . You will regret this act severely."[16]

The great composer had quite a temper and was rightfully protective of his music. I laugh now to think that despite our shared reverence for Schoenberg, neither Glenn Gould nor I realized at the time what a dreadful mistake we were making, how we were, as Schoenberg put it in his angry letter to Dial Records, "going against the artist's wishes, his beliefs!"

When Robert Craft later recorded the *Ode to Napoleon*, he used a male speaker, and it's always done that way today.

Although from my perspective, my glancing collaboration with Gould was minimally successful, one of Gould's biographers, Kevin Bazzana, notes that the concert (the only one Gould mounted during the summer of 1956) was a "tour de force." In *Wondrous Strange*, Bazzana writes that Gould "dazzled his audience with his versatility, appearing in the roles of pianist, conductor, composer, and writer."[17] The critics were evidently impressed by his "virtuosity and versatility." "On paper it looked awful," wrote Ross Parmenter, in the *New York Times*. "But it turned out to be an absorbing evening, largely because Mr. Gould is as gifted as a musical thinker as he is a pianist."[18]

It was such a busy and tumultuous summer—of course Glenn Gould fitted right in. His interlude was a perfect complement to our Jackson Pollock sighting in Amagansett. What is interesting about these two mid-century giants, when you look at them side by side, was their contrasting relationship to performance. Gould's art didn't exist without performance, whereas Pollock's art of painting traditionally has been a solitary one. Ironically enough, Pollock, with his live-action painting, was totally performative. Because he *was* a performer, Gould needed to practice his art in public—but he was painfully reclusive.

That inherent reclusiveness may after all be a quality familiar to many performers. Maybe like Pollock and Gould, all artists have to navigate some kind of interior-exterior balance that never quite feels balanced. Even though I'm not in pain or twitchy like Gould was, or an alcoholic like Pollock, I feel as if I've always had this public-private contrast within me too. Despite the accomplishments of those years with Jacques, I think that by the summer after he left I was in many ways as naïve as the day I'd arrived in New York City. I had learned about performance and cultivated a playful, sincere public game face. But inside I was quite a lot moodier and more insecure than I ever let show. My performing face was a protective shell. I've nursed that dichotomy all my life: My outside self got bolder and

Figure 31. In the apartment on East Seventeenth Street.

savvier and ended up steamrolling through a marvelous singing career, camouflaging an interior that is quiet, reclusive, and serious. The veneer of cheerfulness is almost gone in the later years of my life, as my inner self has taken over.

Milton in particular seemed to see it so clearly in me; it was as if he could see all parts of me at once. He'd tease me, calling me the "Girl Singer from East Lansing"—which was, really, the truth of the matter.

It was to Sylvia that I turned during that year of upheaval, for Milton was not one to give me advice on my personal life. He always treated me as a professional singer of his music, avoiding highly personal issues. And yet I felt his protective presence through Sylvia's mediations and advice. The two of them took me under their wing after Jacques left.

Now that Jacques was gone, I was searching for a new pianist to sing with. It was at that point that I met the composer-pianist Robert Helps, who became one of the musicians with whom I loved best to perform. Bob had played the piano part in *Pierrot* at the first Camera Concert. Our affinity was immediately apparent to us: We got along, we shared the same repertoire of new American music, and we both happened to love French art song. Jacques's stranglehold over my career had ended, and I was free. Immediately Bob and I made plans to start working together. It was a blissful change.

All of us held Bob in the highest regard. He was a marvelous musician, a formidable sight-reader, and over the course of his career would come to be recognized in equal measure for his compositions, performance, and teaching.

Bob came to new music through Roger Sessions, with whom he'd studied composition, and became deeply immersed in the lineage out of Princeton. He'd also studied piano with the great Abby Whiteside and is considered one of her most distinguished pupils. She taught a whole-arm (rather than finger-focused) approach to playing the piano, which gave Bob a remarkable fluency as a performer. He probably should have had a great solo career.

We began to explore the Debussy song cycles. Not only was Debussy a marked change from Schoenberg, but, naturally, practicing with Bob was an entirely different experience than practicing with Jacques—the exact opposite, in fact. Bob did not believe in working through a piece from one criticism to another. He only called my attention to the most urgent error—the wrong pitch, entering at the wrong time. He'd chime in to suggest a different dynamic or point out a phrase he thought should be sung in a single breath. In turn, I'd give him my suggestions. He respected my thoughts, which gave me terrific self-assurance in my musical abilities, something I'm not sure I had enough of at that point. Bob was exactly the gift I needed to carry me through this period of change.

Why should I ever be bullied again, I asked myself? There was no reason for me to have given in to Jacques and I knew it. I was resentful, but something more important was still needling me. I started to understand that I'd been complicit. I had been too dutiful. I'd lost myself in my efforts to please Jacques, to win his approval. I started to wonder if Jacques had ever loved me the way I had loved him, or whether we'd had a domestic professional arrangement—the kind of collaboration he would have formed with any singer? Did it even matter that we were romantically drawn to each other? Or would he have teamed up with anyone, no matter who she may have been?

It was a time of introspection. Being alone forced me to look at myself and take in what was going to change—what I wanted to change. By this point, I knew I was inextricably bound to contemporary music. My identity, my niche, had been established. What's more, I must have known that I had a unique ability for understanding and conveying the new music that I had been singing so steadily over the five years since I'd met Jacques. That said, I saw this life change as an opportunity: a chance to take up more of the classical repertoire I'd so loved to study and sing in college.

After that first Camera Concert in November 1955 with Bob Helps, we performed together off and on for many years. I never treated him, nor thought of him, as my accompanist. He was my partner, a serious composer, dedicated to his work, and an outstanding musician. He was the pianist with whom I most adored making music. When Bob played with me, it felt like a perfect combination—we built off each other in our music making. It's difficult to put into words why our connection worked so well—and yet I'm sure all chamber-music performers understand this kind of shared sensibility and deep mutual respect.

We started working together seriously in the spring of 1956 and gave our first recital that November in Chicago for Contemporary Concerts Incorporated. Even though we both were eager to perform classical art song, the people who hired us requested a new music program—not surprising! We performed Sessions and Babbitt, Carter and Webern, and, of course, Schoenberg, as well as one of Bob's own pieces.

We received several favorable reviews for that concert, but we also got one of the *worst* reviews I've ever had, from Roger Dettmer in the *Chicago Tribune*. Dettmer absolutely hated new music: "Today still, most listeners put fingers in their ears when the label says 'atonal' and stay home to watch television. Last evening at Fullerton Hall, where acoustics imply amplification, Contemporary Concerts, Inc., sponsored a program illustrating why." His review was a lulu. He went on to write about our "tuneless 20th Century seance—a brief but bitter pill even for reasonably sophisticated ears." But the line that stuck with me the most was this one: "Miss Beardslee, a pale young maiden with rhinestone heels on her pumps and a white little soprano, sang . . . nimbly, colorlessly."[19]

On February 16, 1957, Bob and I had our first New York City recital at Carnegie Recital Hall. We kept some of the program from Chicago (despite Roger Dettmer's indignation). Bob played *Pages from My Diary*, a piece by his teacher, Roger Sessions, and also a work of his own, *Fantasy for Piano*. I wanted to include the Webern songs, op. 25, and Milton's *Widow's Lament in Springtime*. We also performed Ravel's *Chansons madécasses*. It was a rather mixed bag already, but we added an entire Schumann song cycle to top it off! We had created our ideal program, combining French and German music, and standard classical with contemporary. We had no idea what we were doing, and I don't think until that point I'd appreciated how good Jacques was at building a program. The *New York Times* critic complained that despite our fine performances, he wasn't sure what the assortment of selections added up to. Program building is a distinct art, as I was learning.

Bob insisted we practice at his Brooklyn pied-à-terre, since I only had the rented upright to work on, no comparison to his Steinway grand. He lived on Montague Street in Brooklyn Heights, a neighborhood of impressive townhouses near the promenade overlooking the East River. Bob often dressed in black. He kept a black sheepskin on top of his piano and had what seemed like hundreds of cans stored in the small kitchen of his one-bedroom apartment. His mother, he told me, was worried he wouldn't eat right and sent him care packages from Morristown, New Jersey (where his family lived) of canned soup and other easy-to-prepare food—none of which he could stand! Bob was twenty-seven years old at the time. When I went out with him one weekend to Morristown, where we were performing, his parents were overjoyed to meet me. I'm sure they hoped that I was Bob's girlfriend.

I think one of Bob's most difficult challenges—especially when he was on the East Coast—was that he was homosexual, and that wasn't an easy path in those days. Bob had turbulent rhythms and sporadic depressive episodes that would suddenly take him out of commission. He was very private. Although we had a close friendship, it was around work. I was never directly involved in his personal life, except for when whatever was happening with him emotionally disrupted our performance schedule or left me scrambling at a late date to find a new pianist. He often disappeared and ended up out West, in the San Francisco–Berkeley area, where he had many friends and seemed much happier.

"Why would you want to work with me?" he used to quip, sphinxlike. "My dear, I'm really quite mad!" To me, he was warm, witty, and boyishly naïve. And it's true that sometimes when he disappeared, he wasn't on a road trip but had checked into a hospital instead because his depression became precipitously acute. He was so dear and so talented, but his instability made him frustratingly undependable. It goes entirely against my character to be patient with that kind of drama, but boy, did I adore performing with Bob. To the extent that he could control it, he was a consummate professional with me. I wanted to work with him forever.

CHAPTER TWENTY-ONE

GODFREY WINHAM

We must step backward in time to 1954, the evening when I first laid eyes on Godfrey Winham. It was an early fall evening at the Babbitts'. As usual I was sitting in the kitchen with Sylvia, listening to her talk about their summer in Europe. They had virtually just gotten off the boat. I interrupted our conversation to ask, "Who is that blond Adonis talking to Milton?" In response, Silvia briefed me on Milton's young protégé, an English prodigy whom she and Milton had met in Austria at the Salzburg Music Festival.

Milton was a charmer who hooked you with his big intellect, whereas Godfrey Winham was precocious, brilliant, and exceptionally well educated. At barely twenty years old, he was already writing reviews for professional music journals, such as the *Score*, studying composition with Mátyás Seiber, and friendly with the influential music critic Hans Keller—a mutual friend of the Babbitts. When the Babbitts met Godfrey and his mother Gwen at Salzburg, Milton recognized an unusual intellect and wanted to bring Godfrey into his stable. He proposed to the Winhams that Godfrey should leave England immediately and come to Princeton, luring him with the influence of Roger Sessions, who was the elder statesman at Princeton and an internationally well-known composer. After Salzburg, the Babbitts visited the Winhams in London and stayed as guests at their Green Street home, just off Hyde Park. It was decided during the course of that visit that Godfrey would move to America, where he temporarily would be under the guardianship of Mr. Winham's close friend and lawyer, Bob Snyder. Godfrey left London with the Babbitts on the *Île de France* at the end of August.

Figure 32. Godfrey Winham right before I met him.

That fall evening, while chatting with Sylvia in the kitchen, I asked for an introduction to the handsome young Englishman. When she presented me, Godfrey looked up for barely a moment to smile and then returned to his conversation with Milton. He was far more interested in what Milton was saying. I was, nonetheless, instantly intrigued. When I left that night, I felt sure somehow that we would encounter each other again—perhaps in Princeton.

In fact, I did see Godfrey again just a few weeks later, at a performance of one of his string quartets at the Martha Graham Dance Company studio. The studio was a beautiful brick townhouse on East 63rd Street that had been given to Graham by her friend and patron Bethsabée de Rothschild. Events were always being held there, and we referred to the studio as B. de Rothschild. After the performance that evening, Godfrey got up to talk about his compositions. He stood before us all, still wearing his hat and scarf, which I found rather amusing, actually beguiling. I was sitting on a Nakashima bench, designed especially for the studio, and was flanked by my friend the composer Leonard (Lenny) Rosenman, and his friend the actor James Dean. At that point, Dean was still unknown in Hollywood, but was studying piano with Lenny. After the program, I went right up to Godfrey to congratulate him. I also told him that if he ever needed a place to stay when he was in the city, he was welcome to stay with me and Jacques.

Godfrey smiled indulgently at me, just as he had before. His smile enchanted me. He had delicate features, beautiful eyes, and a quiet way about him. He wasn't one to make small talk. I think that, despite his offhand manner with me, Godfrey knew who I was. Of course he did. He said he had my Dial recordings back home in England. I remember being so ignorant about international record distribution that I was stunned to hear that they even *knew* about Dial Records in England.

Godfrey reemerged when my relationship with Jacques was crumbling. In the course of events, we went out to dinner several times and one night, on the way home in the back of a taxi, he kissed me. I protested brilliantly that I was too old for him. (I was nine years older than he was.) After kissing me he answered, "It's not important. After all, it's only a number."

In a way he was right. Women between the ages of twenty-five and thirty-five are entirely ageless. I was at the peak of my ageless decade, and Godfrey was a prodigy—and so he was ageless too. Our friends—a combination of my old friends from Juilliard and younger people whom Godfrey knew from Princeton—came together. Soon it seemed as if no one noticed the age difference at all. Even I stopped thinking about it.

And as far as Godfrey was concerned, I was a beautiful young woman who sang the music he loved. I was also the first woman he loved. And that was enough.

Before long, we were spending a lot of time together. He was so attentive to me—I basked in it. Sometimes I worried that I was taking advantage, as if my glamour as a performer had undue influence. But you know, I really didn't care as my feelings for him grew and grew. Foremost in my mind, even if I didn't admit it, was the recognition that Godfrey moved through life totally differently than Jacques did—and I now longed to be part of Godfrey's world.

Over the course of a single month, I arrived at the point where I couldn't bear the thought of losing him. Any doubts I did have had been misleading me. Perhaps I'd even been relying on manufactured doubts because I was scared about falling in love. I panicked one night when he called from Princeton to tell me he wouldn't be able to get back into town for some time. I hung up thinking to myself, "He must be seeing someone else. I'm going to lose him!"

The next time he called me, I told him outright that I thought I was falling in love with him. His reply was monosyllabic and entirely in keeping with his character: "Great!"

Before long Godfrey and I were living together on East 17th Street, sharing my apartment with the photographer and the actress. He'd commute out to Princeton for his classes. I just decided not to worry about all of the reasons that we shouldn't be together and set about figuring out how to enjoy this new and entirely different relationship. Godfrey wrapped me up in his love—and it felt like he would never let me go.

We had only been living together a short while when New York was hit by a February blizzard. Godfrey and I liked to go out for dinner and had planned to go out that night. Undaunted, we decided to brave the snowy streets, donned our winter gear, and ventured out to our favorite restaurant at 17 Barrow Street in the Village. It was a beautiful night. The snow had stopped, and the stars were shining. There was no one on the street. New York was enveloped by a quiet unlike anything I had experienced before. We walked the whole way, often in the middle of the street, for there was absolutely no traffic save the occasional taxi. The proprietor smiled when he saw us, his regular clients. He loved classical music and always had some music playing on the sound system for his guests. We dined by candlelight, being practically the only ones there. When it was time to go home, we trudged out again into the night. This fairyland of white on the city was something I'll always remember. The snow was so white, and the stars, the moon were so bright that there was no need for lights in the street. It was the city reduced to a perfect silence.

When we arrived at the steps to our building we found Mr. Elliott, our fourth-floor neighbor—the cat rescuer—collapsed on the doorstep. He'd slipped and fallen in the snow. We asked if he was all right and he answered that he was, though Godfrey had to lift the eighty-year-old man to his feet. Mr. Elliott seemed completely unperturbed by the event. We helped him inside and walked him up to his apartment. I have no idea how long he was sitting in the snow, or why on earth he was out that night—probably feeding his stray cats.

There was a coffee shop on the corner of 14th Street and Second Avenue where we went for lunch and to play chess. We spent so many hours sitting there playing that I was amazed they never kicked us out. Chess, I found, was a fascinating game that I was terrible at. Godfrey taught me some opening moves, and that was as far as I got. Note the stark contrast to my former life: Instead of spending the day trying to sneak in a little housework on bathroom breaks from rigorous practice, I was squandering hours on end learning games! Chess and then bridge—I was living with a man who had a nimble mind and a remarkable ability to relax and enjoy himself.

This was, of course, the decade after the Second World War. It's worth remembering that both of my husbands, though so different from one another, were European and had been formed in many ways by their experience of the war. Jacques, already a man at the time, had struggled through the occupation of Paris and fought with the Resistance. His family lost a great deal. When I knew them, in many respects their petit bourgeois life was frozen in a kind of emotional and material postwar austerity. Godfrey, on the other hand, was only a child during the war. He was shipped off with his two younger sisters and his mother to the United States when the Blitz started. Not only did he spend those years in complete safety, nestled away in Colorado Springs, Colorado, but the family's wealth was untouched by world affairs, and so he watched the war from a remote lap of luxury. What all of this meant for Jacques and Godfrey as men was that Jacques was driven, as if the devil himself were chasing him, and Godfrey was laid back. He knew his passions and never doubted that everything in his life—his music and me—was exactly the way he wanted it to be.

I remember one day, early in our relationship, when I went over to Godfrey's Princeton University apartment. I'd been looking for something and threw open the closet door, only to be buried in what seemed like hundreds of white, button-down shirts cascading from the closet. "What is all this?" I managed to ask from underneath the load. And Godfrey explained that he hadn't quite been able to figure out how to handle his laundry since his arrival in the States, and so he was resorting to replacing his dirty shirts with brand-new ones.

Godfrey seemed to have easy access to money through his father's New York lawyer. Whenever we ran short of funds, he'd make a telephone call and go over to Bob Synder's office, and just like that our kitty was replenished. Well, that was okay by me. I didn't question it. He took it in perfect stride, and I just assumed he had an allowance from his parents for college expenses. Meanwhile, I was making ends meet the way I always had. I had quit the New York Junior League after Jacques left and took a part-time typing job (transcribing doctor's notes from Dictaphone cylinders) at Beth Israel Hospital, right across the street from the apartment—a far better commute and a great time-saver. I kept my church and temple jobs, though, as I enjoyed both of them too much to stop.

Over the summer of 1956, Godfrey was in London with his family. I was in New York, earning money by singing jingles for radio commercials and trying to get a divorce from Jacques, who was off conducting in Mexico. Jacques had teamed up with the composer Carlos Chávez and immediately launched a whole new series of Monod projects. Jacques even tried to get me to travel to Mexico to sing some concerts for him. Needless to say, I did not go.

In the meantime I was receiving regular letters from Godfrey throughout June, complaining about society life in London. Gwen insisted on Godfrey's being well dressed and disapproved of how unkempt he always looked. He was dragged around London to cocktail parties populated by "bored and uninteresting debutantes," and he wrote to me about the torture of having to wear a tuxedo. He also socialized a lot with the composer Marc Wilkinson (whose songs I'd sung), recently transplanted from New York to London. Marc traveled in the same social circles as Gwen, and Godfrey confided in him about our relationship.

Of course his parents didn't know anything about us yet. They certainly didn't know we were living together, although he listed East 17th Street as his return address on his letters to them after he returned from London that summer. He worried that his mother would decide to come visit, and we'd be discovered.

One day, Godfrey and I went to Coney Island with a group of friends and spent a long, hot afternoon playing bridge at a boardwalk cafe. Dear

Godfrey was so absorbed in the game that he didn't notice the sun on his fair English skin, or that he was only partially shaded by the umbrella over the table. By the end of the day, exactly half of him, one half of his face and neck, one arm, one leg, was burned crispy pink. He exclaimed in pain all the way home. He only found relief in the bathtub. Then I coated him in baby powder afterward to stop the itching. It was hilariously funny once it stopped hurting.

The period after I started seeing Godfrey and singing with Bob Helps was blissful. My routine wasn't the least bit punishing. What was more, because of my hard labor in the years prior, I had memorized a vast repertoire of music and had a solid professional reputation. Composers knew who I was. If you needed a soprano to sing new, atonal, or difficult music, you called Bethany. All of a sudden, there was no struggle to any of it. I wasn't working like a dog. I was happy.

Until the next April of 1957. Everything changed in a single stroke: Everything got more perfect and also terribly serious. I missed my period. How could I have been so stupid? I thought. But when the doctor told me that I was definitely pregnant, I found I was actually overjoyed. I ran all the way home and leaped into Godfrey's arms. I said, "We're going to have a baby!" He replied in understated bewilderment, "Okay." And went back to work.

Jacques had always insisted, "Absolutely *no!*" whenever I brought up the subject of children—no matter how I longed for a baby. Jacques was un-relenting, and so I had always been extremely careful. I'd obviously started to let my guard down with Godfrey. And there I was, pregnant, and want-ing to keep the baby with every fiber of my being. The fact that Godfrey's response was, "Okay," made me unbearably happy. After the first euphoria wore off, we sat down and had to figure out what in hell we were actually going to do about the situation. Here I was, still married to Jacques, and neither the Beardslees nor the Winhams had any idea that we were even together. It *was* a predicament, to be sure.

Godfrey flew back to London to tell his parents about us. I was appre-hensive, thinking they would disapprove of an older girlfriend, and wrote to him—as he did to me—every day. He reported that he'd told his father that we wanted to get married and that I had been married before. His father seemed reasonable but suggested that we decide where we were go-ing to live before getting married. Mind you, I was already pregnant, so there wasn't time to dither. Godfrey said that we wanted to live in America and told his father what he thought were the advantages. Godfrey's father wasn't convinced and made it clear that he could support Godfrey for only another couple of years. But Godfrey still wanted to avoid military service and told his father that he had some teaching work to offset our expenses.

The clock was ticking down, and my divorce still hadn't come through from France! We kept writing back and forth with Jacques, asking him if he'd heard anything about the divorce. The French bureaucracy thought we should all just sit back and be patient, but we didn't have time to be patient. A lawyer advised me to go to Juárez for a "quickie divorce"—not unusual in those days—and so I boarded a plane for Mexico. I remember that my ankles became grotesquely swollen during the flight. That was my keenest memory of the hot, dusty border town—huge, misshapen ankles. The swelling went down quickly after we landed, and I was able to set about getting a divorce. I visited the lawyers and clerks and over the course of two days was able to get an official divorce. Then I hopped right back onto the plane back to New York. I had a wedding to go to!

Back in the city, we scrambled to get our blood tests and boarded the train for Greenwich, Connecticut. Godfrey gave me a little ten-dollar gold band, which I wore throughout our marriage. We rounded up a justice of the peace and got ourselves married. We went back to New York the same day and had a Champagne celebration with our friends Jack Heidelberg (whom I knew from Juilliard) and Kit and Darby Banner (who were Godfrey's friends).

Ever since Juilliard, I'd kept in close touch with my sister Helen. I often visited her upstate in Red Hook—but I hadn't yet updated her on everything that was going on. I was sure she was going to bawl me out for being reckless. Perhaps I was being too sensitive. After all, my family had come to expect the most outrageous things from me: performing music no one could understand (ridiculous), leaving Jacques and getting a divorce, the first in the family (unnerving!), and now showing up pregnant and married to a twenty-three-year-old Englishman (great heavens!).

She didn't bawl me out after all, but she did have our brother Bill come down from Albany to spend the evening with me and Godfrey and officially check out my new husband on behalf of the Beardslee family. "What has Bethany done this time?" was most certainly running through his head as I introduced him to Godfrey. By evening's end, I think Bill had come to understand. He was clearly impressed by Godfrey's maturity. He reported back to Mother that there was nothing to worry about. My husband passed the test, and Helen set to outfitting me in her best hand-me-down maternity clothes. I must have been beside myself with worry about what they were going to think and say, but once it was all out in the open I felt a tremendous weight evaporate from my shoulders.

It seems strange now, as I look back on the mayhem of that year, how supportive my family was, especially my mother. She was as deeply committed to her children as she had been to my father. She lived her life through us—and wanted us to have more than she had. And in many respects we each succeeded, though in different ways. My brother Perry was her comfort and companion when she was old. Walter counseled her, and Helen gave her five doting grandchildren. Bill offered financial support whenever it was needed. As for me, I was her outlet to music.

Despite our achievements, we also had our share of trouble. That's where my mother distinguished herself. She was endlessly supportive. Our mother was, perhaps, always our greatest champion. Whatever was really going on inside her head, she would never let us see it. She was *always* there for us to unload on. She seemed to have resigned herself to the roller-coaster life of her singer daughter—even though the way I lived was certainly *not* how she'd been taught to behave.

As for Godfrey, he was maddeningly unruffled. He didn't seem to think I should have worried as much as I did about my family's response—and I couldn't really figure out whether that was because he knew they'd like him or because he wouldn't have cared one way or the other. Everything amused him; nothing seemed to disturb him. Yet I am pretty sure that he had no idea at all the responsibility that fatherhood would bring.

CHAPTER TWENTY-TWO

LONDON

When I was four and a half months pregnant, Godfrey and I spent the summer in London. I was anxious about meeting his family but brimming with joy. For I was going to be a mother. We stayed in a small hotel near the family house on Green Street. Some mornings I would walk through Hyde Park to their grand townhouse to practice. The family had two lovely pianos, a Blüthner in the living room and a cherrywood Steinway in Godfrey's old room on the second floor. We'd share meals with the family and get to know each other. Godfrey's mother, Gwen, in particular, and her sister Ethel Holroyd, who I was fond of right away, were very interested in music, and queried me about my training and experiences. Ethel was a fine pianist, though to her regret, had never followed a professional career. Gwen had been attentively following her son's work since he began dedicating himself to composing and writing at an early age. I was impressed with her cultivated knowledge of new music. Everyone in the family spoke highly of Milton, who'd impressed them two years before when he and Silvia had visited the Winhams to recruit Godfrey for Princeton's new doctoral program in music composition.

From the beginning, Godfrey's mother insisted I call her Gwen—or Gwennie, which was what everyone called her. She was an impressive beauty. She had aristocratic features—all lines and cutting curves, an exquisite frame to her striking, dark eyes. She wore her brown hair loose, modeled on "casual" but clearly well groomed. She stood half a head taller than me, was slim, and had absolutely gorgeous hands.

Godfrey's father, Francis, would go to the office in the morning—he had real estate companies. Sunday he'd often go around and look at his properties in his brown Morris Minor. At night, he'd have dinner with a business associate or go to the greyhound races at White City Stadium on Tuesday and Saturday evenings. Godfrey often went along, so I proposed that I come too. Francis was amused but seemed happy to have me join them.

Francis hired a car to take us to the races. On our way we'd pick up Henry Savage, a historian and an old family friend. I loved our quartet. We'd eat in a glassed-in dining room looking out over the track—a perfect view. Henry and I both bet on the *tote*, a betting pool where you could put up small amounts of money. Henry was a big talker and had elaborate explanations for how he bet and why he won or lost. At least the Winham men seemed to know what they were doing! I rarely won, of course. This was the first time I'd ever bet on anything. And can you imagine, coming from the background that I had—the Great Depression, the war, my struggling-artist marriage to Jacques—playing games with money? But my tides had changed, dramatically. I could finally play. We had great fun at the races. After dropping off Henry at his apartment, we'd go back to Green Street and have a postmortem over Jackson hardtack crackers, a pat of butter, and tea. These were happy sessions for me. I could observe Godfrey and his father really enjoying each other's company.

Francis Winham was the same medium height as his son. They shared features—a high forehead, beautiful eyes, and soft speaking voices. Francis was rather more square in stature than Godfrey, and his blond hair had gone grayish. Godfrey was a bit in awe of his father, so in many ways he was his mother's son—tending to the arts and an aesthetic culture. There was a warm distance between father and son. Almost immediately, for example, I called him "Daddy" as Godfrey did. But if you paid attention, you'd notice that more often than not when the two were face to face, Godfrey was more likely to call him "you."

In the evenings, we went to the theater with Gwen and her friends. The second day after our arrival, her friend, André, picked us up for an evening ride around London in a convertible sports car. The top was down as we whirled around Big Ben, Westminster Abbey, and Buckingham Palace. Basking in the London lights was amazing and I was enraptured with the beauty of it all.

Godfrey and I also had time alone to explore *his* London. He always wore his raincoat and Lock hat. (Lock is a famous English haberdasher.) It was a habit reinforced, no doubt, by English weather. Parts of London, like Paris, still bore scars. The heavy air raids of World War II had left vacant lots where there had once been homes.

Figure 33. Francis Winham at Joldwyns, the Winhams' country house.

We went to Hampstead Heath in the London suburbs to visit Godfrey's old friend and mentor Hans Keller. Hans, like so many musicians of his generation I had already encountered, was a Jewish refugee from Europe. He'd come over from Vienna in the 1930s and established a strong presence for himself among the musical intelligentsia, mostly as a critic and as music director of the Third Programme for the BBC. He had been Godfrey's violin teacher and was responsible for introducing Godfrey to concert life and especially to new music. It had been through Keller that Godfrey occasionally published music criticism when he was still remarkably young. When Godfrey was in England, he and Hans often attended concerts together.

We spent a wonderful afternoon with Hans and his wife, Milein Cosman, a well-known artist and illustrator. Like the Leibowitz home in Paris, the Kellers' house was modest, with comfortable worn sofas and chairs, stacks of music scores, and good conversation. Milein would show me her portraits of various performers and composers. She had a real way of capturing a personality in her bold, expressive ink drawings. Hans and Milein went on to collaborate on several book projects, his music criticism interspersed with pages of her vivid drawings.

On another afternoon, we took the train out to visit Mátyás Seiber, the Hungarian-born composer with whom Godfrey had studied composition after he left the Royal Academy. Like Gunther Schuller and to a lesser extent Milton Babbitt and Lukas Foss, Seiber was interested in jazz and other popular forms alongside his own compositions. He was a gentle, unassuming man, another great artist who had fled the Nazis. That turned out to be the only opportunity I would ever have to meet him, for he died untimely in a car accident in the early sixties. I wish I had a clearer memory of the afternoon.

Godfrey's best childhood friend was Sebastian Doniach, whose parents, Sonny and Deborah, lived on Alma Square in London. Sebastian played decent clarinet, and his wife, Sarah, was an excellent pianist. Sarah and I would spend long afternoons reading through lieder. They also had chamber-music afternoons. I'd have to sit politely and listen to Godfrey on first violin, Sebastian on second violin, Sarah on viola, and Sebastian's sister on cello, butcher Mozart's string quartets. It was terrible.

Sarah and I got along very well and went antiquing together on Portobello Road. The Doniach parents were both scientists. Deborah Doniach, in particular, was a famous immunologist and a pioneer in the field of autoimmune diseases. Sebastian went on to gain quite a reputation through his career as a physicist. In later years, he and Sarah moved from London to Palo Alto, California. Sebastian still teaches at Stanford. And many, many years after I first met them, I formed a close friendship in New York City with Deborah's sister, Maia Helles.

The time in London raced by. I didn't want to leave at the end. The Winhams enjoyed having fun, and I felt that each day with them brought new adventures.

As much as I regretted leaving London, when I walked into our old homey apartment on East 17th Street, it looked wonderful. It seemed so *tactile*, and all ours. I felt as if we were back in reality. I started practicing again, and Godfrey started composing.

When our first son, Baird, was born on December 17, 1957, Godfrey had just finished a piece for soprano and string quartet called *The Habit of Perfection*, from a poem by Gerard Manley Hopkins, who was one of Godfrey's favorite poets. I would go on to sing it many times. The language was so beautiful:

Elected Silence, sing to me
And beat upon my whorlèd ear,
Pipe me to pastures still and be
The music that I care to hear.

CHAPTER TWENTY-THREE

NEW YORK PRO MUSICA

1958

After the New Year, I received a call from Noah Greenberg, the impresario of early music in New York City. I had met him when I was at Juilliard. Though he wasn't a student there, a group of us singers would go over to his house and sing through madrigals for fun. Noah was an enthusiast, not a financier—a Socialist Jewish kid from the Bronx with a nose for business and a zeal for organizing. When I first knew him, he was supporting himself by arranging choruses for women from a number of different chapters of the Garment Workers Union.

Noah was rather hyper and a chain smoker, but he was charming, too, and knew how to persuade others of his enthusiasm for early music. In 1952, with the mercenary zeal of a used car salesman, he went about creating and financing what would become his very successful early music group, New York Pro Musica Antiqua. His biographer, James Gollin, refers to him as a Pied Piper because he was so good at getting people to follow along with him.

Pro Musica was a small chamber group singing medieval and Renaissance music, accompanied by four players of period instruments. Bernard Krainis, a recorder player (who I thought was terrifically handsome), was Noah's collaborator in setting up the group. Russell Oberlin, my friend from Juilliard and a great countertenor, was involved from the beginning. The repertoire was modeled on the Pro Music Antiqua group that Safford Cape was running in Brussels. Greenberg's concerts at the 92nd Street Y and the New School became very popular. Early-music audiences were classical music listeners who were interested in novelty, but couldn't quite get their heads around difficult new music.

New York Pro Musica was already quite established when Noah called me and asked me to step in for his soprano, Jean Hakes, who was leaving the group to have a baby. He knew my voice from my Juilliard days, and I was rather pleased to be joining the group in the spring of 1958.

I enjoyed the change of pace. For one thing, in Pro Musica, I was able to sing again with my old Juilliard buddies Charles Bressler, Russell Oberlin, and Betty Wilson. Russell was an Irish tenor with the extension of a unique high range. He was our countertenor. His voice had a wonderful, complex sound that distinguished it from the usual falsetto of today's countertenors. Charles Bressler, a legitimate light lyric tenor, often sang duets with Russell; they were incredible together. Charlie also went on to have a major career in oratorio and sang for years with the New York Chamber Soloists. Betty Wilson had a beautiful warm quality to her voice. The two of us blended well and became lifelong chums. Good old Brayton Lewis was our solid, reliable bass; the wonderful baritone Gordon Myers later joined the group. Noah was our "Fred Waring"—our big-band leader. He'd give us the beat. We didn't need him to actually conduct; the music was so easy!

Pro Musica had a busy performance schedule—and that was the pace I liked so much. In addition to traveling, which was wonderful fun, we held three annual concerts in New York City at the 92nd Street Y and the Grace Rainey Rogers Auditorium at the Metropolitan Museum. I also sang in the *Play of Daniel*, a medieval play that Noah and the poet W. H. Auden had resurrected from scraps, with Auden writing the new text. Pro Musica performed this successful play annually, in full costume, at the Church of the Intercession and at the Cloisters.

Recitals, Pro Musica, and our new baby kept me very busy. I was breast-feeding, so at first I brought Baird along with me to rehearsals. Before too long, Baird needed more constant attention, and I had to start hiring baby-sitters. In the fall of 1959, I went with Pro Musica on an extended six-week tour of the West Coast. I left Baird, who was twenty-one months old at the time, with our sitter, Palma. She kept him all day, giving Godfrey a chance to work undisturbed. In the evenings, Baird would come home so that Godfrey could feed him and put him to bed. It seemed like a good arrangement, and off I went down the California coast.

We drove along Big Sur with Charles Bressler at the wheel. The other performers followed, caravan fashion. One stop I'll never forget was at San Simeon, William Randolph Hearst's huge estate, situated high on a hill overlooking the Pacific. Wow! Hearst was, of course, immortalized by Orson Welles in *Citizen Kane*—a movie we'd all seen. The real-life estate was spectacular. Marble swimming pools, rooms done in 1920s baronial style, a forest for keeping wild animals. I had never seen anything like it. Hearst amassed his fortune in the newspaper business, in the days before income tax, when the rich had so much money they couldn't spend it fast enough. Then I knew what the robber barons were all about.

I also remember the beautiful concert hall at the Museum of Contemporary Art–San Diego in La Jolla, California. It was a modern, imposing building, situated high near the Pacific Ocean. I remember looking through a glass door during intermission at the audience standing on a large balcony gazing at the ocean practically beneath their feet.

We traveled all the way down to New Mexico and then flew to Tucson where Betty Wilson, Bobby White, and I had a wild experience while exploring the city. Bobby, another fabulous Irish tenor, was Russell's substitute, filling in for him when Russell had to leave for another engagement. Our small group came upon a massive stone building and a large, old courtyard. It was so peaceful in there. The three of us began to sing in order to hear the acoustics. In recounting this story to Noah's biographer, Betty remembered that we sang the villancico *Si la noche haze escura*. The acoustics were indeed lovely, and as we warmed to the song, heads started appearing up in the windows of the great stone building. At some point, we all realized that there were bars over the windows and that we had wandered into the courtyard of a prison! So we kept singing and singing through to the end of the song and got a wonderful round of applause from the inmates.

When I got home from this long tour, Baird snubbed me the whole first evening, behaving as if he didn't even know me anymore. I had loved seeing the West Coast, exploring with my friends, and performing, but six weeks in that baby's life was an eternity to be separated from his mother. I liked traveling. I didn't feel chained to Baird the way I might have if I'd been less consumed by my career. But Godfrey was not pleased and told me in a very determined way that I'd have to shorten my tours: "From now on, two weeks is the limit on you being away from home." I knew he meant it. Going away for that long turned out to have been bad judgment on my part—maybe Godfrey was jealous that I was having too much fun without him. And of course the crowd-pleasing early music of Pro Musica was the extreme opposite of the new music world that I'd come up in and that I shared with Godfrey.

The conflict was determinative. While I'd been away, I found out I was pregnant again. My family was growing, Godfrey didn't want me traveling, and my career was going to have to take on a different shape. Reluctantly, I told Noah Greenberg that it was time for me to leave Pro Musica. Noah tried to convince me to stay. I'd been with the group for only three years, and I really would have preferred to let Noah talk me into staying, because I very much wanted to go on the upcoming European tour. But I was expecting a second baby, we didn't need the income, and in order to appease Godfrey, it made sense to focus on my solo work.

I didn't know then that just a few years later, in 1966—the same year the Old Met shuttered its doors—Noah would have a massive heart attack and die. He was only forty-seven, but he had been a two-pack-a-day smoker. As popular as it had been, Pro Musica didn't survive without Noah, and the group soon became a thing of the past.

CHAPTER TWENTY-FOUR

THE FROMM MUSIC FOUNDATION

I went back to new music. Half the concerts I sang in those years must have been commissioned by Paul Fromm. He was arguably the most important supporter of American art music during the second half of the twentieth century and, perhaps more critical for a singer like me, he had absolute conviction regarding the centrality of the composer. The mission statement of the foundation, which he moved to Harvard University, begins: "In the cultural life of any period, the vital source of music is the creativeness of the composer." Eighteenth- and nineteenth-century composers had been such a big part of his childhood in Europe. But even in Europe, as in America, there was a schism between old music and new. He believed that something must be added to bridge the schism, and that otherwise, there was no way that "serious art can make its own way in the marketplace."[20] Music needed to be supported. He believed, too, that educating his audience was the key to growth. Hearing Stravinsky's *Rite of Spring* when he was a teenager in Bavaria, he said, "made a twentieth century man of me."[21]

"When I was young," he explained in an interview late in his life with Bruce Duffie, "you learned music as a language. You conceptualized musical history as a kind of evolutionary progression from one period to the other. Each period had a style of its own." It was an evolution that had a name for each stage: Renaissance, baroque, classicism, romanticism. Then, "all of a sudden it ended." This is "the era of Pluralism, which means a very wide spectrum from serialism to hard rock," and everything in between.

Audiences, he explained found themselves in a transitional state early in the century and that transitional state became a permanent condition.[22]

Paul was a lover of new music from a very young age. He had firm ideas about how to cultivate audiences. He faulted big recording houses for failing to raise audiences to higher standards of listening experiences and thought that they played to an uninformed public that didn't have any "syntax" (Paul's word) with which to listen to new music. You can't go from Mozart to Babbitt without knowing Stravinsky, Berg, Schoenberg.

When Paul emigrated from Nazi Germany to Chicago in 1938 at thirty-two years old, he went right into his family wine-importing business. They'd been vintners for generations in Kitzingen. He set up the Great Lakes Wine Company and grew wealthy. He dedicated himself to becoming a one-man patron of composers. He thought of a patron as "someone who is involved in music but also tries to nourish the artistic spirit."[23] In 1952, he established the Fromm Music Foundation.

Paul must have been in his mid-forties when I first met him. He was a tall man, with strong facial features and a big nose. He would always come to congratulate me on my performances in person or send a signed note. I'd had so many newspaper reviews by that point that his compliments meant something more to me. I treasured them. Fromm was the force that made possible the performance of the new music on which I'd built my career. He believed that music didn't *exist* without performance, and so on principle his foundation never funded a piece that didn't have a performance attached.

As a funder he was awesome. He involved himself with both music and the arts. He was an articulate advocate, a lifelong student, and an enthusiast. He enjoyed knowing all the composers, and depended on the more established among them to point him toward worthy new work. He once told the composer Arthur Berger, "I don't want to be thanked for what I do. Nothing embarrasses me more. The composer is the one who deserves *our* thanks."[24] He sought advice on commissions from a board made up of composers and frequently turned to Milton for recommendations because he admired Milton's ideals. They had grown to be close friends. The early concerts Paul underwrote were excellent, and I was honored to sing in so many of them.

In 1958 the Fromm Music Foundation put on its first concert of contemporary chamber and choral music at the New School in New York City. On that program I sang *Sestina* by Ernst Křenek, which Paul had commissioned especially for that concert. A handsome, short man in his early fifties, Křenek already had a major reputation in Vienna before flee-ing the Nazis. Although he wasn't Jewish, the Nazis frequently referred to him as a "Jewish composer." The Third Reich labeled his wildly popular, jazz-influenced opera *Jonny spielt auf* (1926) "degenerate," because the main character is black.

In the late thirties, soon before emigrating to America, Křenek moved into a twelve-tone period. *Sestina* was a big twelve-tone piece for soprano and a large instrumental ensemble to a poem in German that Křenek him-self had written. This highly complex score, in truth, wasn't one of those pieces that ever captured my heart. It was certainly difficult enough to learn. I worked on *Sestina* diligently, mostly while I was still in the hospital after Baird was born. (In those days, it was quite usual to stay a week or so in the hospital with your newborn.) I sat there in my hospital bed with my faithful pitch pipe and metronome, making my way through the score.

The other mother who was sharing the hospital room heard me prac-ticing and thought it was all quite funny. I'm sure she was thinking, "Hey! Where's the tune to that song?"

Sometimes, looking back now, I don't understand how I was able to sing some of the music I learned—pieces like *Sestina*. I can only attribute it to youth and good pitch memory.

I will listen to LPs from that period in my career as I sit at my desk, writing these memories, and think, *Who is* that person singing? Could that really be me?

Křenek had decided to conduct *Sestina* himself, so I had the unique op-portunity to work with him personally. This performance was a world pre-miere, and *Sestina* received excellent reviews. The *Times* said it was "star-tling and perplexing," and described the music generally as having "strange and eerie timbres," "ejaculations of sound" and my part was a "weird vocal line with wide skips."[25] After the concert we recorded it on LP for Epic Records, again under Paul's patronage. Although I later sang Křenek's beautiful concert aria *Die Nachtigall*—an earlier, more tonal work that I loved—I never sang *Sestina* again.

The conductor and composer Lukas Foss and I spent a lovely evening with Paul in his beautiful Chicago apartment years later, in 1966. We were there performing Lukas's piece *Time Cycle* with the Chicago Symphony. I'd worked very hard preparing, and the performance went well. The *Daily News* wrote: "Foss, not so surely a conducting talent as an eloquent propagandist for avant-garde works, including his own, stole the show with his 1960 masterpiece *Time Cycle*, sung with gripping intensity and tuning fork certainty of pitch by soprano Bethany Beardslee."[26]

Although *Time Cycle* does get performed a lot, I never sang it again. And there are many, many other pieces like it that I sang once and no one ever took up again: Křenek's *Sestina*, Phil Batstone's *Mother Goose Primer*, even Stravinsky's *Threni* for that matter. It was and continues to be one of the most unfortunate aspects of the new music scene. Pieces, big and small, important or minor, only get a single performance. It was demoralizing for everyone! The "one-performance syndrome" was likely the driving impetus behind the trend of composers forming their own performance groups in the 1960s and seventies. By mounting their own concert series and doing their own conducting, composers ensured that their music, as well as the music of their colleagues, would get numerous performances. Two such organizations that were particularly successful included the Group for Contemporary Music at Columbia University, founded by Charles Wuorinen and Harvey Sollberger, and the Fires of London, founded by the English composers Peter Maxwell Davies and Harrison Birtwistle. Other groups organized by the performers themselves were: the Da Capo Chamber Players, the New York New Music Ensemble, and Continuum.

Part of Paul Fromm's mission was to defeat the single-performance syndrome. He firmly held that one part of the burden lay with him, in funding the creation of new music, which he did by commissioning more than three hundred composers over the years. The other part fell to the performers, who had to really adopt a composer or a work and champion it through repeat performances. In 1975, the Fromm Music Foundation conducted a comprehensive survey called "Music of the Last Forty Years Not Yet Established in the Repertoire." In the introduction Paul wrote: "If our survey has in some way served as a catalyst to impress musicians to probe into the catalog of contemporary music, we will have accomplished our purpose." (It would be an even longer list today.) Without performance music dies.

Jacques and I had built our repertoire on the same principle—it's one of the reasons that learning all that difficult work by heart was a fundamental part of my career. Once a piece was in our repertoire, we would program it again and again.

CHAPTER TWENTY-FIVE

EARL KIM AND RUSSELL SHERMAN

E rnst Křenek had originally hired another singer to perform *Sestina*, but she backed out when she saw the music. It was over her head. So they called me, as they always did, when there was something modern and difficult to sing. It was hard to ignore the fact that I was the new music girl; it was a niche, also known as a "pigeonhole." I started to wonder if anyone knew that I could sing a C-major scale! The time had come for me to prove myself and in the process to fulfill an old vow that I had once made.

And so that spring, I turned to Franz Schubert and to my dear friend from the Princeton faculty, Earl Kim. Earl was a Korean composer who had come to Princeton from the West Coast, where he had studied with Schoenberg. He was a real aesthete, with immaculate taste in everything, food, clothing, even the way he decorated his home. He loved composing for voice, and through the years I sang his music many times. Earl was my coach for Schubert's song cycle *Die schöne Müllerin*.

Schubert was Earl's favorite composer; when Earl taught analysis, he used Schubert's works as his examples. Earl also had very particular ideas about how lieder should be performed; specifically, he insisted on a full range of dynamics. Working with him, I learned how to sing all the gradations of *piano*, from **mp** to **ppp**. At first, I thought he was pushing the soft singing too much. There were times in our practice sessions that I'd burst out, "Earl, I'll never be heard in a hall singing this softly!" I thought that Earl was imposing his own minimal aesthetic onto the music. But he reassured me. He told me never to underestimate the audience. *You* determine the dynamics, he said, and the audience will be drawn into your world. I trusted him; of course, he was right.

Earl and I performed Schubert's cycle at the Phillips Gallery in Washington, DC, on April 27, 1958. I can remember a very large Renoir painting hanging behind the piano in the room where we performed. It was an intimate room, seating only a few hundred people. Earl was not a professional pianist, but he played well. We performed the cycle together again in Princeton at Proctor Hall and got very high compliments. I asked Earl to play with me in New York City, but he refused. Like Jacques, he had terrible stage fright. Probably he had performed with me in DC and Princeton only because he loved the music so much. He wasn't prepared to take our show on the road.

But I had worked hard on *Die schöne Müllerin*, and I didn't want to lose all that work. I wanted to perform Schubert and incorporate this song cycle into my repertoire. Unfortunately, Bob Helps was having one of his periodic crises and was unavailable. I didn't have a pianist for my Schubert and was in a quandary.

The solution came to me through Frida Kahn. Frida was the widow of Erich Itor Kahn, a German Jewish composer and pianist who was only fifty years old when he died in 1956—before he'd really had a chance to establish himself. To those of us in the thick of the new music world, Kahn was known as a serial composer, but he really made his living as a chamber musician. I knew him primarily as Jennie Tourel's accompanist and a founding member of the Albeneri Trio. Jacques once had told me that Erich had introduced René Leibowitz to Webern's music when the Kahns were first exiled to Paris in the thirties. If true, this would have made Erich a very important link in the chain that brought *me* to the Second Viennese School.

Erich Kahn had a gentle nature; he wasn't one to force his music on anyone, which meant that hardly any of us knew his compositions. Frida was determined to change that after her husband died and mounted several memorial concerts to introduce his music more widely. She wrote to ask if I would sing a group of Schubert songs along with Kahn's four *Marien Lieder*. Since I had sung Kahn's *Music for Ten Instruments and Soprano* with Jacques on an ISCM program, I knew that the music would not be easy. We would need a first-rate pianist. Frida brought on board Russell Sherman, whom we all called "Buddy."

As soon as we started rehearsing the Kahn, I realized what a truly wonderful pianist he was. And I thought to myself, *Here* is my Schubert pianist! Russell was a student of Eduard Steuermann and had made his performance debut at Town Hall when he was only fifteen years old. We had a lot in common—he loved the music of the Second Viennese School. He played Erich Kahn's music as magnificently as he played the Schubert songs.

It was fascinating to rehearse *Die schöne Müllerin* with Russell after having learned it with Earl—fascinating and completely different! Russell was a concert soloist, and I took advantage of his wonderful assertive playing to really sing out. I was, however, mindful of Earl's soft-singing principle, and I insisted we use it whenever it was really appropriate to the song—which wasn't to quite the same degree as I had done with Earl.

I felt lucky to play with Russell early in his career, for he was still an emerging performer. But he soon went on to have a substantial solo career.

We first performed the Schubert cycle in Carnegie Recital Hall on November 17, 1958, and had excellent reviews. The *Tribune* said, "Bethany Beardslee sings Schubert as well as she sings Schoenberg."[27] The *Times* was even better:

> New York is hardly lacking in song recitals, of which many are quite good, but it seldom hears one in which singer and pianist are so wonderfully matched as on this occasion. Mr. Sherman was neither submissive accompanist, nor signal-calling coach as he played the piano part of *Die schöne Müllerin*. He and Miss Beardslee were an equally matched team whose contributions complemented each other at every turn. As a result of their collaboration the great song cycle was endowed with enlivening warmth, color, sentiment, and drama. With skill, intelligence, and imagination, she made it the attractive servant of Schubert's miraculous lyricism, and she did it masterfully.[28]

Hooray! I thought. Now I can change horses and do just traditional song recitals like Elisabeth Schwarzkopf, Irmgard Seefried, and Dietrich Fischer-Dieskau.

I had such moments overcome me more than a few times throughout my career; they were especially keen when I received a fabulous review after a traditional recital. You must remember that when you sing new music, the critics are reviewing the composer as much as the performance. So, for example, when Russell and I had many years earlier appeared on the same program at an ISCM concert, Howard Taubman's *Times* review began: "[Although] the elapsed time was no longer than that at the normal evening of music, one felt as though one had been listening for hours and hours." And before roundly complimenting my performance, Taubman had to qualify: "The I.S.C.M. enthusiasts cannot be blamed for trying to concentrate as much music by as many composers as the average concert will allow. But the composers they present require concentrated listening and an effort at absorption. These requirements would not be too burdensome if the listener were helped along with a little more contrast in style and a little more music with a warm, human impulse."[29] I was split by diverging desires for my career. Should I abandon new music for traditional concert formats, which would mean many more engagements and reviews that would focus on my singing? Or should I stand strong and uncompromising? Would I be the singer who gave my audience something different, something it couldn't get elsewhere? It was a complicated decision, one that I had to consider over and over again through the years. I loved all music, and yet I had branded myself as a specialist—a contradiction? But they were performances of "difficult" music. There was a way, too, in which I felt isolated in new music. Except for Valarie Lamoree, who was just coming on the scene, the other New York singers seemed to avoid the hard twelve-tone scores. There were a very few other new music specialists, Phyllis Curtin, for example. But even Phyllis tended toward the new music composers who were working in more traditional styles, such as Ned Rorem and Carlisle Floyd.

Oddly enough, I felt in a way that I was quite an old-fashioned singer. For until the end of the nineteenth century, singers only sang the newest music that was being written in their time. It wasn't easy for a singer to have access to scores from all periods of music and pick and choose. I, like them, sang the music of my time.

I don't think realistically I could have ever refused a new work, saying something like, "Sorry, I don't sing contemporary music anymore."

First and foremost, I'd gotten to the point in my life where I was surrounded by new music. It wasn't just my husband, but all of our dearest friends, mostly composers, were part of new music. I was not going to turn my back on them.

There is a kind of magic about new music that you can't quite grasp when you're singing masterpieces. The work arrives as a score, just marks on paper—from the composer's mind to you. I always learned my music *a cappella*, committing the vocal line to memory. I often did not know what the music would sound like until it all came together for the first rehearsal. Together at last, the soloists, the instrumentalists, a pianist, or an orchestra would combine the mysterious elements we'd been practicing in isolation to make a whole—something brand new. Something that *no one had ever heard before.*

Bob Helps called. He was out of the New Haven clinic, recovered, and playing again. He had set up a program for the summer Starlight Festival of Music at Yale. He wanted us to again perform Schumann's *Liederkreis*, op. 48; Godfrey's *Habit of Perfection*; and his own Two Songs on texts by Herman Melville. It was a luxurious setup, because Godfrey had the chance to coach the quartet in rehearsal, and the result was that we got a fairly decent performance of his piece. Even though Sessions had been Bob's composition teacher, Bob's new songs showed the influence of Debussy; French music was part of Bob's gestalt.

At least until his next disappearance, it was great to have Bob back playing again, though I'll never forget how sublime it was to sing with Russell Sherman.

CHAPTER TWENTY-SIX

WORKING WITH
MARTHA GRAHAM

In 1956, I had sung in the premiere of Vivian Fine's small opera *A Guide to the Life Expectancy of a Rose*, a quirky piece set to an article from the *New York Times* garden section. Vivian had been drawn to the title and used the text about tending rose bushes as a metaphor for romantic love. It was a fun show to be part of. It was the first work to be commissioned and performed by the newly created B. De Rothschild Foundation for Arts and Sciences.

Vivian wrote the opera. Martha Graham directed and staged it first at the Donnell Library for Vivian's Composer's Forum and then at Bethsabée's—that is, Martha's studio on East 63rd Street. I was singing opposite the tenor Earl Rogers. For the show, Martha cloaked the studio practice barres with pleated gray curtains. She put the instrumentalists on one side of the stage and Earl and me on the other. Martha also designed the costumes, dressing us in formal clothes from the Edwardian period. As the opera opened, I was reclining on a chaise longue. During section pauses, three male dancers performed at center stage.

Vivian's music was smartly composed and atonal, yet had a Mozartian flavor. The way it worked, with the text describing different species of roses, was playful. Meanwhile, Earl and I were playing out a dialogue about marital relations, expressed in terms of cultivating roses: what will survive; what's bound to wither; what has to be pruned away. The critic and fellow composer Wallingford Riegger described it perfectly: "By use of exaggerated stress and clever prosody, she has transformed the pedestrian seriousness of the words into something hilariously funny."[30] "Serious" phrases included "There are no tables of life expectancy, there are so many conditions that influence longevity," and "even under these conditions, some varieties do not thrive." This was indeed the funniest libretto I've ever sung. Keeping a straight face while singing and acting it was not easy!

Vivian studied with Ruth Crawford Seeger as well as with Roger Sessions. She was also a piano student of Abby Whiteside. I liked her music. Vivian, along with Miriam Gideon and Marion Bauer, were some of the important women composers in those days and on a par with any man. Marion had been Milton's composition teacher before he went to study under Roger Sessions. Milton respected her a great deal. I was fond of Vivian, and got to know her because she was Martha's music director at the Rothschild and organized the concerts there.

When Martha was developing a new production, *Clytemnestra*, in 1958, Vivian asked me to be part of it. Martha was sixty-five, and this was to be her last major choreography. In terms of her entire career, many consider this piece to be her masterpiece. The music was composed by the Egyptian composer Halim El-Dabh. The sets and costume were designed by the sculptor and frequent Graham collaborator Isamu Noguchi. Robert Irving conducted. I was the female part in the two-voice Greek chorus. Robert Gross sang the male part. In April we opened for a two-week run at the Adelphi Theater on Broadway.

Clytemnestra was not a hard score. A Greek chorus narrates, through *Sprechstimme* and intoned speech, the story of the evil Clytemnestra and her murder at the hands of her children. Halim rather deliberately had composed the score to sound primitive, which suited Martha's interpretation of the Greek tragedy. Although he worked closely with Martha during rehearsals, he was very unassuming about our singing and never had many notes.

In his *New York Times* review the day after the opening, John Martin described our role like this: "Part of the time a chorus of two, a man and a woman, dressed in impeccable modern evening clothes, sits just inside the proscenium, scores in hand, half-singing, half-speaking explanatory passages and introductions of the central figures. Sometimes they resort to wordless chanting with almost Kabuki vocal coloration. The air of remoteness and objectivity they contribute is remarkably valuable."[31]

There is one scene though where Clytemnestra has a nightmare, and I let out a screaming *Ya, ya, ya, ya, ya, ya, yee.*

Oh, the tribulations of performing new music! . . . Actually, that section was more fun than you can imagine. Halim really knew what he was doing, and the overall effect was stunning.

In her memoir *Blood Memory*, Martha explained that to put *Clytemnestra* together, she spent evenings on her studio floor placing great pieces of red material all around. Isamu Noguchi then developed a corresponding way to use fabric as both a costume and a prop—as a triumphal cape as well as the entrance to Clytemnstra's bedchamber. "I had used fabric in movement before, but not in such an intense way," wrote Graham.[32]

Martha had an amazingly expressive face, with large, full lips painted deep red, and startling black eyes, thick with mascara. Martha revealed so much of Clytemnestra's character, her voluptuousness, her anger, fear, and seduction. Every body movement, even her face, was a reflection of the evil woman.

Modern dance was new to me. I had a wonderful view of the whole company from my position on stage. Martha Graham was famously still vital, and it was fascinating to watch her work. She was quite a gal. Her lead male dancer for *Clytemnestra* was Paul Taylor. The rest of the company consisted of Bertram Ross, Ethel Winter, Helen McGee, Linda Rhodes, Matt Turney, and Glen Tetley—all legends. She was authoritarian with her dancers and worked them hard, pushing them to their limits. She made me think of Jacques, another hard-driving perfectionist. But she was, however, perfectly lovely to me and very gracious.

Nonsingers seldom realize how physical singing is. There was no way that Martha Graham didn't understand. She knew hard physical work. In *Blood Memory*, she wrote:

> I believe that we learn by practice. Whether it means to learn to dance by practicing dancing or to learn to live by practicing living, the principles are the same. In each, it is the performance of a dedicated precise set of acts, physical or intellectual, from which comes the shape of achievement, a sense of one's being, a satisfaction of spirit. One becomes, in some area, an athlete of God. Practice means to perform, over and over again in the face of all obstacles, some act of vision, of faith, of desire. Practice is a means of inviting the perfection desired.[33]

She is right: it's all practice. Although with Martha Graham I really do think there must have been some magic in the mix, too.

CHAPTER TWENTY-SEVEN

THRENI AND THE ALTENBERG LIEDER

The first weekend of January 1959, as Castro rolled into Havana and Khrushchev's foreign minister arrived in Washington to meet with President Eisenhower, and the *New York Herald Tribune* declared: "History was made yesterday!," the New York City premiere of Igor Stravinsky's new piece *Threni: id est Lamentationes Jeremiae Prophetae* took place at Town Hall. I had the soprano solo part.

This large choral work, Stravinsky's first considerable composition since *The Rake's Progress*, had been commissioned two years earlier by the North German Radio of Hamburg. Paul Fromm's foundation, of course, produced the New York City concert, which was conducted and probably programmed, too, by Robert Craft. The program positioned *Threni* alongside major works by Berg and Schoenberg—an interesting combination, given that this was Stravinsky's first exploration of serial music.

When Stravinsky and Bob Craft were organizing the concert, they approached me because they knew of my reputation as the singer of new music in New York—or maybe they remembered my singing from when they had attended Jacques's all-Webern concert. Stravinsky was always curious about new ideas and was impressed by Webern's music. Either way, Bob Craft and I met, and he graciously invited me to have lunch with Stravinsky. It was so long ago that I don't remember the lunch terribly well. I know that I was nervous and had a chance to show off my French, trying to impress the Master. I remember the sweet way that Stravinsky had about him, and his evident delight in sharing a pretty girl's company.

I always admired Stravinsky's wisdom in continuing to grow as an artist in his later years, exploring new compositional techniques rather than just rehashing the same ideas. *Threni* was twelve-tone music, and according to many critics a departure from the most familiar applications of twelve-tone music. Stravinsky himself described it rather as a "music of intervals." In *Conversations with Stravinsky*, Craft asked Stravinsky to explain what he meant in this specific instance by "interval" and received the following answer:

> Let me tell you about a dream that came to me while I was composing *Threni*. . . . After working late one night I retired to bed still troubled by an interval. I dreamed about this interval. It had become an elastic substance stretching exactly between the two notes I had composed, but underneath these notes at either end was an egg, a large testicular egg. The eggs were gelatinous to the touch (I touched them) and warm, and they were protected by nests. I woke up knowing that my interval was right. (For those who want more of the dream, it was pink—I often dream in color. Also, I was so surprised to see the eggs I immediately understood them to be symbols. Still in the dream, I went to my library of dictionaries and looked up "interval," but found only a confusing explanation which I checked the next morning in reality and found to be the same).[34]

I love that answer, but it doesn't explain anything. Stravinsky was more helpful in a subsequent answer, and able to position himself better with regard to twelve-tone music: "Always I have been interested in intervals. Not only horizontally in terms of melody, but also the vertical results that arise from the combinations of intervals. That by the way is what is wrong with most twelve-tone composers. . . . They are indifferent to the vertical aspect of the music."[35]

Threni was a very challenging piece. The composer Claudio Spies described it as standing out among Stravinsky's other compositions of the period "by virtue of its elaborate interweaving of small formal schemes, adding up to large, continuous movements, as well as its predominance of unaccompanied choral and solo vocal music."[36] The premieres in Venice and Paris had not gone well. Stravinsky described the Paris event, which was met with jeers, as "the unhappiest concert of my life," and argued publicly with Pierre Boulez about the disaster. Stravinsky blamed the performers, who he thought were not up to the difficult parts and the inadequate rehearsals. It was too complex a piece to put together on a couple of rehearsals. But *Threni*'s inauspicious European debut meant that it was twice as important to get it right in New York.

Of course I arrived at the rehearsals having studied my part. I remember vividly Stravinsky shouting during one of the rehearsals with the soloists: "Listen to the soprano!"

Hugh Ross's chorus was well prepared and sounded in tune. But there were six of us soloists, and I really sympathized with the rest of them. I'm sure it was one of their first experiences singing that new dissonant Stravinsky. The male soloists in particular had unaccompanied sections of highly dissonant harmony.

The *a cappella* male solo sections never blended or sounded in tune to me. That's one of the particular challenges of Stravinsky's *Threni*. It needs lots of rehearsal by a very good professional group like the Swingle Singers, who sang Bach's polyphony *a cappella* and beautifully in tune. When you have soloists who are set in their own individual timbre, it doesn't always result in good blending.

On the same program, Alexander "Sasha" Schneider, who'd been the second violinist of the Budapest String Quartet, and who I believe contracted the performers, asked me to also sing Berg's *Altenberg Lieder* in what would be its American premiere. These songs were sometimes called the "Picture-Postcard Songs," because the poet Peter Altenberg had originally sent the short poems to the composer on postcards. The songs were composed in 1912, the same year Schoenberg wrote *Pierrot lunaire* and Stravinsky *The Rite of Spring*. As with those notorious pieces, the audience rioted when the *Altenberg Lieder* were premiered in a 1913 concert mounted by Schoenberg. The musicologist Mark DeVoto labels this early piece, by the still young Berg, as the first *real* twelve-tone piece. DeVoto explains, "These five orchestral songs are an amazing leap into the visionary unknown, representing Berg's heroic and fully successful effort to declare his independence from Schoenberg's guidance after seven years of dedicated expert instruction."[37]

I was more nervous about singing against a full orchestra than I was intimidated by the piece's complex harmonies, and I was hesitant to take it on. I usually backed away from such big instrumentations. Sasha, however, insisted that the songs fitted me—I must have been among the few singers in New York who could have undertaken such a complicated score. There's a sustained *pianissimo* high C in one of the *Altenberg* songs. I got a big round of applause from the orchestra every time I did it in rehearsal. I guess not many singers sing that note *pianissimo*—everyone else I've ever heard hits that note loud. Earl Kim had really taught me not to fear those soft dynamics, and I had a strong ethic for honoring the composer's instructions. If Berg wrote *pianissimo*, then that is the way it should be sung, right? Right!

Despite my nerves, I'm so glad that I agreed to do the *Altenberg Lieder*. It was an exquisite pairing with *Threni* and a major triumph for me. After marveling over *Threni*, Jay S. Harrison described the Berg as "a wondrous series of five songs which, in their expressionistic bite, sting and quiver like an exposed nerve." He went on: "They were gloriously sung by Bethany Beardslee, a young soprano whose intervallic sense is not matched by anyone in this writer's acquaintance."[38] Robert Craft, too, simply fell in love with the songs and later that summer sent me one of his signature postcards of congratulations.

After that successful concert, we went on to record both *Threni* and the *Altenberg Lieder* for Columbia Records with Fromm's sponsorship and under the supervision of John McClure. Stravinsky himself conducted the recording of *Threni*—I believe it was at the insistence of Columbia Records, with whom he had an exclusive contract. This was the first time soloists and chorus worked under Stravinsky's direction.

We were working in January, the dead of winter. Stravinsky was a tiny man and would appear at the recording rehearsals in a huge overcoat with a massive fur collar that practically buried him. In his conducting, his beat was short and awkward as he hunched over the score, his eagle eyes watching us. Yet he brought out the music's form and rhythm in the way only a composer can do. When he smiled it seemed to engulf his face, for he had a large mouth and big teeth. But those eyes didn't miss a trick!

Stravinsky was a cosmopolitan and a good businessman, and was worshiped by his audience. Would that all composers had his success. Through his long career, from *Firebird* to *Threni* and the *Requiem Canticles*, Stravinsky left an unparalleled legacy. He was really the last composer of the twentieth century whose lifestyle was as elegant as his music. In Europe he was fully immersed in the Paris scene of the 1920s. He lived in an era in which he was able to be a "successful composer." More important, *The Rite of Spring* was genuinely epic. That piece changed music. *The Rite of Spring* closed out the nineteenth century more completely than Schoenberg's work had. Schoenberg's style may have been more advanced, but *The Rite of Spring* had impact. It was a landmark in the development of modern music.

Craft tacked the *Altenberg Lieder*, which he now loved, onto the *Threni* recording session. It didn't take that long, maybe forty-five minutes, almost as if it was recorded using overtime from *Threni*.

Figure 34. In my costume for the *Play of Daniel* while recording the *Altenberg Lieder* at Columbia Records.

While I was recording *Threni*, I was also performing with Pro Musica in *The Play of Daniel* at the Church of the Intercession, way uptown. We did the *Altenberg* on the same weekend as the Pro Musica show. I had to jump into a taxi right after the performance and rush from 155th Street and Broadway to the midtown Columbia recording studios. I made it just in the nick of time, still wearing my medieval *Daniel* costume. Of course, the Columbia recording was a big deal and everyone was interested in Stravinsky right then, so a photographer popped into the studio while we were recording the *Altenberg*. Wouldn't you know that I was still wearing my medieval costume! For years, whenever newspapers needed a picture of me, they'd run those foolish pictures, first the wedding dresses and then the monastic felt.

In this period, between the Stravinsky and Pro Musica, I also had opportunities to sing more traditional repertoire. I loved at last that my career had turned into one where I sang both classical music and new. Godfrey's father was in town that spring on a business trip and came to hear me sing at a city-sponsored Handel Festival. It was the first and only time he heard me live in concert. Thank goodness it was Handel he came to hear and not Křenek! I did a group of German arias with Sasha Schneider on violin and Thomas Dunn on harpsichord. Daddy was a businessman, and his knowledge of music was short of nothing. Who knows what he would have thought of a Křenek program? But I was so pleased and proud to know he was in the audience.

CHAPTER TWENTY-EIGHT

PRINCETON
AND SASKATOON

We decided to move to Princeton the summer of 1959. I brought little Baird along with me on my summer singing engagements and left my husband with the chore of moving us out of 315 East 17th Street. At first I wasn't crazy about the idea of leaving New York. It was my city, and since my reputation as singer of new music had grown, I was in demand there. But Godfrey had his master's degree now and was staying on at the music department to pursue a doctorate, the first year they were offering the advanced degree. He had the commute out to Princeton timed to the second: Grab a cup of coffee, dash down the stairs, hail a taxi to Penn Station, hoping to catch his train. Godfrey had had it up to *here* with having to time every morning.

He found us an adorable cottage on Hodge Road, right in the borough of Princeton. With the money from my singing and a monthly allowance from Godfrey's father, we could afford the rent, and so we settled in. The Hodge Road area was one of Princeton's most affluent neighborhoods, and our little cottage actually sat in the backyard of a string of mansions. We were set back from the road by a long driveway of rhododendrons. We had flowering dogwood and cherry trees, plus a tiny fishpond. I loved the grounds around the house, with bamboo bordering one wall and all the flowering plantings in the springtime. Baird had a sandbox that we filled with hand-me-down toys from my sister's five children. For the next fifteen years, Princeton was the center of our life. I called our home the Enchanted Cottage.

Figure 35. The Enchanted Cottage on Hodge Road.

It had a spacious living-dining area with a side kitchen and hall. Upstairs there was a large bedroom; a bath; an open, small room for Baird; and a separate, round tower off the upstairs hall where Godfrey could spread out his papers and work. He preferred to work at night when it was quiet. His studio accommodated bookshelves, a fireplace, his chair, a lamp, and all of his many notebooks detailing his thoughts in pencil. While the children slept, Godfrey worked.

He sharpened his pencils with the smallest pencil sharpener that he could carry in a pocket in order to have countless sharpened pencils ready at all times. I still have some of his pencil sharpeners, and they work like a charm. He'd also keep a fly swatter nearby in the summers for the occasional visiting bumblebee. Godfrey's work attire was a pair of shredded shoes worn down to the sole, a soft plaid cotton shirt, a cashmere cardigan, and pants worn until the seat shone. Sometimes he'd wear his robe and slippers, too! He loved comfortable clothes, never shopped, and abhorred looking like a dandy. My husband was interested in his work, in philosophy, logic, music theory, game theory, chess, poker, and Go. He even invented games. He adored mysteries and would devour entire novels at bedtime. He was a Renaissance man.

Evenings at the Enchanted Cottage, Godfrey would often visit with his classmate James K. Randall. They mostly discussed music theory,

Schenkerian analysis, and the like, but their conversations could roam. Godfrey and Jim were two peas in a pod—in some ways. Whereas Godfrey favored comfortable, time-worn clothes, Jim had a very loud style for a Princeton student. He wore Hawaiian print shirts, was always battling his weight, and smoked heavy cigars; once he started teaching he grew a long beard. The combination of that beard and his blue eyes gave him a startling resemblance to Johannes Brahms. He was like Milton in that he enjoyed teasing me. He had a biting wit, and I was never quite sure whether he was mocking me. Thank goodness he had a perfect companion, his wife Ruthie. She was smart and down to earth. The two of us often enjoyed a good laugh at the expense of our husbands' wacky personalities.

During the day, when I would practice, Baird went to stay with Palma, the wife of a Princeton graduate student. She adored Baird, who had many other young children and babies to play with in the graduate housing complex. At least, I think Godfrey worked. He was often asleep during the day, having worked all night long. Sometimes we passed like ships in the night. I never knew what time frame he was operating on!

Princeton was very different from New York City. Among other things, we suddenly were faced with the obstacle of not being a block from a grocery store. Since I always did the shopping anyway, I had to learn how to drive, and we bought a little red VW convertible. Godfrey decided to hold off learning until it seemed absolutely essential (typical).

The summer we moved out of the city and into the cottage, I took Baird to Tanglewood, the summer epicenter of classical music, where I was singing Bach's Cantata no. 51, *Jauchzet Gott in allen Landen*, with Charles Munch and the Boston Symphony.

I love singing Bach, and this cantata is a showpiece for the voice. It's not easy, as all the coloratura must match the articulations of a solo trumpet. I found that by using *non legato* (every sound articulated like a shotgun), I could render each pitch clear, no matter how fast the tempo. That kept my coloratura clean, and never sounded messy. It wasn't as if I'd invented anything. I've heard Marilyn Horne, Cecilia Bartoli, and Joyce DiDonato use the same technique in their coloratura in the years since then.

I was still singing with Pro Musica that summer, and their concerts at Tanglewood fell the same week as my Bach. After Tanglewood, we went on with Pro Musica to Ravinia, the summer music festival in Chicago.

Traveling with a toddler on a professional music circuit is not a cakewalk. We had two big "incidents" that summer, Baird and I. The first was at Lake Michigan. Betty Wilson and I had taken Baird down to the beach.

When I went into the water for a swim, Baird became hysterical. I guess he thought I was going to disappear into the water and never come back. I had to rush back out of the water to reassure him that I still existed. He was really still so small. And I was a new mother.

After Ravinia, Baird and I split off from my Pro Musica pals, and headed north to a music festival in Saskatoon, Canada. Baird wandered away from me while I was checking our tickets at O'Hare Airport in Chicago. I turned back around from the ticket desk—and he was gone! This time I was the one who thought I'd never see him again. I was hysterical. It seemed as if I corralled everyone in the airport to join the frantic search for my baby. I'm not sure I've ever experienced such terror. In the end, a girl working at the candy counter, just a few feet away from the ticket counter, came up to me and announced, "Your little boy came over to visit me. *Here he is!*" Baird toddled out from behind the candy counter with a big grin, and I snatched him up. I thought I was going to faint on the spot.

Later that evening, as we were flying over the thousand lakes of Wisconsin and Minnesota toward Canada, I could see the gaslights glowing in the hunters' cabins below. They reflected off the lakes and twinkled all together like so many stars at night. As I watched the scene sweep past, I kept one hand protectively resting on the soundly sleeping boy at my side.

We were headed up to the Saskatoon Music Festival, a jubilee celebration marking the fiftieth anniversary of the University of Saskatchewan at Saskatoon. Murray Adaskin, who was then the director of the Saskatoon Symphony Orchestra, had invited my friend Jim Bolle to be the guest conductor at the festival, and Jim invited me.

My long friendship with the conductor and composer Jim Bolle had begun a year earlier, when the Princetonian Michael Steinberg introduced the two of us at his Mulberry Street walk-up on the Lower East Side, where Michael lived with his wife, Jane. In those years, it was common for young couples to live cheaply in old tenement apartments; I can distinctly remember the smell of urine in the hallway of that building the first time I climbed the stairs. The squalor disappeared once you crossed the threshold into the Steinberg apartment. It felt like another world. Jane had artful taste and had beautifully decorated what could have been a real dump.

Michael had invited me over specifically to meet his old buddy Jim Bolle, who lived in Chicago but wanted to start putting on new music concerts in New York City. Jim was an energetic young musician who had married into a wealthy New Hampshire family, giving him the resources to really launch himself in an interesting way into the new music world. He was a large fellow, with stooped shoulders and a huge head. He was also a composer and very likable, and talked incessantly about music! I knew from the start that I would enjoy working with him.

Although his primary interest was in new music, Jim didn't burst onto the scene with a roster of all–new music programs. In fact, I sang a lot of early music on his first New York concert series—three concerts at the 92nd Street Y under the name Musica Viva Ensemble.

The first program, in February 1959, was Purcell's *Fairy Queen*. I had the privilege that night of singing with the very young Judith Raskin, who would go on to have an impressive opera career. Just a few years later, I heard her sing Pamina in *The Magic Flute* at Glyndebourne, England, and she was Stravinsky's Anne Trulove in the CBS recording of *The Rake's Progress*. She died far too early of cancer, at only 56—a great loss to the opera world.

On the second concert in March, I sang the part of La Musica in Claudio Monteverdi's *Orfeo* with my old Pro Musica buddy Charles Bressler. The last program in early April emphasized new music and included compositions by Darius Milhaud, with whom Jim had studied; Hans Werner Henze; and Luigi Nono. Nono's *España en el corazón* in particular remained with me from that concert. It was set to the wonderful poetry of Federico García Lorca and Pablo Neruda, and spoke out against the Spanish Civil War. Nono, who had married Arnold Schoenberg's daughter Nuria, was a real activist. I've always admired his kind of dedication.

As for Jim, I think he was clever with his programming in terms of arriving on the New York City stage. The programs were interesting, and he got good press coverage. Unlike Noah Greenberg, who always had to raise funding in order to make his way in the music world, Jim had the luxury of money backing him.

Those concerts marked the beginning of a long and fruitful professional relationship. Jim's far-reaching love of music from all periods had a great influence on me. His encyclopedic knowledge of the canon was incredible; under his baton, I learned many works that I never would have otherwise pursued. I would go on to sing for him many times in Chicago, particularly at Monadnock, a summer music festival in New Hampshire that Jim and his wife, Jocelyn Faulkner, formed in 1966.

In Saskatoon, Jim rented a small house for us and hired a babysitter for Baird. The Canadian countryside was miles and miles of flat open prairie land and endless fields of Canadian wheat. As Kansas is in the United States, Saskatoon is the breadbasket of Canada.

The Saskatoon Music Festival was a huge affair, with over eighty works performed, many of them new music. I sang the same Bach I had done in Tanglewood the week before. I also sang a beautiful cantata by Jocelyn, who like Jim had studied composition with Darius Milhaud. Since Michael Steinberg was also in Saskatoon for the festival, I got it into my head that Michael should play *Die schöne Müllerin* with me at a small concert in Regina that happened to coincide with the festival.

Regina was a pretty town alongside the flat railway tracks in this astounding land of broad vistas. I don't think we went around a single bend in our trip, but just straight as an arrow to our destination. Michael of course was a musicologist and critic, not a performer, and was nervous every second that he was on stage—in front of an audience that essentially consisted of well-behaved Canadian farm ladies. They loved us, even though Michael was not a professional pianist. He vowed to me afterward, "Bethany, I will never play in public again. It's too full of *angst* for me!"

I was eager to perform the Schubert again and really put poor Michael on the spot. It wasn't entirely fair. I knew him and Jane from Princeton, where Michael had studied musicology. He was quite literally a Jewish refugee, one of ten thousand children smuggled out of Germany into Britain on Kindertransport in the months before the Second World War began. Michael was one of the miracle stories. His mother and brother survived the war, and the family was reunited after only four years. They all emigrated together to the United States.

I don't think Michael ever did perform again in public after I'd forced his hand that one time, but he did go on to become an influential music critic, first at the *Boston Globe* and then at the *San Francisco Chronicle*.

While we were all in Saskatoon, Michael published a humorous piece in the local paper describing the festival and praising it for going beyond the "usual festival," featuring "the usual repertory by the usual people, but under-rehearsed and with tickets scaled to at least twice their normal price." He went out of his way to compliment me in the article: "the extraordinary soprano whose virtuosity keeps her in constant demand to tackle jobs that are simply too hard for other singers."[39]

CHAPTER TWENTY-NINE

THE RUSSIAN
DELEGATION

It was the 1960s, and the Cold War was on. President Eisenhower had been the leader of the Allied forces through World War II and warned against the arms race, the "military-industrial complex." But despite his warnings, the country began building up its war machine; the Soviets kept pace right through the Reagan era. We had become caretaker to the world and found ourselves embedded in foreign wars. It was all such a huge expense, a tragic folly. I see it so clearly now. But back then, I was fully a musician and didn't read or even think about politics. I looked at the *Times* to read the music news in Section Two of the Sunday paper. In those days an entire section of the paper was devoted to serious music. I'd pore over the advertisements for concerts during the upcoming week and read reviews and articles by writers I was interested in. I couldn't have cared less about what was happening in the world. To make matters worse, I was married to an Englishman who had even less interest in affairs of government. I think the only time I ever saw him fully engaged in the evening news was during the Watergate hearings, which he watched with the same kind of eager absorption he devoted to his spy novels.

That fall, I was invited to the Library of Congress in Washington, DC, to perform Schoenberg's String Quartet no. 2 with the Budapest Quartet. You can imagine how delighted I was to appear with such a prestigious group, having first heard them years before when I was a student at Michigan State. To make the event more momentous, in our audience that night would be an impressive delegation of Soviet composers, including Dmitri Shostakovich, whose Fifth Symphony I'd loved since college.

Schoenberg's second string quartet is a milestone piece. It is the first work in which Schoenberg departed from tonality and wrote without a key. The key shift comes in the final movement, which opens with the words from the Stefan George poem "Entrückung," "Ich fühle Luft von anderem Planeten" (I feel air from another planet). The air marked the beginning of Schoenberg's new sound—his transition into modernism.

Schoenberg wrote this quartet in the aftermath of a terrible period in his marriage, and it's filled with turmoil. When the quartet premiered, the audience exploded in disapproval by the start of the third movement, what Schoenberg subsequently characterized as "brutish and bestial." Writing in 2009 in the *Guardian* about what was referred to as the "Schoenberg Scandal," Christopher Fox said:

> What is perhaps even more remarkable than the scandal of the "Schoenberg affair" is that this string quartet, born out of the most intense personal trauma, should have exerted such a profound influence over the subsequent evolution of modern music in the 20th century. In the second and third movements, the gradual dissolution of the music's connection to any secure sense of tonality is a potent expression of Schoenberg's anguish, and the final movement embraces atonality as a metaphor for a psychological haven beyond suffering.[40]

The players were especially keen for suggestions from me during rehearsals. I don't think Schoenberg was part of their repertoire yet. The Kolisch Quartet had played far more Schoenberg than the Budapest players had. The difficulty of the rehearsal was further complicated by the fact that two members of the quartet were not speaking to each other. I never found out what was going on, but everything was rather awkward and funny all at the same time. Although the quartet was originally all Hungarian, the players had turned over several times and, at this particular moment, they were all Russian. The violinist Jascha Heifetz famously quipped: "One Russian is an anarchist. Two Russians are a chess game. Three Russians are a revolution. Four Russians are the Budapest String Quartet."

Even though the Cold War hadn't really ended with the signing of the Warsaw Pact, artistic exchanges were part of Khrushchev's post-Stalin attempts to improve relations with the West. In 1958, Roger Sessions had been part of a delegation of American composers to the Soviet Union, and we had our entourage of Soviet composers at the concert that evening. After the concert they came backstage to meet us.

For me the real honor was meeting Shostakovich, who was a retreating kind of man. He was slight and wore steel-frame glasses; he spoke softly and seemed to have an air of sadness. He didn't smile and stood to one side while the others did most of the talking. For someone so famous, it must have been repressive composing in Russia under Stalin, and I wonder what he was thinking after hearing our advanced music and talking to our composers.

The others in the entourage were Dmitri Kabalevsky, Tikhon Khrennikov (the powerful head of the Union of Soviet Composers), and Fikret Amirov, along with the musicologist Boris Yarustovsky. Kabalevsky congratulated me on my performance, and then asked me through his interpreter if my part was difficult to sing. I replied, "Why, Mr. Kabalevsky, this is an old *classic* of contemporary music. It's really *quite* old fashioned." I don't know if I was being cheeky or was just entirely immune to the challenges of atonal music, but I guess for the Russians it was a new listening experience.

Meanwhile, I'd grown tired of seeing myself everywhere—the *New York Times*, *High Fidelity*, *Musical America*, you name it—in my medieval Daniel costume. Half the time I couldn't figure out how they'd gotten hold of all those Daniel photos! I assumed they came from the press office of Columbia Records. That said, I only had one decent publicity photo, of me in one of my discount-rack Altman wedding dresses. So I decided to get new photos. I hired the photographer Harold Bergsohn, who had shot for *Vogue*. I wore my French wedding dress with a blue stole, and a red silk chiffon. He wanted action shots, so I recited *Pierrot lunaire* while he snapped away. The photos he took would follow me for years. They were glamorous, as a singer's photo should be—though I have to admit that I found my expressions in the two I selected as my primary publicity photos to be imperious in one and smilingly sweet in the other. I am neither.

As I have said before, Godfrey was never entangled in my career as Jacques was. We each had our own independent work: He composed, I performed. Sometimes I asked his opinion about scores I was considering and occasionally turned down work based on his recommendations.

In the early years of our marriage, he handled the business aspects of my career, such as negotiating fees. He was a shrewd negotiator. When I was discussing the recording of *Pierrot lunaire*, for example, he insisted I receive a 4 percent royalty, which was more than even Bob Craft got. I would never have pushed that hard on the money end. I considered my work with Craft at Columbia to be my big opportunity to be heard by a major recording label and felt that it really sealed my reputation in New York City. From my perspective, it was a trophy I won for all of my years of grueling work with Jacques. But Godfrey had a nose for business and knew just how hard to push. He knew I could *both* get the compensation I deserved and also leap forward in my career. Ultimately, though, Godfrey hated all the letter writing involved in being my manager and didn't stick with it for long.

In 1962, I hired Jay Hoffman to be my new manager. Jay was young, just getting started, and was handling only one other singer, Claire Watson. She sang opera in Europe. Besides Claire, he also managed a handful of pianists and conductors. Jay was excellent. He understood what I was all about.

Once you sign with a manager, you have to pay him 20 percent of all engagements he sets up. Jay also sent out brochures advertising my work to the concert-buying public. To stimulate interest, he supplemented those with flyers whenever I'd get a rave review. Jay took care of booking my hotels and travel. My fees had gone up quite a bit by this time and could have put me in a precarious situation with most of the city's new music groups, such as the ISCM, which operated on very slim budgets. But colleges had money, and that was where I was giving most of my recitals at that point. Regarding the new music groups, Jay and I had an understanding. Even though they couldn't pay high fees, the concerts were always reviewed and New York City reviews had cachet. So Jay left me to set up those venues at my discretion. He didn't take a cut, and he didn't get involved.

Jay was my manager until 1969, when he left the business. He handed over his client list to Sheldon Soffer, who didn't have any idea what to do with me. I ended up relying on one of his assistants, Mary Lou Tiffin, to handle my bookings while Sheldon collected his twenty percent. I stayed with Sheldon longer than I should have. We were a bad fit from the beginning, and Sheldon was no Jay Hoffman.

During the last few years of the 1950s, I had only learned nineteen new works. In the same amount of time, during the Monod era, I learned fifty-nine! The pace of my life had certainly shifted. I concluded that I'd finally reached a higher degree of normality. The next fifteen years were wonderful. I had a new manager to handle administration, and I was making money. I had a large repertoire to draw on and a busy schedule of prestigious engagements. My programs were perhaps unusual—I stuck to my

Figure 36. The front of the publicity circular my agent, Jay Hoffman, made up for me.

principle of combining classical music with twentieth-century repertoire. Sure, I always had concerns about being trapped in a niche, but my convictions about what music I should be performing weren't going to change. I was still on a mission and wanted my recitals to offer the public a new listening experience. Everything seemed at last to be falling into place.

CHAPTER THIRTY

RECORDINGS WITH ROBERT CRAFT

During the winter of 1960, Robert Craft and I went back into the studio for Columbia Records. In December, we recorded Alban Berg's *Der Wein* and the *Seven Early Songs* (*Sieben frühe Lieder*), which Jacques and I had recorded for Dial Records. These early recordings of music of the Second Viennese School, made for such a big label, reached an even larger audience. I was delighted to be a part of this wave. It turned out that I was still on the same mission that Jacques and I had embarked on all those years before.

Robert Craft was still a young conductor. He was building a career and essentially working as Stravinsky's factotum. He had a special talent for making things happen and knew how to take advantage of good opportunities. Stravinsky had an exclusive contract with Columbia. That gave Craft some leverage and leeway, which he used to record all of Webern in the West Coast Columbia studios. He used local singers for these recordings, including Marni Nixon, a wonderful singer with absolute pitch. She worked with Stravinsky and Craft early on before going to Hollywood, where she dubbed actresses in all the big musicals. Our voices were very similar—in fact, her voice sounds *so much* like mine that for years I got credit (often in print) for her Webern.

Craft used excellent freelance players and took advantage of the Columbia orchestra, so all the musicians were less strictly reliant on his conducting skills. He accomplished a lot with Stravinsky as his supporter—more than many other new music conductors would have, even those with far more experience. He and I worked well together.

The Second Viennese School was still unfamiliar territory, even with the best freelance musicians stepping up. The only reservation I had about Craft's conducting was his choice of tempi for the *Seven Early Songs*. Jacques and I had of course performed the songs with piano, as they were originally conceived. Later on Berg had orchestrated them. Craft was using the orchestra version, which I had never done. Singing with an orchestra is like pulling a huge elephant along beside you, and I felt that some aspects of the music had gotten flattened out. The original tempi were much faster and had variation from song to song. To get the kind of dynamics and *rubato* that Jacques and I achieved would require hours of rehearsal for Craft and the orchestra. That would have been totally unaffordable. The recordings were very well received nonetheless. But even Craft knew it would have been better if we'd had more rehearsals.

Craft was forging ahead on his ambitious projects and was planning to record all of Schoenberg for Columbia. He asked me to do *Pierrot*, but I was frankly feeling a little gun-shy at this point. I had just received a scathing letter from dear Michael Steinberg criticizing my German diction on the *Altenberg Lieder* I'd recorded with Craft. Michael wrote:

> The sound itself, the musicality, the vocal technique, all that is simply too good and too rare to be so cavalierly annulled by that amateurish disregard of language. There are performers from whom one doesn't expect much, but given everything that Bethany Beardslee has come to stand for, I should like to think that I could count on you for clean intonation, good phrasing, and so on, but also for a reasonable pronunciation of "Plötzlich ist alles aus."[41]

Good God, I thought, if this isn't a kick in the butt! Why hadn't anyone ever pointed it out? Why hadn't other critics? I had always gotten glorious reviews for my performances, but there had never been a single word about my faulty German. At Juilliard I took a course in diction with Madame Edith Braun. She was German, so I always just assumed my pronunciation was fine. But Michael was German, too, and obviously that made the critique more pertinent. Michael also truly loved music, and I think that made him a much more exacting critic. Some performers couldn't take it. After he'd become the music critic for the *Boston Globe*, the Boston Symphony tried to have him banned from Symphony Hall. But I had the deepest respect for Michael; he was my favorite kind of critic. He'd study the scores before coming to the performances and was a musician first, then second a journalist.

When learning *Pierrot* with Jacques, I must have been too caught up with the musical issues. And Jacques was certainly no help on the matter, because his attention would have been on the music, too. What I really needed was a year or two living in Germany to master the language, as so many of my colleagues had done. A lot of American opera singers trained abroad. Some stayed in Europe, but others—the most successful ones— went on to sing in big US houses, including the Met.

I decided I had to prepare before going back into the studio with Craft for *Pierrot*. I enlisted Paula Fleischmann, a German actress from Vienna, to become my diction coach. She was a wonderful little old lady—easily seventy-five or even eighty years old. She was a very strict teacher and didn't miss a thing. She taught me theater German (also known as *Hochdeutsch*, or High German). We worked and worked on *Pierrot*. I believe that's the first German recording I did that I don't have the slightest qualms about.

We recorded *Pierrot* in March of 1961 as part of volume 1 of Schoenberg's music, along with other works such as the violin concerto and *Erwartung*. I told Craft that I wanted to work with the same musicians who had trained under Jacques for the Camera Concert performance. Craft agreed. I was determined to record *Pierrot* according to the aesthetic standards that Jacques had set when we first learned the piece and, more important, the musical instructions that the composer had intended. We had Bob Helps on piano; Isidore Cohen, violin and viola; Charles McCracken, cello; Ernest Bright, clarinet and bass clarinet; and Murray Panitz, flute and piccolo. I hadn't worked with Ernest or Murray before, though I knew Murray's playing from the early ISCM days.

We got to the end of the session, and Craft had to dash out to catch a plane—which was when I realized that we'd neglected to record no. 7, for voice and solo flute. I will never forget the look on Murray's face when we realized what was not done and that our conductor had already left. Murray laughed and said, "Well, okay, let's get to work." No. 7 is my favorite section of *Pierrot*, so I felt some confidence that if we set about working on the part by ourselves, moving at our own pace, we could do it. I'm always amazed at these freelance players and their wonderful playing, their remarkable ability to produce first-rate performances with just a few rehearsals. But I feel that there was some kind of unique synchronicity in the music that day in the studio. We did it—we produced a beautiful no. 7. Murray was surprised and delighted with our results. We would go on to work together several more times in the next years.

Michael sent me a letter complimenting my German after he heard *Pierrot*. And Craft sent me another postcard (he always sent postcards) on which he wrote: "Your performance of *Pierrot* is the first performance of that work that anyone can listen from beginning to end with total pleasure and belief in the sprechstimme medium. Really, it's terrific. You have made a permanent document."

Reviews for volume 1 of the complete music of Schoenberg appeared in *American Record Guide, High Fidelity*, and the *New York Times*. William Flanagan, a composer and a critic for *HiFi/ Stereo Review*, gave me a glowing review:

> Craft's readings give every aural evidence of scrupulous care: the music projects frequently blazing intensity and, in the vocal works, great power. It is hard to imagine any singer of the future surpassing Bethany Beardslee's performance of the text of *Pierrot*. Quite apart from Miss Beardslee's characteristic and uncanny control of the work's severe technical problems, she here possesses astounding dramatic force. With this recording of *Pierrot Lunaire*, Miss Beardslee stakes an authentic claim to recognition as a great performing artist.[42]

And Alfred Frankenstein in *High Fidelity*:

> Arnold Schoenberg is, of course, the hero of this album, and I am opposed on principle to placing a performance or performer ahead of the music. In connection with *Pierrot Lunaire* however, I am constrained to say first that you have never heard it at all until you have heard it with Bethany Beardslee. She is, to put it simply, the greatest interpreter of "Pierrot" I have ever experienced on records or in live performance. Sprechstimme, that fantastic amalgam of speech and song which Schoenberg invented for "Pierrot" has never been handled so subtly as it is handled here, and its value as a musical, expressive, and coloristic device has never been so marvelously displayed. Add to this a fine instrumental performance and a perfect recording, and you have the last word in *Pierrot Lunaire*.[43]

Much of the credit for these reviews goes to Jacques, for the work methods he taught me and for insisting on *how* I learned *Pierrot*. It is also not insignificant that three of Jacques's original performers were involved in the Columbia recording. Credit, of course, also has to go to the invention of the microphone. I had an unlimited range of dynamics—levels never available to a live performer in a concert hall. Take the microphones away, and the pop singers in today's music world have *nothing*.

This recording of *Pierrot* is the classic version now, used in the Norton anthology, taught to music students in school, and referred to in books on contemporary music. Since then, *Pierrot* has been recorded numerous times and is one of Schoenberg's most often performed pieces. Over the course of my career, I, for one, gave over sixty-five live performances of *Pierrot lunaire*.

CHAPTER THIRTY-ONE

TO PROVE MY LOVE

O n March 8, 1960, pregnant with my second son, I gave my fourth New York recital with Bob Helps at the 92nd Street Y. I sang two of the three settings of Shakespeare sonnets that Godfrey had been working on, a cycle dedicated to me and titled *To Prove My Love*. The rest of the program was traditional: Handel arias; a Mozart concert aria, "Bella mia fiamma, addio!"; Schumann's song cycle *Frauenliebe und -leben*, Debussy's *Fêtes galantes* (book 1); and five songs by Schubert. I always sang well when I was pregnant. The evening was a huge success, with many composers— "my boys"—in attendance. I was thrilled to hear that Jennie Tourel, whom I idolized and whom I'd gone to hear so many times at Town Hall, was in the audience that evening. Afterward she came backstage to congratulate *me*. There I was, flushed and so excited to meet this grand old lady, that I brashly told her that she too should learn the *Seven Early Songs* of Berg— that they were just right for her. What chutzpah! Imagine me telling Jennie Tourel what *she* should sing! In my heart it seemed that, whether I'd admitted it or not, I would always be dedicated to my mission.

Championing the literature of the Second Viennese School used to make me feel like a pioneer. But now, all these years later, it's far more common for singers to include this music in their repertoire—though I'm not sure it's being entirely well represented by the new generation of singers. For example, it doesn't seem to my ear that all of the dynamics that Berg wrote into his music are being observed. Singing this class of music is really a matter of tuning intervals, and that is what builds its integrity. Harmonically, the music of the Second Viennese School is utterly musical; if it is tuned right, whole sections of phrases sound clas-sical. Tuning to the interval is an intuitive approach when you're learning classical music, because classical systems are part of you—you just know them so well. This intuition doesn't always carry over into atonal music. When you get into atonality or serial music, you should be singing it just the same way you'd sing Schubert or Mozart. Most people don't do that. They sing *pitches* instead of musical intervals.

That April, Godfrey and I drove up to Dartmouth College in our little red VW convertible. I was going to sing Luigi Dallapiccola's *Divertimento* and Godfrey's *Habit of Perfection* at a new music festival that seemed to feature everyone from Percy Grainger (on the influence of folk music on art music) to Milton Babbitt. Milton was on his own mission: the synthesizer and the wonderful possibilities it opened to the composer. His talk at Dartmouth was entitled "Electronic Music: How and Why?" He'd been traveling the country delivering variations on this same lecture; he'd even appeared on TV with David Brinkley.

Godfrey rehearsed *The Habit of Perfection* with the Phoenix Quartet and found them to be a shoddy group of players as well as uncooperative. This was the second group we'd done the piece with. It is a hard piece, es-pecially the big cello cadenza that comes at the end. The first time we had done *The Habit of Perfection* was in New Haven with Julius Schiers's string quartet (a pick-up group), so we had concrete evidence that it could be played reasonably well. The Phoenix Quartet at Dartmouth had a terrible attitude and despite Godfrey's careful coaching gave us a bad performance. It seemed clear that they didn't like the piece and didn't care for contempo-rary music. I don't know why the festival organizers hired them! Such were the risks of the business, and sadly it was out of our control.

The Habit of Perfection was recorded again recently for Albany Records with a very good group of Juilliard musicians—young people who'd grown up immersed in contemporary music. Even though they had to run through many takes to get it right, they did. My singer on that recording was the pitch-perfect Tony Arnold, who puts her whole soul into all she sings.

To offset the dismal performance, we spent an enjoyable afternoon lunch with Sarah Delano and her husband, Anthony di Bonaventura, the pianist who was also appearing on the festival. I asked Sarah if she was related to the presidents' famous family, and she was. You couldn't imagine a more charming woman. The Delanos were an old Hudson River family going as far back as such early aristocrats as the Livingstons of colonial times.

Young Sarah had grown up bathed in the history of her famous grand-mother Eleanor Roosevelt. I was also surprised to find she was acquainted with my nieces, my sister Helen's daughters, from the Edgewood Club.

That wasn't the only memorable moment of our excursion. When we were on our way home we encountered one of those freak spring blizzards. I was driving, and the roads were slippery. Our car swerved off the road and plunged into a snow bank. Baird's toddler bed was tucked on the floor in the back of the car—there were no seat belts then. I had thought he looked so adorable nestled up and sleeping. But then there we were, run off the road and stuck in the snow! Fortunately a group of college students were passing by, saw us in trouble, and stopped. It seemed like an impossible feat, but the six of them literally picked up our little VW convert-ible and put it right back on the road. Baird slept through it all! That was when I learned to turn into a skid and not against it. Thank goodness, the rest of the trip was uneventful, but it continued to trouble me that our car weighed *so little* that those boys could just lift it back onto the road!

Martha Graham called me to do *Clytemnestra* again. It was another two-week run that started in early May, with *Clytemnestra* occupying the first week and other dances for the second part. It was Martha's last triumphant year of dancing publicly. By this time, I was quite pregnant, so Martha ad-justed my costume and had me in a flowing gold, brocade robe. I felt quite regal. Martha Graham operated at the highest artistic level in everything—even her friendships. One day I arrived early, as usual, at the theater, and found her having tea in her dressing room with one of her great admirers, Katharine Hepburn, the dressing room door standing wide open. Hepburn had a townhouse in the Murray Hill section of New York so it was quite likely she was in New York for a period between films. Why is it one gets rather excited being introduced to a film star when a singer's work is just as hard and publicly less rewarding? But yes, I was thrilled to actually look into the eyes of this famous movie actress and say, "I'm so happy to meet you," on my way to my own dressing room.

A third and last time, Martha called on me to do *Clytemnestra*. On this run she wasn't going to dance the principal role, as she had retired. I agreed to the performance but with much less interest. I was there one afternoon, sitting in the empty rehearsal hall with Martha, watching the new dancer who would take over her part. I turned to her and said, "It's just not the same with you not in the role." And she recoiled, abruptly putting me down for criticizing one of her dancers. I was rather shocked by her belligerent reaction. Despite her fierce reputation, she had never been anything other than gracious to me.

It was an illuminating moment. That was when I understood how Martha and I diverged as artists. All of her intention was on the product, the performance, whereas what I loved was working in collaboration with the creator. That was the quality of my career that ultimately made me, deeply and steadfastly, a composer's singer.

CHAPTER THIRTY-TWO

BAIRD AND CHRISTOPHER WINHAM

Life in Princeton

O n July 8, 1960, our second son, Christopher Winham, was born. He was a beautiful baby boy with blond curly hair and blue eyes. From the moment of his arrival, Christopher's disposition was sweet and undemanding. He was just the opposite of his older brother Baird, who was high strung and got anxious whenever I'd leave to sing. I suppose I will always be paying for that six-week tour with Pro Musica.

My mother had come to help right after Christopher was born but once she left, it became very evident that I was going to need more help. It was crystal clear that Godfrey would not be central to rearing the boys. He had been raised by a nanny. It never occurred to him that things might be different for his own children than it had been for him. He was clearly totally uninterested in tending to babies day after day—most especially in the early years. Godfrey's work was Godfrey's main priority—and that was the ethos in which our children would be brought up. Fortunately (in one sense) he did most of his work at home, so that despite all of his working, the children never felt as if he was far away. He was certainly not constantly heading out, suitcase in hand—like their mother.

And yet, Godfrey's work necessitated "keeping the house quiet"—*that* was really the essence of what it meant to live with Godfrey. During the day, there could be no noise, and of course that's a virtual impossibility for two young toddlers.

When they got older, the boys would come to love, as I did, listening to their father play the piano for us before supper. He'd often play the compositions he was working on. And then after supper, they'd play games, something we all enjoyed. Christmas Day was a big exception, though. Godfrey always dedicated Christmas Day to the children.

Quite apart from Godfrey's needs for his work, I had my own rigorous practice routine to contend with. I had always worked first thing in the morning and that's exactly the time—right after they wake up—that small children need the most attention. We were overdue for a child-care solution.

We hired a young married woman from Trenton named Mrs. Dessie McCleese to be a full-time nanny. Dessie was southern and observed the formal mannerisms of the South, always addressing me as "Ma'am," for example. She had the most beautiful smile and was very pretty, but mostly she was kind and calm. My children loved her, and I was so grateful to have her. Dessie would arrive early in the morning, around eight o'clock, and stay until four in the afternoon, five days a week. Once in a while Dessie would show up on the weekends with her husband, Paul, and their son Robert Earl, all dressed up and out for a Sunday ride. Dessie would go on to help me for many years to come in Princeton.

Outside of our friends and colleagues on the music faculty at Princeton, we socialized with the parents of our children's friends. Baird often played next door with the four Donaldson boys, who took him under their wing, because he was the youngest. But there were a number of families with children on Hodge Road at that time. There were the Bordens at the end of our block; the Blairs, who had a bevy of little girls two houses down; the Penicks; the Peytons. All the children went to the famous Mary Mason's School for Toddlers, on the corner of Hodge Road and Route 206.

In the summers we'd often go to the Jersey shore for two weeks to visit Ellen and Eberhard Faber. Eb, of the Eberhard Faber pencil company, was a friend from Princeton. Eb's mother, who was running the business at the time, had a large summer home on the shore at Mantoloking, New Jersey. The men had two things in common: chess and poker. I have fond memories of many long evenings of poker at the shore. We wouldn't start until after Baird and Christopher were in bed, then the four of us would play, sometimes until two in the morning. After cards, Eb would run down to the ocean and dive in for a refreshing dip before bed. To this day I have never known a better poker player than Eb Faber. But those late hours are highly inadvisable for a singer.

Figure 37. Godfrey and Eb Faber at the New Jersey shore.

The Fabers lived a couple of houses down from us in Belle Mead on River Road. We saw each other regularly for dinner and games. Until Godfrey discovered computers, games were central to our marriage and our social life. Ellen and I were devoted to each other and have remained lifelong friends. In those early days, she was a dutiful housewife and, like me, raising two boys. Ellen grew discontented—especially watching the way that I pursued my career in music. It made her feel unrealized somehow.

It was an unsteady time for us all. We were in our forties, and marriages seemed to be falling apart around us. I was Ellen's primary confidante during this time—which was also when the conductor Lukas Foss was apparently pursuing me, so we had a lot to gossip about. But then Ellen really exploded into feminism and started studying mandolin, fell in love with her teacher, and left Eb. After they divorced and after her brief career as a bluegrass musician waned, she went back to school and got a degree to counsel alcoholics. She met her second husband, Steve Rubin, a psychologist, through the counseling world, and they are still very happily married.

In the late 1970s, Ellen and Steve got deeply involved in Werner Erhard's EST movement, which had just come onto the scene. She convinced me to come along to a few meetings. I remember returning from my very first meeting late one night and creeping into the bedrooms where the boys were fast asleep. While they slept, I kissed each one. I whispered to them that they were my darling children and I told them how much I loved them. I *never* did that sort of thing. It really wasn't my style. I was reeling slightly from the meeting and probably drew courage from the fact that everyone was sleeping and couldn't see me acting so ridiculously.

Before they were divorced, Ellen and Eb came to London with us on one of our summer visits to Godfrey's parents. Daddy lent them an apartment. That summer, Ellen, Ellen's sister, Anne Scurria, who was twelve, and I took the children on a long car trip in Wales. We left Godfrey and Eb back in London to play chess. We stayed one night in a tavern in a room over the pub and they were playing music from *A Hard Day's Night* so loudly we couldn't sleep. On that same trip we went to visit a castle; Baird had an appalling tantrum when he wasn't allowed to visit the dungeon. He remembers it to this day; he was so upset, as was I. Ellen and I bickered the whole time about my driving. I had Christopher in the front seat with me and drove very slowly. Ellen was in the backseat, screaming, "We'll never get there!" When I finally relented and let her drive, she was like a mad-woman at the wheel. And I suppose then I was in the backseat screaming at her as we careered down narrow country lanes bordered by Welsh farm-ers' stone walls. On the way back to London we ran out of gas and money in Chester and were marooned. That village seemed as if it was right out of Shakespeare—I remember those all-white houses with their dark wood beams. Eb and Godfrey had to wire us money to get home, and by the time we got back into London, we were furious at them. We'd had what had turned into a horrendous trip and they'd just sat around London the whole time, playing chess and eating at expensive restaurants.

One Sunday, I went out driving through the city with Daddy in his small brown Morris Minor to look at his real estate projects. He would tell me about his construction projects and I would listen with great interest. Of course, I love to look at properties. It's a hobby that I picked up long ago from Sunday-morning drives with my own father.

Christopher had his third birthday party that summer at his grandfa-ther's home in London. Gwen arranged a wild, overblown affair, complete with a carousel set up in the hall at Green Street. She'd invited a slew of small children, who all arrived in the company of their nannies. Christopher knew none of them, but they were all three-year-olds and in no time were happily romping together like the best of friends. After much play, the chil-dren trooped into the dining room and took their seats at the table, their nannies standing correctly behind. There appeared a sumptuous birthday cake decorated with little Beefeater figurines. (We use these same Beefeater figurines on birthday cakes in our family to this day.) I remember Daddy and Gwen standing together, enjoying the whole spectacle. Christopher wore a gold paper crown and at three years of age was overwhelmed. He remembers it after all these years—even though he didn't know any of his guests at all. I have no idea where Gwen dug up all of those children for her true English-style birthday party.

The early 1960s were a bustling time for me professionally: Shortly after Christopher was born, I was named the singer for the Second Princeton Seminar in Advanced Musical Studies, a large residency gathering around forty-two composers and eleven of us musicians. Bob Helps was the seminar pianist. The Lenox String Quartet (I wish *they* had played *The Habit of Perfection*; it would have been fantastic) were among the instrumentalists in residence. The program began in mid-August, which meant that I had just over a month to learn a large piece for voice and string quartet, recover from childbirth, and get back into singing shape. The seminar was being sponsored by Princeton University and the Fromm Music Foundation. The subject matter covered everything from electronic music, to setting text, to new music string technique, to "Polyphonic Time in Stravinsky." The heart of the seminar was the series of talks delivered by various distinguished composers—Roger Sessions, Milton Babbitt, Earl Kim, and Edward T. Cone, as well as Karl-Birger Blomdahl, Elliott Carter, Luciano Berio, and Felix Galimir. We musicians were to learn works that had been submitted ahead of time. My piece was for string quartet by the young Princeton composer Philip Batstone. However, in the context of the seminar, his work was programmed only for rehearsal and not for performance.

Phil Batstone was an unusual person. He had served in World War II, married a German girl, and come to Princeton (perhaps on the GI bill) to study with Sessions and Babbitt. Phil was the second composer to receive a doctor of music at Princeton, Godfrey being the first. Even though Phil was a serial composer, his music was very tonal. He wrote beautiful lyrical music and, like Schubert, could compose quite fast. Magda, his wife, aided me with translations of complex German poetry, such as that of Stefan George. She was a great help when I was working on *Das Buch der hängenden Gärten*.

I got the impression that the Batstones were always in need. He was poor but had a gregarious personality and seemed not to worry that he was continually broke. A serious, sensitive musician, absorbed in his own world, Phil also had a great capacity for friendship. For several years after

Figure 38. Composer Phil Batstone.

Godfrey's death, his confidences and encouragement were a great comfort to me. Phil's downfall was that he liked to drink, which enraged Magda, drove her away, and ultimately led to his early death. He was a major talent, short lived and unknown. Thanks to his close friend Mark DeVoto, Phil's music, what there is of it, is housed at Harvard.

In 1961 Milton wrote a spectacular piece for Bob Helps and me entitled *Sounds and Words*. It was a virtuosic work for voice and piano, blending nonsense syllables with vowel sounds. This was Milton's first attempt at a serious piece with—for want of a better description—nontext elements. *Sounds and Words* gave the singer a sweeping vocal line and splashes of high notes; vowel colors; and short, syllabic texts. It was a stunning piece to include on my recital programs.

Later he composed *Phonemena*, based on—guess what—phonemes. Milton always had puns in his music titles. It was elegant scat singing, laid over Milton's jazziest style. But somehow, when I was trying to learn it, I just couldn't remember all the phonemes and stumbled around helplessly, lost in the gibberish—so I gave up! I never learned *Phonemena*, and I still regret it.

During that period, Milton also composed *Partitions* for Bob Helps. The opening of that piece is perhaps one of the most spectacular moments in piano history, with its startling separation of bass and high treble notes in the first measures. The sonic separation and virtuoso playing is unbelievable. I always enjoy hearing that piece.

I don't know why Milton trusted me, but that's the strongest impression of our working relationship that I have to this day. I always arrived with my part learned—unless I encountered some kind of really unusual problem, as with *Phonemes* or, more controversial, *Vision and Prayer*. Other than that, he never helped me or critiqued my work. He knew his music wasn't easy. I think the same was true of his relationship with many of the performers who championed his music, Bob Helps, or Bob Miller, or Bob Taub (all those pianists named Bob); the extraordinary pianist Alan Feinberg; and the conductors Gunther Schuller and James Levine. He worked with other singers, such as Judith Bettina and Lucy Shelton, not to mention the many instrumentalists—William Purvis, David Starobin, Lois Martin, Curtis Macomber, Jayn Rosenfeld—who came to him for solo works later in his life, when his output was at its most prolific.

In the early years, when Jacques and I were first performing *Du*, I was in awe of Milton. I delighted in his wit and his brilliant mind. But I did not like his music. Back then, I didn't like any serial music. But over time, as each piece of music dropped into its proper place in my brain, I discovered that there was more to life than tonality. A performer who limits herself to the classics is missing out on the joy of creating music.

The following March, Malcolm Peyton offered me the opportunity to sing in his concert of chamber works at the 92nd Street Y. He had written a violin concerto, and the program opened with Malcolm playing the first movement with Joseph Kovacs, who was the violinist in the reduced violin-piano score. I always welcome singing, and for that matter, hearing Malcolm's music. On the same program, Bob Helps and I were also able to give the first performances in New York of *Sounds and Words* and *Partitions*. Also on the program were four songs by Edward T. Cone on poetry by the Greek writer George Seferis, which I sang accompanied by the composer. Bob played two of his own compositions, and we also performed for the first time the complete cycle of Godfrey's *To Prove My Love* as well as selections from *Das Buch der hängenden Gärten*. What a marvelous program—and very Princetonian.

My feisty friend Ralph Shapey, from Juilliard days—and a student of Stefan Wolpe—asked me to sing at his 1960–61 Composer's Forum, which he was sharing with Charles Wuorinen. Milton was the moderator. Ralph's piece was *Incantations for Soprano and Ten Instruments*, in four movements. (Some of the movements didn't have a voice part.) Oddly enough, Ralph was also playing with the nontext concept as Milton was. The vocal part was just syllables, plus a movement involving humming and staccato singing. It had a central C-sharp in the first and second movements. This C-sharp was decorated with nontext vocal lines, returning to C-sharp and were in duet with a solo cello and other instruments. The third movement is purely instrumental. The C-sharp comes back in the last movement, always the center of extended phrases of humming interspersed with soft staccato pitches against delicate percussion and gong. It was really a unique piece. In a rave review in the *New York Times* the next day, Allen Hughes likened it to "a composition of abstract expressionism that seems to lay bare the most secret and elemental doubts, yearnings, torments and despair of the human soul." Hughes went on to say that Ralph's new piece proved that "conventional sources of musical tone are still far from exhausted as means of achieving acutely modern expression."[44]

Ralph was such a sweet person underneath all of his showy bluster, and he loved my singing. Shortly after the Composer's Forum, Ralph was inspired to give me the opportunity to sing his piece *Dimensions*. The *Dimensions* concert took place on May 13, 1962, on a program that also featured compositions by Arthur Berger, Stefan Wolpe, and Ernst Křenek. All four new works had been commissioned by Paul Fromm.

Ralph went on later to teach at the University of Chicago, where he formed the school's contemporary music ensemble, again (surprise!) under Fromm's sponsorship. Ralph and Paul had become close friends in Chicago. Ralph was a meticulous conductor, very outspoken, and my good friend. He married the painter Vera Klement; they divorced, and he later married the lovely singer Elsa Charlston. Elsa became Ralph's singer of new music in Chicago, working with his ensemble and premiering more of his vocal music. She was the heroine of contemporary music in Chicago for many years and continues to teach there today.

The busy pace kept up into the summer. Robert Koff, who was the former second violinist of the Juilliard String Quartet, asked me to perform *Pierrot* with his colleagues from Brandeis, where he was now teaching. Martin Boykan played piano, Phil Viscuglia played clarinet, and Elinor Preble was on flute. Madeline Foley was the cellist. I would always marvel at how Madeline played *Pierrot* on gut strings. She'd studied cello with Pablo Casals; after that, she never wanted to switch over to modern strings. Gut strings are much harder to manipulate—can you imagine playing the Serenade, no. 19, with all its difficult cadenzas and glissandos? I couldn't imagine, but Madeline mastered it.

On the same program, Marty Boykan played Schubert songs for me; we also performed Schubert's *Der Hirt auf dem Felsen* with Phil's wonderful clarinet alongside. Switching gears from *Sprechstimme* to pure singing was never an obstacle for me. I repeated this program on an East Coast tour with the Brandeis group. Later, they would also perform *Pierrot lunaire* with me for Aaron Copland's televised exploration of twentieth-century music. I'm amazed now when I think of my audacity, bringing together such different sounds, as if it weren't any big deal. But I didn't think of those things back then. Marty Boykan is now retired. He no longer plays piano but is an important composer, the only person, besides me, left of the group. We keep in touch. Just recently we had dinner together and reminisced. How nice to still have an old friend. They are fewer and fewer these days.

Looking at some of my old programs, I realize now the high quality of the music being performed in the 1950s and 1960s. Schoenberg's method was prevalent, the continuation of a tradition that began with the polyphony of Bach and led through Beethoven and Brahms right to Schoenberg—who was the true modernist. Music had become more complex. The new compositional styles challenged the listening audience. But I don't believe that audiences were ready to totally abandon the comfort of tonality. Understanding a new piece of music from this period takes courage and more than one listen. Listen many times over, follow with the score, and you will be amazed at how the music reveals itself.

CHAPTER THIRTY-THREE

D A S   B U C H   D E R
H Ä N G E N D E N   G Ä R T E N

Opus 15 by Arnold Schoenberg

By November of 1961, Bob Helps and I had finally learned Schoenberg's magnificent 1909 song cycle *Das Buch der hängenden Gärten*, which many consider the beginning of his atonal period. It became standard fare on our recital programs; we performed it more than twenty-four times. In 1961 we performed it on two separate programs in New York: first at the New School as part of a Berg–Schoenberg program; and then in Carnegie Hall's New Artist Series, for which I also sang Schumann's cycle *Dichterliebe*. That program would become one of our favorite touring concerts.

It takes a great deal of vocal stamina to sing those two pieces back to back. Unlike in an opera, you're singing for the entire program, so the physical demands are incredible. Those two grand cycles together on a program made for a real showy recital: a gentle reminder that recitalists aren't merely singers who can't do opera, but quite another breed of artist.

In his program notes at the premiere of *Das Buch* in Vienna, Schoenberg wrote: "With the George Lieder I have for the first time succeeded in approaching an ideal of expression and form which has been in my mind for years. Until now, I lacked the strength and confidence to make it a reality. But now that I have set out along this path once and for all, I am conscious of having broken through every restriction of a bygone aesthetic."[45]

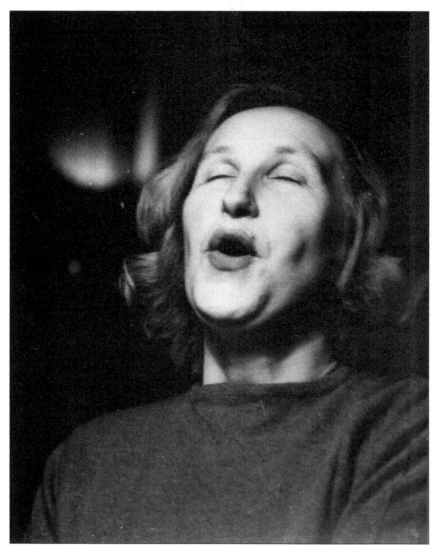

Figure 39. Me, ca. 1962.

Das Buch is set to fifteen poems by Stefan George. These short songs must be performed in immediate succession and together. Schoenberg created this challenging cycle during his middle period. There are no triads, no fixed tonality; the voice floats in a line that has the rise and fall of natural speech. So a good amount of the music lies in a singer's middle range, and the singer must tune constantly to blend her voice line into the underlying

harmonies of a highly chromatic piano part. In this cycle, the barline is of
no consequence whatsoever; the music flows along with the poetry in a
recitative-like manner, entirely intertwining the voice and piano. You must
have a first-rate pianist to perform this cycle. With this music, Schoenberg
did indeed create a new standard of musical expression, by which I mean
that the voice line is not self-contained as in a Schubert song but brought
into the context of the piano part.

Later in 1962, we recorded *Das Buch* for Elliott Wexler's small record company, Son Nova. Elliott had previously worked for Warner Records. Before
his untimely death, he issued perhaps a dozen excellent recordings with
Son Nova—including one of Bob Helps and me doing *Du* and some new
songs by Mel Powell on haiku texts.

Mel's songs were a perfect fit for my voice; I sang them many times.
I loved being around Mel. He was such a wide-open, warm person, you
couldn't help but fall in love with him! Before he became a serious composer and began teaching at Yale, Mel had been the pianist and arranger for
Benny Goodman's band. If caught in the right kind of informal situation,
Mel would sit at the piano and play jazz for us all. Of course, as fellow lovers of jazz music and show tunes, Milton and Mel really hit it off. I am convinced that if those two hadn't become serious composers, they would have
been snapped right up by Broadway. It was great fun to listen to them try
to one-up each other when they'd banter about show tunes and American
popular music.

Mel was married to the actress Martha Scott, whom he'd met when he
was working in Hollywood. They eventually moved from New Haven back
to Los Angeles, where he became founding dean of the school of music at
CalArts, founded by Walt Disney. Many years later, I had a week-long residency at CalArts; the president, Nick England, and Mel asked me to come
and teach there. I had to decline. A move to California would have been
quite a drastic change of scene for my family, not to mention the fact that I
knew Godfrey would *never* leave Princeton.

Several small recording companies emerged in those days, focusing on
contemporary music: Dial Records, Bartók Records, CRI, and Son Nova.
All of them eventually fell by the wayside. Son Nova was a pilot project
that could have been so important to many composers—in particular to
help move contemporary music composers out of the trap of single-performance syndrome. Today, New World Records and Bridge Records are the
champions of contemporary music.

I think those were important recordings, even though they've never been reissued. Apart from the fact that Elliott was a wonderful producer, *Das Buch* was a dedicated part of Bob's and my performance repertoire; we performed it many times in addition to doing the recording. There weren't many other duos performing *Das Buch* that I know of and there are only two other recordings of *Das Buch* from the period. Glenn Gould and Helen Vanni recorded it in 1966; Jan DeGaetani and Gilbert Kalish recorded it in 1976. In his *High Fidelity* review of Jan's recording, David Hamilton mentioned our recording, saying that of the three it "captured to near perfection the intensity and mystery of these subtly erotic songs."[46]

Glenn and Helen certainly had never performed the piece and didn't work together habitually as Bob and I did, which I do think has an influence over how performers will interpret a given piece of music. Jan and Gil, on the other hand, worked together constantly. Jan was a true recitalist. Sometimes our repertoires overlapped. She recorded *Pierrot*, too, though I'm not sure how often she performed it. Jan recorded frequently because she was close friends with Tracy Sterne, the head of classical music at Nonesuch Records in the 1970s. She was also a fine voice teacher at the Eastman School of Music, where she taught Dawn Upshaw and Renée Fleming. It was another blow to the new music world when Jan, like Elliott, died in her fifties.

This was a wonderful period all told, marked by *Das Buch*, the Mel Powell songs, the recordings with Son Nova. Perhaps the nicest part was that I got to work a lot with Bob, which always pleased me. Our mixed programs found appreciative audiences among college students and faculty. It's hard to tell how they would have gone over at a more conventional community concert, but we knew that our programs were setting a new standard for the art-song recital.

PART FOUR

NEW MUSIC
(1963–75)

Figure 40. My new publicity shot. Photograph by Harold Bergsohn.

CHAPTER THIRTY-FOUR

VISION AND PRAYER, OR, MY FIRST ADVENTURE WITH ELECTRONIC MUSIC

The second ISCM Duo Concert in 1955—the one that Jacques canceled—had a new composition by Milton on the program: *Vision and Prayer*, for voice and piano. Fortunately, it was still incomplete when the concert was called off. Milton ended up abandoning the piece shortly after, but then returned to it with fervor in the early 1960s. He had by then found an ideal instrumentation for the setting of Dylan Thomas's highly formal poem: the RCA Mark II Sound Synthesizer.

Vision and Prayer was the second piece Milton composed for synthesizer and one of the first major compositions ever written for machine and voice. I premiered *Vision and Prayer* in 1961. It is a fourteen-minute work for soprano and synthesized accompaniment, commissioned, naturally, by Paul Fromm, and set to a long poem cycle by Dylan Thomas about birth, death, resurrection, and the rejection of redemption. The poem is considered concrete poetry, which means it relies heavily on its arrangement on the page. *Vision and Prayer* is meticulously typeset into several different triangle-based patterns—triangles joined at their base to look like a diamond, joined at the tips like wings, arranged to look like tiles in a Spanish bath, and so forth. There are twelve shaped stanzas in all: The first half of the cycle explores increasing and decreasing—one syllable added per line until the line hits nine syllables, then decreases back down to one. The second half of the poem reverses the process, moving from decrease to increase. The precise formalism of this poetry must have really appealed to Milton. It was the visual representation of a sonic principle. Even though he didn't finish the original version for piano and voice, when he got involved in electronic music, the poem clearly still held its fascination—if not more so, given the added layers of conceptual aesthetics.

Milton—along with fellow composers Otto Luening and Vladimir Ussachevsky and the engineer Peter Mauzey—had been working since 1958 on the RCA Mark II Sound Synthesizer. This machine was a second generation to the RCA Mark I, which had been too primitive and mechanical to interest Milton. That "first machine was ridiculous," he explained in an interview. It "involved splicing tape and playing with oscillators" and didn't interest him musically. Milton found much more to be interested in with the Mark II. "The idea of this machine," he said was "perfect for me because you were punching in every aspect of the musical event, the mode of succession from one event to the next."[47] Although the machinery, at $500,000, would prove far too expensive for any university to adopt, RCA wanted to pursue the synthesizer and wanted musicians to be involved. The machine had been donated jointly to Columbia and Princeton Universities.

Milton produced his first piece for synthesizer in 1961. For that work, Milton explained he wasn't even concerned with the new timbres from the synthesizer but focused primarily on the tempo. It was an early effort, and Milton felt as if he still wasn't enough in control of the equipment to do what he wanted to do and so he kept to very simple principles. *Vision and Prayer* was destined to be a more complicated piece and included an important variable—me! He was worried as he approached his new composition that the synthesizer would "throw the singer," that I wouldn't be able to hear the music behind me. It was an interesting preoccupation, given what would turn out to be my *actual* experience of singing alongside a recorded tape track.

Vision and Prayer was an important piece for both of us. With it we were truly venturing blindly into new territory—a new landscape of performance, preparation, interpretation. There was nothing to do but proceed boldly. Milton wrote a score for me, which I had for a period of time to prepare before he sent the tape that would be my synthesized accompaniment. As I always did when I was preparing a song set to poetry, I began by studying Dylan Thomas's text. It was a process that I had learned how to do in earnest when I was working on Godfrey's *Habit of Perfection*. Gerard

Manley Hopkins was a complex poet. Godfrey had talked me through the poem, teaching me how to read lines and understand poetry's workings. Unlike, say, Emily Dickinson, or some of the German romantics that I had sung—work whose meaning is right there in front of you—the poetry of Hopkins, John Donne, George Herbert, and Dylan Thomas had buried movements, double meanings, and complex, insistent themes.

When I look at this poem today and read the final lines of the final stanza, "The sun roars at the prayer's end," I can't help but hear Milton's crashing last chord—the poetry and music inextricable. And as long ago as it all was, it is still almost unbearably lovely.

Milton created the music on the Mark II, housed at the Columbia-Princeton Electronic Music Center, of which he was the cofounder. The synthesizer was a huge machine that occupied a good-sized room and required several walls of equipment. The circuitry received instructions from a large punched-paper roll (like a player piano). Milton was thrilled with his room-sized toy, his robot orchestra. Working with the synthesizer gave him the opportunity to realize his compositions exactly as he'd intended them. Given the difficulties that new music composers experienced getting accurate performances of their music, an electronically generated performance was a unique satisfaction. Every musical event in the piece was notated on the paper roll and recorded onto an audiotape. The composer could build his music in the studio and then head home, carrying a perfect performance under his arm.

There were huge challenges with the score—it wasn't immediately apparent to either of us how to notate this new form. The score that Milton first sent me to start working with turned out to be quite skimpy. He claimed it was "complete." When I heard the final tape, he predicted, then I would know, in his words, "what I was getting." The real missing component, however—the much more important element in that spare score—was the minimal representation of the synthesizer's music and, especially, its rhythmic values. It was quickly evident that the materials I had were not enough. I couldn't just take that preliminary score and forge ahead.

Milton was struggling with the score: "I could get rhythmic values which I knew I could differentiate, receive, distinguish—and yet which no instrumentalist could ever play. Not because they were unplayable—though some of them probably were—but because *there was no way to notate them*."[48] It was as if back at the lab, Milton had stumbled onto the need for a new system of encrypting musical time in order to score his new music. He posed himself the question: "How do I notate these ridiculous rhythms? I could put them down as something like 19 in the time of 17—but didn't want to write that. Not only would it be terrifying, but I couldn't have read it myself." At issue, he continued, was that "I knew that what I'd conceived and that what I put on the tape was eminently *hearable* and distinguishable." So when the time came, he "faked it" (his words), and sent me a final score with precise values for the vocal line and approximations for the synthesizer. Nothing was off by more than a sixtieth of a second, he explained; "they were reasonable values," he thought, his approximations were carefully calculated.

Later, after we'd gotten through *Vision and Prayer*, Milton would be quoted as saying about me, "She manages to learn music no one else in the world can. She can work work work. She's a perfectionist. If you say, 'That's fine, stop,' she says she was off a sixteenth note. I don't know any other such person."[49] Perhaps Milton and I had our deepest affinity in the perfectionism of that sixteenth note.

When at last I received the recorded accompaniment and sat down to work with it alongside the score, it didn't go well. I called Milton and told him that something was wrong. I said, "Either the score is wrong or the tape is wrong." It was obvious to me that the score didn't line up with the music. Milton was surprised that I could hear it. His "approximations" had been so very slight and shouldn't have been audible to anyone—at least not to someone who wasn't an engineer, someone like Peter Mauzey or Vladimir Ussachevsky in the computer lab. They'd been training their ears to hear such very small variations. Milton had calculated the discrepancies, and I shouldn't have been able to hear them.

Maybe I wouldn't have heard just one approximation, but the score was filled with them! What's more, he had really barely notated the synthesizer's score. In other words, Milton had not written out a full score. Instead he gave me a sort of "cue score" indicating the pitch and rhythmic events of my voice line, alongside a very vague representation of the score involving the electronic music. And to make matters more intricate, there were tape interludes between the different sections of the poem that represented compilations of the music that had come before. He'd sent me out into the unknown territory of electronic music with barely anything to work with!

I protested. We discussed it and decided that the best solution would be to make a rhythmic click track for each vocal section of the piece for me to rehearse with. Godfrey helped by notating certain chordal lines in the final section where it was almost impossible to follow Milton's score. We all *hated* the click track. It really seemed like a bush-league solution to a highly sophisticated problem. And yet, it was the only way that I could rehearse and learn the piece—which I did. With Godfrey's help and the click track, I learned *Vision and Prayer*. Then, with practice, I liberated myself from the click track and began to enjoy, to hear, the extraordinary sound of this music. It was suffused with pitches, high and low, and speeds—sounds my ear had never experienced. It was in some ways *Du* all over again, but this time my partner was *always* right—my partner wasn't human. If any mistakes were made in a performance, they would be mine.

You can see here where Godfrey added notations in pencil to help me follow the score:

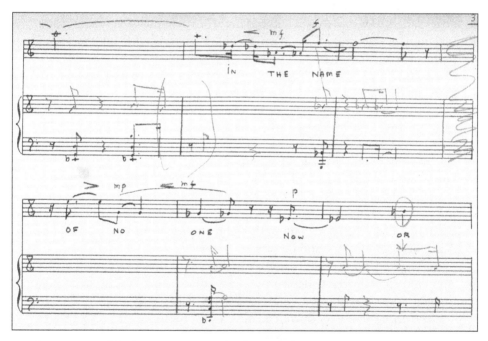

Figure 41. Godfrey's notations on Milton's original score for *Vision and Prayer*.

I have always loved *Vision and Prayer*. It is, in retrospect, my favorite piece of Milton's. What I like in particular is the way Milton handles the poem. The piece begins with a spoken word, followed by *Sprechstimme*, and then finally breaks into full song. He reverses the progression at the end of the piece, moving from singing through *Sprechstimme* to spoken word. The closing section swells with beautiful, chordal bell-like sounds.

By the time the last words, "The sun roars at the prayer's end," are spoken, the music has built into a huge, three-second-long, chordal ending. It truly does sound to me like the sun's roar. It is a long poem with many sung verses whose variety, especially in terms of what he pulls out of the synthesizer, is really Milton at his best. There is such a wealth of electronic colors. Each stanza has its own unique setting to dramatize the words. Sometimes I would sing over a one-line accompaniment of deep bass notes, and then a verse with harpsichord-like sounds and percussion. There was even one section where I sang a duet with the same rhythm as the accompaniment.

It is a curious example of Milton's predisposition to embellish for the sake of a good story, but he likes to claim that I premiered *Vision and Prayer* with that click track. And he also says that over fifty performances, I never sang *Vision and Prayer* without my score in hand—a very significant exception to my reputation as a singer who memorized difficult music and performed whole recitals never looking at sheet music. In Milton's version of events, I always sang *Vision and Prayer* with a score and never once performed *Philomel* with a score; that was because *Philomel*, written only two years later, was simply much more accurately notated, and so I could read it better, hear it more clearly, and memorize it. *Philomel* was also, as Milton explains, a much more complex piece, much longer, more elaborate electronically, with "every kind of befuddlement in it," including modified voices and mutated sounds of all kinds. The score had all the crazy rhythms written right into it. It's an interesting theory about "hearing and learning to hear," and Milton says that it's one of his favorite stories on the subject. I could memorize *Philomel*, Milton thought, because there was a correspondence between the tape and the score.

It's a good story—but it's not true. The fact of the matter is that I did sing *Vision and Prayer* with a score at the premiere and then only once after that. But I *never* performed *Vision and Prayer* with a click track.

The thing about performing with a recording is that once you've learned the music, you've learned it. There are no variables. It's ultimately quite a bit more straightforward than singing with a human. There's not a lot of room to roam or experiment but by the same token, there's no room for error.

Because of the complexities and challenges of Milton's score, even today singers need more information in order to perform this vital piece. Fortunately, now there is a beautifully engraved score by David Dies with annotations by Mimmi Fulmer, a professor of voice at the University of Wisconsin, complete with singer's notes (published by Subito Music in

2016). I believe that there are not many engravings of Milton's vast out-put—especially, as in later years, he refused to have his work transferred from his handwritten drafts to computer. Between the singing annotations and the corrections, I think this publication is an important part of carrying Milton's legacy forward to future generations of singers.

The premiere of *Vision and Prayer* took place on September 6, 1961, in Grace Rainey Rogers Auditorium as part of the (believe it or not) Eighth Congress for the International Society of Musicologists—*musicologists!* You can just imagine 850 musicologists sitting in the concert hall that night, experiencing electronic music—perhaps for the first time. The *New York Times* identified it as "What must have been one of the most distinguished audiences ever to attend a concert in this city."[50] The experience would give them all quite a bit to write about in the years to come. For they were listening to a singer, standing alone on stage, accompanied by four KLH stereo loudspeakers.

I was robed in the black butterfly gown Stanley Seeger had bought me for *Pierrot*. Milton was backstage the whole time, nervously supervising the launching of the tape—he was on guard against anyone who might trip over or step on his precious cords. He'd grown absolutely paranoid about anyone stepping near his speakers. He was like a speaker-wire guard dog during rehearsals. But good old Milton was making history!

I am sure that the experience of hearing *Vision and Prayer* was far more startling for the audience than it was for me. I'd practiced it to death and only had to worry about hearing my cues so I wouldn't miss an entrance. Electronic music was in its infancy. Milton was its fierce pioneer—and about to be famous for it—but the audience would be ambivalent for years to come. In the *New York Times* the day after the premiere, Eric Salzman's qualified response was quite hard to read. He wrote, "The quality of Mr. Babbitt's musical thought is the same whether he writes for instruments, voice or the electronic music synthesizer. There is an expressive quality to the very purity of his musical thinking."[51]

I performed *Vision and Prayer* again in May of 1963 as part of a three-day festival sponsored by the Princeton-Columbia Electronic Music Center. This time I had twelve speakers accompanying me, mounted all around the periphery of the McMillin Academic Theatre at Columbia. It was astounding. The whole time I was singing I felt as if I were emerging from a vortex of electronic sound. The audience, too, was surrounded by the music, coming at them from twelve different directions. Milton must have been in seventh heaven. I think he would have liked for all of his beautiful electronic scores ultimately to be experienced this way, a sensory blast.

I was fully caught up in the excitement. *Newsweek* came to interview me before the premiere—my friend Fay Lansner's husband Kermit was the executive editor. The article ran with the title "A Composer's Singer" and described my particular niche and the difficult work I'd become known for. I was so brazen. In one section they quote me as saying, "I don't think in terms of the public. Music is for musicians. If the public wants to come along and study it, fine. I don't go and tell a scientist his business because I don't know anything about it. Music is just the same way. Music is art and not entertainment."[52] I still stand by what I said but I have to admit that I was just a bit over the top!

I had a bit of a funny experience the evening of the *Vision and Prayer* premiere, which perhaps sheds light on what it felt like to be one of electronic music's first performers. I sang on the first half of the program and then stayed backstage to listen to Elliott Carter's *Double Concerto*—also being premiered that night, and entirely not electronic. As I listened to the music, I kept wincing. It sounded as if everything was out of tune. I thought my ears were playing tricks on me. But then I realized, *Of course!* I had been working exclusively with the purity—or maybe better, the precision—of synthesized sound for three weeks. In comparison, conventional instruments sounded *wrong*. It was a completely bizarre sensation, and it passed quickly. But it left a deep impression. With this piece, Milton had given me a whole world of new musical sounds.

CHAPTER THIRTY-FIVE

CAMELOT YEARS

1 9 6 2

I n January 1961, John F. Kennedy became president. His beautiful
wife, Jacqueline, brought elegance to the White House with her perfect interior renovations, and she incorporated culture and the arts—
music, too—into the presidential social calendar. The first lady hosted
concerts, carefully, and politically, curating her musical guests: the
Spanish cellist Pablo Casals, the African American mezzo-soprano Grace
Bumbry, the racially integrated Paul Winter Sextet, and the Korean pianist Han Tong-il. Composers, from Bernstein to Stravinsky, thought
the world of the Kennedys.

And yet in the background, the 1960s were not easy years. The constant threat of nuclear war, in the aftermath of World War II, was a shadow
that never left you. You had to push it out of your mind, into your subcon-
scious, so that you wouldn't walk around scared all the time. You'd go crazy
if you didn't. Godfrey and I read about Bertrand Russell's peace movement
in London and the antinuclear demonstrations. Russell's philosophy made
perfect sense to me: There were two paths—obliteration or common sense.
I was in favor of the commonsense solution: Get rid of the bomb entirely.

In the first year of JFK's administration, the Princeton Symphony
Orchestra commissioned Godfrey to write *Composition for Orchestra*, in
which he was able to demonstrate musically his theory of "composition
with arrays"—a mathematical ordering he devised for writing music, which
was also the basis of his doctoral thesis. The twelve-minute *Composition
for Orchestra* was premiered on March 8, 1962, under the direction of

Nicholas Harsanyi. Thank goodness I have a tape of that performance—it's the only recording, or performance for that matter, in existence. The one-performance syndrome hit our family as well.

My husband was not a very prolific composer and reticent about promoting his own music. With the exception of my performances of his song cycle *To Prove My Love*, Godfrey's music was seldom heard. I think his problem was that he was interested in too many things! He had grown increasingly intrigued with the vast potentials of electronic music too. He became fascinated by the RCA synthesizer and started going into New York all the time to work at the Electronic Music Center. He'd often just stay the night in town at Ben and Naomi Boretz's place.

Later that year, Godfrey received the first doctorate of music at Princeton, a program that had only begun the year before. He was elected to Phi Beta Kappa but never picked up his key. How typical.

In that season of accolades, I was presented with the Laurel Leaf Award by the American Composers Alliance for "distinguished achievement in fostering and encouraging American music." It had been twelve years since I first sang Ben Weber's *Concert Aria*—twelve years of singing new music. I deserved an award.

In the wake of the award, Howard Klein interviewed Valerie Lamoree and me together in the *New York Times*. The premise of the interview was that the two of us, champions of new music, had more in common than just both being blonde! I talked about coming to new music through Ben Weber, and the excitement of having just worked on *Vision and Prayer*. We both talked about how people were always remarking on our ability to learn and sing these difficult works—but I had to remind myself (and others) that we had the advantage of knowing the composer.[53]

That summer, Charles Munch asked me back to Tanglewood to perform in the opening concert. I did Bach's Cantata no. 51 again. This time, though, I sang in the great Music Shed, which was an open-air venue and larger than the concert hall, and accommodated an additional ten thousand people on the lawn. The Music Shed and the lawn at Tanglewood can seat over 14,000 people, though opening night in 1962 had a smallish audience of 3,690. "Small" is relative; it was still quite a departure from my usual recital audience. In a rave for the *Berkshire Eagle*, Jay C. Rosenfeld, who covered Tanglewood for years, called me "the sensation of the evening."

It was Munch's last year at the festival, and this event was a real send-off, a *beglückend* occasion in Munch's honor. He was a darling of a man and

Figure 42. With Maestro Charles Munch when I sang the Bach cantata, *Jauchzet Gott in allen Landen*, in the big Shed at Tanglewood, 1962. Photograph by Heinz Weissenstein, Whitestone Photo. Courtesy of BSO Archives.

told me, to my enormous surprise, that he preferred New York State wines to French wines. I wholeheartedly agreed. What did I know about wine?

We spent time with my sister Helen in Upstate New York that summer. Baird and Christopher played with their five cousins and got a chance to let off some steam and scream and yell without worrying about disturbing their father. Godfrey had some uninterrupted time to work, and I could visit with Helen in her beautiful Queen Anne home in the center of the small village of Red Hook. It was important for Godfrey to have this working time when the children were small. We both knew that, and the children really looked forward to the summer, because they got to go to camp upstate and play to their heart's content. Having a father who is an intellectual, no matter how much you love and respect him, is not really a great deal of fun!

I was also performing the role of Rosina in *The Barber of Seville* with the Turnau Opera Company, based in Woodstock, near Red Hook. Turnau was a small opera theater that had been founded in the fifties by the New York philanthropists Joseph and Sally Turnau, with a mandate to perform the classics and promote performers of color. George Shirley, who would be the first African American singer to perform at the Met, had his stage debut at Turnau in 1958.

The composer Yehudi Wyner, who'd been vacationing in Woodstock and had become enchanted by the company, had just been convinced that year by the executive directors Marie and Ward Pinner (who were devoted music lovers without a great deal of background) to take over the artistic direction along with Barbara Owens, the stage director. In an interview, Yehudi described Owens and his first season like this:

> There was no way when first looking at her to guess at her level of achievement. Here was a young woman resembling a "bobby soxer" who wielded the most formidable sensibility I've ever encountered in the form—which happened to co-exist with a marvelous sense of humor. Barbara demanded the essence of opera and cut to the emotional truth of every scene. When I was offered the directorship I simply felt unable to refuse. Of course, the schedule was all but super-human. We did eight full operas in eight weeks. Large chorus sections naturally had to be cut, but the essential opera was performed complete. . . . At the beginning I performed the scores alone—grand piano half tucked beneath the stage, facing the singers with a weak little bulb glaring down upon these monumental scores. It was a profound musical education—one of the two or three most uplifting episodes of my career. And I would be so bold as to say that with our pianos the audience did not miss an orchestra.

Owens was the one who convinced me it would be fun to do a bit of opera—and why not? I would always find it hard to turn down Mozart. Yehudi explained:

> My first opera ever was *The Barber of Seville*, featuring the small, exquisite voice of Bethany Beardslee. Her husband was a mover and shaker in the most advanced contemporary music, and he persuaded Bethany to sing much if not most of the important new pieces to arrive in New York. Her first love remained the classics but she didn't have the vocal power to

fill a large opera house. So it was our delight to have her fill the Turnau's small hall.[54]

My Count Almaviva in that production was the young Nico Castel, who later became the famous diction coach and *comprimario* at the Metropolitan Opera. But my most important and enduring connection from the interlude at Turnau was meeting and working with Yehudi. He was an elegant and musical performer, somewhat like Jacques. And like Jacques, he was also a more serious partner than Bob Helps. Bob was always half boy, and Yehudi was an adult. I admired his gentle seriousness. For years to come I would also depend on dear Yehudi to be my pianist when Bob disappeared.

CHAPTER THIRTY-SIX

LE MARTEAU
SANS MAÎTRE

Arthur Weisberg, a bassoonist and another Juilliard alum, wanted to turn his talents to being a conductor. In 1961, he formed a group devoted to new music called the Contemporary Chamber Ensemble. He took me out to lunch one afternoon and asked if I'd be interested in taking on Pierre Boulez's work *Le marteau sans maître* (The Hammer without a Master). *Le marteau*, on early surrealist poetry by René Char, was a rather talked-about work at the time. It was particularly noted for its exotic instrumentation and the shadow of some unpleasant French musical politics around its debut at the 1955 International Society for Contemporary Music in Baden Baden. Even Stravinsky (in his reticent way) had been impressed by *Le marteau* when he heard it in 1957 at its Los Angeles premiere under Boulez's baton: It "is an admirable, well-ordered score despite all the aural and written complications (counterpoint, rhythm, length)," he wrote to Nadia Boulanger. "Without feeling close to Boulez's music, I frankly find it preferable to many things of his generation."[55]

I had already sung *Improvisation II sur Mallarmé*, from Boulez's *Pli selon pli*, with Jim Bolle in Chicago, but I was hesitant about *Le marteau* because of its extravagant vocal line, written for contralto, and I wasn't sure I could navigate the range. What's more, Arthur warned me from the get-go that I'd have to accept a smaller fee than what I was used to. The attractiveness of the offer, nonetheless, was that we would be putting on the New York premiere of this important piece.

The music was, as I had anticipated, difficult to learn. Boulez's vocal lines are similar to Webern's, which meant that they have wide intervals. Boulez, like many others, had been caught up in the Webern craze but had his own individual style. In truth, the instrumentation for Le marteau did not overwhelm me. For this piece, Boulez was particularly interested in the setting of the poetry: "It is better, I think, when the poetry is not imprisoned within the music, as it is with romantic song, but when music and poetry can interact more freely."[56]

As a conductor, Arthur, like Jacques, favored many rehearsals, so I came to feel quite at home with some of the great players working with me: Ray Des Roches and Max Neuhaus, fabulous percussionists; Jacob Glick on viola, Sam Baron on flute; Paul Price on vibraphone, and Stanley Silverman on guitar. The piece was a big success when we premiered it April 2, 1962, at the 92nd Street Y.

We performed the piece again at Hunter College, with Boulez discussing the music. He said, "I am bothered and bored with the idea that there can be only one relationship between a poem and its music. In Le marteau I have tried to find the deep roots of poetry in music, in the instrumental parts even more than in the vocal sections."[57] Ned Rorem elaborated on that point when he wrote about Le marteau as a turning point in American art song:

> The past years have seen a crop of American singer—not properly a recital singer—skilled to deal with current vocal concepts. These concepts stress words as sound no less than as sense, and inevitably enmesh the voice in a jungle of instrumental hues. The parent work is Boulez' Le Marteau sans Maître (1954), and the spinoff interpreter in America is Bethany Beardslee, who could always do anything, as could Julius Eastman, Cathy Berberian, Jan DeGaetani, and Phyllis Bryn-Julson. The pieces are not songs, because they do not restrict themselves to piano and lyric poem. They are shows—narrational, terrifically up to date, yet still using texts from another time and place.[58]

The Hunter College performance was part of a big Boulez-Babbitt concert tour we did the following year. The program was made up of Le marteau sans maître and Vision and Prayer. It was interesting to work on those pieces together and to have the opportunity to compare the two great composers. Milton's music stood out from that of his peers of this time in that my voice line was absolutely diatonic; all of his most complicated material was happening in the electronic background. There was none of the hopping and skipping all over the place that these other guys made you do—the intervals in *Le marteau*. Singing Milton was like singing Schubert in comparison.

My manager, Jay Hoffman, had been amenable to my taking a reduced fee for the New York premiere, but he negotiated my fee for the tour—especially since I was singing both works—which had eight performances. These were two very different compositions, by two very different composers, who both happened to be on hand to speak about their works, as Boulez and Milton toured with us. The players again gave great performances of *Le marteau*, and our success with that piece was entirely due to Arthur's preparation and them. I'm sure the tour went a long way toward establishing both Milton and Boulez on a national platform.

While we were on tour, I had the chance to ask Boulez what he thought of *Vision and Prayer* and he answered laconically, "It seems to me like a long song cycle." That was all. I laughed, because it didn't seem like much of an answer. I wondered whether he noticed the whole new electronic medium, the unusual formalism of the poem as well as Milton's setting. Boulez's response at the time seemed so noncommittal. And yet just a few years later, Boulez built IRCAM, his own electronic music center in Paris—so I have to assume that he was indeed totally aware of, even tracking, Milton's involvement in the medium and its endless possibilities.

Over the next decade Pierre Boulez would come to really establish himself stateside. In the late sixties, I was asked to appear with him in a concert in which he featured as a soloist, conductor, and composer. He asked me to perform Webern and Debussy songs with *him* at the piano. I didn't know Boulez even played the piano! He apologized to me during rehearsal, explaining that he wasn't a professional pianist. He didn't have to tell me that. The concert was at Hunter College in March of 1969. It opened with Boulez conducting Webern's *Concerto for Nine Instruments*, then we did the Webern songs op. 3 and the 1913 Mallarmé settings by Debussy. This was very late Debussy, practically the last thing he'd written, and I think Boulez was attracted to them because they were almost atonal. Next, Charles Rosen played Boulez's third piano sonata, and we ended with Boulez conducting me in *Pierrot lunaire*. The concert went very well, and he immediately engaged me to do *Pierrot* in Cleveland, where he was the conductor of the Cleveland Orchestra.

Although Boulez was a very prominent figure at this point, singing under him was disappointing. He had come out of the same training as Jacques, and I had assumed (or hoped) that working with him would be equal to singing with Jacques. But it wasn't. You couldn't read Boulez's expressions at all. He had such an elegant face but never revealed any emotion. He just seemed so far away. Boulez had studied at the Paris Conservatory, and like Jacques, he'd worked with Olivier Messiaen. I wasn't sure if Jacques and Boulez happened to be in the same classes at the Conservatory—Boulez was two years older than Jacques. Neither one ever mentioned to me that he knew the other. They also had very different temperaments. Boulez was polished. He had impeccable manners and treated his fellow musicians with respect. Later, when I rehearsed with him, I'd discover that, like Jacques, he would sing solfège syllables when correcting a player's mistakes. It was no doubt part of their training.

From my association with Boulez, I can say that I found him standoffish. He seemed like someone you couldn't get close to, and his music had that very same distance. It was unemotional but elegantly conceived. However during these years he was a driving force throughout the world for contemporary music, with an emphasis on the music of the Second Viennese School. When he was director of the New York Philharmonic and the Cleveland Orchestra in the late 1960s and early seventies, his programming demonstrated a commitment to the work of Schoenberg, Berg, and Webern. He was a major conductor well into his eighth decade and influential as the director of IRCAM. He was a diplomat and played politics in the music business, but he never seemed to compromise his beliefs and brought integrity to his work without being fussy or angry. At the height of his career, he was mounting big, gorgeous concerts and making impressive canonical recordings.

One night backstage during that era, when Boulez and I were chatting, he told me that he had "laid out the course of his career for the years to come." Ambitious man. I was impressed by his seriousness and determination of his future, but frankly—even as I was well into my professional career—it all seemed rather too businesslike to me. Nonetheless, he had a plan for himself, and it worked out terrifically well.

I've always thought that Jacques should have had the success that Boulez did. But Jacques's demanding rehearsal schedule and the economics of the music business never jelled. Jacques eventually left conducting, although he was often asked to come back, and began teaching at Columbia University. Like Schoenberg, he took on private students in his later years and even became quite reclusive. Jacques was a great musician, handicapped by a self-destructive streak in his personality. Boulez was, on the other hand, shrewd, and diplomatic. He knew how to maximize his opportunities and get what he wanted.

CHAPTER THIRTY-SEVEN

THE SIXTIES

N ovember 1963, the world fell into shock after the assassination of President Kennedy. I look at my old issues of the *New York Times*, photos of Jacqueline and the funeral procession from all of those years ago, and I still can't describe the feelings we had when Godfrey and I heard the news that afternoon at Hodge Road. I remember Walter Cronkite announcing in a tearful voice that Kennedy had died, and suddenly it was as if the whole country came to a halt. We were stunned, and we cried. Camelot was over.

That evening at Philharmonic Hall, before starting the scheduled program, Bernstein played the beautiful *Adagietto* from Mahler's Fifth Symphony, in honor of our young president. More than fifty years after Kennedy's tragic assassination, our country and the world still pay homage to his memory.

Lyndon Johnson became president, and in March 1965, he ordered the first American combat troops into South Vietnam. "I guess we've got no choice," he announced, "but it scares the death out of me. I think everybody's going to think 'We're landing the Marines! We're off to battle!'" There were so many who thought the war could have been avoided. Would Kennedy have taken the same action? Kennedy had defused a confrontation with Russia during the tense days of the Cuban Missile Crisis and was in the process of pulling a thousand troops *out* of Vietnam—but that document was still on his desk, unsigned, when he was assassinated. It would be the beginning of years of war spending, and many lives lost.

The sixties were wonderful and tragic all at once. The civil rights movement and the protests against our involvement in Vietnam were in full bloom. Martin Luther King, Jr. was assassinated in April 1968. Riots broke out. Later the same year, JFK's brother Robert F. Kennedy ran for president and was killed in June. But amid these tragedies though, the wonderful part was that as a nation we weren't passive; we were responding.

Berkeley was one of the hotbeds of protest and radicalization. In the 1962–63 school year, the same year that Aldous Huxley delivered a lecture entitled "The Ultimate Revolution," the composer Luigi Dallapiccola was Visiting Professor, Chair of Italian Culture at Berkeley. Dallapiccola stayed that semester with David Lewin, a brilliant music theorist and one of Godfrey's Princeton classmates. The university mounted an all-Dallapiccola concert in his honor.

In the spring of 1963, I went out to California to sing two of Dallapiccola's pieces, *Sex carmina Alcaei* and *Concerto per la notte di Natale dell'anno 1956* with chamber orchestra. Despite the fact that Dallapiccola's music is quite accessible—a lyric twelve-tone style that tends toward Berg's romanticism—it is not played often enough. I was shy about singing Dallapiccola's music, because I knew that Magda László was singing him all over Europe and that she was doing wonderful work. I hoped he would like my singing as much.

We had a great evening in the Lewins' kitchen, sitting around the table listening to Dallapiccola hold forth—he told fascinating war stories. He was a rather small man, with piercing black eyes. There was something so tangibly European about him, he reminded me of Jacques. He seemed proud and not in the least bit insecure. He was a heavy smoker and used a toothpick to hold his cigarette butt so that he could smoke it down to the embers—a habit picked up during the war. I kept thinking he was going to burn his fingers, but he had his technique down to a science.

Bob Helps often was in the San Francisco–Berkeley area and that summer was renting a friend's home. He drove me around Marin County, with its sheep farms and soft old hills. I will never forget the scent of the eucalyptus trees up in the hills by the campus. Bob loved this area and had, by this point, come out of the closet. He had many friends there and felt as if he composed better when he was out West.

While I was in Berkeley, Bob and I gave another recital at the university, and I had the chance to sing *Vision and Prayer*. I put it on the program with Debussy's *Proses lyriques*. Bob played a Mendelssohn sonata and repeated Babbitt's *Partitions*. I never really knew when Bob was going to be in New York or whether he had gone off to San Francisco—but I had come to accept his capricious cycles.

Figure 43. Bob Helps with the children at Hodge Road, ca. 1965.

That winter, 1963, I had a unique opportunity to appear on television for a series called *Recital Hall*. It was hosted by Ben Grauer, who had been the announcer for the NBC Symphony Orchestra on the Toscanini broadcasts that I'd sung on at Juilliard—the first time that I was on television. I was excited about this appearance, particularly because I wasn't going to be hidden in the chorus this time. I sang Strauss, Webern, Mel Powell's *Haiku Settings*, Brahms, and Debussy. Bob played for me.

Godfrey and the children and I watched the broadcast back at Hodge Road. I was embarrassed, but my family seemed pleased to see Mom on TV "doing her thing." Why is it that you have these feelings watching yourself perform? I was embarrassed in the same way when people complimented me backstage. For some reason it made me question whether they'd even understood the difficult music I was singing. I could never accept compliments. The moment I walked offstage, I could always see with glaring clarity everything that had gone wrong in the performance. Even though I had moments when I was working alone in which I felt like the perfection I sought was just within reach, I was never satisfied by the performances. Those perfect moments are always just out of reach. I often wonder if all performers share this sense of being always just shy of perfection.

My TV recital is one of the only documents of me singing and I would love to see it again—I don't know if I'd be embarrassed the same way. But I do think about the fact that today's singers are constantly filmed and their performances can be easily seen. In their retirement they'll be able to see themselves at their prime, which seems like it would be a great treat—like an old movie star watching her great films.

At this point in my career I had done seven recordings. But they had all been of new music. Jim Bolle gave me the opportunity instead to record a recital of eighteenth-century arias with orchestra for Monitor Records, a small label out of New York City specializing in hard-to-find music. Jim loved the music of Haydn and programed an LP with arias by Giovanni Pergolesi, Stephen Storace, and Haydn for me to sing with the Musica Viva ensemble under his baton—in particular Jim uncovered a beautiful but unknown Haydn solo cantata, *Miseri noi, misera patria*. The Pergolesi aria had an obbligato duet played by Basil Reeve, a fabulous oboist. The LP got excellent reviews and compared me with the young Elisabeth Schwarzkopf. The project came about because Jim and his wife, Jocelyn, moved from Chicago to Francestown, New Hampshire, and decided to start the summer Monadnock Music Festival. They asked me to be the singer for their 1966 inaugural season, thus the Monitor recordings. For me it seemed as

Figure 44. Jocelyn and Jim Bolle, ca. 1966. Courtesy of Monadnock Music Festival.

if something endearing and pleasant was always in the cards when Jim was around. Jocelyn was also such a dear person. She was from an old established Keene, New Hampshire, family. At Monadnock she always seemed radiant, with her exquisite skin and abundant blonde curls. She wore the most beautiful summer clothes, rich with color, and would *always* be sitting in the audience and cheering us all on. It was one of Jocelyn's talents— her wonderful ability to make every musician at the festival feel important.

The Monadnock Music Festival grew very successful. Jim's musicians returned again and again, in particular because of the beautiful New Hampshire location: fern-bordered dirt roads, cool summer nights that meant getting to wear comfy summer clothes, the white and green shuttered houses nestled in rolling hills, the ambience of the small town halls and churches with perfect acoustics where we held our performances—the sheer informality of it all made this festival very special to us all. For me it was a real breather from the hard labor of having to learn difficult new music. Jim conducted the orchestra and found pieces for me that I would never have had the chance to sing otherwise; for example, Benjamin Britten's *Les illuminations,* and Sam Barber's *Knoxville: Summer of 1915.* I in turn could give suggestions for music that I wanted to do. Jim and I would have long telephone conversations about composers or performers and still do today.

I returned to Monadnock after a six-year absence, in 1973. That summer Rudolf Kolisch, a champion of Schoenberg's music, was on the faculty. In terms of Schoenberg, Rudy was the closest you could get to the master himself. He had been a student of Schoenberg when he was a young man and, later, his brother-in-law for a period. Rudy and his famous Kolisch Quartet had played the premieres of Schoenberg's quartets before World War II in Vienna. When Rudy coached players, he would spend unlimited time on a few bars of music, but in those few bars he gave the student more information on performance principles than by the usual run-through commentary of most coaches. Rudy always called me "Betty" and loved watching hockey on TV. He said that hockey resembled polyphony in music—with the continual weaving in and out of the players. (I could never see the resemblance myself.) He played a mean game of chess and beat me constantly. I never should have told him I knew how to play. I'm not sure I really did. Godfrey had tried to teach me chess, but it takes a great deal of time and deep concentration—it's not a game you enter into casually. Russell Sherman and Gunther Schuller admired Rudy, as did Bob Helps. It was an honor when Rudy was our onstage page-turner for our performance of *Das Buch der hängenden Gärten* that summer.

Jim also founded the New Hampshire Symphony Orchestra, which he ran for twenty-nine years, I was his soloist four times, singing Mozart arias, Berlioz's *Nuits d'été,* Mahler's Symphony No. 4, and the four last songs of Richard Strauss.

CHAPTER THIRTY-EIGHT

PHILOMEL

1 9 6 4

A mutual friend recently wrote to me and asked for memories of Milton. I have so very many. But the first one that flashed to mind was the night we performed *Philomel* at Wheaton College. I had forgotten my lipstick and insisted that I couldn't go on without it. I remember sending him dashing out to the drugstore to get some for me—I told him firmly to get me the darkest coral he could find. He was so gallant.

I think, however, the dearest memory I have of him is the night we premiered *Philomel* in New York City at the Grace Rainey Rogers Auditorium of the Metropolitan Museum of Art. We had actually premiered the piece in Amherst, then at Wheaton, but New York was the big event, and one of the most important concerts of my career. We had a grand party afterward at Claus Adam's apartment; it felt as if every composer in New York and Princeton was there. *Philomel* became Milton's *Clair de lune*. I've never seen him as happy as he was that night.

If I could say I was spoiled by a single piece of music, it would be *Philomel*, which Milton wrote for me and I performed in New York City on February 21, 1964. That was the night I gained a signature piece.

Philomel is an electronic work for live voice, recorded voices, and synthesized accompaniment—again realized on the RCA Mark II Sound Synthesizer—and set to poetry written expressly for the piece by John Hollander, based on the legend of Procne and Philomela in Ovid's *Metamorphoses*.

The piece was part of a Ford Foundation grant for concert soloists that I had received, after being selected as one of fifteen out of 231 nominated by a selection committee of conductors, composers, singers, critics, and other music professionals. It was a tremendous opportunity that allowed me to commission a new work from any American composer of my choosing, and then mount its New York premiere at the Metropolitan Museum of Art. I was very proud to be chosen, and have to assume that my involvement with new music distinguished me among soloists.

I had sung in the Grace Rainey Rogers Auditorium before, when I was working with New York Pro Musica, and I knew it had excellent acoustics. More important, it was where I'd premiered *Vision and Prayer*, so I felt not only at home but that there was a lucky star hovering over that venue.

Godfrey and I programmed the premiere concert. At nineteen minutes, *Philomel* is a long cycle, and took up the whole second half of the program. I would also sing Handel's solo cantata *Lucretia*, with harpsichord and continuo. Lucretia, like Philomel, was a deranged woman character (though of a different variety). I also sang Schubert's *Der Hirt auf dem Felsen* for piano and clarinet; and a new work by Malcolm Peyton, *Four Shakespeare Sonnets* for two clarinets, violin, viola, and cello, which Malcolm conducted.

Malcolm was a friend, a fellow Princeton graduate and a pupil of Roger Sessions. In later years he would be a great champion of Godfrey's music. I had sung Malcolm's work before, but these Shakespeare settings were one of his best pieces at the time, and I was honored to include them on the program. Malcolm would go on to compose songs on beautiful settings of Walt Whitman poems for me, which we performed several times and recorded for CRI.

The acoustic works started the program; during intermission, we cleared the stage of the music stands and piano and replaced them with four KLH stereo loudspeakers (each one about three feet high) set in the four corners of the stage. I changed my costume, too. I was wearing a beautiful salmon-pink chiffon gown with a gold brocade coat designed by my dressmaker, Eleanor Ambos. For *Philomel*, I would switch out the coat and wrap myself in an antique silk Japanese stole that had an embroidery of birds, branches, around a large peacock. It seemed to cry out, from the moment I first saw it, *I am your Philomel stole.*

Philomel is a monodrama similar to Schoenberg's *Erwartung*. I had memorized the score, giving me the chance to focus on the dramatization of the story. I loved performing this part—it was my own little opera role. I

Figure 45. The premiere of *Philomel* at Amherst College, 1964. Courtesy of Amherst College Archives and Special Collections.

played Philomel, the sister of Procne, who is raped by Procne's husband, Tereus, king of Thrace. Tereus cuts out Philomel's tongue and locks her away to keep her silent. But Philomel secretly weaves her story into a tapestry and sends it to her sister. Together the sisters concoct revenge. Procne kills and cooks Tereus's youngest son and serves him to Tereus for dinner. Tereus finds out what's happened. Procne frees her sister, and the two escape into the forest, pursued by Tereus. The gods transform all three characters into birds: Tereus is turned into a hoopoe, Procne into a swallow, and Philomel into a nightingale—upon which she finds her voice again. "Gradually achieving coherence, she echoes the birds with her song, and the world responds with the final words of her questions. Finally she sings in a strophic aria of the redemption of her now fully evolved voice and celebrates her flight, as in her refrain."[59]

> I sing in change
> Now my song will range
> . . . .
> As it once flew
> Thrashing, through
> The woods of Thrace.[60]

John Hollander explained that from Ovid's story, "the nightingale has sung all night of her tragedy, becoming allegorically the poet who figuratively out of pain and literally out of darkness transcends suffering."[61]

I knew my accompaniment would always be flawless, because as with *Vision and Prayer*, I was singing with a synthesizer! Milton's setting had me singing against my own recorded voice and synthesized music, which represented the birds and echoes of the forest. This also meant that I could move around freely onstage, interpreting the character of Philomel. The aural textures were both a dramatization and an immersion into a fantastical environment. It was a perfect coming together of form and content. Hollander wrote about the project, "Long ago I had wanted to use the myth of Philomela for an elaborate aria because I had always thought that the story was quintessentially operatic, with a great transformation scene in which a soprano, who has been singing nothing, but vocalizes choppy syllables suddenly can break out into both sustained melody and language. But after having heard *Vision and Prayer*, the possibilities of a synthesized accompaniment for dramatic purposes seemed enormous, and when the Ford Foundation commissioned such a piece and Babbitt asked me for a text, the metamorphosis of the nightingale seemed the obvious subject."[62]

Milton, as expected, sent me the score in 1963 but the taped part came incrementally—or "progressively," as it was being realized on the synthesizer. Each new tape arrived with additions and corrections that had come up along the way. As always, and as with *Vision and Prayer*, I worked my voice line along with the metronome first; once it was really solid, I matched it to the tapes Milton was sending. I had to learn it in that order, because I didn't like the intrusion of taped music when I was checking and rechecking my voice line. With my relative pitch, I wanted to have the voice line like steel in my ear running against the complexities of Milton's taped music.

The dress rehearsals were something else. Milton would be hovering about on high alert that none of the players would step on one of the electrical cords leading from the speakers. He was always in a panic about it. Of course, at the performance itself, he'd have to stay backstage to make sure nothing went wrong with the tape machine. And I, as usual, would arrive early to the theater before the concert. Ever since I began performing, I arrived early. I got used to being the first one there. I like to have time to review my music, and if I have my own dressing room, which I did that night, sit in the dark. Over years of performing, I have found that sitting in the dark for a few minutes is restorative and calming. And I was particularly keyed up for this concert—for it centered entirely on me and on the piece I had chosen to commission through the Ford Foundation.

My voice was in excellent shape—probably because I was so excited. The house would be full. All the composers were there. My sister and her husband came down from upstate for the event. Even Godfrey left the children with a sitter and came into town—a special occasion in and of itself, because he seldom showed up for my New York performances. This was one concert I insisted he not miss. I booked myself into the St. Regis Hotel for the week, because I really wanted to celebrate the concert with glamour. How often in the early days of my career had I longed to stay in such a first-class hotel. There we were the next day, tucked into the downy bedding at the St. Regis, eating breakfast in bed, reading the morning papers. The reviews were fabulous!

I couldn't believe my eyes. Eric Salzman of the *Herald Tribune* wrote: "Bethany Beardslee is Philomel." Well, golly, that's like when they say "Callas is Tosca."[63]

Howard Klein in *The New York Times* wrote: "It should be said that Miss Beardslee is unique among singers today. Her technique, taste, and sense of style are flawless. The unfailing beauty of her tone, sure sense of rhythm and pitch were marvels. She commanded attention like a sorceress weaving spells. It was a concert to remember."[64]

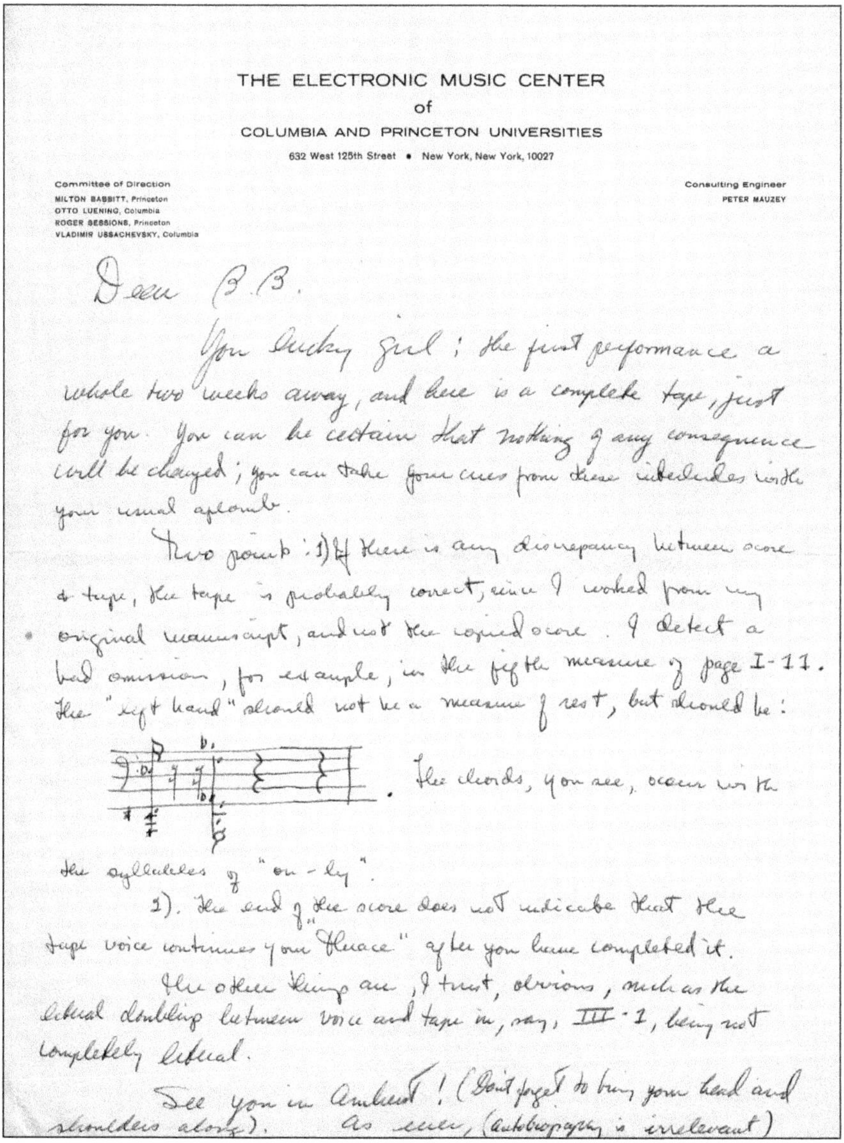

THE ELECTRONIC MUSIC CENTER
of
COLUMBIA AND PRINCETON UNIVERSITIES
632 West 125th Street • New York, New York, 10027

Committee of Direction
MILTON BABBITT, Princeton
OTTO LUENING, Columbia
ROGER SESSIONS, Princeton
VLADIMIR USSACHEVSKY, Columbia

Consulting Engineer
PETER MAUZEY

Dear B.B.

You lucky girl; the first performance a whole two weeks away, and here is a complete tape, just for you. You can be certain that nothing of any consequence will be changed; you can take your cues from these interludes with your usual aplomb.

Two points: 1) If there is any discrepancy between score & tape, the tape is probably correct, since I worked from my original manuscript, and not the copied score. I detect a bad omission, for example, in the fifth measure of page I-11. The "right hand" should not be a measure of rest, but should be:

[musical notation]. The chords, you see, occur with the syllables of "on-ly".

2). The end of the score does not indicate that the tape voice continues your "fluace" after you have completed it.

The other things are, I trust, obvious, such as the actual doubling between voice and tape in, say, III-1, being not completely literal.

See you in Amherst! (Don't forget to bring your head and shoulders along). As ever, (autobiography is irrelevant)

Figure 46. Letter from Milton while we were preparing *Philomel*. Courtesy of Betty Ann Duggan.

Figure 47. Me and the synthesizer.

I had sung my best that night. My voice responded to all of the coloratura in Handel's dramatic cantata and the long, sustained phrases in the Schubert. Mac's sonnets were beautiful. People rushed up to me backstage to congratulate me. Milton was besieged with compliments. Even Godfrey was beaming. We were the toast of New York City that night.

Needless to say, it was a moment to savor in many ways. I finally had a signature piece. I loved *Philomel* and had the opportunity of singing it many times again. With *Philomel*, Milton consolidated his reputation not only as an important composer but also as an innovator in using the synthesizer to make serious music. *Philomel* became his watershed work. As of 2017, it is in the canon of American music and in the Library of Congress's archive of historic recordings.

I would use *Philomel* often as the second half of my college recital programs, following a more traditional first half of Schubert, Brahms, or a song group from the Second Viennese School. I performed *Philomel* many times, as there was a great deal of demand for it. Everyone had read about this unique piece. *Philomel* became the most performed composition of the fifteen commissioned by the Ford Foundation.

·

In addition to Godfrey, other young composers, such as Mario Davidovsky, Bülent Arel, Vladimir Ussachevsky, Otto Luening, Pril Smiley, and Alice Shields, started writing for the RCA synthesizer at the Columbia-Princeton Electronic Music Center. Articles were written about the center, highlighting Milton's work. And I had my photo taken with the synthesizer. . . . I don't know who upstaged who.

CHAPTER THIRTY-NINE

A COMPOSER'S SINGER

I 've said it in other places, but it bears repeating: Being able to turn to a composer for coaching has been a defining aspect of my career. I found great coaches in composers: Jacques, Bob Helps, Yehudi Wyner, George Perle, Earl Kim, Mel Powell. I am a composer's singer. I always worked alone in the learning process, but so many of my accompanists were also composers and invaluable in the preparation and final details for performance.

With many of the works for voice and large ensemble, I had to wait for that first rehearsal to hear how the music all came together. It was an *aha!* moment and was typically an exciting, almost magical, epiphany. Only very rarely was I disappointed instead—as when I was working on Peter Maxwell Davies's *Revelation and Fall*. The piece had such a lovely vocal line, but I hated what happened when the instruments came in.

Composers would often attend the first rehearsal, where their attention would be primarily on coaching the instrumentalists. The instrumentalists were freelance, and mostly union, which customarily meant they hadn't even seen their parts before. As a singer, I could never have walked into a first rehearsal and sight-read. Bob was like me. As soloists we really had to know the score. But orchestra musicians generally see the music for the first time at the first rehearsal. Seldom do they work on their part beforehand. Freelance musicians like those I worked with were wonderful players and very competent sight-readers, yet this music had difficult rhythms and phrasing. From the contemporary composer's standpoint, getting a good

Figure 48. On the steps of the Schoenberg Institute in Los Angeles.

performance was perennially the greatest challenge of writing new music. Milton was always explicit that his interest in the synthesizer and recorded music came out of his ongoing quest for perfect performance in a culture of underrehearsing.

In his autobiography, *A Life in Pursuit of Music and Beauty*, Gunther Schuller "reveals" (because there is an element of dirty laundry to it) the frustration of a composer-instrumentalist in the face of the business of professional musicians:

> The vast majority of orchestra musicians, probably 98 percent, never look at a score, never study a score. These are generally fine musicians, who know their individual parts very well, but whose interest in the music

does not extend to the work as a whole. On the face of it that means that orchestra musicians are not interested in finding out what is in a score, how their part fits into the rest of the orchestration (harmonically, melodically, thematically, rhythmically, dynamically), how the composer put the whole piece together, and what a vast amount of vital information is actually notated in a score.[65]

Composers came to understand they had a better chance of getting a good performance when they were working with soloists. That is one of the main reasons so much chamber music was written during the twentieth century.

By the height of my career, I'd built up an enormous catalogue of composers. There were a number of composers whose work I premiered whom I didn't know personally—Wladimir Vogel, Gilbert Amy, Klaus Huber, Ruth Schönthal, Michel Philippot, Krzysztof Penderecki, and Heinz Holliger—a composer from Switzerland and a fine oboist. I sang the wonderful music of Nikos Skalkottas, who was perhaps the only composer whose work was already in the canon—but he was dead. Then there were very good friends— Earl Kim, Milton Babbitt, Bob Helps, the gentlemanly Claudio Spies (who adored Stravinsky), George Perle, handsome Mel Powell, Phil Batstone, and Jim Randall. Jim was Godfrey's dearest friend and an excellent theorist. Oddly, his music is hardly known, although he composed like crazy after he retired from teaching. Other composers were dear to people near me, such as Donald Sur, who was close to Earl Kim; or Frank Brickle and John Melby, friends of Godfrey who worked at the computer lab; or David Winkler, who studied with Jacques, and George Edwards, who taught at Columbia.

Ed Cone was another Princeton gentleman and a lifelong member of the music faculty there. He was also probably the richest guy in our circle. His family owned Cone Mills, a huge fabric manufacturer. Eddie was a wealthy kid who fell in love with composition as a student at Princeton. I had sung his music several times. Strangely enough, he even wrote a piece called *Philomela* for voice and instruments that I enjoyed singing—it was quite different from Milton's *Philomel*, and set to different poetry but still based on the Ovid myth. I think he kept a respectful distance, knowing that I was Milton's "girl singer." He was shy and gay, and I feel that it was years before we really got to know each other. We did make friends eventually, and in the 1980s we did a lieder recital together. His music was rather conservative, but he was a first-rate theory teacher. In 1968, he wrote a very good book, *Musical Form and Musical Performance*. Eddie's most important legacy, however, was the Cone Foundation, which he established in his will; it is to this day a huge supporter of new music. He was decent; he

Figure 49. Milton, Roger Sessions, and Ed Cone in a panel discussion at Amherst College, 1975. Courtesy of Amherst College Archives and Special Collections.

never played music politics, as Milton did, or used his fortune to promote himself, as Elliott Carter did. We all respected him.

The composer and conductor Lukas Foss was my biggest "intrigue" during that period. He was gorgeous and an irrepressible flirt, a wonderful pianist and a former boy genius. He had great gifts, but he somehow never managed to consolidate them. Even though Lukas had the benediction of the powerful Aaron Copland and Serge Koussevitzky, he never really found himself as a composer. He vacillated among too many different styles. There was no trajectory. When you listen to early Brahms and late Brahms, you can hear where he was going as a composer, getting richer and more mature—there's a continuum. Lukas was like a child, reckless in his discipline. He was a very good though erratic conductor. He absolutely butchered Milton's *Correspondences* in its 1968 Carnegie Hall debut. The last time we had coffee together, when I was in Buffalo to sing Leoš Janáček's *Mass*, I told Lukas, "You know what's wrong with you? You should have gone to Princeton and studied with Sessions!"

Although I knew all of these composers, it was working with them on their music that made a difference. What kind of person a composer is has nothing to do with the kind of music he or she writes. Earl Kim may have been the distinct exception to this rule. He was exactly like his music. One of Earl's signature phrases was, "I am reducing everything to its maximum."[66]

My reputation as a "composer's singer" was secured, which meant I was learning new music all the time and had many composer friends. My repertoire grew and was always revitalizing itself. More than all of that, I was working with this music and these composers because I wasn't afraid of taking a risk. I wanted the public to share my love of music of the moment. I was stubborn in my conviction that good new music was being composed and must be heard!

There were heavy-hitting funders in the sixties who shared my idea about new music. This was a golden period of funding for the arts. Other than Paul Fromm's vital support, the National Endowment for the Arts was established in 1965 under the Johnson administration. Nancy Hanks, who headed the new entity, was aggressive in building up government endowments. She increased NEA funding from $8 million to $114 million over her eight-year tenure. She was successful because she understood politics and diplomacy. It was said that she ran her organization like a well-oiled machine. The musicians couldn't have been more grateful. "A great orchestra or a fine museum is a natural resource, like a park," she said in a *New York Times* interview. "It must be maintained."[67] These were prosperous years in America. So much of the globe was still recovering from World War II. American goods provided a steady revenue stream, which trickled down to the arts!

The Rockefeller Foundation, which had been instrumental in building the NEA, and the Ford Foundation both actively supported performing groups, composers, and solo performers. In 1963 the Rockefeller Foundation announced a plan to finance composers-in-residence with several symphony orchestras. The idea was that composers would compose pieces for the orchestra, thereby teaching the players something about twentieth-century music and new playing techniques. This coincided with an increase in my own confidence in my ability to sing against a larger ensemble. My voice had become heavier over time, and I was appearing with orchestras, singing more Mozart and Handel as well as premiering new work.

John Huggler was selected as composer-in-residence at the Boston Symphony, where Erich Leinsdorf was the music director. As part of that project, John wrote a piece called *Sculptures*. Leinsdorf had put Mahler's Sixth Symphony on the same program, and I'm afraid John's piece, only twelve minutes long, looked a bit pale by comparison. Unfortunately, the critics were not enthusiastic about the work. Harold C. Schonberg complained in the *Times* that although the piece had "modern textures, it was basically tonal," and that was "one of those compromises that does not come off very well, being neither good traditional music nor good contemporary music."[68] Reviewers were getting more fluent in new music, criticizing it with more confidence and nuance. This was both good and bad. John Huggler caught it on the chin from Alan Rich in the *Herald Tribune* after the premiere of *Sculptures*:

> Mr. Huggler took his bow at the end of the piece wearing faded corduroy slacks and desert boots, which might be a testimonial to the new spirit in Boston, except that there wasn't very much new about the work itself. It is a 15 minute chunk of everybody's twelve-tone music these days, full of points made for coloristic purposes, attractive blocks of shifting harmony, a song for soprano in one movement that alternates long repetitions of one disjunct interval with passages on a monotone. Terribly old hat it was and rather black tie. Mr. Huggler was wearing the wrong costume.[69]

It wasn't just reviewers. Because of the recordings on big labels and the enthusiasm among conductors, major orchestras started playing more Berg, Webern, and Schoenberg. With Stanisław Skrowaczewski and the Minneapolis Philharmonic, I sang Marie in *Wozzeck*. Hermann Uhde, a fine singing actor, was Wozzeck. We did a semistaged version of the third act, which has the harrowing music that dramatizes Marie's murder, and the perfectly tragic ending—the child on stage alone singing his "hop hop."

If I could have sung any operatic roles, Berg's *Lulu* would have been my top choice. The music was close to my heart. At Berg's death, *Lulu* remained unfinished. Helene Berg insisted that only her husband's completed music could be performed, and so *Lulu* was mounted with a truncated third act. After Mrs. Berg died, it was discovered that the Austrian composer Friedrich Cerha had edited and completed the orchestration of the third act while Mrs. Berg was still alive. The composer George Perle and the musicologist Douglas Greene were instrumental in bringing this completed *Lulu* to light. In February 1979, Pierre Boulez conducted the complete *Lulu* for the first time at the Paris Opera. Teresa Stratas sang the role of Lulu; the opera was immediately recorded for Deutsche Grammophon. Opera houses began mounting complete productions of *Lulu*—this was a major addition to the opera canon. I had a chance in 1985 to hear Teresa Stratas sing Lulu at the Met with James Levine conducting. She was marvelous.

At the time, George told me to learn the role of Lulu, but I retreated. I was afraid of the whole opera scene—it was an entirely unfamiliar world. I know now that I could have done *Lulu* in one of the small European opera houses, as the music was well within my voice range and Berg's musical language was so familiar to me. But somewhere in the back of my mind, I could always hear Bernardo De Muro's prophetic words: "It eez a verreey pretteey voice, butta not for zee ohperah."

CHAPTER FORTY

DARMSTADT

1964

With its summer festival, Darmstadt, Germany, had become the European hotbed of new music. In my time, the festival was lorded over by such composers as Bruno Maderna, Karlheinz Stockhausen, Luciano Berio, Pierre Boulez, Henri Pousseur, and György Ligeti. The focus was definitively European; hardly any new American music was played. When Milton was finally invited to Darmstadt in the summer of 1964 to give a series of lectures, he asked me to come and perform *Vision and Prayer*. Godfrey and I were in England visiting family, so it was convenient enough. Godfrey and his mother flew with me to Darmstadt.

When we arrived, we found Milton quite perturbed by the whole Darmstadt scene. Boulez and Stockhausen seemed to be running things, but they did not always see eye to eye. Stockhausen was a rather intolerant character who had a famously erratic temperament. He did seem, however, to hold influence over a cadre of young composers. This young faction was unreservedly caught up in musical politics—and would loudly boo or cheer performances depending on which composer they were siding with. It was totally uncalled-for behavior. The performers were caught in the middle of a truly hostile scene.

I was booed when I sang *Vision and Prayer* at Darmstadt that summer. It was a shock, for I had never been booed before. And it was also, when I had some time to cool off, rather amusing. I later came to understand that I would have been booed no matter what I sang. It was a kneejerk response to anything American.

You have to remember that the best of Europe's musicians and intellectuals had fled to America in the 1930s and '40s. We took in many composers and performers, which meant that our young American composers significantly benefited from the teaching of wonderful European musicians—Ernst Křenek, Paul Hindemith, Darius Milhaud, Stefan Wolpe, and especially Arnold Schoenberg at UCLA. Young composers such as Leon Kirchner, Earl Kim, Dika Newlin, and Pat Carpenter were able to study with the Master. To my mind, we had the crème de la crème on our side of the Atlantic, but as far as this group was concerned, we were still a new frontier populated by cowboys and Indians. With the exception of Boulez, who'd been to the United States and certainly had an inkling of what was going on, I think they were totally unaware of the American new music scene.

It was the height of the Cold War, and the sentiment at home and abroad was insular and basically xenophobic. Generally speaking, the scores for new music by American composers were not available in Europe. In London, I went to Foyles, a major music store, to see what they had to represent American music and only found two composers—namely Elliott Carter and Aaron Copland. I suspected that Elliott, who was independently wealthy, funded his own international distribution. Copland was a celebrity. Because of the political mood, governmental interest in supporting cultural exchange in the early sixties was minimal and did nothing to boost our profile abroad. In 1963, the *New York Times* cultural reporter Henry Raymont wrote:

> Washington has only allotted $2,500,000 to finance a cultural exchange program. This is the amount Congress authorized the State Department to use for cultural presentations overseas. [The State Department] has fashioned a program intended to be modest and noncontroversial of representative American artists and entertainers to foreign audiences. Thus it includes no major symphony orchestra or opera company. Nor are there any spectacular innovations, such as a sample of electronic music or of the new generation of singers and artists who have impressed many critics as unrivaled for their technique and musicianship.[70]

That year, my manager, Jay Hoffman, approached Columbia Records about recording *Philomel*. Debby Ishlon, who had been instrumental in producing the Stravinsky and Craft recordings, had since left the label, and Columbia was reluctant to take the risk. They wrote:

> The suggestion in your letter to Mr. Lieberson that Columbia record Miss Beardslee in Milton Babbitt's "Philomel" and "Vision and

Prayer" is a good one and we have just given it full consideration in our Masterworks department. Unfortunately, our conclusion is that we are unable to undertake this at the present for reasons of budget and very full commitments with our own roster. We regret this in view of Miss Beardslee's superb performances for Columbia in the past and because of our continuing interest in bringing important contemporary music to the public. Etc.[71]

I have often wondered since then whether they were afraid of putting a piece of electronic music into their catalog at the time—or whether it had to do with the fact that I would have asked for an outrageous royalty again. Was it an artistic or economic decision? Regardless, they missed an opportunity, for *Philomel* was the only piece from the Ford Foundation project that had made an impression on the public.

Meanwhile, the composer Lukas Foss, the music director of the Buffalo Philharmonic at the time, was fishing around about me through Milton. Lukas and I had met many years earlier at Tanglewood, but he wanted an insider's perspective. Milton told him, "If you want Bethany, engage her to sing Mozart. She would never say no." He was right. I jumped at Lukas's invitation to sing the role of Ilia in Mozart's *Idomeneo*, one of Mozart's late operas, full of wonderful choruses, arias, and solo quartets. I was at once appalled and secretly amused to see the biographical notes that Lukas had invented for me on the glossy Buffalo Philharmonic program: "Bethany Beardslee has built an enviable reputation singing Oratorio and some of the more important world premieres of contemporary music. She comes to Buffalo for this performance from England where she has been working with the noted British composer Benjamin Britten."[72] Benjamin Britten! Fantastical. I wonder whether Lukas thought the Buffalo audience was too provincial to be impressed with anything less and gullible enough to believe anything he wrote.

A month later, Foss asked me back to sing *Messiah*. On several occasions Lukas asked me to perform with his group of contemporary players, also based in Buffalo. The group experimented with improvisation, a medium I was not terribly interested in, and so I declined. Lukas hired me several more times over the next few years. His interest wasn't exclusively in my singing, and as the state of his marriage got rockier, his flirtation got a bit too insistent.

At the time, his wife, Cornelia, a visual artist, had gotten involved with Glenn Gould. But Lukas was a rake—even without the excuse of his wife's exotic affair. He was also quite good looking, and for a period he was fun to flirt with. The first time I went up to Buffalo, Lukas and Cornelia were driving me to a reception after the concert, and Lukas commented to her that I "looked like a Botticelli." Cornelia agreed with him and then added, "I know what you're thinking. Behave." I found the whole dynamic to be bizarre.

I never would have actually had an affair. It would have been immoral. Godfrey and I were really straight. He knew all about Lukas's attentions and for the most part didn't think it was worth worrying about. From Godfrey's perspective, Lukas was "beneath discussion."

Lukas and I were friends. I found his attention flattering but not compelling. When I heard someone in *Downton Abbey* described as "irritating and beguiling in equal measure," I couldn't help but think it was a perfect way to describe our relationship!

When Lukas was the director of the French-American Festival at Lincoln Center he asked me to take on Boulez again. He wanted me to sing *Improvisation II sur Mallarmé,* which I had performed before with Jim Bolle in Chicago. I was happy to sing it, for I found it a very pretty piece. The vocal line is quite effective against an accompaniment of piano, harp, celesta, bells, vibraphone, and gong. All of the instruments are treated like percussion, creating an unusual, almost impressionistic, transparent texture that complimented my voice.

The players for that performance were from the Group for Contemporary Music of Columbia University; Richard Dufallo conducted. This group was an early model of the solutions that composers came up with to get their music heard. As I have said, it was founded by Charles Wuorinen and Harvey Sollberger in 1962 and was the first contemporary music ensemble run by composers and based out of a university. Sollberger directed the group for twenty-seven years. Later, they mounted a number of meaningful concerts of new music—their own music and that of others.

One evening during the early 1960s, I had the occasion to be invited to dinner with Edgard and Louise Varèse in their charming historic home on Sullivan Street in Greenwich Village. This cluster of brick colonials shared a beautiful, parklike backyard that extended the whole block. Edgard had a recording studio on the ground floor, and the couple lived in the parlor level.

Edgard was on a big bandwagon for getting contemporary music performed and had clout in the community. He was also one of my big supporters early on. He came to all of the ISCM concerts in the 1950s, and because he was French, Jacques and I had several occasions to be invited to dinner with him and Louise. The two men would sit and talk French while Louise and I chatted. Over dinner that night, Varèse told me about a piece he was writing for me based on texts from Anaïs Nin's *House of Incest*.

Varèse's reputation grew quite a bit after he died, but even then and despite really liking him as a person, I thought he was a terribly overrated composer. He was an outspoken, iconoclastic musician who really wanted to explore the newest boundaries of music. He was particularly interested in working with taped sounds, and was using noises from the port in Brooklyn in the early days of experimenting with taped sounds. He was a visionary of new music, but he was not, in my judgment, on the musical continuum of Bach, Beethoven, Brahms, Babbitt. Dare I say it was a relief that he never finished the Anaïs Nin piece before he died? But I was touched nonetheless by his dedication, and I sentimentally kept the sheet of stationery on which he had outlined the instrumental and percussion assembly for the work.

Varèse paid me perhaps the nicest compliment I've ever received. He said about me that I was "a musician who sings."

CHAPTER FORTY-ONE

AARON COPLAND, *IMENEO*, AND MAX

1965

Aaron Copland was working on a series of television programs for WGBH, the PBS station in Boston. The series was called *Music in the 20s*, and he asked me to do portions of *Pierrot* for it. There were twelve episodes in the series, and I appeared on the first. It was produced by public programing and ran on the six stations that made up the Eastern Educational Network, and it was carefully archived. I recently found the whole series rereleased on DVD and was able to see it again. Watching your younger self performing so late in your life is quite an experience. It didn't exactly live up to my notion of being an old movie star! I sat there in my big armchair and saw this young me appear on the screen, and I could only think, "Well, she certainly hams it up." I had no idea that I assumed so many different facial expressions when I was on stage. I wasn't even singing *Pierrot*, I was doing *Sprechstimme*!

Copland had studied with Nadia Boulanger in Paris—as had Virgil Thomson—and he represented the conservative side of American music. He became a powerful figure to young composers and helped many to establish themselves. He was a gentleman in all respects; even if he wasn't part of the twelve-tone movement, he never criticized his colleagues who wrote in that tradition. His exploration of the 1920s, and the height of the Second Viennese School, in the documentary was really a quite comprehensive and earnest exploration of the period. Late in his career, like Stravinsky, Copland too would venture into serialism.

That season (1963), I sang quite a lot of Handel and Haydn with orchestra. I sang Handel's *Judas Maccabeus* and the Haydn "Lord Nelson" Mass. Coloratura suited me, and this music was full of it. Princeton University mounted Handel's opera *Imeneo* under the direction of Merrill Knapp, in what was rumored to be its first US performance. More important, I finally got to be onstage, singing a true operatic part, in full costume, with an orchestra in the pit. I loved the acting and the singing.

I would tell Godfrey later that I thought I could have sung in small European opera houses, like the ones in Glyndebourne and Salzburg. We had been to Glyndebourne in Sussex several times on our summer visits to London, and I found the European houses had an intimacy that the Metropolitan lacked. Given the right venue, my voice would have been perfect for certain operas!

Another great gentleman advocator of new music had come into my life the year before—although at the time I didn't know what a huge career my friend Max was destined for. I first met Peter Maxwell Davies in Princeton in 1962, where he'd come on a two-year Harkness Fellowship, a program set up to reciprocate the Rhodes Scholarships. In those early years, if Max was known for anything, it was as "Britain's angry young man of modern music." But his hunger and commitment to dissonance and systems wouldn't have distinguished him at Princeton as much as it might have at Manchester. In his March 2016 obituary for Max, Ivan Hewett summed up Max's music this way:

> Though he never said as much, Maxwell Davies seemed to believe that if the constructive basis of a piece of music was strict enough, comprehension on the part of the listener would be guaranteed. . . . The characteristic Maxwell Davies "sound" is very distant from the pointilliste, splintered musical world of the European avant-gardists. It is a tensile, highly dissonant combination of lines, etched in primary colours, with absolutely no harmonic or colouristic padding to ingratiate the listener.[73]

In 1965, Max and two fellow up-and-coming British composers, Harrison Birtwistle (who had a Harkness Fellowship the year after Max) and Alexander Goehr, mounted a summer music festival at Wardour Castle in Tisbury, Wiltshire, in southwest England. Max was after me to come perform. I wanted to do *Pierrot* with Jacques, but the Melos Ensemble, whom

Max had contracted to perform with me, were reluctant to work with him. They were wonderful players who had been Jacques's core ensemble in the years that he had worked at the BBC. But I gathered they'd had enough

After many letters back and forth, we finally came to an agreement about fees and programming. We would make a summer trip out of it. I took along my niece Gretchen Beardslee (Walter's daughter) to help with the boys, still only seven and five years old. Godfrey's father let me have a car to get around and a beautiful flat on Cadogan Place in central London, which would be our home for six weeks of work and visiting the family.

Godfrey, as usual, stayed home in Princeton to work on a massive set of piano variations on *Jingle Bells* that he had promised the children. Suffice it to say that what started out as a notion one Christmas Day captured his imagination and turned into a thirty-minute piece, comparable to the *Diabelli Variations* of Beethoven. In any case, my husband hated to travel. It disrupted his work habits. I loved traveling. I liked to just sink into the seat of an airplane, leave my domestic duties behind, and look forward to singing.

When we arrived in London, Max told me he had also set up recitals for me on the BBC Third Programme as well as the festival. I would have the opportunity to do *Philomel* and a recital of American art songs. Stephen Pruslin, a Princeton alum who had taken up residence in England, would be my pianist both at Wardour and on the BBC.

Performing *Pierrot* with the Melos Ensemble at the summer festival, under the baton of Edward Downes, was a high point. I did it in costume and, for the first time, cabaret style, sitting on a stool with a glittering crescent moon in the background. This was how Schoenberg had conceived *Pierrot* for Albertine Zehme, the actress who'd commissioned it—a true cabaret piece.

In 1972, Boulez asked me to perform *Pierrot* with him in Cleveland, using that same intimate cabaret-style staging. It was a much bigger hall, and we had Schoenberg's orchestral tone poem, *Pelleas und Melisande*, on the same program. For *Pierrot*, Boulez put the players behind a screen on stage and stuck me on a stool under a long spotlight. The stage of Orchestra Hall in Cleveland is vast, and without the glittering scimitar moon behind me, a costume, or a cozy hall, it just didn't have the same magic as it had at Wardour Castle. I never called out Boulez on his theatrical misjudgment, but I wasn't thrilled about it, either.

Baird and Christopher had a wonderful summer in Tisbury on the farm where we were staying during Max's festival. The countryside was postcard beautiful. The farm had animals and lots of activity to keep them occupied. The woman who ran the farm made the most wonderful homemade marmalade, something the British are famous for. (I still have her recipe.) She was warm and friendly, the sort children liked to be around. A young Frenchman with a guitar on his back fell for Gretchen, and he even followed us to London after the festival ended.

Once back in London, Max introduced me to my producer, Stephen Plaistow of the BBC. Max helped with these BBC broadcasts, especially with getting a perfect balance for the broadcast of *Philomel*. Steve and Max would come over for "tea," which consisted of the most outlandish display of pastries from Harrods's food department. Harrods, the elegant department store, was not far from where we were staying.

In later years, Max would form his own contemporary music ensemble, called the Fires of London, modeled on the *Pierrot* ensemble. Like Harvey Sollberger and Charles Wuorinen with the Group for Contemporary Music at Columbia University, Max shrewdly set up the perfect way to distinguish himself among emerging composers. He was a very ambitious musician. The Fires not only provided a venue for his music but also established him in the public eye. They gave concerts in England, throughout Europe, and in the United States. Their programs featured only new music, much of which was composed by Max or one of his colleagues.

The night before our departure from London, Daddy came to say goodbye. I handed over all of the English pounds I'd earned from my engagements, which made him laugh. I thought it only fair and a pittance compared to all he had done. Daddy enjoyed meeting Gretchen, who showed a real interest in painting and had raved about the wonderful collection of Turners we'd seen at the Tate Gallery. Daddy appreciated this, because Turner was his favorite English painter. Daddy stayed quite a while that evening, reclining on our bed while I packed and Gretchen ironed. I think he enjoyed just being with us, and a part somehow of our domestic chores.

We were all sorry to leave London, but I was eager to get home too. It had been my first summer in England without Godfrey, and I missed him.

CHAPTER FORTY-TWO

BELLE MEAD

Back in New Jersey, the four of us were beginning to outgrow our Hodge Road cottage. The space had gotten too small for us and two children. Because of his usual nighttime work, Godfrey often slept through the morning. But that was when I liked to practice, and the children had to play out on the patio. We both knew the cottage was too cramped. We needed a bigger house, perhaps something with a separate studio for Godfrey.

Daddy offered to help us with a down payment, and we began looking for something better suited to our needs. We found a house on River Road, beside the Millstone River and the Delaware-Raritan Canal in Belle Mead, near Griggstown, just fifteen minutes from Princeton. I could carpool with other mothers to get the boys to Princeton Day School. Most important, our noise problems were solved! The house was set high on a hill and had a separate room over the garage that Godfrey could use as a studio. There was a huge living room, 30 by 20 feet, with towering ceilings, that I could work in. There was even a large yard for the children to play in and a hill that was perfect for sledding when it snowed. Once Baird went sledding all the way down the hill into the tiny brook at the bottom. He actually landed in the brook—not much fun on a cold winter's day. In the summer they would slide down the hill in cardboard boxes. I remember planting so many daffodils on that hill that Ellen Faber called me the Daffodil Queen of Belle Mead.

The Millstone River was notorious for flooding homes. It had a shallow bed and when there were successive rainfalls, it turned into a floodplain. But we never had a problem. Our neighbors, the Shermans, lived next

Figure 50. The living room at Belle Mead. Notice the towel over the lamp. Godfrey always did that to cut the glare when he was reading. It's a wonder the house didn't go up in smoke. You can also see his beloved Shetland wool ottoman here—he always wanted to be cozy.

to the canal running parallel to the river—the river spilled into the canal and flooded their house. Baird and Chris would often be on hand to help them move their things upstairs when they flooded. After that happened one time too many, the Shermans abandoned that house and moved into Princeton.

Our new home was an old farmhouse, built around 1900. The people who'd lived there before us had given it a Swiss chalet look. There were carved Breughel-style heads set into the unusual wooden mantel over the large fireplace in the living room. The wall sconces revealed portions of an oil painting, blackened with age. A massive wrought-iron chandelier that had never been wired for electricity was suspended in the middle of the living room. On special occasions we'd set candles in its many holders. With the chandelier lit and a fire going, our house took on an especially festive air during the holidays.

As I said before, my husband loved to play games in the evening after supper. Because of Godfrey, I learned to be an atrocious chess player, a fair poker player, a decent bridge player, and a good player of Broker—a stock market game invented by two bright fellows from MIT. We also played Diplomacy, Stratego—which the children played too—and a family board game that Godfrey invented and called "Escalate." Escalate was a war game and was named after a term we heard in the news from Vietnam. The children loved these evenings when their father was available.

Godfrey's working in the studio over the garage was a short-lived idea, as he kept coming back to the main house for coffee. When he worked he chain-smoked Gauloises and drank too much coffee. It wasn't a good combination for anyone, but he was young and felt invincible.

In the fall of 1966 Daddy passed away suddenly one evening, sitting in his chair. We'd had no sense that our time with him was so limited. Godfrey flew to London for the funeral, and I stayed home with the children. Godfrey was never able to express his feelings on how his father's death affected him—the English do not express their feelings very well. But I missed Francis Winham terribly, especially when we went back to England for family visits. It was never the same after that, and Godfrey never wanted to go at all.

That year brought another era to an end. In 1966, the doors of the old Metropolitan Opera House on 39th Street were closed for the last time. It was a nostalgic event, featuring a gala concert of young and old divas singing great farewell arias. There was a huge spread in Life magazine, with wonderful photos of the performers, arms entwined and singing "Auld Lang Syne." I remember one photo in particular of Licia Albanese kissing the stage floor goodbye. Enrico Caruso, Giovanni Martinelli, Elisabeth Rethberg, Lotte Lehman, Amelita Galli-Curci, Kirsten Flagstad, Rosa Ponselle, Eleanor Steber, and many, many other great singers had built their careers there. The "old Met," with its horseshoe interior and red velvet seats, had been built in the late nineteenth century and was modeled after the old European opera houses. Months after the farewell event, it met the wrecking ball and was demolished American style. It should have been preserved. Instead we have a skyscraper in its place.

In the meantime, I had the chance to sing Alban Berg's beautiful *Altenberg Lieder* with the St. Louis Symphony under Eleazar de Carvalho. Apparently Carvalho and his wife had loved my Craft recording. I also sang in Webern's *Kantate II*, op. 31. The *Altenberg* were so successful that we repeated them in encore. These songs are beautiful and too rarely performed live. The glowing review by Clark Mitze opened with the line:

"The strangest concert in the recent history of the St. Louis Orchestra was given Saturday evening in Kiel." At the last minute, Carvalho omitted the Schoenberg piece that he'd programmed, which allowed him to repeat the second half of the program—the difficult part: "Such intellectual serial-type music defies correlation to the cantatas of earlier composers—at least at surface hearing. It is fiendishly difficult to perform and only the very brave or the very foolish will attempt it." The strange part of the evening, according to the reviewer, was that half the audience fled before the encore, but for those who stayed: "The repetition was so magnificent that the remaining few gave her a true ovation. This was equaled by the applause and appreciation of the musicians on stage as they recognized the true artistry of her performance."[74]

Jean Martinon, music director of the Chicago Symphony Orchestra at the time, invited me to do the *Lulu Suite* with him in Chicago and Milwaukee. He'd heard me previously, when I performed *Pierrot* with a chamber group made up of players from his orchestra. The concert was a lovely production. The dramatic music is harrowing even unstaged: "Miss Beardslee, who had coped superbly with the high tessitura of her part, and its jagged leaps, also interjected Lulu's cries at the moment of the trollop's stabbing by Jack the Ripper. It was somebody's shrewd idea to have the soprano let out her bloodcurdling screams while seated, thereby taking the audience by surprise and multiplying the shock effect."[75] The same reviewer, though, lamented the poor attendance: "Programming such a work, modern classic though it may be, is still risky in Chicago. Bizet and Handel were the other two composers of the night, but many patrons stayed home." This music was still not standard listening fare for audiences in the 1960s.

Both concerts stand out in my memory as triumphs. I didn't notice the audiences the way the critics did. I was singing beloved pieces from my repertoire with extraordinary musicians and conductors. The Chicago Symphony is a great orchestra. It was a tremendous privilege to appear with them. I was delighted to return later in the season to sing the *Three Fragments from "Wozzeck."*

In early 1966, Lukas called me to do Madame Golden Trill in *The Impresario*, a short comic Mozart opera. He was mounting a concert version in Buffalo and then at Avery Fisher Hall in New York. I turned it down at first because the part was for an extremely high coloratura, running around on high Es and Fs. I did think, however, that the other soprano role would be perfect. Alas, my friend Helen Boatwright had

Figure 51. Practicing in the living room at Belle Mead.

already been assigned to that part, so I let Lukas talk me into taking Madame Golden Trill against my better judgment.

When Lukas picked Helen and me up for the rehearsal in Buffalo, he leaned right over and kissed me full on the mouth. Helen was certainly taken aback, and I guess I was in a silly mood, because I just laughed and kept laughing as Lukas drove us to the rehearsal, taking every route that didn't involve the actual road—such as someone's lawn. The whole thing was kind of a disaster. Cornelia Foss deliberately spilled her drink on my new Ambos formal in the reception hall (it was the dress I wore for the PBS program with Aaron Copland), and Lukas wouldn't stay away.

Even though Godfrey wrote new, more appropriate cadenzas for one of my arias, I shouldn't have been singing that part. The tessitura and the role were all wrong. The critics were kind but honest, and I had to vow to myself that I'd never make this mistake again. My passion for Mozart led me right into a big professional blunder.

Mozart was hardly ruined for me, though. I'd had a wonderful success the summer before singing Mozart songs with Jörg Demus at the annual Mozart Summer Festival in Philharmonic Hall. And I'd sung two of Mozart's concert arias, namely "Bella mia fiamma, addio!" and "Ch'io mi scordi di te?" with Jim Bolle at Monadnock. The truth was that I absolutely loved to sing Mozart. As Milton had already predicted, I would always perk up my ears if Mozart was on the program. He is one of my favorite composers, and he adored the soprano voice. Of course all of those high pitches were half a tone lower in Mozart's day. Many were written for Aloysia Weber, the famous coloratura, his wife Constanze (Aloysia's sister), or Nancy Storace, the original Susanna in *The Marriage of Figaro*. I've always held that the Mozart concert arias are full of every technical hurdle a soprano can confront. I am of the opinion that if you can sing those concert arias beautifully, you can sing anything.

CHAPTER FORTY-THREE

GODFREY AND THE COMPUTER

In 1967 Godfrey abandoned the RCA synthesizer for the computer. Up to this point, he'd been making frequent trips into the city to work on the Mark II Synthesizer at the Columbia-Princeton Electronic Music Center, but now he wanted to learn more about what seemed to be the unlimited possibilities of the computer. Hubert (Tuck) Howe and Godfrey began working in an early computer language, to develop the Music 4B program and its successor, Music IBVF, foundational early music software. I remember him telling me that they were going to figure out how to make computers talk and sing, and I got upset because I had no intention of being unemployed. He also tried to convince Milton, who'd become the composer most tightly associated with the Mark II after *Vision and Prayer*, to leave the synthesizer and come over to computers. But Milton protested, "You can't teach an old dog new tricks!"

Godfrey and Tuck, joined by Jim Randall, worked on the IBM 7094 at Princeton—another machine that took up an entire room in the basement of the engineering building. The IBM 7094 was cutting-edge technology; other machines were installed at MIT and NASA. Unlike the Mark II, this computer also needed constant icy air conditioning to keep its processors from overheating. It wasn't until the late 1970s that these machines started getting somewhat smaller, which isn't to say that they no longer needed dedicated rooms to house what now fits in a laptop.

Even if Milton was intractable on the matter, many of Godfrey's colleagues were interested in the developments at the Princeton sound lab— Mark Zuckerman, Joel Gressel, Richard Meckstroth, Richard Cann, John

Melby, Charles Dodge, Frank Brickle, and Paul Lansky. However, from Godfrey's perspective, perhaps the most important one was Professor Kenneth "Ken" Steiglitz of the Electrical Engineering Department, who tutored Godfrey on the principles of engineering that related to this new field of music technology. Ken and Godfrey became very dear friends. For years, Tuesday-evening dinners with Ken Steiglitz were a sacred men's night out. The two men relaxed in town and talked shop.

During that period Godfrey and Jim Randall would make frequent trips to Bell Labs to consult with Max Matthews. Max would show them computer programming. Bell Labs was the nexus of everything happening in early electronics. Godfrey grew interested in analog-to-digital conversion. He'd bring home discarded computer paper for the children to draw on—giant stacks of connected pages, with feeder pin holes all along the edges to run through early printers. He'd say to me, "Darling, one day there will be a computer in every home in America." I laughed, not believing a word of it. And if he were here today, he'd say, "I told you so!"

Meanwhile, I was busy with older technologies. Lukas Foss called on me to perform some early orchestral songs of Webern at Carnegie Hall. They had been written in 1913 or 1914, and I don't think they had an opus number. I took the xeroxed score I'd been sent to show Earl Kim, my coach. Composers are always fascinated to see unknown works by a major composer. Earl's fascination was contagious. He set about analyzing the music and coached me on how to express its beauty.

I would always go to Earl for help preparing any orchestral pieces. Godfrey wasn't interested in coaching me, but I really did feel that I needed feedback. I needed, too, to hear how the piece sounded. Earl was an excellent pianist and could help me hear the whole. He was also a terrific coach. I remember him in particular helping me with Desdemona's aria from *Otello* when I sang it with Jim Bolle in Chicago. When we performed the Schubert songs together, Earl taught me that the music could bear much more *pianissimo* than I'd thought. We worked in the same way on orchestra pieces. Earl was convinced that most singers just yell, and so they can't take advantage of their whole *piano* dynamic. When it came to working with an orchestra, Earl taught me that conductors would follow my lead and bring the instruments down. Along with Jacques, Bob Helps, and Yehudi Wyner, Earl was one of my most important influences. I missed him terribly when he left Princeton for Harvard later that same year.

For a period, I thought I might be premiering unknown Webern works—we performers love to be part of a premiere—but I found out that

Lukas had already performed them in Buffalo with the marvelous Marni Nixon. After the concert, Godfrey and Gwen, who happened to be visiting us in Belle Mead, came backstage. This was the night that Godfrey's temper flared about Lukas's obvious interest in me, just around the time that Cornelia was gearing up to leave him for Glenn Gould. Godfrey flagrantly snubbed Lukas. It was all terribly embarrassing. Because Gwen was there and I had to get on a plane with the orchestra right after the concert to perform the Webern again in Montreal, Godfrey and I weren't able to talk about it. It nagged at me while I was away, and when I got back Godfrey and I talked. I reassured him that he needn't worry about Lukas. He was angry and talked about me as if I were his property, but at the end I felt as if we'd closed the matter.

The Foss marriage was defined by an unusual dedication. Lukas was a noted womanizer, and Cornelia had a famous affair. But even when Cornelia was packing their car and children up to move to Canada in order to be closer to Glenn Gould, Lukas just stood out in the driveway, calmly watching her. She asked him, "Why are you smiling? I'm leaving you for Glenn." He answered, "Don't be ridiculous. You'll be back." In the aftermath, he went out of his way never to estrange her and was vindicated. After four and a half years as Gould's consort, she returned to Lukas, and they stayed together until he died in 2009.

But Lukas kept after me. I was set to do *Philomel* in Buffalo as part of a big festival supported by a grant from the Rockfeller Foundation. Sylvia Babbitt had already warned me to stay away from Lukas, and Milton hovered over me during the entire Buffalo sojourn. I nonetheless quite enjoyed the whole event. I got to spend some time talking to John Cage and couldn't help finding him charming. We talked about his new hobby of studying various species of hallucinogenic mushrooms, with which he was totally fascinated. He had a soft, smiling voice and seemed so pleased with life in general, I don't think he would have noticed if a bomb went off next to him. He talked about Zen, meditation, health foods—you know the type.

A perfect antidote to my Mozart blunder: Paul Paray, conductor of the Detroit Symphony, gave me the opportunity to sing Claude Debussy's *The Blessed Damozel*. Now *that* score was just right for my voice! Being in Detroit, I also had the chance to visit Aunty Verna, Uncle Jay's wife, who was still living there. She was amazingly well preserved, immaculately dressed, and very proud of my career. We went out for drinks after the second performance and reminisced about the wonderful days at East St. Joe and holiday visits.

In the meantime, Jacques had returned to the States from England with his new German wife, Margarit, and their daughter, Caroline. (Jacques *was* a father type in the end!) He had resigned from the BBC and was now teaching at the New England Conservatory. The faculty in Boston were urging him to conduct—he'd grown into quite a masterful conductor—but I think Jacques really wanted to leave the performing world for good. After all, William Glock at the BBC had given him freedom to program contemporary music, and he wouldn't have left the BBC if he had still wanted to program and conduct. That said, we had a marvelous *Pierrot* reunion over the summer at Harvard's Sanders Theatre; Jacques gathered the same players from our Camera Concert, Bob Helps played the piano, and Jacques conducted. It was just like old times.

CHAPTER FORTY-FOUR

MARLBORO AND PENDERECKI

1 9 6 7 – 6 8

I spent the summer of 1967 at the Marlboro Music Festival in Marlboro, Vermont. The children were off at sleep-away camp, and Mother came with me. She made it a practice to visit her children every summer, to leave the heat of Lake Worth, Florida, where she and Perry were now living permanently. Between rehearsals and concerts, there was music in the air twelve hours a day, so Mother couldn't have been happier. She was especially flattered when the pianist Rudolph Serkin, one of the festival's founders, went out of his way to welcome her.

Meals at Marlboro were just great. Huge bowls of freshly picked local raspberries, wonderful food, great poker players, spitball fights at lunch time, and such camaraderie as only performing musicians do well. Serkin set the tone with a kind of shy, sincere charisma. It was an exhilarating, hard-working summer camp set against a perfectly lovely backdrop of rolling hills and dairy cows. But it was hardly a paradise for new music.

At Marlboro I sang Bach, Mahler, and lots of chamber works. I got to know the composer Leon Kirchner, the Italian violinist Pina Carmirelli, the Uruguayan pianist Luis Batlle, and many others. Leon and Earl Kim had been students of Schoenberg. Leon's music was, in fact, very Schoenbergian in style, whereas Earl had taken his composition in a totally different direction. It's a credit to Schoenberg as a teacher that his students were independent thinkers. But for Leon, most of the players there were performing the classics.

One night as I was singing a group of Mahler songs, the cellist and conductor Pablo Casals, who must have been ninety, started grunting. He was in the front row, and I found the grunting quite annoying, to say the least. I complained to Leon afterward about this insulting behavior. He replied that I should be honored: "The old boy grunts when he is really enjoying a performance." Well, that's the strangest way I can imagine of showing approval, I thought and laughed.

According to the New York Times, "Marlboro came to stand for musicianship of a special ardent type."[76] I think it's safe to say that the Marlboro aesthetic on the whole was classic, old-fashioned, mainstream. There were marvelous musicians there, a charming environment, and dedication to classical chamber music, but except for Leon, most players had conservative tastes. The politics, under Serkin and Casals, were not congenial to contemporary composers. They paid token attention to new music by performing pieces that were contemporary classics, such as Schoenberg's Verklärte Nacht. Casals had actually refused to play a cello concerto that Schoenberg had written for him—a great disappointment for the composer.

The festival also always hosted a young composer in residence. This was good—they couldn't entirely ignore new music. That summer it was Henry Weinberg, a Princeton colleague of Godfrey and a student of Sessions, whose music I was happy to get to know. He became one of my composer friends. Henry had three songs for me to sing, so I enlisted Richard Goode, who could sight-read and play almost anything, to do them with me. Thankfully, Henry was on hand to give us plenty of help. I don't believe Richard had encountered anything as rhythmically difficult as Henry's music before. I found the songs beautiful and well composed, but without a doubt, the rhythms were difficult.

Henry was an especially great raconteur. Because he was gay, a terrific gourmand, and constantly fighting his weight, he reminded me of my old friend Ben Weber. In later years he would live with the famous Italian chef Giuliano Bugialli and help him to publish a large collection of gorgeously illustrated cookbooks. The two ran famous cooking schools in New York and Florence, Italy. They also had a passion for buying property, especially in New York, that they would renovate, live in for a while, and then flip for a nice profit. Henry should have composed more, but his new life with Giuliano brought those creative expenditures to an end—a shame.

In November of 1967, the conductor Stanisław Skrowaczewski, with whom I'd sung *Wozzeck* three years earlier, contacted me. He wanted me to perform in the US debut of Krzysztof Penderecki's *St. Luke Passion* with the Minneapolis Symphony Orchestra. It was a flashy premiere. The new piece had had a lot of success in Europe and arrived stateside with due fanfare. After the New York premiere, in a gushing appraisal for *New York* magazine that began "I had predicted months ago that Penderecki's *Passion* would be the season's most distinguished event. I retract nothing," Alan Rich wrote:

> The *Passion* is an extraordinary piece, powerful, genuinely moving, able to engage both mind and gut. At a time when non-involvement is often prized, it is an extremely involved piece. I think, for example, that its startling ending, that great gleaming diatonic chord, constitutes for the composer a genuine Statement on the import of the events he has dealt with in his score: not an ending (as in Bach's *Passions*) but a beginning.[77]

I imagine Skrowaczewski wanted to perform and celebrate a fellow Polish composer. But Skrowaczewski was an excellent composer in his own right and by the night of the performance, I dearly wished I had been singing Skrowaczewski's music instead.

Penderecki's score itself was not hard; however, I remember working terribly hard on a complex cadenza that made absolutely no musical sense. At the first rehearsal I proudly sang it for Penderecki and was pleased that it came off note perfect.

"Oh *no!*" he cried—to my total dismay. "It must only be a *smear* of those pitches," he corrected me. Musically, it seemed he wanted the opposite of the precision I had worked so hard to achieve, both for his piece and for all of the new music I sang. What's more, any direction indicating his intention to have a *smear* was neither notated nor specified. As a performer and on principle, I always put great faith in what I could see in the score—it was why I was a "composer's singer." I honored the notes as they were written and always assumed that the composer meant exactly what he'd written—except in this case, where I was supposed to intuit that Penderecki wanted a smeared cadenza. All that great effort in vain. I was furious.

Despite its phenomenal success, I was never impressed by this piece. When I performed the *Passion* again with Robert Shaw and the Atlanta Symphony, then again in Toronto, I sang every pitch in the cadenza *as it was written*, because Penderecki wasn't there to correct me. No one seemed to notice the missing "smear."

The next summer, 1968, I returned to Marlboro and this time the composer in residence was Fred Lerdahl, a twenty-five-year-old Princeton graduate student. He was working on a chamber piece on texts from Joyce's *Finnegans Wake* and wanted me to sing it. Fred's music wasn't easy, and the piece was long. With all of my other commitments, I had misgivings. He wanted the first performance to be at Marlboro, which meant that time was very short. I like to learn slowly or at least at my own pace and would never have been able to learn *Wake* without Fred's help. We both were under the gun—Fred was still handing me sheets of score at the last minute. Jacques had said that you needed "at least one hour of rehearsal for every minute of music. Less than that, and you cannot do justice to the piece. You also need good players."[78] Fortunately we had excellent players for the premiere on August 14: Hidetaro Suzuki on violin; Scott Nickrenz on viola; Ronald Leonard, cello; Heidi Lehwalder, harp; and three percussionists: John Wyre, Russell Hartenberger, and William Cahn. Fred conducted.

It was such a rush and bumble to learn that piece that I was very gratified to be able to sing it again a year later on a recording for the AR Contemporary Music Project, which was a collaboration between the speaker company Acoustics Research and Deutsche Grammophon. Milton Babbitt, Elliott Carter, Aaron Copland, Gunther Schuller, and Roger Sessions were advisors to the project. I was especially pleased that it afforded me the chance to record *Philomel* at last (and to show up Columbia Records for not having had the nerve to take it on themselves). We put Fred's *Wake* on the second part of the LP. We had plenty of time to rehearse this time and had a terrific conductor for the piece in David Epstein. All of my recording legacy is on vinyl, though some has been remastered.

While we were in Boston recording *Wake*, a young fellow stuck his head in to listen to the rehearsal. It turned out to be Michael Tilson Thomas.

We recorded *Philomel* in New York, and Milton of course kept close watch over the session, making comments and checking everything out. In the end, I don't think the production values were as good as they should have been—even with Acoustics Research behind the project. New World Records rereleased *Philomel* recently, and I can't help thinking that the balance between voice and tape is not good, with the voice too dominant. There are moments when my voice drowns out the tape. It seems to fall far from the perfection that Milton was always seeking for his electronic music. I have much more perfect performances in my private archives.

The fall of 1968 was very busy. Philip Batstone had recently finished a beautiful chamber work called *A Mother Goose Primer* to be premiered at the University of Colorado in Boulder, where Phil taught. Phil was a serial composer and, like Milton's, his vocal line is diatonic. *A Mother Goose Primer* was based on portions of Mother Goose rhymes and scored for solo soprano, flute, clarinet, cello, piano, percussion, and second voice. My second voice was a young soprano, Victoria Bond, who today is quite a well-known composer. I had a large opening section for unaccompanied voice before the instruments enter. The playful Mother Goose texts are accompanied by instruments, bells, and a few percussion instruments.

Phil's notes for the piece describe it as "a dramatic music-word poem" that "contains no music which is independent of the words; no words—beyond merely individual lines—which in any way be thought of as independent of the music."[79] It was a narrative piece, beautiful, fanciful, and I loved it.

I sang *A Mother Goose Primer* again at the big contemporary music festival hosted by UCLA. Alden Ashforth, yet another Princetonian, was teaching there and was one of the organizers of the festival. After the festival was over I stayed on to record Alden's *Unquiet Heart* together with Phil's *Mother Goose Primer* for CRI. The two composers treated me like a diva. They both dedicated their pieces to me, and it couldn't have been nicer being around them.

Phil had such confidence in me. He'd write long letters to us about what he was composing. Godfrey regarded Phil as an exceptional musician. When I would start to have doubts toward the end of my singing career about "the voice," Phil wrote me a long letter. After Godfrey died, when I was at a low point and even felt my singing was not up to snuff, his advice and support gave me renewed strength.

I have a fond memory of being with Phil one day in Boulder. He was in a contemplative mood, and we were looking at the huge mountain range nestling Boulder. He turned to me and said, "Look, Bethany, sheer Beethoven!"

While in Los Angeles for the festival, I visited my old friend, the composer Lenny Rosenman, and spent an enjoyable afternoon in his luxurious Hollywood home. Lenny wanted all the news from back East. We talked about Milton and other composers Lenny knew. I wanted to hear more about his career as a movie composer; it seemed important to him to make it utterly clear that he didn't think he had somehow "sold out" of "serious music." He assured me that he continued to compose his serious music.

Lenny was known as the movie composer who introduced avant-garde music to Hollywood and won two Oscars, for *Bound for Glory* and *Barry Lyndon*. His 1955 score for *The Cobweb* is considered to be the first major film score to use twelve-tone technique. His 1966 score for *Fantastic Voyage* is heavily influenced by Berg. He managed to be a success in Hollywood, while at the same time keeping true to his composition teachers, who included Sessions, Dallapiccola, and Schoenberg.

It's worth noting—when thinking about Lenny's quirks, the choices he made in his life, and the consequent frustrations—that Lenny was one of Schoenberg's dissenting students. He was easily fed up with Schoenberg's insistence on teaching sixteenth-century counterpoint. He wanted to learn twelve-tone technique! I, on the other hand, have always admired the way that Schoenberg brought his composition students to their own original music through a solid understanding of tradition. Ultimately, it made them all more sure-footed composers. Lenny was more neurotic than sure footed and had more expensive tastes to boot.

I couldn't resist asking about his friend James Dean—whom I'd met a decade before at Godfrey's concert—and the cult around him that had risen up after his sudden death. Of course, Lenny's music was in two of Dean's movies, *East of Eden* and *Rebel Without a Cause*. "That kid lived fast and died fast," Lenny explained. "Rather stupid when he had so much to give to the industry!" I was surprised to hear him speak of Hollywood as the kind of place where an artist could make "significant contributions." It seemed to contradict the way he characterized his screen work as "just a day job." Lenny was a conflicted person. Despite his nonchalance, I think he did struggle with trying to keep a foot in each world of concert music and film. He was quoted in a 1982 *New York Times* interview describing his experience as "schizophrenic."

Soon after I visited him, he published an article in the journal *Perspectives of New Music* describing the distinction between film scoring and composing concert music as a nonissue. It's sort of his position paper and has aspects of defensiveness.

> Several years ago I was invited by a university to teach a course in musical composition for films. I declined the offer saying that composition is composition and that I felt such a course would be better taught under the aegis of the Business Administration Department. My reply to this invitation was only half-facetious for, in functional

music media, there are in fact no special compositional techniques to be learned.[80]

But he would become less optimistic about his ability to move between the two in later years. When he won his second Academy Award in 1976 for *Bound for Glory*—the score was an adaptation of Woody Guthrie songs—he quipped, "This is really almost on the borderline of absurdity because I do write original music too!" I wonder if any one in the audience there knew what he meant.

Lenny shouldn't have been so neurotic about his Hollywood status. There was a strong tradition of important, serious composers working in movies, some of whom were part of the flight from Europe: Erich Wolfgang Korngold, Miklós Rózsa, Aaron Copland, Sergey Prokofiev, Ernest Gold (Marni Nixon's first husband), Georges Auric, and even Charlie Chaplin—to name a few.

During the UCLA festival, Bob Helps flew down from San Francisco, where he was staying at the time, because we had a recital at Royce Hall. The festival was a ten-day affair; Bob and I were there to present a program of lieder of the Second Viennese School.

We met up with Bob's old friend Ian Underwood, who was then playing in Frank Zappa's band. Frank Zappa said he wanted to meet us, so the three of us headed over to Frank Zappa's home in Laurel Canyon. He had a magnificent studio in his basement with all kinds of recording equipment, and I assumed that was where he composed as well. He played some of his "serious music" for us and then sat back to receive our comments. I didn't say much; Bob was, as ever, reliably diplomatic. I felt that here, in Zappa, was a man who wanted recognition as a serious composer, especially from another serious composer. (It seems that a lot of rich composers struggled with this insecurity in Los Angeles.) Then Frank Zappa suddenly had a brilliant idea: I, of all people, would appear with his band! He was, mind you, very serious. He described the stage setting: I could wear a brown leather jumpsuit and emerge from a suds-filled washing machine, singing one of his pop tunes.

I thought, Good God, the man is crazy. I think he was pulling my leg, though, and I told him in no uncertain terms that I would have none of it. Bob and Ian thought it hilarious, and brilliant indeed. But I stuck to my guns. When I got home and told my sons about Zappa's idea they laughed: "Mom, you missed a golden opportunity!" By their lights, maybe I had. Chris and Baird had found their own way in music—responding to, or intimidated by, their parents. They took piano lessons and studied music in college but ultimately stuck to their element. They listened to Jimi Hendrix, Joni Mitchell, and Bob Dylan. They were both Frank Zappa fans and into the whole world of pop music. They *would* have loved it if I'd climbed out of a washing machine in brown leather singing a Frank Zappa song!

CHAPTER FORTY-FIVE

OLD FRIENDS AND NEW PIECES

I t was starting to be clear that with every passing year, learning new music got harder. It was as if I couldn't cordon off the repertoire I already had in my memory bank from new material. I much preferred at that point to rework pieces I already knew.

My old friend Peter Maxwell Davies, who was rocketing in a determined but gentlemanly way through his career toward a well-deserved knighthood, had been given a commission by the Koussevitzky Music Foundation. The commission resulted in a piece for voice and a large instrumental group, set to six prose poems of Georg Trakl and called *Revelation and Fall*. The instrumentation was wild and the piece not entirely convincing. Some of the instruments in the ensemble turned on amplification in designated passages, which I didn't understand. I was using *Sprechstimme* as well as singing, and the opening phrase took me from G below middle C to a high C-sharp. I had a bullhorn that I had to seize and scream into at one point. It was a striking work, filled with sheer, blood-curdling drama, and unlike anything I'd heard from Max before. Trakl's poetry was filled with gory hallucinations and obsessed unrelentingly about death. One passage in the poetry ran: "Let the blood flow from the moon-clad feet that tread the paths of night, where the rat screeches and scurries on." Dark stuff. In *New York* magazine that week, Alan Rich praised it:

> A piece of extraordinary emotional power; its musical language is that
> of contemporary atonality, and it is brilliantly used to thread its way
> through the underbrush of Trakl's imagery, pounce on words and their

implications, and drive them deeply under the skin. Bethany Beardslee's performance of the vocal line, excruciatingly difficult and ranging all the way from a kind of gloom-haunted Mahlerian lyricism to a couple of minutes of wild shrieking through a bull-horn, was in itself one of the most extraordinary things I have ever heard in a concert hall.[81]

The New York premiere was at Avery Fisher Hall; we repeated it in Washington, DC, at the Library of Congress. Max's favorite English singer, Mary Thomas, later performed the piece famously wearing a bright red nun's habit. But I wore a flaming red dress when I performed it. (Max knew better than to ask me to wear a nun's habit.) The premiere was a huge success, but I have to confess, I didn't like the piece much.

On the same program a young singer named Phyllis Bryn-Julson was singing a new piece by David Del Tredici, called *Syzygy*. David had studied composition with Roger Sessions and piano with Bob Helps. David and Phyllis had been having success with a series of pieces he'd written based on texts from *Alice's Adventures in Wonderland*. Phyllis was astounding. She had absolute pitch and could toss off phrases the way Marni Nixon did in the early days on the West Coast. I believe Phyllis is now retired as Chair of Voice, though still teaching, at the Peabody Conservatory at Johns Hopkins in Baltimore. I have always admired her voice, which was a bit heavier than mine, and her musicianship.

The University of California, Berkeley, marked the opening of its new Zellerbach Hall in 1968 with a celebration of Stravinsky's music. My manager called and said that Robert Craft wanted me there to sing in *Les Noces*. Word was that Stravinsky himself would conduct, but I thought that highly improbable. These were Stravinsky's last years, and I think everyone knew it. Craft was, of course, on hand and ultimately did conduct that night. The other soloists and I went to Stravinsky's room backstage before the concert to greet him. He recognized me and we exchanged smiles. He looked so small and tired, slumped in his chair. Many in the group I was with wanted him to autograph their scores and ask him questions. They had him talking and were tiring him out. I didn't say a word, put his hand in mine briefly, and then left. It would be the last time I saw him, but I felt as if we'd had our moments together. Memories mean a great deal more than autographs.

Perhaps my richest memory of Stravinsky is from April 1963, when Stravinsky called Milton asking if he could hear *Vision and Prayer*. Stravinsky, always of a curious mind, had heard the buzz about electronic music. Milton and I met up with Stravinsky at the Columbia Records studio on 30th Street, where I gave a private performance for the Master. Afterward, while Craft was talking to Milton, Stravinsky and I had a separate conversation quietly in French. He expressed his great respect for Milton and how much he admired his intellect, but he confessed that he didn't understand the complexities of his music. It was beyond him.

Bob Helps was by now living full time in San Francisco, so I was starting to work more with Yehudi Wyner. Bob came back to the East Coast in 1969 for a concert we had scheduled at Swarthmore College. He wanted to put together a new lieder program for it. We began with a group of new Schubert songs, followed by Schoenberg's *Das Buch der hängenden Gärten*. After intermission there was a wonderful new Brahms group, followed by more Schubert. I must say that it was one of our most beautiful collaborations. We repeated the concert at Princeton as a benefit for the Friends of Music. Bob played marvelously in his special way. I recall vividly certain programs with him, including this one, as well as our tribute to Maurice Ravel and some of our all-French recitals. Sometimes I really did just want to sit on him to make him stay put.

That same spring of 1969, Arthur Weisberg decided to mount an all-Webern program at Carnegie Hall—I loved singing in that hall. I performed some of Webern's early tonal songs with the pianist Gilbert Kalish, as well as Webern's Opus 15 with instruments. There is no doubt that Webern's musical language influenced a whole group of composers in the 1960s, though I couldn't understand quite why. For me, the music of Berg and Schoenberg was rich, growing out of the tradition of Mahler, Bruckner, and Brahms. Webern's sparse serial music, with its pointillist style, was different, all in short time durations. It appealed to a whole new generation. This said, my opinion of Webern—why I hate his music—is formed through a performer's perspective.

Jan DeGaetani sang on the program with me. With her light mezzo-soprano, she had been launched into the world of new music specialization through her appearances with Arthur's group. Like me, Jan had relative pitch. I often wondered how *she* learned new music. Did she have the same approach in learning a new score? Were her methods different? Jan had also chosen not to enter the opera world and was a bona fide recitalist. She worked only with Gilbert Kalish, a wonderful pianist and I think her only partner throughout her career. Over the years she sang music by Elliott Carter, Charles Ives, George Crumb, and many others. Along with Phyllis Bryn-Julson, Jan made significant contributions to the contemporary music scene. She left a substantial recorded legacy and worked for years at the Eastman School of Music, where she taught Dawn Upshaw and Renée Fleming, before dying too young of leukemia. Appearing with Phyllis and Jan, and hearing other wonderful singers such as Valarie Lamoree and Benita Valente, I no longer felt alone in my niche. At last singers with beautiful voices were not afraid to learn contemporary music, and, more important, they wanted to.

The LaSalle String Quartet was another marvelous group, dedicated to the work of the Second Viennese School. They'd started at Juilliard in the 1940s but had moved to the University of Cincinnati Music Conservatory, where they were the teaching quartet in residence. Among their most important students, perhaps, is the conductor James Levine, who had studied with the first violinist, Walter Levin. Walter was also instrumental in having Alexander Zemlinsky's manuscripts and archival material housed at the University of Cincinnati. The quartet were deep into the music of the Second Viennese School, having made their reputation with it. They called on me to come sing the second Schoenberg Quartet.

I had sung Schoenberg's magnificent second quartet only once before with the Budapest String Quartet, but went on to sing it twenty more times. The LaSalle Quartet and I performed it twice that season, first at Severance Hall in Cleveland as part of a music festival in which the group was performing the complete Schoenberg quartets and then at the conservatory in Cincinnati, where Yehudi Wyner and I did a full recital of music from the Second Viennese School.

Yehudi approached me with an idea for an unusual program to be performed at the recently opened Alice Tully Hall at Lincoln Center. He wanted to put Debussy and Webern songs on the first half, and I wanted *Vision and Prayer* on the second. The juxtaposition of the Webern and Debussy cycles was particularly enticing, and the whole program was a real conceptual deviation from standard New York vocal fare.

This concert was the culmination of my career, combining the difficult classicism of Debussy, the expressionism of Webern, and of course, Milton's strange, groundbreaking first work with recorded sound. Harold Schonberg wrote a lovely, complete review in the *New York Times* the next day:

> Debussy might come under the heading of conventional song literature, except that not many singers concentrate on his music any more.

Figure 52. With Yehudi Wyner at Paul Jacobs Memorial Concert in 1984 at Symphony Space. This snapshot was sent to me by Nonesuch record executive, Teresa Sterne.

Hardly anybody specializes in the difficult, highly organized and concentrated songs of Webern. A program like this was a risk in several ways. Debussy's songs often go along in a quasi-parlando manner, and, exquisite as they are, they do not provide much variety. The Webern songs, too, are very much of a piece. Only a very skillful singer could dare to bring together both composers in what amounted to an entire program, and avoid monotony.[82]

Schonberg gave due credit to Yehudi's marvelous playing. He was "a perfect partner for Miss Beardslee, playing with superb control, with absolutely flawless rhythm, and with a complete range of dynamics. . . . He really made music rather than provide a bashful, discreet accompaniment."
Schonberg went on to explain why this program was so perfect for me:

Ms. Beardslee is a very canny singer. She has been before the public for many years now, yet her voice sounds fresh as ever, and she has not lost her silvery timbre. That is because she sings easily and never forces. A voice as well placed as hers does not need much volume, and

Figure 53. With Michael Tilson Thomas in 1970, performing Ernst Křenek's *Die Nachtigall*. Photograph by Heinz Weissenstein, Whitestone Photo. Courtesy of BSO Archives.

Miss Beardslee was able to make all of her points without any suggestion of strain.

For the most part she sang the Debussy songs in a sweet, pure and simple manner. Her interpretation was full of subtleties, but she never made so big a thing of them that the purity of the line was lost. As song succeeded song, it was amazing how well she was able to sustain interest by delicate applications of color, or a word stressed here, a phrase there.[83]

Ernst Křenek came back into my life with his concert aria *Die Nachtigall*. It is one of his early tonal works, completely different from *Sestina*, the big twelve-tone piece that I'd learned in my hospital bed right after giving birth to Baird. The instrumentation consisted of strings, flute, and high voice. The idea for the performance came from Michael Tilson Thomas, who had just taken over the Boston Symphony Orchestra at the precocious age of twenty-five. The BSO's previous conductor, William Steinberg, had gotten too sick to finish the season, and Thomas rose to the occasion. He may have been a prodigy, or landed in his destined place a little ahead of schedule, but regardless, Thomas went on to be an important conductor for introducing and supporting new orchestral music.

He programed *Die Nachtigall* for the opening week at Tanglewood and also asked me to do Bach's Cantata no. 51 again—which didn't appeal to me at all. I'd already sung it twice under Charles Munch. Instead, I wanted to do Bach's Cantata no. 202, which I'd just sung with the Princeton Symphony and was fresh within me. In Bach's day, no. 51 was sung by boy sopranos. My voice had grown heavier over the last few years, so it didn't feel like the right match. Not to mention that I just wasn't that thrilled about doing it a third time in the same place. But he was insistent and won out.

There's a long opening phrase in the Křenek aria that culminates in a high C-sharp. My ten-year-old son Christopher had come with me to Tanglewood that year and sat through all the rehearsals and both concerts and must have heard me practice that opening phrase a hundred times. The night of the second performance he turned to my brother Bill and said, "Well, she flubbed it." My high C-sharp wasn't up to his standard. It was an impressive observation for a ten-year-old, but I was able to hear that performance recently on a Tanglewood anniversary CD—and my C-sharp was entirely true. Christopher must have heard a bird squawking out on the lawn. It certainly wasn't me he'd heard.

CHAPTER FORTY-SIX

ERWARTUNG

I n the summer of 1969, Irving Hoffman, who'd been associate conductor of the Chicago Symphony under Jean Martinon, asked me to
Chicago to perform *Pierrot* at Grant Park, an outdoor theater where they
held free concerts in the summer. It was similar to the public concerts they
held at Lewisohn Stadium in the fifties in New York. In an uncontained
outdoor venue, I would have to use a microphone. I really used it to my
advantage. Having the microphone allowed me to work wonders with all
of the dynamics—I'd be heard at any level. If you only knew what a ball it
was for me to do *Sprechstimme* with a microphone!

It started to rain in the middle of the concert, but nobody left. The
newspapers reported that the organizers had tried to close down the show
on account of the rain, but the audience refused to leave. By the time I
came out on stage, I was looking over a sea of black umbrellas. The combination of the rain, the umbrellas, and *Pierrot*—I felt like I was in a French
New Wave movie.

The next summer, Irving invited me back to Grant Park, but this time
he wanted to do Schoenberg's *Erwartung*. The only time I'd ever heard
Erwartung performed live was at Carnegie Hall in 1951, when Dorothy
Dow sang it with the New York Philharmonic and Dimitri Mitroupolous
conducted. *Erwartung* was a daunting piece of music. Craft himself recorded it several times with Anja Silja and Helga Pilarczyk. I had to believe that
Irving thought I *could* sing it. But before I agreed, I got assurances from
him that I could use a microphone, as I had with *Pierrot*. He said soloists
commonly used microphones when performing in the park and promised

me I could use one again. So I answered yes quickly—before I could change my mind—and then it was too late to back down.

It was the right kind of vocal challenge for me to be taking on. I was forty-five. Years of recital singing had given me a larger lung capacity and stronger bracing muscles. My voice had a much bigger sound throughout my middle range than it had in the beginning of my career. As a recitalist, I also had developed tremendous stamina. We recitalists are alone and often sing straight through a good hour and a half of concert. Song cycles and long stretches of uninterrupted singing had changed my voice. I had more power and more confidence, but Schoenberg's *Erwartung*, a twenty-minute monodrama for solo soprano, was nonetheless an intimidating piece of music to learn.

Erwartung is, like *Philomel*, a highly dramatic, intense work of music. It is an atonal piece that Schoenberg composed in 1909, during the same period as *Das Buch der hängenden Gärten*, before he started writing twelve-tone music. Its particular beauty is the wonderful orchestration, but for me that meant that I would be singing nonstop against a large orchestra: sixty-four strings, seventeen woodwinds, twelve brass, a harp, a celesta, a glockenspiel, a xylophone, and six percussion. I was scared to death.

Schoenberg wrote that his aim in *Erwartung* was "to present in slow motion everything that occurs during a single second of maximum spiritual excitement, stretching it out to half an hour."[84] I think it's one of Schoenberg's most effective scores, and I've always been particularly drawn to how deeply he goes into the heroine's desperate emotional state. The libretto, by a young poet and medical student, Marie Pappenheim, is pure psychological hysteria—which would have been a very "hot topic" for a young medical student and feminist in the early days of Freud. It tells the story of a woman wandering the woods in a state of total confusion; she doesn't know whether she has just murdered her unfaithful husband in a rage or whether, to her horror, someone else has. She trips and thinks she might have stumbled on her husband's dead body, or maybe a log, which is like a trigger for her: "Do not be dead my beloved. Only do not be dead!" She pours out her feelings. It's a great work of musical expressionism.

I set about learning *Erwartung* that spring the way I always approached a new score. I worked unaccompanied as usual: I spent weeks repeating, checking, and tuning my vocal line, blocking out as many of the harmonies as I could on the piano. Range was no problem. I didn't have to push my sound in the lower register because the microphone would help me with volume. The high range is never a problem, as it always cuts through the orchestra. But that's mincing words: That voice line is an unrelenting

Figure 54. Sample page from my *Erwartung* score with singing notes. Schoenberg, *Erwartung*. Used with kind permission of European American Music Distributors Company, US and Canadian agent for Universal Edition.

twenty minutes of continual singing, without a single interlude to recoup (as I had in *Philomel*). It was a test of vocal stamina for a lyric voice like mine. And yet I grew to love the music more and more every day that I worked on it.

Maestro Hoffman and I had our first rehearsal at his apartment. I sang my line unaccompanied while he conducted, showing me how he would cue me. We pored over the various tempo changes—there are a great many in this score. Then we had two working rehearsals with the full orchestra and a dress rehearsal. The orchestra was largely made up of Chicago Symphony players in whom I had tremendous confidence, and Hoffman had everyone extremely well rehearsed. But I was still nervous just before stepping out on stage, quite nervous—for perhaps the first time I can remember. The voice part begins almost immediately and then you're off to the races, singing nonstop until it's over.

Chicago weather didn't disappoint the second year in a row. Linda Winer's review in the *Chicago Tribune* began:

> As if Arnold Schoenberg's horror monodrama "Erwartung" wasn't eerie enough on its own, Chicago's dirty air settled on the downtown area last night, giving the Grant Park stage a halo of nightmare gray.
>
> And as though Bethany Beardslee's portrayal of the distraught deserted lover wasn't chilling enough, she sang ". . . how heavy is the air from in there . . . like a storm that stands still, so horribly calm and empty . . ." and (honestly) the sky responded with sudden strokes of lightning.[85]

In *Chicago Today*, Kenneth Sanson wrote: "There are some sopranos able to pick difficult notes out of the air, there are others capable of deep pathos, and there is Bethany Beardslee who does both better than just about anyone. She is a vocal phenomenon."[86] I'm so happy to have a pirated recording of that performance.

Nineteen seventy-one was a grand year for Schoenberg. Georg Solti had taken over as conductor of the Chicago Symphony and programmed a concert version of Schoenberg's opera *Moses und Aron* at Carnegie Hall. The concert was a memorable occasion. For me it was like the first performance I'd heard of Berg's *Wozzeck* under the baton of Dimitri Mitroupolous in the 1950s. I'm always wondering why it takes so many years for these great works to be realized by a first-rate orchestra and conductor!

After the triumph of *Erwartung*, I was invited back to Grant Park the following August. Brian Priestman was the guest conductor this time and gave me carte blanche to select my piece. I decided on Křenek's concert aria *Die Nachtigall* and *Miseri noi, misera patria*, the little-known Haydn cantata that Jim Bolle had unearthed and that we had recorded for Monitor Records. These were two works I really enjoyed singing. Brian was the essence of the likable Englishman, but his element was really oratorio. The *Chicago Tribune* described his performance as "competent but without face." I was complimented for the audacious program—unknown Křenek and obscure Haydn. It was a solid concert and my favorite kind of blending of old and new—but it was hardly as electrifying an experience as the Schoenberg had been the summer before.

Roger Sessions tells the story of hearing Maurice Ravel's *Daphnis et Chloé* performed by an orchestra for the first time—when he'd only known it from the piano score. Hearing the piece performed full strength was like hearing it entirely for the first time. I think of the concept of loudness, being encompassed by sound at an orchestra performance at the beginning of the twentieth century, versus the same experience today after all of our advancements in audio technology. Massive volume is everywhere. How does that diminish the potential of an orchestra's sound?

During the second half of the nineteenth century, orchestral music was a primary social activity for the cultivated European bourgeoisie. Most people had pianos in their homes, read music, and knew classical music intimately. But there is only so much volume one can make with a piano. If you think about it, an orchestra would have been the loudest thing around. And new instruments were being invented and introduced into orchestral scores all the time in order to build on this marvelous acoustical machine. For nineteenth-century concertgoers at a performance of a symphony by Bruckner, Mahler, Strauss, or Schoenberg, the sheer enormity alone of the sound must have been quite an experience.

CHAPTER FORTY-SEVEN

HOW THINGS
WIND DOWN

1973

The summer after *Erwartung*, I rented a large house on Martha's Vineyard for the children and me, along with my mother, my brother Perry, and Helen. My sister had fallen and broken her wrist. The doctor recommended sun and saltwater to speed up the healing process. She was in terrible pain, and I could hear her sobbing at night. But we spent our long summer days on the beach, and I could see the sun and sea working wonders on Helen's slow recuperation.

That fall, a number of bonds that Godfrey had received from his father's estate matured, and he suddenly had a large sum of money. "Well," he announced to the family, "we are rich!" We decided to look for a larger house. I was anxious to move back into town because carpooling from Griggstown had become a real annoyance. We were several miles from Princeton Day School, and the children had to leave every morning at seven. I began looking at houses in Princeton and found a beautiful old mansion, Guernsey Hall, on Lovers Lane, right in the borough and listed at $160,000. I saw its potential immediately and thought it could be a perfect home for us. I could already see us entertaining there, holding musical evenings. It needed some painting and updating, but it was right next to a public park that at one point had been part of the property. It was perfect for the children to play in, and we would be near to their school—they could even bike to school and still be on time. Or I could drive them in a matter of minutes

Figure 55. Me, ca. 1971. Photograph by Jane Szathmary.

and would be home in a snap to get down to practicing. Godfrey, however, was not impressed when I took him to see it. "Darling," he complained, "Christopher would get lost in this huge place." So Godfrey nixed the idea, and the broker who had shown it, Bill Stewardson, seized the opportunity. He bought it in a flash and converted it into million-dollar condominiums.

After much fruitless searching, Godfrey decided instead that we would expand the house we already had. (Maybe that had been his intention all along.) He hired a Princeton architect, Perry Morgan, to help. We built a large studio off the living room for Godfrey to work in. It was well insulated from my singing, with its own foyer and separate entrance; it even had a nook that could house a small computer. We added a large wing to the other end of the house for the children; it had two bedrooms, a large play area with an upright piano, and another small room with a sink for Christopher's artwork. He'd started to demonstrate a real gift. We built a billiard room with a snooker table—Godfrey had played snooker back in England and insisted that we needed one. In the end, everyone was delighted with our new Belle Mead, except for me, because I was still stuck driving back and forth to Princeton Day School and still had my tiny kitchen.

My old friend and singing coach Earl Kim had left Princeton for Harvard in 1967. He had been hired away by his Schoenberg buddy Leon Kirchner.

Whenever I went to sing in Boston, I'd make it a point to visit Earl and Martha, often staying with them rather than in a hotel. While I was visiting one time, Earl pleaded with me to consider taking on a piece by his friend Donald Sur, who was a doctoral candidate at the time. *The Sleepwalker's Ballad* is a long poem by Federico García Lorca that Donald had set for voice and instrumental accompaniment. I loved García Lorca's poetry but found the music totally puzzling. Donald was known as a quirky composer of minimalist, atonal music, with a penchant for unexpected instrumentations. In rehearsal, my conductor, Charles Wuorinen, ended up rebarring many sections because Donald had the strangest way of notating his rhythms. What started as a favor to Earl turned into a nightmare for the rest of us. Thank God for the rebarring. We wouldn't have been able to sing and follow Charles's conducting otherwise.

Earl also set me up with a summer appointment at Harvard that turned out to be surprisingly unsatisfying. I had never coached singers before, and perhaps I had unreasonable expectations about the level that the students would be working at. Despite having the delightful young pianist Jerry Kuderna helping me in the classroom, I was disappointed—but glad for the learning experience.

Later that same year I became involved with a benefit concert at Alice Tully Hall to support the Francis Thorne Fund, run by the composer Francis Thorne. The Thorne Fund had been active since 1965 and by this point had handed out $220,000 in fellowships and commissions to twenty-seven composers. Our goal with the benefit concert was to raise a lot of money so that we could keep up this kind of funding. In the *New York Times* the next day, Donal Henahan quipped that the "performing cast looked like a Who's Who of new music."[87] It was quite a to-do, a formal gala, with a big audience and several large premieres. I performed songs by Ben Weber and *The Running Sun*, a new cycle that Bob Helps had written for me. It was a setting of poetry by James Purdy, a well-known modernist writer who lived in Brooklyn and was a friend of Bob's.

Bob and I always worked in Brooklyn. When we had a performance in the city he'd make me a big dinner of steak and rice before the concert and regale me with a slew of off-color jokes. Bob had a huge repertoire of funny stories and an endless list of hilarious names he had plucked out of the telephone book—real names!

In May 1972, the ISCM asked me to do a solo recital. I agreed on the condition that I could choose my own program. Godfrey loved the music of

Nikos Skalkottas, but it just wasn't that well known in America. Godfrey had first heard Skalkottas's music on the BBC Third Programme, where Hans Keller would often present it. The two of us saw this concert as an opportunity to bring Skalkottas's music to New York. I programmed his *Five Songs*, excerpted from a larger cycle of sixteen songs on poetry of Christos Esperos. We also programmed *Du* and songs by Arlene Zallman, Peter Westergaard, Alexander Zemlinsky, and Jim Randall. Yehudi Wyner and Jerry Kuderna were my pianists.

Nikos Skalkottas was a pupil of Schoenberg and had died at the early age of forty-nine. He was included on a special and very small list of composers whom Schoenberg felt were his most gifted students, composers he unreservedly endorsed. Skalkottas left Berlin before World War II and at thirty-three returned to his native Greece. He was aware that no one, except for a very few friends, would accept his twelve-tone compositional style. He literally composed in isolation and kept his music in a drawer. He was very prolific, though totally unperformed, during the war years. To earn a living, he played in the Athens orchestra, in the back row of the first violin section. That was his day job; he used all of his free time for composing. He was poor, mind you, in comparison with most American orchestra musicians who were paid union rates.

Skalkottas was married to a pianist, Maria Pangali, who would perform his music for their private salons. He also had some success with Greek folk songs that he'd scored for orchestra in a tonal style. His serious music is harmonically rich and polyphonic. Because he uses multiple rows in his works, I've sometimes thought on first hearings that Skalkottas's music was almost too thick, but the more you listen to it the more it reveals and becomes beautiful.

Gunther Schuller was an important influence in the United States in keeping Skalkottas's music vital. In the 1980s, Gunther went to Greece to negotiate with John G. Papaioannou, who was looking after the estate, to have the scores brought to the music publisher Margun (Gunther's own company). There is now a Skalkottas Society, and most of his major scores are available through Universal and Margun Music Publications. There is a Margun CD of Skalkottas's complete piano music, *32 Piano Pieces*, performed by Idith Meshulam—a lovely collection. Hopefully as the years progress his music will often be recognized, played, and increasingly incorporated into the canon.

I was getting into my late forties. My performance fees had gotten so high, I'm afraid, that I priced myself out of the new music market. Phyllis

Figure 56. Interview at WEFM for a performance of *Pierrot* with Pierre Boulez, 1972.

Bryn-Julson, Jan DeGaetani, and Benita Valente were stepping in to fill my shoes. New pianists were also appearing on the scene, such as Alan Feinberg and Ursula Oppens. Along with the violinist Paul Zukofsky, the extraordinary violinist Rolf Schulte, and many other instrumentalists, all of them were performing new music.

Instead I was starting to deliver lectures on new vocal techniques. I gave one at Harvard and was surprised to see Leonard Bernstein in the audience. It was in 1973, the same year he was delivering the Norton Lectures. I'm sure he was simply curious to hear what I had to say—with my atonal perspective. Bernstein had been a protégé of Aaron Copland and Serge Koussevitsky at Tanglewood and was definitively a tonal composer. His Norton lectures ended up praising tonality and demolishing serial music. He was a masterful conductor of the classics, Mahler in particular, but he always seemed to be overly emotional when he was conducting. I would have thought that as a twentieth-century composer, he would have had more interest in the music of his contemporaries. I think instead that he couldn't enjoy twelve-tone at all. I have a newspaper clipping from the 1970s, a review by Alan Rich, criticizing Bernstein's dismissive posture toward new music. I've scribbled "traitor" under the photo caption.

Bernstein had such massive natural talent, but he squandered most of his energies on conducting when he should have dedicated himself to composing for Broadway. *West Side Story* is a masterpiece.

Much later in my life, I was at a party at the esteemed music editor Claire Brook's, and Lenny arrived late, his arms laden with bracelets and several young boys. He walked right up to me and gathered both of my hands in his. "Bethany Beardslee," he said and looked me in the eye. It was a flash of communion. We both knew what we were about. And I was too deep into my life and career to worry about whether he was a traitor anymore or not.

In the 1974–75 funding year, I served on the selection committee for the National Endowment for the Arts that gave grants to composers and librettists. There were six or seven of us, with the composer Ezra Laderman as our chairman. Nancy Hanks was still the director at the time and my admiration for her was unabated. Although I found the process vexing, we ended up distributing $419,925 that year. Many of the grants were very well deserved. However, I felt that we'd neglected a number of deserving young composers in favor of more established composers and musicians who happened to live in the right places. As with many governmental grants, the law of democratic giving was observed. There was a fair geographical spread—every state had recipients, and the monies ranged from $1,000 to $10,000. The larger grants went to opera projects, many of which were never realized. I was only a committee member; it wasn't up to me to redistribute!

Around this same time our friends Ellen and Eberhard Faber found a house near us on River Road. That meant that many evenings were now taken up with Ellen and Eb for dinner and poker, our favorite game. If we had moved, I reasoned, we probably wouldn't have seen them so often. There were several other couples we entertained frequently, including Arlene Zallman and Gregory Proctor. Greg was a graduate student in music theory at Princeton, and Arlene was getting her doctorate at Penn, where she was studying composition with Vincent Persichetti. A few years earlier, she'd been in Florence studying with Luigi Dallapiccola on a Fulbright. Our friends Roger and Priscilla Maren would often bike over to see us; they lived in Hopewell, so the bicycle trip was at least twenty miles. They were really the original hippies, long before that was fashionable.

Figure 57. At the Jersey Shore with Baird, ca. 1963.

They grew their own vegetables. They even had an outhouse and lots of cats, plus a Steinway piano that Roger lovingly played. They could often be seen on the corner of Witherspoon and Nassau Streets handing out their flyers protesting the war in Vietnam.

My days started to fill up with Baird, Christopher, and my work. My evenings were full of friends, or sometimes just us. Oddly, even though Godfrey now had a room entirely barricaded from noise, he continued working at night. I was working less. Our revamped home and my relaxed lifestyle lulled me away from my singing. Call it the inertia that comes from having money—a very corrupting influence.

I was getting ready to call it quits. I performed one last *Clytemnestra* with Martha Graham; Stravinsky's *Pulcinella* with Lukas Foss and the Chicago Symphony; and another *Erwartung* with Irving Hoffman. My career was solid and mature. I could see my new music mission winding down. I wanted to enjoy my family and settle down into the good life.

By this point, I was on several panels concerning the future of new music. Milton was often with me, which was a comfort. Surprisingly enough, I do not have an easy time talking in front of an audience. I'd find myself up in front of everyone, all eyes turned to me, waiting for me to *say something*, and I'd think, "What in hell am I doing here?" Often I'd pull out some familiar shopworn sentiment, such as: I feel that no matter whatever period a piece of serious music comes from, the main thing is that it is well composed. . . . The performer must recognize this as his responsibility and not be indiscriminate in what he chooses. . . . Meanwhile, Milton would speak about how he lived untouched by the showbiz aspect of music, as he worked under the protection of a university. I was always dubious about the point or usefulness of these discussions. I felt a great deal of agency over my own involvement in new music—I always had. I was very selective in choosing what I sang; I didn't have to worry about supporting myself or my family financially, and I was already famous. I wondered what, realistically, I could have to pass on to the next generation? I thought my legacy, if anything, would be coaching the twentieth-century repertoire that I found to be most significant.

In 1974, the ISCM mounted a centenary Schoenberg concert in New York at Alice Tully Hall. It was a big affair, and many composers were in the audience. The program comprised just two pieces: *Das Buch der hängenden Gärten*, which Bob Helps and I performed on the first half, and then the *Serenade*, op. 24, which Jacques conducted. The baritone Richard Frisch sang the Petrarch sonnet in the fourth movement. Jacques had many rehearsals, and did an extraordinary job. That evening, the *Serenade* fairly bounced with joy and lightheartedness, catching a rhythmic transparency of incomparable beauty. Bob and I had many years experience behind us on that song cycle. It was one piece that the two of us wore like a glove. I wish the old man could have heard the performances that night.

David Hamilton published a long and extremely knowledgeable article on the concert in the *New Yorker*. He stressed the importance of Schoenberg's rhythm and wrote generously about our interpretation of the master's work as well as acknowledging Jacques's unparalleled conducting:

> Bethany Beardslee and Robert Helps (one cannot say "accompanied by Robert Helps," for it is a complete partnership) have performed the "Fifteen Poems from 'das Buch der hängenden Gärten,' by Stefan George," Opus 15, on many occasions, but rarely as advantageously. They know how to make every phrase of these spare, allusive, asymmetrical songs shiver with life and color. Next, Jacques-Louis Monod conducted a young ensemble (led by the superb violinist Jeanne Benjamin) in the Seranade, with Richard Frisch as expert baritone soloist in the movement that sets a Petrach sonnet (in German translation). All the rhythms sparkled here,

like the pigments in a freshly restored painting; the wit of the discourse, the variety of the textures, Schoenberg's delight at his own virtuosity in coaxing new patterns from traditional formulas were made startlingly accessible. Mr. Monod is the best Schoenberg conductor around, and we do not hear enough from him; his rare performances give listeners more precise aural images of the music's expressive potential.[88]

When Jacques conducted Schoenberg, he made it seem so easy.

Westminster Choir College in Princeton decided to put on its first Art Song Festival in June of 1974 and asked me to be one of the participants representing contemporary repertoire. I sang Claudio Spies's *Three Poems on the Poetry of May Swenson*, Milton's *Vision and Prayer*, and Godfrey's *To Prove My Love*. The other singer participants were: Eleanor Steber (American art song); Jerome Hines (Russian and Italian); Martial Singher (French), and Elly Ameling (German art song). We gave performances and then held workshops.

My lecture stressed tuning in both advanced styles and classical song, and that the singing voice is uniquely able to reveal harmonic relationships in a piece of music. Singers and string players are the only musicians able to modify pitch without reattacking. I wanted to emphasize that a singer can "show" how pitches lean into each other and in that way bring out more of the harmonic beauty of a piece. Most musical singers feel this intuitively. It is one great advantage that the voice has over the other instruments such as the brass, winds, and piano, with their fixed pitch—though as I've said, string players, too, are aware of and utilize this fine art of tuning.

I also spoke about new vocal techniques, including *Sprechstimme*, phonemes, and the use of nontext, and about the computer as a new medium. Then I played portions of *Vision and Prayer* to illustrate how Babbitt used spoken voice at the beginning, then moved into *Sprechstimme*, and then into full singing. For examples of how phonemes, or nontext, might be used, I played *Phonemena* and Ralph Shapey's *Incantations*.

After the festival, I took off for six weeks of singing at Monadnock. I hadn't been back to Monadnock since 1966. It was lovely to be there. New Hampshire was a relief from the hot, muggy New Jersey summers, and I was absolutely bewitched by the beauty of the area. I always felt very special, singing in the wooden meeting halls of Jaffrey, Peterborough, Harrisville, and Nelson, with their perfect acoustics. I loved being with Jim Bolle and his wife Jocelyn—as before, they gave me the chance to sing music I wanted to sing. And I started to really get to know Boston-area performers, such as Lois Shapiro, Elinor Preble, Marc Schachman, Laura Stepman, Dan Stepner, and Craig Smith, Ken Ziegenfuss, Linda Quan, and John Gibbons.

The summer of 1974 I sang everything: Hugo Wolf's *Italienische Liederbuch* with James Maddalena, baritone, and pianist Craig Smith; duets with the soprano Neva Pilgrim (a dedicated singer and organizer of new music in the Rochester area); Samuel Barber's *Knoxville: Summer of 1915*; Mozart concert arias with the orchestra; *Philomel*; and a set of Handel arias with the flutist Elinor Preble.

After Monadnock, I hopped down to Chatham in Cape Cod to sing in the Monomoy Chamber Ensemble's festival with Eleanor Lawence Steindler, flutist and director of the festival. It was one of the many times I appeared at Monomoy; over the years Eleanor became one of my dearest friends. In other words, the summer of 1974, I spent an unduly long time away from Godfrey and the children.

CHAPTER FORTY-EIGHT

GODFREY

M y children had stayed home that summer with their father. They had gotten to the age when they wanted to be with their friends during the vacations and were old enough to be left to their own devices. Godfrey was spending the summer working on a wonderful tonal orchestral piece, *Sonata for Orchestra*, which we had been listening to him play before dinner all spring. One of the central aspects of the piece, as he had conceived it, came in the big string section that opens the second movement. He set the *Hauptstimme* (the main voice) into the middle voice, so that instead of being on top, the theme is moved back and forth in the inner voices.

When I returned in late August, I was alarmed by Godfrey's physical appearance. He looked extremely tired and complained to me that he'd been having night sweats. I knew he hated going to doctors, but this time I insisted we go. There were to be no excuses. He relented. He knew he was ill.

At first they thought he might have mononucleosis and ran a battery of tests. It was a lab technician who discovered that he had Hodgkin's disease, a form of lymphoma that was considered curable if caught early enough. I felt ashamed and guilty for having been gone for such a long stretch. I still do.

I was overwhelmed. I got in touch with Godfrey's mother, Gwen; she arrived a week later. We knew it was serious, and at the beginning everyone had ideas about what we should do. Our friend Arthur Komar had had Hodgkins and had recovered. The doctors recommended radiation treatments over Godfrey's whole upper torso, and they were awful. Godfrey could scarcely swallow and lost his voice. Then he lost his appetite, so I'd

Figure 58. Godfrey.

make him protein shakes that were easy to swallow and would give him strength. Godfrey didn't want to stay in the hospital; he wanted to be at home. We set up the bedroom so that he could listen to music and be comfortable. I nursed him, keeping track of the various medications he needed and arranging visits with his close friends to keep him distracted and in good spirits. Once the music department found out he was sick, the house flooded with visitors. Jim Randall and Roger Maren came often. Paul Lansky brought a pile of LPs. Anita Cervantes and her boyfriend Mark Zuckerman were a big help. Anita would stay with Godfrey when

I had to go off to sing. She had given the first performance of Godfrey's *Variations on a Theme by James Pierpont* at Princeton and now performs all over South America. The house filled with good will. We were hopeful, optimistic even.

Gwen returned to London after three weeks. I found I missed her quiet support. When Christmas approached, I invited Godfrey's family back to New Jersey to spend the holidays with us. Godfrey protested, "Darling, what are we going to do with all these English?" I don't know how exactly, but the house opened up to accommodate all of us. I slept in my dressing room, next to our bedroom, so that I could be near Godfrey. It was a strange Christmas. We were all drinking a lot. And Godfrey was in rare form, propped up on pillows in his bed, playing bridge and making all sorts of witty remarks. It seemed as if he couldn't do enough to make his family happy, somehow making us all laugh despite how anxious we were inside. The English left after New Year's, expressing many wishes that he would get well.

In February he had a small remission, and his full voice returned. He said to me, "Darling, when I get well I'm going to make this all up to you." I knew what he wanted to say. He would change his dear old habits. But then he began the chemotherapy.

It was a year of great sadness. I saw my husband waste away from cancer. The treatment seemed primitive at the time; they knew so little compared with what they know today. Radiation treatments are delivered in very small doses now and closely monitored—nothing like the excessive radiation he received. The chemotherapy immediately seemed to do far more damage than good. Godfrey wasn't a strong person to start with. The chemo made him vomit, and he hardly ate. The treatment was horrific, and more than anything I was helpless. All I could do was to sit by his side, follow the doctor's orders, and give him love and encouragement.

Through this incomprehensible time, my sister would often come down from Red Hook to help me. I was trying to keep my singing engagements but also be with Godfrey. Because of Schoenberg's centennial, I had scheduled many concerts, including *Pierrot* recitals and appearances on the West Coast with the LaSalle Quartet. I didn't want to leave him. I canceled many of those performances.

Godfrey died on April 23, 1975, after six months of heroically fighting his cancer. I have never really recovered from Godfrey's death.

Princeton University held a beautiful memorial service for my husband and renamed the computer laboratory the Godfrey Winham Laboratory for Computer Music. He had only just turned forty that December. Our friends were shocked.

I have a pile of condolence letters from after Godfrey's death. The names on the return addresses included almost everyone I've talked about in this book: Paul Fromm, Miriam Gideon, Donald Martino, Ed Cone, Claudio Spies, Pierre Boulez, and on and on. While Godfrey was sick, some people backed away, as is so common in the face of dreadful illness. Others, such as Paul Lansky, Roger Maren, Arthur Komar, and Jim Randall, came to see Godfrey frequently. Jim Graves, who was going through a divorce and living in the apartment over our garage at Belle Mead, was a most considerate friend; he would come help me move Godfrey when I couldn't lift him.

I think that death became a strange experience for me because of Godfrey. In the years since he died, I have lost so many friends. My sister, who lived to be ninety-nine, died recently. Her life was complete, and I *will* miss her. But the only loss I have really felt so intensely was the death of Godfrey. Perhaps it was because of the way he died—the way I had to watch him waste away in front of me. It was so plain and in my face every day. His absence is with me even today. Often in my dreams at night, I will hear a particular piece of music that he loved, like the Brahms *Variations on a Theme by Haydn*, and I'll find myself crying. There were many years that I couldn't bring myself to go to funerals. There were years in which I harbored so much anger that he was gone. Godfrey was my soul mate, and I wanted him back.

We often played the game Diplomacy with the children when they were little. Godfrey was very strict about not favoring the children or overlooking mistakes in a game—which often left young Christopher in tears. For Godfrey, rules must be obeyed, and there were no exceptions for the children. They observed his work time and his desk as sacrosanct. His work demanded deep concentration, and he worked around the clock.

Keeping quiet in the house was all important. My work was the exception. I could sing. Other than that, the only background noise he could tolerate was the sound of the ocean. He loved hearing the surf. Otherwise, all noise was unbearable—especially the ticking of a clock.

Godfrey's idea of exercise was walking from the studio in our home to the kitchen to renew his cup of coffee. I asked him once, puzzled, "Darling, why do you always run up the steps of the Engineering Building?" His answer, "It takes less energy!"

He had this marvelous sense of humor, and everyone who got to know him adored him. When we visited Ellen and Eberhard Faber at the Jersey shore, he would walk down to the edge of the beach, take one look out at the ocean—often standing there musing for a long time—turn around, and come back to the house to sit down at the chessboard. Godfrey and Eb loved chess by day and poker by night. Godfrey was shy and hated small talk. When I spoke of many famous singers I was in awe of, he said that they were all just cogs in the music business.

I'm hardly an intellectual, and I'm sure he regretted not being able to discuss his work with his singer wife.

He was a man of deep habits. He always took us to the same restaurant when the family ate out, the Chinese Tea Garden on Witherspoon Street in Princeton. There were his Tuesday nights out with Ken Steiglitz. Wednesdays with Arlene Zallman and Gregory Proctor. After Godfrey died, Roger Maren and Ken kept up the Tuesday night tradition for a while, but it wasn't the same. I'm sure Ken missed Godfrey a lot.

For years, Roger tried to turn Godfrey on to jazz. But my husband invariably objected, "Roger, it goes nowhere."

PART FIVE

FAREWELL AND FAREWELL

Figure 59. Publicity photo, ca. 1979. Photograph by Jim Graves.

CHAPTER FORTY-NINE

REMEMBERING
MILTON

At Godfrey's memorial service, Milton had told me that he was going to compose a requiem for Godfrey. He had a commission from the New York State Council of the Arts and a grant from the American Music Center by the Andrew Mellon Foundation to write a piece for the performance group Continuum. Instead of the usual large choral work that most requiems are, this one was for solo voice with a two-piano accompaniment—an unusual combination. I received my score for the *Solo Requiem* two years after Godfrey's death. The dedication read, "In memory of Godfrey Winham" and Milton had included a sweet note along with the manuscript, "For Bethany, For Everything. For Christmas. Milton (12/13/1978)."

The piece arrived just at the period during which I was starting to sing again. The timing could not have been better.

Solo Requiem is a large piece. It includes Shakespeare's Sonnet 71 ("No longer mourn for me when I am dead"), as well as poetry by Gerard Manley Hopkins, George Meredith, August Stramm, and John Dryden. The Dryden is recited in *Sprechstimme*, and the sonnet repeats at the end. Milton's selections were perfect; these were some of Godfrey's favorite poets.

I had learned my part alone in my usual manner; but putting together three separate ensemble partners was hell. The pianists Cheryl Seltzer and Joel Sachs worked together like dogs for weeks on the *Requiem*. We practiced in Cheryl's apartment in New York. She always had wonderful cheese, crackers, and apples for respite during our long rehearsals. Our problem

Figure 60. With Milton, possibly discussing *Phenomena*, which I never ended up learning, ca. 1963.

was synchronizing Milton's rhythms, which were not easy, to say the least. Whereas Milton's vocal line is always easy, his rhythms demand rehearsal. Of his repertoire, *Solo Requiem* is considered a piece with "intense emotionality," in other words, not as intellectual and abstruse as some of his other works.[89]

These rehearsals brought me back to the early days of learning *Du* with Jacques. And there were moments during our struggle to perfect this piece that I longed for my old friend the synthesizer, who never complained and was always accurate. The synthesizer made life a lot easier. The three of us performed the *Requiem* many times that season.

It seems strange when I think that I knew Milton for a longer time in my life than my own father. You could say that Milton and Sylvia were my musical parents, inasmuch as they were so much a part of those early days in New York, and then even more a part of my life when Godfrey and I moved to Princeton, where Milton was teaching. This wonderful man was at my side every time I sang in New York. He was always in the audience, and I could depend on him being there. On more than one occasion, Milton called me Betty Ann—his daughter's name—by mistake, and I was flattered.

In the early days, when I was married to Jacques, I was always scared of saying something dumb, making a boo-boo, in Milton's presence. I was never an intellectual and knew enough to just listen and not air opinions. Not that Milton would have embarrassed me if I did. He had an innate respect for good manners and loved good company, even in his later, more reclusive years.

Milton was a true southern gentleman, born in Faulkner country—Jackson, Mississippi. He was slightly built, rather bald, and always well dressed. I never saw Milton in a turtleneck, blue jeans, sneakers, or a pair of shorts. I remember him only ever abandoning his jacket and tie on hot summer days when we were at the annual summer picnics held by the Princeton music department.

Although Milton had an enormous love of good food and good beer, he never gained a pound. I have fond memories of sitting with Milton in his favorite Chinese restaurant on 125th Street (near the synthesizer lab during the *Philomel* era), listening to him expound on the merits of Chinese cuisine. I thought Wah-Kee in Chinatown was superior. Milton probably never went down to Chinatown, but who knows? He had *his* place, his own hole-in-the-wall restaurant, where he went with Vladimir Ussachevsky. I'm sure the chef catered to both of them.

Figure 61. With Milton onstage after the Philomel premiere, Amherst College, 1964. Courtesy of Amherst College Archives and Special Collections.

Milton had contemporary tastes. If he could have afforded it, he would have been delighted to live in a Manhattan penthouse, with a painting or two by Mondrian, earn lots of money, and have uninterrupted time to compose.

I loved the sound of his rich baritone voice and his witty asides. I never experienced him as sad or depressed. To me, he was just gregarious and exciting to be around. Sometimes he could become angry or cynical about the "show biz" aspects of the music world, but he was basically an optimist. I imagine his genius mind took him into realms of thinking where he didn't have time to think about his complaints, or most other earthly matters.

Milton saw music as an intellectual discipline. Princeton, where he taught for so many decades, was his haven for exploring and analyzing music without having to worry about the pressure of public reception. Teaching was his livelihood as it continues to be for many composers today. The generations of composers who either studied with him or were influenced by him are formidable and include many prominent figures. Even after he retired from Princeton, he exerted his influence over students at Juilliard. He brought new terminology into the language of music. He believed in the continuity of the art form, as did Schoenberg. His lineage was the German aesthetic carried to its furthest with serial music.

I once asked Milton to describe his music to me. He smiled and answered, "It's the density of complexity." It took me a while to understand that one. For me his music is lyrical. Yes, it is complex and unexpected with the jazz elements in his rhythms. (When Milton was very young, he played jazz clarinet.) It has always struck me that when I first heard a piece by Bach, I couldn't get my brain around it, as polyphonic music isn't easy to listen to first time around. Milton's music needs even more listening. But repeated listening brings out the wealth of details, a kaleidoscope of musical events. He never composed an ugly note. You must give Milton's music many opportunities to reveal itself. It is unique, like nothing you have heard.

In the early days when the Princeton music department occupied a small Greek temple called Clio Hall on the campus, Jacques and I would often find Milton, Roger Sessions, Earl Kim, Ed Cone, and students in the downstairs office, joking. Milton would be smoking his favorite brand of cigarette, Picayune, and usually had one leg draped over an armchair. We would often perform in the upstairs lecture room, which was the department's concert hall in those days. I sang so much music by the faculty and students in that hall. Later, when the Woolworth Center for Musical Studies was built, Bob Helps and I would often perform there, or in Alexander Hall with the student orchestra.

Milton's favorite Princeton destination was the Balt on Nassau Street, a subway-tiled restaurant where Milton, Jacques, and I would congregate for coffee, food, and conversation. I favored the Annex, a restaurant that only closed in 2006, making it practically a landmark. Milton often ate there, too. It was in the basement, also on Nassau Street, easily accessible for the students, and with good reasonably priced food. No matter where we ate, I was of course always the listener. My ears filled with opinions of the work of other composers and the latest new music. I once asked Milton about a certain composer's piece and his answer was, "It doesn't probe deep enough," which I loved as an answer.

We who adored him loved to just be in Milton's presence, listening to his marvelously articulate thoughts, expressed in his beautiful English. He spoke rapidly and usually dominated a conversation. He was, as you might expect, an avid reader, constantly buying books, and he had an enormous library. His inquiring mind pursued mathematics, philosophy, logic, and music theory. His social conversation was lighthearted. He enjoyed talking about old pop songs from the 1930s and 1940s. (He adored Rudy Vallée for his intonation and diction.) He had an encyclopedic memory about jazz, baseball, old movies, and the better show composers, such as Rodgers and Hart, George Gershwin, Irving Berlin, and so on. When Milton was with Mel Powell, they would share their passion for good popular music and horse around. Hearing Milton playing show tunes on the piano is among my fondest memories. When we were working on *Philomel* he signed one letter to me "Irving Berlin." Despite the German lineage in his formation, he was as American as they make them!

I often thought he created an intentional distance with his social banter, so that he didn't have to reveal how he composed or assume a serious air. But even if he had, I doubt any of his students would have really been able to *understand* how he composed. Milton, like Schoenberg, was private in this respect. The last time I visited him, the week before he died, he actually showed me music he was in the middle of composing. There were many worksheets covered with numbers in columns and diagrams. I couldn't possibly have understood what he was showing me. Those notes are now catalogued with the Library of Congress. But at the time I was astonished to be allowed in on his work process—me, of all people. Godfrey had tried for years to get Milton to explain the way he composed but to no avail. Sometimes Milton would throw Godfrey a bone—something to speculate about—just before boarding the bus in Princeton after a long day of teaching to return to his New York apartment.

One of the best descriptions of Milton's music and his process I've found is in the liner notes to the recording of *Phonemena* on the album *New Music for Virtuosos*: "In all important ways his most recent works use the same basic premises as his early ones: that music is a suitable medium to show the strategies of the human mind to create order and to impose this order on the imperfect external world. Of course all art does this to some degree, but in Babbitt's music this is the overriding principle."[90] It always amazes to think he taught until his ninetieth year and still attended new music concerts. We all just assumed Milton would always be with us, sitting with head bowed as he listened to a new or older contemporary score. He was a compulsive concertgoer of new music.

Milton had poor eyesight. I once asked him, "Milton, did I look all right on stage?" And his reply, "Darling, how would I know with my lousy sight? But you sounded great!" Despite his poor vision, Milton's scores are all handwritten. He never wanted to use the computer as so many do today with their beautifully engraved scores. Aside from his published scores, my Babbitt scores are photo offsets of his handwritten manuscript.

In his later years, he wrote solo pieces for performers he admired. The soprano Judith Bettina and the pianist Robert Taub were among his favorites, along with David Starobin and William Anderson, guitar; Sam Rhodes, viola; William Purvis, French horn; and Jayn Rosenfeld, flute. Judith Bettina became Milton's "girl singer" when I had more or less retired. Robert Taub has recorded many of Milton's solo piano works, and Milton's music is well documented on the New World, Naxos, and Nonesuch labels.

Another point I feel I must make is how many letters of recommendation Milton wrote for young hopefuls looking for their place in a university. He truly gave of himself. I remember how appreciative he was to those who performed his music, and how supportive a beam to young composers. Young composers knew Milton would be in the audience to hear their new pieces. I remember his love of the synthesizer—the instrument on which he could realize his music perfectly. I remember his concern when Godfrey was ill and the beautiful requiem he wrote for Godfrey.

Figure 62. With Milton and Joel Sachs on a panel at Juilliard, ca. 1985; we were cracking up after a hilarious comment Milton had made.

Anyone who knew him will always remember him, for he was indeed unforgettable. And I am so very thankful to have had Milton and his music in my life as intensely and consistently as I did. As I am writing these memoirs in 2016, it is Milton's centenary celebration year, and there has been a flurry of concerts remembering him. At one centenary concert of Milton's music, I looked around the small Symphony Space auditorium and remarked that not only did I see the same faces there that I saw in the 1960s (those who are still alive at least) but that the size of the group hadn't changed that much—minus perhaps the several music critics from major papers who were dependably in attendance once upon a time. The audience for contemporary music is constant, yet small and rarefied. Composing isn't work that one does for either glory or gold; one does it for urgency of artistic expression. I suspect convincing oneself that the expression needs to be made sometimes requires a little bit of fairytale. If you have the notion that a singer or player is out there, waiting breathlessly to perform your music, perhaps that's all the fairy dust that's needed to keep on. Perhaps that's what Milton meant when he said to me—his last words to me—"This is the end for us."

CHAPTER FIFTY

AFTERMATH

What happened to my life after Godfrey died? What changed, in my house, my career, my music? Well, everything changed, absolutely everything.

Losing Godfrey ruined me for grief. I was fifty years old, and I would never again have the same capacity for devotion, guilt, negotiation, caretaking, relenting, or funerals. My boys were at a loss and in very different ways would have to be rebuilt. The beautiful house at Belle Mead was too big to be a refuge, too isolated to be a comfort. On the other side of the ocean, Godfrey's father's estate was in limbo, something too enormous to contemplate.

I needed to work, and work a lot. But for me, work had almost always been as part of a team—a duo, a marriage, a counterpoint. Jacques had organized, catalogued, conducted, produced, and pushed. Godfrey was a teacher and an artist, a thinker and a mentor; he tethered me. In the years to follow, I would have to chart my own course, follow my own instincts (whatever they were), and build where I had been only a visitor before.

All of which is to say that my career changed profoundly in its last chapter. I became a producer, a teacher, a benefactor, an organizer. I sang with friends rather than with institutions. I sang music I loved—Berg, Ravel, Schoenberg, Mahler, Schubert, Brahms—with musicians I admired. My voice carried me into my sixties. And it took me over a decade to retire. Life is too long and too short to mark endings with ceremony and Champagne and then stand aside. I've never had the patience for goodbyes.

The timing may not have been exactly this (but this is the way I remember it): After Godfrey's memorial service I asked my niece Gretchen to stay with the boys, and I got on a plane for Austin with his unfinished orchestra piece in hand. Godfrey had left incomplete his biggest piece, the *Sonata for Orchestra*, a thirty-minute, three movement, orchestra piece. I still had fairly good recall of Godfrey playing it at the piano, and I thought I could help someone reconstruct it. It was a matter of urgency: I wanted to rescue the piece before the echoes of him working on the third movement, not even fully sketched out, disappeared from my memory.

He had been working at the piano on the *Sonata* for two years. The first movement was finished and completely orchestrated. The second was 90 percent finished—there were just a few missing notes to be filled in. As for the third movement, I had the first fifty-seven measures orchestrated in his notebooks. There was also a piano reduction but no final section. He didn't bother to notate it. It just dropped off. Godfrey was deep into orchestrating—as if he had all the time in the world. Standing in the kitchen, preparing dinner, I had heard him play through the music so many times; even the children remember this. But I wasn't a pianist, and it was so frustrating not to be able to play the notes I heard in my head.

The composer Paul Lansky (a student of George Perle at Queens College who'd gotten deeply involved in the computer lab), was the only person who had heard Godfrey's idea for the complete piece. He came out to Princeton to visit right after Godfrey started his treatment, and Godfrey played through the whole piece for him. Godfrey had spent the entire summer—the summer I was away too long—working on the piece. The day Paul came over was the last time Godfrey ever worked on the piece. The radiation treatment that followed took everything out of him. If only I'd had the good sense to turn on a tape recorder that day.

I went first to Milton, then Jim Randall, and then George Perle to ask them if they would finish the piece for me. I trusted them. They all knew and admired Godfrey; they understood how he thought. I felt one of them would do right by him. Yet they were all adamant in their refusal. A composer's work was sacred. A composer can't interfere with another composer's work! In retrospect, none of them shared the same sensibility as Godfrey.

I don't know how much at that time I had in mind Bach's unfinished work *The Art of Fugue*, Puccini's *Turandot*, Schoenberg's unfinished *Moses und Aron*, or even Alban Berg's *Lulu*—the stories of those massive incomplete works and the generations of animated debates they inspired. Truth be told, my focus was on Godfrey's legacy and on the fact that he hadn't done everything he was supposed to before he died, not music history. His *Sonata for Orchestra* would have been a masterpiece. I wasn't going to let go easily of the idea that it needed to be finished and performed.

At the time, my dear friend Arlene was living in Austin with her husband, the music theorist Gregory Proctor (another Princetonian), who was teaching at the University of Texas. Arlene was frustrated. After whirlwind years at Juilliard, a Fulbright with Dallapiccola in Italy, and the first blush of her new marriage and graduate school life between Princeton and Penn, she wasn't settling easily into the role of faculty wife and mother of two small children.

In terms of aesthetics, Arlene probably had more in common with Godfrey than with Milton, George, or Jim—she wrote tonal music and loved language, especially the language of poetry. Arlene was instinctive where Godfrey was deliberate. In his notes to a 2013 CD of Godfrey's music, Benjamin Boretz wrote, "Every musical work by Godfrey was an essay on music, showing by example the content and implications of his complex evolving philosophy of music."[91] One of Arlene's primary musical values seemed to be rooted in interpretation, or variation, and especially the ways that music mimics the human experience. She also had deeply admired, even loved, my husband. What's more, there was an aspect of puzzle-solving and dramatic play to this project, the spirit of mimicry, that intrigued her—an elaborate, oversize board game, like the ones the four of us used to play together deep into the night at Princeton.

Fortunately, Godfrey had left an outline of the third movement. We never would have been able to get as far as we got without it. Arlene finished the movement of *Sonata for Orchestra* over the next year. In the final stages of composition, Arlene flew up to New Jersey so that we could hear an orchestral run-through of the piece with the Princeton Student Orchestra, conducted by Michael Pratt. Jim was there to listen and give feedback. Less than half the orchestra showed up, and for some reason players kept darting in and out of the auditorium. It was a total disaster.

But I did hear Godfrey's piece in some form, and all of the memories flooded back. Finally, I resigned myself to letting it go. Many years later in 1993, the conductor Joel Subin, who at that time was working in Europe, paid me a visit and asked to see the score. He was curious. He said, "Bethany, I want to do the first two movements." Despite the few missing notes in the second movement, he said it was perfectly reasonable to perform, although he refused to perform the problematic third movement. So the first performance of Godfrey's piece took place in Poland under Joel's direction. Gwen, Godfrey's sister Francine, Baird, and I all went to hear it. The orchestra was not the finest, but Joel did understand the music and gave us a good performance.

I couldn't let go of the idea that I had to hear the complete *Sonata* performed for real. So in 2010, I went to the arranger and music editor Randa Kirshbaum, who worked for Boosey & Hawkes. Together we filled in the few notes that had been left out of the second movement. She also made a computer-engraved score and parts. At least then I had a complete, performable version of the part of the piece that Godfrey had finished, and Arlene's third movement.

In 2011, Leon Botstein conducted the American Symphony Orchestra in the whole piece at Bard. There were two performances scheduled, but the night of the first performance, there was a huge snowstorm, which canceled out the second performance. A sign, to be sure!

In truth, there's very little of Godfrey in that third movement. It's too much Arlene. Instead of completing Godfrey's masterpiece, I had inadvertently commissioned a companion piece to Godfrey's *Sonata*.

Godfrey was not ambitious about getting his music performed. *Sonata* would have been his longest piece and only his second orchestral work. Despite being a compulsive worker, he did more working than he did completing. He never even published his own book of theory, so much of which was original and challenging.

There seemed to be so little left, compared with the hours of thought and work Godfrey had invested in his music, his writing, and his computer research. After I returned from working with Arlene in Texas, Roger Maren encouraged me to archive Godfrey's papers properly in the Firestone Library at Princeton.

The first step was to take Godfrey's notebooks and organize and transcribe them. Princeton wanted typed notes. Some of these writings went as far back as Hodge Road, when he and Jim Randall were interested in Schenkerian music theory. I bought an electric typewriter and set myself up in his study. Every morning, for almost a year, I'd wake and get to work. I typed clean copies from loose sheets and thick spiral notebooks. Godfrey always wrote in pencil, never pen. I think he wanted the convenience of erasing a mistake and that it was just an old habit. There were many pages of penciled thoughts in his notebooks and loose sheets among the enormous amount of writing he left. There were papers on music theory, criticism, a system for teaching tonal music, a notebook on psychoacoustics (how one listens), his doctoral thesis (*Composition with Arrays*), his analyses of many classical works, and so on. I typed up all of these papers as best I could and included them alongside his manuscripts in the archive of Firestone Library at Princeton University. Sometimes his writing was illegible, and I would leave an empty space for an incomprehensible word. Fortunately, with Roger Maren's help, we were able to solve many of these word puzzles. Later, Leslie David Blasius (known as Lee), a Princeton graduate student, used Godfrey's papers as a basis for his thesis. He issued a book, *The Theory of Godfrey Winham*, published by Princeton University Press. And yet that was only the smallest glimpse into all that Godfrey had written.

I worked on it until it was done. I'm compulsive about finishing things; I managed my feelings by diving into Godfrey's beautiful, musical mind.

The aftermath of Godfrey's death was complex and disordered. It can't be depicted as if it all happened within a reasonable, sequential amount of time, in a coherent, identifiable way. Finishing the archives and completing the *Sonata* were both perhaps the closest I came to a chapter of mourning. They were both tangible projects with evident endpoints. What happened in my family, my house, and to some extent my work, for better and worse, was much more drawn out and often hard to see in the moment.

For the entire year of Godfrey's illness, I had been depending on Baird. Christopher was only fourteen at the time, and I kept him away from Godfrey's sickroom, but Baird had been by my side and watched his father waste away. It all must have been so frightening. For months before Godfrey died, Baird had been telling friends at school that his father was getting well, which meant that he'd spent the entire tragic experience in deep denial. And yet I turned to him for help and support during that time, and then just as easily turned away from him so that I could focus on Godfrey. By the time I came back from Austin, he'd been on his own dealing with his grief as poorly as you might expect of a teenage boy. He was a mess, paranoid and delusional, unable to focus on school, strung out on anguish and hallucinogens.

Now I can look back and see what was happening, how Baird began self-medicating. I blame myself for not having monitored him better. Neither Godfrey nor I had ever smoked pot or done drugs of any kind at all. We had a glass of wine at dinner; that was the extent of it. But that wasn't true of Baird and his friends. They were children of the sixties, affluent Princeton teenagers. Beer and marijuana were everywhere. They experimented with harder drugs. Over the two years since his father had died, Baird had gotten broken and dependent. The consequences of that period would reverberate well into his adulthood.

We brought him to the Carrier Clinic, where he was treated for nervous exhaustion and drug abuse. He was critically ill for three months and lost almost a year of school. As soon as he was released, still fragile, from the hospital, I took him and Christopher, along with Baird's best friend, Tom Tate, to England for Christmas. I wanted to be with Godfrey's family but far away from Belle Mead. By the following April, Baird was able to return to school, and I got back to work on the archives. Being busy with Godfrey's papers, I felt a sense of his closeness and even more of his powerful intellect.

Godfrey was an intellectual and an artist. His interest in money extended only to his immediate circumstances. He never paid it much mind when it was there, and it was never really not there. He certainly didn't live ostentatiously—with his shoes full of holes and his pants shiny from wear. He couldn't tolerate anything new until it was "broken in," as he used to say. When Daddy gave us the money that we used to build an addition to the Belle Mead house, Godfrey was grateful for the opportunity to live more comfortably. When we had money left over from that, Godfrey set about learning how to invest it as if he were studying new strategies for chess. He was a quick study, and he invested our money well.

The way I handled Godfrey's estate can probably best be described in the context of grief. There were periods in which I was involved—organized, curious, vocal—and there were periods in which I couldn't think about it. I was overwhelmed, or had spent all of my energy on dealing with Godfrey's papers and music, activities that somehow allowed me to live with the fact of Godfrey's death and the horrible circumstances surrounding it. Grief is capricious.

After Godfrey's funeral, our old friend Eb Faber came up to me and started talking to me about the estate and how it would work with the co-executor, who was my sister's husband, Jack Maynard. Jack had come down with Helen from Red Hook while Godfrey was sick and helped him draw up a will. Of course Godfrey didn't have one at the time; he was too young to have thought about such things. And I was too distracted with worry to pay much attention to what they had set up. In my naiveté I didn't really know anything anyway about executors, legal matters, or fees. I was in fact surprised to learn that my brother-in-law would take over my family's affairs. I felt that the will had been drawn up behind my back. I remember distinctly that I exclaimed to Eb in the course of our conversation, "I don't need an executor! I can take care of everything."

All my life I'd been resourceful and independent. I'd left Lansing with the intent of forging my own career as a singer. I'd left my first marriage without the slightest reservation about my ability to take care of myself. Here I was, suddenly on my own again, and no matter how confident I was in myself, I also knew that our life had grown more complicated: We had a house and children, we had investments overseas. In truth, I didn't really have the slightest idea what I could actually take care of by myself and what I couldn't.

What I learned—not right away but over the course of many years—is that I am self-reliant and can handle a great many things well, especially money. But self-reliance also means being able to identify situations where you're out of your league or element, situations where you need professional assistance, and it means knowing where to go for good advice. I didn't start out knowing all of that. There were mistakes to be made along the way.

Godfrey had invested our money in the stock market and had positioned us extremely well. Eb Faber then recommended me to an extraordinary broker, Julian Robertson, and encouraged me to become a charter investor in the new hedge fund that Julian was setting up. It meant selling some of the assets that Godfrey had put us in and was for that reason a colossal risk. But I thought to myself that this was my only chance to actually ever make some money.

I was right. The Tiger Fund that Julian started turned out to be one of the most successful hedge funds of all time. Between 1980 when the fund started and 2000 when Julian finally closed it, we earned very well. My fortunes were set, and I had done it myself. I didn't need taking care of at all. I was right all those years before at Godfrey's funeral. What I needed and what I had was very good advice and astronomical luck.

Perhaps it will strike some as unseemly to talk about money in a book about music. There is no inherent synchronicity between hedge funds and music, yet I don't think I could possibly overstate the degree to which being wealthy defined the course of my career. From the moment I met Godfrey, and through all those years of singing rarefied new music to a select audience of minute proportions, I didn't once have to worry about making a living. That liberated me entirely into my art, putting me and the music that I performed into a distinctly privileged position. Very few artists (especially these days) are able to chart a path that is completely unpolluted by practical concerns. I went from barnstorming the country with the literature of the Second Viennese School, to performing difficult, often obscure, new music, to a last golden chapter singing lieder because that's what I loved to sing. I could *never* have had the career I had without financial security. It would be guileless to think that artists and their art inhabit a sanitized bubble uninflected by the world of commerce.

CHAPTER FIFTY-ONE

SINGING AGAIN

In my experience, dancers take advantage of musicians. It's strange, though, because you'd think dancers and singers would have an unwritten pact, or at least an affinity. And it's always been clear to me that dancers have a great deal of respect for the intellectualism of musicians and especially composers. That said, you can't steal a dancer's performance as easily as you can a singer's. For years after I sang in Martha Graham's *Clytemnestra*, I'd come across evidence of her company using a bootlegged tape of my live performance. I have a program from the first tour the show made in Jerusalem where I am credited as the singer even though I wasn't there, meaning that they used a recording, one that I never went into the studio for. I received a letter in 2002 from a scholar working on a biography of Halim El-Dabh, who wrote the music for *Clytemnestra*. The scholar was looking for permission to use a portion of a reel-to-reel recording of the music that she had unearthed. It strikes me that she was the first person involved with *Clytemnestra* who ever requested permission for what must have been the unofficial recording used many times over for live performances of the ballet.

In 1961, Glen Tetley choreographed a ballet to *Pierrot lunaire* and for years after used my recording of it in performance without acknowledgment or permission—that I know of. The "theft," though, led to a wonderful opportunity. In 1977, the great dancer Rudolf Nureyev approached me because he wanted to mount Tetley's dance but wanted me to perform it live.

Working with Nureyev was quite different from working with Martha Graham. I wasn't on stage but down in the pit with the instrumental ensemble. I had a microphone and felt in total control—I could watch Rudy's pacing and respond with my own tempi. Some evenings I would slow down phrases on the part with solo flute, "Der kranke Mond," just to watch his intuitive response. His movements were always in perfect sync with my voice, and that's when I was impressed with how musical he was. I also indulged the feeling of being the powerful one—dancers are so dutiful when it comes to following the music. It's their organizing principle.

We started with six weeks in New York at the Uris Theatre, and the whole experience was as glamorous as you'd hope. We moved on to Los Angeles, where I introduced my friends Clara Steuermann and Leonard Stein to Rudy after the performance at the Hollywood Bowl. Then on to Paris at the Comédie-Française for two weeks. Rudy always brought me onstage for bows at the end, treating me as his collaborator. If flowers were thrown, he would pick one up and give it to me.

There is a lovely poetry to my having started this long, final chapter of my career with Nureyev and this choreography. Nureyev was already advanced in years when he took on this solo piece. Much of Tetley's gymnastic dance takes place on a cubist jungle gym—so the little clown's feet don't touch the ground.

Physical artists, dancers and singers, are constantly battling their bodies. When Lotte Lehmann gave her farewell performance at Town Hall in 1951, she famously said, "It is really tragic that just at the time when I understand singing so profoundly, the ability to do it the way I would like is taken from me." I was only in my early fifties at that point, so I was beginning to feel the decline only in little measures. But as my diary pages from those years till now would begin to flag with increasing frequency, my body and its limitations were a source of frustration. Aging is not for the weak!

My voice was still strong in 1977. I went to Greece that year as representative of the United States section at the ISCM World Days Festival. I was there with the conductor Robert Black and the composer Brian Fenneley. I sang *Philomel*, representing American New Music. We had a wonderful time in Athens. We took a ferry out to some of the islands where we ate salad and drank local wine. The memory of that culinary delight lingers. But the memory that I will treasure forever was standing on a hill over the Acropolis one afternoon and listening to Nikos Skalkottas's Violin Concerto being rehearsed in the open-air theater below. It was like a dream. We heard many works by Skalkottas on that trip and saw an exhibition of his manuscripts. The Australian pianist Geoffrey Madge played the complete set of Skolkattas's thirty-two piano pieces in one concert. I couldn't help but think how much Godfrey would have enjoyed the experience.

In some respects, these were to be the most interesting years of my life. Baird and Christopher were in college; I didn't have to keep a homestead the way I once did; I was by myself and free. It seemed somehow that the more I drew away from the performance battlefield of new music that I had abandoned abruptly when Godfrey got sick, the more interesting new opportunities seemed to come my way. My career had matured; I was being recognized for my achievements—I received honorary doctorates and was asked to speak and to serve on panels—which was a deeper kind of appreciation than a rave in a daily newspaper.

Princeton gave me an honorary doctorate in 1977—I took my brother Walter, who was delighted to be able to spend the evening talking to the civil rights activist and congresswoman Barbara Jordan, who was also being honored. The citation on my degree read: "She has been a constant source of encouragement to a host of 20th century composers—a spur to their creative endeavors and, not least, a cause for their gratitude. In her, our serious contemporary musicians have in the truest sense an ally. Her brilliant voice is an instrument of praise to the brightest products of the human spirit." If my dedication, though occasionally (and privately) grudging to contemporary music has indeed been a spur, then it was well worth the battle.

I lost a lot of weight in 1977 and eventually had my first affair after Godfrey. I also started really singing again. Singing freed me from my sorrow and loss. I had to get back to singing as it was the best therapy to recover from Godfrey's death. But my career had shifted, or rather, my desires for my career had shifted. The shift is probably best expressed in terms of Godfrey's death. I came out of that period with less time to waste, less patience for music that didn't transport me, and more affection for the people around me. I think of those as years in which I did a great deal of singing with and for friends of music that I wanted to sing—whether new or classical.

My first official concert in this new chapter was Claudio Spies's *Shirim le Hathunatham* (The Wedding Songs), which I performed with the Da Capo Chamber Players at Carnegie Recital Hall on April 21, 1976. Da Capo is now in residence at Bard College, just up the street from where I live.

Claudio Spies was a gentle man who I particularly remember had the most beautiful hands; his manuscripts were always gorgeously copied. He was a lovely person with a lovely wife and four children. He taught at Princeton with Milton and was particularly interested in Stravinsky. Claudio was born in Chile to German Jewish parents and spoke many languages. When I started working on lieder again, he would step in and help me brush up my German. Especially in the period right after Godfrey died, Claudio was a loyal friend and a big fan.

In that first year back to singing, I tackled a few new pieces, including David Winkler's *Three Shakespeare Sonnets*, and Frank Brickle's *Varioso* for soprano and computer-synthesized sound. I also did John Melby's *Two Stevens Songs* for soprano and computer-synthesized sound. John and Frank had both been colleagues of Godfrey and students of computer music at Princeton. I liked Frank's work and his unusual take on what the computer could bring. He saw the electronic evolution moving in a different direction. I loved John's music, too. The computer sound had a beautiful warmth to it that the synthesizer lacks. I compare a synthesizer with a harpsichord. It's percussive, whereas the computer has a warmer timbre.

At the end of 1980, I *finally* sang in the recital hall at the Arnold Schoenberg Institute in Los Angeles. Clara Steuermann and Leonard Stein were codirectors of the institute, which housed Schoenberg's manuscripts, important documents, books, and letters. The occasion was a concert by the Sequoia String Quartet. They were young, wonderful players. As a guest artist I performed in Schoenberg's Second Quartet, which I had done often with the LaSalle String Quartet. Mel Powell, who taught at the California Institute of the Arts, wrote some *Little Companion Pieces* to fit the program. We repeated the program in New York at Alice Tully Hall and, under Mel's coaching, recorded them both for Nonesuch records.

I had spent a lot of that first period after Godfrey died seeing friends and going to concerts, when I wasn't working on the archives in New York City. I would visit with the Perles frequently. I first met George Perle, you might remember, all those years before when Jacques and I were on our Second Viennese barnstorming tour in Kentucky, and I was stuck waiting for a steak to defrost while Jacques and George endlessly talked shop. By 1976, George was teaching at Queens College and living with his wife, the sculptor Barbara Phillips, in a large, gorgeous apartment right on Central Park West.

One of my recurring laments in the immediate aftermath of Godfrey's death was that I had never taken enough photographs of him—clearly, because it had never occurred to me he'd suddenly not be there one day. So Barbara decided to undertake a large-scale portrait of Godfrey, working off

Francine's photos of him from Hodge Road. I hope it's not ungrateful to say that it's difficult to capture a person's essence from a photograph. Hers was such a sincere and generous tribute, but the finished charcoal sketch was painfully two-dimensional and stirred nothing of Godfrey in me.

Tragically, Barbara already had cancer. She became ill very soon after that and died. Before she died, George took her to Europe to see the medieval sculptures in Spanish cathedrals that had been her lifelong ambition to see. George and I were suddenly young widows together. We spent a number of evenings soon after Barbara's death reading through songs—Fauré, Wolf, and late Debussy. George had similar inclinations to mine and took solace in composing. Between that and the sight-reading, he decided to write a new song cycle for me on the poetry of Emily Dickinson, only the second of two pieces for voice and piano he ever did.

The opportunity to debut the Dickinson cycle presented itself during the summer of 1978 at the second Westminster Choir College Art Song Festival. I planned a full program with Morey Ritt, a wonderful pianist and a friend of George's. In addition to the Dickinson, we performed Debussy's *Trois poèmes de Stephane Mallarmé* (the ones I'd sung with Boulez), and we closed the program with Schumann's *Liederkreis*. George had requested we include the late Debussy songs, which he loved in particular. Mallarmé's poetry is practically untranslatable, and the late Debussy songs are rather atonal. Yet it was all familiar music and a program that I could approach with confidence, my preferred strategy now that I was in my fifties. I was frankly starting to notice differences in my sound. It was as if my voice had lost its girlishness and was getting darker.

George's music was easy to hear but rhythmically difficult. Morey was a wonderful pianist and a great help; I confess that I relied on her heavily. Many of the rehearsals were with George in his apartment and he gave us wonderful coaching. My brain had been overloaded with all the new music I had learned and a part of me just wanted to sing lieder. But I admired George's cycle and persevered, and I'm glad I did. I think it's an important addition to the canon. We were able to record the whole cycle for CRI. George was by our side the whole time, checking on his metronomic wristwatch to make sure each song was in its proper tempo and that all tempo changes were exact. He trusted me implicitly on the pitch and interpretation, but he didn't leave rhythm to chance. Some composers are very fussy about certain details of their music, and George was one.

Parenthetically, it is an interesting phenomenon that throughout my career the composers whom I have been closest to, whom I have adored as people and as artists, often claim that I asked for them to compose something for me. I know of many pieces that were composed for me, with my voice and my aesthetic in mind, but I have only ever formally commissioned one piece, *Philomel*. The other exception was that in a burst of enthusiasm, I asked the composer George Edwards if he'd write me something after I'd heard a beautiful performance of *Moneta's Mourn* at Tully Hall. He produced several songs on the poetry of George Herbert, *A Mirth But Open'd*, and I performed them at the Composers Guild with the pianist Christopher Oldfather in 1987. George was a student of Milton and Earl's at Princeton, and a great friend of Fred Lerdahl. Of course, his beautiful music was difficult. I don't know what possessed me to ask for such a work. But again Chris bailed me out during many rehearsals with his coaching. He is such a fine pianist and a gift to new music.

Having been married to two composers, I should know how difficult it is to keep up morale. The audiences are so small and it's so rare for new music to be performed more than once, let alone for a new piece to join the canon. Perhaps things like commissions, even the enthusiasm of performers, help to keep a composer working in an artistic world that must feel like a desert more often than it should.

The Dickinson songs were among George's most successful works and were included on the tribute CD compiled for me by CRI in 1997. For the liner notes, George wrote a particularly thoughtful comment on my career and these songs:

> Bethany and I met frequently during the eight months it took me to write the *Thirteen Dickinson Songs*, and I was able to experience firsthand something that I already knew: that Bethany could make the most difficult problems of intonation and the most intricate rhythmic relations seem effortless and natural. But our collaboration actually began before I had even found a text, when I would prime myself for the composition of the song cycle that Bethany had asked me to write by reading through songs of Beethoven and Schubert, Debussy and Wolf, with her. And indeed, a perceptive reviewer of the original release of the present recording observed that "Perle can be said to be working within, even paying homage to, the Lied tradition," as Bethany herself had done in her performances of the "atonal" songs of Schoenberg, Webern, and Berg. In fact, Bethany's career has earned a place for itself in the history of music and is to be treasured above all for the connections it has given us. Without

connections we would be without tradition, and without tradition we would have no language, neither of music nor of words. So it is worth noting that the same artist whose rare and special gifts we first came to know through her incomparable performances of the music of the second Vienna school, including the world premieres of several song cycles by Webern and the American premieres of Berg's Altenberg-Lieder and Schoenberg's Three Songs, Op. 48, and who showed us how this music is continuous with an earlier tradition, also gave the premiere performances of the works that are heard on this disc.[92]

George's sincere praise means the world to me, and I was proud to have the Dickinson songs at such a late period of my career.

I began to feel more and more that I wanted to be working with people I enjoyed and admired. When I look back on this period in my performance career, I think of it as my "singing with friends" chapter. I performed with chamber groups such as the Sequoia and Pro Arte string quartets, and Earl Kim's group the Ariel Chamber Ensemble. I sang contemporary composers I wanted to sing—Milton (on his many birthday occasions), Mel Powell, and Schoenberg and the classics.

The oboist Marc Schachman, from Monadnock, had formed a very good baroque group called the Aulos Ensemble. They were like Pro Musica, traveling everywhere and playing early music. Most of the time, they didn't do vocal music, but occasionally I would join them and we'd perform Bach together. We toured with a lovely program called "A Baroque Christmas." I would move soon into a glorious period of singing lieder. I felt more in charge of my repertoire than ever before.

In 1977 I went back into the studio for New World Records. Bob Helps and I, along with the wonderful baritone Donald Gramm, recorded an album of American art songs entitled *Yesterday Is Not Today*. I sang work by Israel Citkowitz, Aaron Copland, Theodore Chanler, Roger Sessions, and Samuel Barber. I also did Bob's new cycle *The Running Sun* on verses by the novelist James Purdy. Donald sang Theodore Chanler, as well as Paul Bowles and John Duke. Ned Rorem wrote the comprehensive liner notes, a warm and concise appreciation of the American art song.

Soon after, I was able to be part of my friend John Huggler's big redemption concert in his honor at the Sanders Theatre in Cambridge, Massachusetts. You'll remember how poorly received John's piece *Sculptures* had been received in the early sixties. Critics weren't content to pan

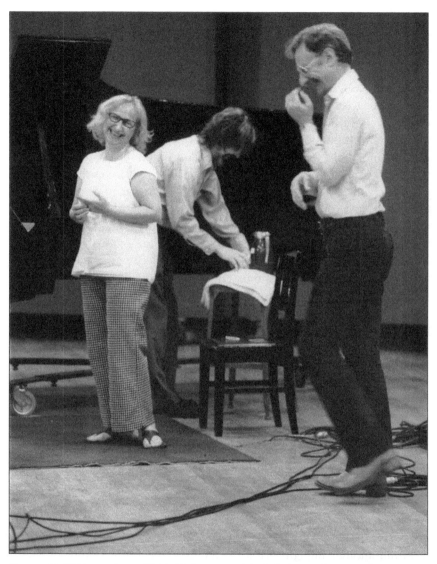

Figure 63. With producer Keith Holzman and Bob Helps at the recording session for *But Yesterday Is Not Today* for New World Records, 1977. Courtesy of Barbara Jaffe.

the pieces back then; they drove the point home by reviling John's too-informal attire that evening. I may not have liked *Sculptures* that much, and he was wearing sloppy brown corduroys, but I adored John.

His new work, Seven Orchestral Songs, was a great improvement on *Sculptures*. They were beautiful settings of poems by E. J. Leavenworth. These were easy pieces to sing, and I could learn them even with my old brain. John had experienced a great deal of early success. He won a Guggenheim Fellowship at the start of his career and then had the extraordinary opportunity to be composer in residence with the Boston Symphony Orchestra when he was only thirty-five years old. The aim of that residency program, which was a pilot program at the time, was to give composers the chance to work closely with an orchestra, to hear their music as they wrote. Many of the composers I collaborated with over my entire career wrote for small ensembles. That was what the cultural industry supported. It was exponentially harder to get an orchestra piece produced than it was to mount a concert with a few musicians. John stood out among my friends for his access to such large-scale productions. Unfortunately, he died very young, just a few years after the concert at Sanders, of lung cancer. He was only sixty-four.

After Godfrey's death, I had grown very close to Arlene Zallman, who was now teaching composition at Wellesley College. Between her and Earl Kim, I was up in the Boston area a great deal. Arlene belonged to the composers' group Griffin Music Ensemble; I sang a few concerts with them. Arlene was heavily involved with the concert programming at Wellesley College. I went on to make a number of appearances at Wellesley through the 1980s, beginning, I believe, with a December 1982 performance with the Atlantic String Quartet. That concert was a combination of friendship and tribute, for not only were the chamber musicians my friends, but the program was Godfrey's *Habit of Perfection*, Schoenberg's Second String Quartet, and Berg's *Lyric Suite*.

I did another big concert at the Sanders Theatre in Cambridge with the Ariel Chamber Ensemble. The program was perfect: Webern, Mozart, Maurice Delage, Brahms, and my triumph, Schoenberg's *Herzgewächse*, which Richard Dyer aptly referred to in his review as "the most difficult challenge ever posed to the human voice by a great composer." The piece is built on vertiginous intervals; I had bragged to Dyer that I had learned it while standing at the kitchen sink, washing dishes. That image of me, working away at the difficult vocal line, while doing my chores must have

Figure 64. Me and Arlene on the porch at Belle Mead, ca. 1977.

struck him as especially hilarious—but also reinforced a point about what it was still like to be a professional woman in those days. "All of this," Dyer wrote, "Beardslee managed with the greatest mastery: this most diaphanous of voices has only grown more beautiful during the singer's nearly 30 years before the public—certain tones in it now seem to be dissolving in light." Dyer's review, in its effusiveness, all summed up the central conundrum of my career—the conundrum I was spending my final chapter trying to resolve: Had she chosen, he wrote, "to spend her career singing Delibes' "Bell Song" rather than Babbitt's "Nightingale," Bethany Beardslee might have become one of the most famous as well as one of the best singers of our time."[93]

Because of George Perle, I was also singing Berg's *Lyric Suite* frequently in this period. Berg was one of George's areas of expertise. He had written

Figure 65. Shirley and George Perle at the Perles' weekend house near Tanglewood, ca. 1998. Photograph by Bethany Beardslee. Courtesy of Shirley Perle.

extensively about the composer and, along with Douglas Green, was key in discovering the hidden love letter to Berg's married lover, Hanna Fuchs-Robettin, that he had embedded into the music. The story was almost fantastical and scandalous. George had been going through Berg's papers and discovered clues that the last movement of the *Lyric Suite* was set to a Baudelaire love poem. There were no words, but the notes were there. George went to good old Louise Zemlinsky to ask whether she knew anything. Mrs. Zemlinsky indicated that she did know *something*—but she'd have to consult with her husband before revealing anything to George. Well, Alexander Zemlinsky had been dead for over forty years at this point. But he nonetheless relented, and Mrs. Zemlinsky was able to help George put together the puzzle pieces.[94]

George was like a little boy who'd discovered the golden Easter egg. His enthusiasm for his historical detective story was delightful. He extracted the notes and the setting from the score and rehabilitated the secret version, which I performed a number of times. I sang it for the first time with the Columbia String Quartet; George appeared with me, lecturing about the story. We did it again with the Vermeer Quartet at the All-Berg Conference in Chicago and finally with the Emerson Quartet at the Chamber Music Series of Lincoln Center. The buried love poem is musicologically interesting, but in terms of great music, I think it should be said that the *Lyric Suite* is much better off without the sung version.

The Berg brought me full circle. I was getting less and less interested in debuting music. I resisted when the young Princetonian composer John Peel brought me his new piece, *La pythie*. It was a monologue for soprano and chamber ensemble based on French text from Paul Valéry's poem. I knew from the outset that it represented hours of work—the kind of work that was getting increasingly difficult for me. But John played it through on the piano, and I could hear right away how glorious the music was. I couldn't *not* do it. I premiered it in Boston with the ensemble Collage, conducted by Richard Pittman. I was able to perform it only one more time after the debut, in New York with the contemporary-music group Parnassus, conducted by Anthony Korf. I loved that score and have often wonder if John found someone else to sing it. Or did it end up with all the other neglected scores on the shelves?

You see how perfectly cyclical the rhythms of my career had become? Singing Berg again in the eighties; singing *Pierrot*; singing new music that languished with too few performances. And then there was of course, the perpetual pull toward classical music.

CHAPTER FIFTY-TWO

LIEDER WITH RICHARD GOODE

1 9 8 0 – 9 0

One night in 1980, I went to a dinner party that Shirley Rhoads was holding to celebrate George Perle's birthday. George and Shirley had fallen in love and were about to get married. Shirley is a fine pianist who appears often in Ned Rorem's many diaries, as they had been friends since early on in Paris, and she'd always been in the midst of musical society. Her first husband was the composer and cellist Seymour Barab—their marriage was annulled—and her second was the painter George Rhoads, with whom she had two children.

Richard Goode was the other guest at dinner that night. I was delighted to see him again. Richard ended up the evening at the piano playing Chopin and some Brahms intermezzi for us. I remember thinking as I listened to him play that night that the time had come for the "old gal" (me) to live a little. I wanted to indulge myself, go back to the classics. I was tired of memorizing new music, all that work for all those pieces that would never be played again. I was also tired of waiting for Bob Helps to be around. Shortly after the party, I decided to call up Richard and find out if he might be interested in doing a lieder series with me—an idea I'd been toying with since doing a Schumann and Brahms recital recently with Eddie Cone at Princeton.

As with Bob, I didn't want Richard to be *just* an accompanist. I wanted a creative collaborator. He started coming out to Belle Mead, or I'd go into

Figure 66. In my London apartment in the early eighties.

New York to his apartment, and we'd read through lieder and listen to LPs. We read through many, many songs. We finally chose the ones we wanted to do for three concerts of all Brahms, all Schumann, and all Schubert.

We decided to model our concerts after those of Artur Schnabel—whom Richard was often compared with—and Schnabel's wife, Theresa Behr, a well-known recitalist in Europe before World War II. Each program had a large group of songs combined with a piano work by the same composer: songs, a solo piano piece, intermission, songs. For the Brahms program, we did a group of five songs. (Brahms didn't compose cycles, but would give an opus number to a group of songs.) Then Richard would play the *Variations and Fugue on a Theme by Handel.* After intermission we did a large group of eleven songs. The next program was all Schumann. We began with a large group of Schumann's individual songs and ended with my old favorite, *Liederkreis*, op. 48. Richard played the C-major *Fantasie*. For the Schubert program, Richard played the C-minor Sonata, D. 958, flanked again by two large groups of individual songs.

Richard and I started with that concert series in New York and went on to perform together many programs from German and French song literature. Since Richard could read anything, I think I enjoyed our sessions of reading through lieder as much as the concerts themselves. It brought me back to my old college days when Dr. Lucas and I used to read through songs.

We gave our first program in November 1980 at Merkin Concert Hall in New York. It was the beginning of several years of collaboration. The critics noted right away that Richard was a gorgeous soloist and "as an accompanist he functioned as a partner, turning each song into a kind of chamber duet that underscored every emotional point."[95] As for me, in 1980 I was only fifty-five years old and to my mind nowhere near retirement. My voice had a great deal of stamina, especially compared with those of some of my contemporaries who'd tested their big sounds against years in opera houses. In a review from the same period of a performance that I gave of Mel Powell's songs with the Sequoia String Quartet, Donal Henahan described my voice as "now darker than it once was … able to exploit the work's prevailingly somber moods." I knew that my sound had changed. But the darkening was important and was something I could use dramatically. "A first-rate lieder singer must be a first-rate vocal actor, must be able, with a minimum of operatics or none at all, to convey the emotional and intellectual content of the song with the full power of the theater. … This last was the heart of Beardslee's achievement. The recital was a series of interior visions, completely characterized and conveyed with absolute conviction."[96] I began thinking (for the millionth time in my life) that I should have just made a career out of this repertoire—the music I'd loved in college.

After a Schubertiade program with Richard at the Frick Art and Historical Center in Pittsburgh, the *Pittsburgh Post-Gazette* wrote: "Now Beardslee has turned to Romantic songs, with, if anything, even greater success. In the offbeat Brahms songs, she inflected every word with the precise color to communicate its emotional core. In Schubert she commanded a near perfect legato and made the familiar Romanze from 'Rosamunde' as fresh as if it had been written yesterday. Not one phrase was less than the very highest artistic accomplishment."[97]

Peter Davis of *New York* magazine gave us an extensive write-up:

Throughout most of her career, Bethany Beardslee has been associated with new music, and the contemporary composer could scarcely hope for a better interpreter—committed, intelligent, and, unlike so many specialists in this field, blessed with a real voice. Beardslee has been so busy with premieres that she seldom finds time for more conventional repertory, but over the past few years the soprano has allowed herself that luxury in a series of joint recitals with the pianist Richard Goode at Merkin Hall. . . . And how wonderfully she sang them all, with a voice still striking for its intonational purity and silvery clarity.[98]

I thought to myself that I had finally gotten to where I wanted to be a long time ago.

But things are never simple. Richard was very different from any other collaborator I worked with. He was a big personality—not demure like Earl Kim or Eddie Cone, or industrious like Lois Shapiro or Christopher Oldfather, deadly serious like Jacques, or dear like Yehudi Wyner or Bob Helps. Shirley Perle always spoke of him in most adulatory terms. Richard was charismatic, with a warm. He was big and rumpled, voracious in his tastes—a big eater and a huge reader. Books littered the halls of his apartment for want of space. We would dash through so much music, as he could sight-read anything. I really relied heavily on his formidable musicianship. But I wanted him to stop and work through things meticulously as I had done with Jacques. "People are always concerned," he told Bruce Duffie, "that this has to be *the* way the piece goes, rather than this is *one* way it goes . . . most of the piano records we listen to were made fifty years ago, and they have wrong notes in them. But they also sound inspired, so we keep listening to those. It's not, somehow, playing every note in its absolute place that seems to matter, but something else."[99]

I couldn't possibly have invented a more anti-Jacques perspective. Whereas Jacques rehearsed us to death, overprepared us, in his massive effort to stave off nerves, Richard had the exact opposite approach. Despite lavish encouragement from his peers and mentors, such as Rudolf Serkin and the gang at Marlboro, Richard had spent his early career hiding himself in chamber music, where he was highly regarded. He played with the Chamber Music Society of Lincoln Center. When we reconnected at George's party, he was starting to venture out as a concert pianist and had just won the prestigious Avery Fisher Award. His big solo break was when he did the Beethoven sonatas at the 92nd Street Y. Then he recorded them for the Book of the Month Club. That launched him into the major part of his career. In the process, he turned what came naturally to him into an aesthetic—that important "something else" that had nothing to do with playing every note in its place. What Jacques found in precision, Richard found in a performance style.

When it came to our partnership, it was divisive. We were forever doing battle with what did work: a shared passion for that repertoire and a flair for dramatic interpretation. As one critic put it: "All this time, Richard Goode was providing accompaniments with a tremendous warmth and power of their own. His style is visually distracting—bending and swaying, mouth working all the time, almost like a singer's—or rather, it might be distracting if Beardslee did not grip the listener's attention so absolutely."[100] Alone on stage, he made perfect sense, the way he swayed, rocked and, hummed, as if he couldn't contain the music. Glenn Gould was the same way—he'd sing and conduct and practically hug the piano. Someone, though, probably his manager, must have put the screws to Richard about his performance style, because as he advanced in his career, he stopped moving around so much, and his technique grew distinctly cleaner. Nonetheless, in the period we were together, his performance style was intrusive. He'd sing when he played; I'd get furious with him. We'd come off stage and I'd say, "You know, Richard, there's only one singer on this program." He'd reassure me and then keep on doing his singing. I finally decided to leave well enough alone. He was such a wonderful artist.

Critics are funny—as is, I presume, my relationship to them. I collected every review from my early years and put a great deal of stock in what they said, until I became confident enough to know for sure that I was good at what I was doing and that, more important, I could trust my own impressions of when I'd done well and when I hadn't. Godfrey used to say, "Darling, the time you stop reading your reviews you will have grown up." I stopped caring so much about (and cataloguing) all the reviews in my mid-career, which isn't to say I didn't celebrate a smart, lovely review. I did. But I also knew better that critics have their own musical memories, the ways their minds fix. If they've heard and fallen in love with another singer doing a certain piece, they're never going to give you a good review on it. I've been on the receiving end of that—a 1985 review of Jessye Norman's performance of the *Altenberg Lieder* was criticized because she didn't take the high C at the end pianissimo as I had on my recording with Robert Craft thirty years earlier![101] If critics like big, beefy voices, they're never going to give a singer like me a good review no matter what. Similarly, some critics had heard me as a young singer and then heard me again in my fifties, and they couldn't help but compare. They heard change. It was during this period that I starting paying attention to the critics again, considering their opinions more than I had been. I was probably waiting to hear someone tell me it was time to retire—or not, and I was also reassuring myself that singing lieder was more satisfying and important. I mention this here because this period of collaborating with Richard was defined by the unpleasant matter of my retirement. Still strong in my fifties, I certainly didn't feel ready to retire, and yet I had to plan it. Lotte Lehmann did fifteen years of lieder recitals after her opera career, before retiring at sixty-three. I wanted to retire *before* my voice failed me, not after. Which is why my relationship with the critics shifted again and I grew a little more dependent on their perspective.

As early as 1980 in my first recital of Brahms with Richard, small critiques of my voice started to appear. John Rockwell reviewed our Brahms recital with reservations. Although he praised the musicianship of my long career of interpreting contemporary music, he noted that my "Brahms lacked the ideal security of support and tonal control." His qualification was that mine had been "a long career." He added that my command of style was most convincing and that my "intensity of involvement" on the passionate songs of the program was "uncommonly moving."[102] At the time, I dismissed the criticism.

In 1983 Richard and I mounted another series in New York. We decided it would draw on my contemporary repertoire. I was now in my home court and had a reputation behind me. My voice was darker and heavier but still honed. On the first program was the Schoenberg's *Buch der hängenden Gärten*, Ravel's *Trois poèmes de Stephane Mallarmé*, and Benjamin Britten's cycle *On This Island*. Richard played late piano pieces by Brahms (capprici and intermezzi). Then I shifted gears and did the second program with the Atlantic String Quartet. We performed Schoenberg's String Quartet no. 2, Godfrey's *Habit of Perfection*, and Berg's *Lyric Suite*, with the hidden poem by Baudelaire. I had done this program several times, but it was new to the Atlantic String Quartet.

Allen Hughes wrote a glowing review of our *Das Buch der hängenden Gärten*. The review started with the assertion, "Bethany Beardslee is a phenomenon. A soprano who has probably done more than any other singer in America to aid the cause of difficult 20th century vocal music." His critique: "There was really only one thing that troubled some of Miss Beardslee's performances: She occasionally found herself on the lower side of the pitches,

Figure 67. Milton speaking about Godfrey's song cycle, *To Prove My Love*, at Merkin Hall, ca. 1984. Richard Goode on piano. Photograph by Jim Graves.

rather than square in the middle of them. Though hardly serious enough to be called flatting, the result was bothersome nevertheless."[103] The review appeared on Christmas Day, my fifty-eighth birthday. It stung. I thought to myself, Perhaps it's time.

The third program in the Merkin Hall series fell in May 1984. Richard began with Beethoven's Sonata in E, op. 109. I sang a group of Schubert songs and Godfrey's cycle *To Prove My Love*, and closed with a Poulenc cycle. I announced to my audience that I was retiring. The final encore was *Die Nachtigall*, one of the *Seven Early Songs* of Berg with which I had begun my career. Gwen Winham and André Deutsch came over for the occasion, and I dedicated one of my encores to them.

So that was that. I had had a long career, and it was time. My friends Ellie and Frank Steindler threw a great party with not enough food, but who cared? I don't think Ellie and Frank expected so many guests. People kept running out to get additional provisions. It was a hilarious and good-natured evening.

Then people kept asking me to do things, and it felt wonderful because my voice was still good. I began to realize that by announcing my retirement,

I didn't have to keep working on building a lieder career. I could just start doing what interested me—which brings me to my falling-out with Richard Goode. We'd been playing together sporadically since my retirement in May 1984. He got married in 1987, and then his solo career started taking off. Critics marveled at his inexplicable late blooming. For my part, I was scheduling leisurely, in keeping with my grand plan of singing what I wanted to in lovely venues: my golden chapter.

In the late winter of 1990, we were asked to do a recital at the Metropolitan Museum of Art and planned a program of Wolf, Brahms, and Debussy. While we were practicing, Richard told me, "You're flat. We can't do this recital." We canceled the show, even though we were already on the season calendar, and returned our six-thousand-dollar fee. I was devastated and angry at Richard for years after. He was right, of course. I wasn't singing well. But right or wrong, it felt as if he was plunging a nail into my coffin.

CHAPTER FIFTY-THREE

PIERROT RECORDS

New Ventures

I n the middle of Godfrey's sickness, when I was beyond distressed, I received a questionnaire-survey about singing technique. I certainly didn't have the presence of mind at that point to respond to a survey. But I did have an intense ability to focus. So on March 18, 1975, I sat down and wrote this letter in response.

Dear Ann Chase,

I received your letter of March 3rd. Instead of putting down some kind of answer to questions on your questionnaire, I would like to just state a few beliefs that I've always had as a professional singer. First and foremost, I believe a performer has a real responsibility to his art to perform the best quality music that has been written and is being written. It is not a question of singing Baroque Romantic Contemporary or whathaveyou but good music. I feel this attitude must prevail above all. With this in mind, students must know the fine basic repertoire of the past, from Josquin to Schoenberg. Then they develop taste and a value system by which to select music being written today. Performers should know how to write music, composers should know how to perform music, and the listener, ideally should be the most sophisticated of all, as he receives the music third hand. Of course these conditions do not exist but one can strive toward these ideals.

And now about singing itself.

1. A singer must have a fine ear. A good singer tunes. In tonal music one does not sing a tonic C sharp the same way as a leading tone C sharp. Tuning sometimes is difficult for singers who have absolute pitch. They can't always make these subtle distinctions.

2. A singer must have a good background in piano, so that they can play their score. One must hear the total piece and not just their line.

3. One finds their own learning process, using your ear as your guide. You have your unique sound and you must find what works best for you. This is your voice technique. It is a balance between what you wish to achieve musically and the physical ease of doing it.

4. Three things hurt a singer: bellowing, singing beyond your range, and age. Otherwise, born with a good ear and healthy body and good sound, anyone can have a professional career. Your sound should be tuned legato and free of distortion (i.e., breathiness or wobble).

Most singers sing with an unbalanced line. By that I mean that you can always hear the high range while the middle and lower range often disappear. Acoustically this middle and lower range must be reinforced to balance with the higher range. Either one sings with less volume higher to make for a smooth line dynamically, or one twangs more in the middle range to reinforce the upper partials of those pitches. Neither solution is ideal but should be noticed and worked on. A balanced line makes for beautiful singing.

A good diet, lots of rest, and a happy life, make for good singing. Music is a lifetime study and with each new piece one is learning musicianship. The control of a voice is a lifetime study and with each new musical problem, one is learning technique.

Voice teachers everywhere are going to say that I don't know what I'm talking about. And yet, in this last chapter of my career, one of my great pleasures came from occasional opportunities to teach.

Starting back long before my retirement, I made my first foray into teaching. In 1978, I taught and coached art song at Westminster Choir College in Princeton. My class was made up of both singers and pianists. I worked in conjunction with Marty Katz, who was teaching accompaniment to the pianists. I had many talented students there. Some went on to be professional accompanists; one that I know of became a rehearsal pianist at the Metropolitan Opera. My course covered a wide range of song repertoire from Schubert to Schoenberg (but nothing after the Second Viennese School) as well as French repertoire. For the first time I had to do research and prepare lectures on whatever composer we were covering. I left technical matters to the students' individual teachers and concentrated on coaching the music. It was very enjoyable to see the students phrase beautifully and watch their dynamics. I also made them listen carefully and make sure their pitch was always true.

One day in 1981, Arthur Komar, an old friend, called me because there was an opening in the Voice Department at the University of Texas at Austin. I applied for the position, never imagining I would be accepted—I had had such limited teaching experience. Either Arthur pushed my application through, or they were impressed by my performing reputation, but they did hire me. It was the perfect transitional opportunity. Belle Mead was making me sad. I sold the house in Belle Mead, put my furniture in storage, and drove down to Austin in my small, brown Datsun.

Until then, I had only coached at Westminster, so I got in touch with my friend Jo Estill, hoping to get a crash course in teaching college students who wanted to learn how to really sing. Jo was in the vanguard of the field of vocal pedagogy. She came from a singing background, but embarked on a remarkable course of scientific research late in her life to map the musculature of the voice and incorporate that information into voice training. She divided sound into different categories: speech, falsetto, sob, twang, belting, and something she called "opera ring." The last is what most professional singers are taught. I armed myself with some of her personal advice, her manual, what I remembered from my lessons with J. Herbert Swanson, and my own common sense, and I became a voice teacher.

Also in 1981, I was awarded a residency at the University of California, Davis from January to March, so for that period, I commuted back and forth. It was a mighty busy time. They gave me an apartment in California, and I was adopted (temporarily) by a beautiful cat. Everyone biked because the campus was so flat, and they'd imported red double-decker buses from England—the bright color complemented the landscape perfectly. Davis had real charm. I called it the Princeton of the West Coast. I hope it's still as charming now as it was in 1982.

Davis is in the middle of the Napa Valley, so I had some grand excursions. I went wine tasting with the composer Richard Swift and Bill Valente (a cousin of Benita Valente). Bill was a connoisseur and wanted to prove to me that California wines stood up in every respect to French. As I had by that point visited several vineyards for tastings and was a little tipsy, I wholeheartedly agreed. I also had a casino adventure at Lake Tahoe. It was one of my days off, and I decided to test my gambling skills. I had played poker quite a bit when Godfrey was alive and I wanted to try my luck. I waltzed in and sat down at the poker table with six men. In the space of fifteen minutes I had dropped a hundred dollars, so I got up and left. That was my last experience with casino gambling!

Sightseeing aside, the residency at Davis was primarily for performance. They wanted *Philomel*. Richard Goode came out to do a lieder recital with me. He performed a new piece that George Perle had composed for him, *Ballade*. Our lieder program was in a beautiful, small hall with wonderful acoustics. It was perfect for soft dynamics, and I was able to take full advantage of everything I had learned from Earl Kim. Years of experience singing in different halls gives you an awareness of how precious a good hall is. Audiences appreciate a dynamic range and listen differently. This time you could hear a pin drop.

I also had the opportunity to sing Mahler's *Songs of a Wayfarer* with the orchestra. It's a beautiful cycle, but I'd only ever done it with piano accompaniment. There's one especially dramatic song for which you might as well resign yourself to being buried by the orchestra. I tried to boost the volume of my lower register by using my chest voice whenever possible. It works to some extent, but those brasses were still overwhelming.

My faculty recital at the University of Texas was *Philomel*, coupled with lieder. On this occasion, David Garvey played for me—David, whom I knew so well from my voice lessons with Catherine Aspinall at Juilliard. He was now teaching at UT and playing for Leontyne Price.

The year in Texas and California was one of great transition. I learned a lot from teaching. I found that I had something to offer to voice students beyond coaching, and I had the distinct impression that it helped my own singing. The experience was probably most useful for me as a catapult out of Princeton. Ultimately, I wasn't happy in Texas. It was such a different atmosphere from that in the Northeast, and I was homesick for New York and my children. I stayed away a year and then packed myself back into my Datsun and went home.

I returned to New York City, rented a beautiful classic apartment overlooking Riverside Drive, and started trying to figure out what I was supposed to be doing, besides battling aging and spending money in that pricey city. I loved being there, because it was so easy to see old friends and hear music. I saw a lot of Jo Estill, who was finishing her PhD coursework at New York University and developing what would eventually become her significant (and patented) voice-training technique. Jo was a wonderful and

Figure 68. With conductor D. Kern Holoman after singing Mahler at University of
California, Davis, in 1982.

supportive friend. I really admired her. She used to tell me that I could do anything I wanted with my voice, that I could sing opera if I wanted to, but that I was just too timid. She said I indulged the little-girl part of me too much and let myself be intimidated by all the big cheeses. Jo was smart, as smart as some of the impressive men I surrounded myself with, and having her words in my head helped me keep my spirits up during all of the changes.

Jo and my sister Helen helped me throw my first big New York City party after I got back, a dinner to celebrate the marriage of Marni Nixon and Al Bloch. Marni and I sang Rossini and Purcell duets, and Marni sang a love song to Al. As of this writing, Marni has died—July 24, 2016. Another good friend gone.

I started looking for a permanent New York apartment, as my lovely West Side apartment was only a two-year lease from a Columbia professor who was on sabbatical. I stumbled on a quaint mews, a row of historic cottages nestled in between West 94th and West 95th streets. It was called Pomander Walk, and it was just going co-op. I bought a cottage there in January 1984 and spent the next year restoring it. I had been accustomed to big spaces. The living room alone in Belle Mead was thirty by twenty feet. New York City spaces didn't come that big. The first night I moved into Pomander Walk, I sat down and wept amid the boxes. What a horrible mistake I'd made! It wasn't just that everything was so small, or even so small and charming. It *was* perfectly charming, with its little flower boxes and its little fence and its little cottages. It was also just perfectly wrong. My piano didn't fit right and seemed to always be glaring at me accusingly, saying "Why did you do this?" The neighbors complained when I practiced or coached. I had to drape the windows with quilts to dampen the sound, which just made it darker and more depressing. New York had changed. It wasn't the city I'd loved in the fifties. It was crowded and expensive, with many homeless on the streets. Another romantic illusion gone. I held out for three years and then abandoned New York City for good.

I moved upstate to Rhinecliff, near Christopher, who had settled there after graduating Bard. I bought a sweet old house, just up the hill from the commuter train. If I needed to get to the city, I just waltzed down the hill to the station.

One day in the fall of 1992, a professor from Vassar College appeared at my door. There was an emergency in the music department, and they needed a voice teacher. It turned out that my friend William Parker was sick with AIDS. I'd been on the jury when Will won the John F. Kennedy

Center Rockefeller Foundation International Competition for Excellence in the Performance of American Music. He had a beautiful natural baritone and was in the prime of his career. Although I was grateful for the opportunity to teach again, I told Vassar that I would step in for Will only temporarily. As soon as he was better, they had to give him his job back.

Will didn't recover. He died shortly after, in 1993. I stayed on teaching at Vassar for another three years. I grew very close to several of my students, Sarah Hackenberg, Tara Loughran, and Catherine Viscardi. Of the three, only one, Catherine Viscardi, became a professional singer. When I told Vassar that I wanted to stop teaching, I realized that this time, I meant it. It was gratifying work, but I didn't need the income, and I wanted more freedom.

I started traveling in earnest—finally exploring places that I chose, rather than just following the itinerary of a concert tour. Jim Graves and I went to Mexico. I had a great trip with my brother Walter to England and Europe. Arlene Zallman and I spent a lovely long week in my apartment in England. Over the next decade, Arlene and I became devoted traveling partners and inseparable friends. She was divorced at this point, and when her daughters were on extended stays with their father in Ohio for Christmas or the summer, she was happy to have some kind of adventure to focus on. We went to Provence and Paris, England and Italy—especially to Florence, where she had spent several years on a Fulbright in the late fifties studying with Luigi Dallapiccola. We got into a groove: She'd finish up her semester teaching at Wellesley, and the next day we'd meet at an airport to catch our plane. With the exception of swimming, which I absolutely adore and Arlene couldn't have cared less for, we had highly compatible preferences for eating, sightseeing, relaxing, and laughing. Arlene had a canny sense of humor and loved to laugh and feel lighthearted—or, as I used to say, "to frolic." Without a doubt, the opportunity to travel is what I love most about retirement.

Of course the business of new music was never far from my attentions. Arlene and I were involved with the Association for the Promotion of New Music (APNM), one of good old Jacques's most successful and important "projects." Jacques started APNM in 1975 with Robert Pollock—another Princeton graduate. A cooperative publishing house run by composers, mostly for unpublished composers, APNM turned out to be the functional incarnation of the Composer's Catalog. This was during the period when Jacques was teaching at Columbia and had gotten especially chummy with Mario Davidovsky; they were both Marxists and shared musical affinities.

Jacques was still married to Margrit Auhagen at the time and making a good living, teaching first at the New England Conservatory, briefly at Queens, and then Columbia. He was in a good position to start again—yes, my friends—Monod Projects.

Jacques had first approached me about APNM right after Godfrey died. He wanted to help me organize Godfrey's music and to publish Godfrey's works. He got Godfrey placed with the music rights agency BMI and put the scores with APNM. I thought it was the right thing to do. I suppose you're wondering why Jacques was back in my life and telling me what to do, *again*. Sure, he always had to be boss of whatever he was doing, but his ideas and services were always right. I was grateful for his assistance and happy to have a revived friendship.

During that same period, Jacques was running a new music group that he called the Guild of Composers. The guild was a small organization, operating on a shoestring budget (of course), and mounting concerts in Christ & St. Stephen's Church on the Upper West Side, where the acoustics were just adequate. The programming was entirely under Jacques's control, as usual, but he managed to get new works by many young composers from Columbia University performed through this series. Jacques wanted me to come on as president of the Guild, which I agreed to do. Being president meant holding up the organization financially as well, which I did for several years, until it folded. It's so difficult for these little organizations to survive. I wonder whether the ISCM has done so well because it's an international organization.

APNM also survives. Rob Pollock ran it for years, operating it out of Ship Bottom, New Jersey. Jacques and Rob Pollock had a falling-out. Jacques's paranoia literally forced Rob to resign. Looking back, I can see it was wrong. Rob had done a fine job but had obviously crossed Jacques at some point. Rob now lives in Maui and has his own new music scene. Jacques was president when I got involved, and I began helping with administration. I managed the arrangements with Subito Music, which housed and distributed composer scores. I kept the books, collected dues, filed taxes, and so on. Arlene took over the presidency from Jacques; the two of us worked on it together until she died.

It was on one of our trips (I remember a beautiful view, delicious wine, and batting away mosquitoes) that Arlene came up with the idea of Pierrot Records. Arlene knew me well by then and had heard all of my regrets several times over. I had some greatest hits: that I hadn't loved new music unreservedly; that I hadn't done enough for Godfrey's music, despite having approached several record companies (with no success); and my old standby, that I hadn't recorded as many lieder as I'd wanted to. Arlene, who despite everything always seemed to come home to the conviction that anything is possible if you want it badly enough, finally shut me up by saying: "Bethany, why don't you make some lieder recordings and put them out on your own label?"

Her solution was inspired. She pointed out that there was nothing stopping me. I didn't realize that a person could just form a small record company. Arlene was right, of course. There was nothing stopping me. I had just come off a year of singing lieder with Richard Goode, publicly announced my retirement (although the announcement turned out to be some premature high theatrics on my part, but we'll come back to that), and my hedge fund was doing well. I was throwing money around—on my children, real estate, traveling, Jacques's projects. I had just built a recording studio for Baird in the outbuilding at Rhinecliff. There was no good reason not to get some kind of return on my investments.

Altogether, we made six CDs under the Pierrot label, and kept the project going for about a decade. I wasn't especially savvy about the business end, and I incorporated rather than setting up as self-employed. This was far more expensive. That misstep ultimately led to the financial collapse of my tiny company. But for a while, it was a blast.

The first two lieder CDs we made were Schubert and Schumann songs. I worked with the wonderful pianist Lois Shapiro, a colleague of Arlene's. I'd stay with Arlene in Wellesley and go over to Lois's house (bearing coffee and donuts) to rehearse. We practiced doggedly and then recorded the Schubert songs at Houghton Chapel on the Wellesley College campus. For the Schubert we used a historic Viennese piano. The piano was the result of a crazy impulse the two of us had to attract people to the CD by using a period instrument. We approached Edmund Michael Frederick, who with his wife had built up a historic piano collection housed in Ashburnham, Massachusetts. The Conrad Graf piano that we selected was an antique, dated 1828–29, that couldn't hold its pitch, so we had to have a tuner on site during the recording session to make constant adjustments.[104] For the Schumann, we used Wellesley's beautiful Steinway.

The third lieder CD was Brahms. Richard came up from New York to record it with me. Rather than the Steinway piano, he insisted we bring a massive Bösendorfer—the Rolls-Royce of concert pianos—into Houghton Chapel. It was an expense, but Richard was volunteering his time (in itself a substantial donation), and so I acquiesced. In retrospect, I might have done better to pay him for his time. He volunteered only one day for the recording. Even though the two of us had performed a number of the Brahms songs the year before, there were a few that we hadn't, and so once again, we relied rather too much on his prodigious sight reading. After such an intense rehearsal period with Lois, I felt that we were just knocking out the Brahms.

Pierrot Records not only satisfied my long-held ambition to record lieder but also kept me busy and interested, two things that were otherwise on the wane in my life. I got myself my first computer, created a logo, supervised the selecting and remastering of the CDs, and produced them. I can't remember if I was feeling especially elegiac at the time, but the last song on the first CD was Schubert's "An die Musik"—the same song with which Lotte Lehmann had ended her final Town Hall concert.

The orders came into my little Rhinebeck Station post-office box—many from college libraries. The first three CDs were selling, so I decided to keep going. I put together a Christmas-themed CD of Scarlatti cantatas and Godfrey's piano variations on "Jingle Bells." After building the backyard recording studio, I built a pool, then a deck, added a screened-in porch to the back of the house, and then built on an outsized modern kitchen. Arlene used to tease me by describing my house as a "kitchen with a house attached"!

Arlene spent a great deal of time with me in Rhinecliff, especially on the holidays. She wrote most of her formidable song cycle *Vox feminae* on my piano. Those songs were written for me—in a way. She had my voice in her head. Of course by that point I was too old ever to sing them.

And Jacques started calling a lot. He wasn't doing well, was now divorced, and often just needed to complain. I had a long cord on the phone in the giant kitchen, but it wasn't long enough to allow me to dedicate myself to Jacques's breathless diatribes. Sometimes I would have to just set the receiver down on the island so I could prepare the pot roast. Jacques didn't know I wasn't there, because he was characteristically not waiting for a response from me. I'd get dinner in the oven and come back to the phone, and Jacques would still be talking. Before long, I would extend myself and invite him up to stay near me to work on another CD project. But before *that*, I had to buy a mansion.

I am skipping back and forth in time a little, but bear with me. My sister Helen, who'd lived in Red Hook, New York, for her entire adult life, had moved to Seattle to be closer to her children. Shortly before her move, the historic Maizeland house in the center of Red Hook (just down the street from where she used to live) came up for sale. It was cheap because the taxes were high and it needed restoration, and of course it was a beast to heat. It had a grand French entryway with a formal staircase. It had been years since I'd lost the argument with Godfrey about buying Guernsey Hall in Princeton, and I couldn't pass up this opportunity to at last have the entryway I'd always dreamed of. We sold the house in Rhinecliff and I moved into Maizeland—where I will live out my life.

Jacques had been the one to teach me all those years ago to keep scrupulous track of my work—the recordings, programs, reviews, correspondence. Of course, he did the same. He had kept documentation and all his tapes of his BBC radio performances and wanted to put them out on Pierrot. We had great plans. We wanted not only to put out his BBC performances but also to reissue the Dial recordings. But I had to secure permission from the BBC. We negotiated the price for the permission of one piece, Schoenberg's *Chamber Symphony*, op. 9. It was seven thousand dollars. Well, I said to myself, we won't be able to do more than one CD.

  With Pierrot Records, I learned I wasn't a very good businesswoman. Then Julian Robinson dissolved the Tiger Hedge fund in 1998. We didn't have any more extra money. I had to close up shop on my CD company. But I still have those recordings that Jacques and I wanted to do. I listen today to the Webern songs that Jacques and I worked so hard on when we were still students at Juilliard, and I catch my breath as the music moves through those passages—the ones that broke us. His playing is so precise as it edges into and against those perilous swoops only barely resolved—so precise you almost can't hear it. It's as if the sounds we were making together always existed like that and we just fetched them out of the air.

CHAPTER FIFTY-FOUR

ENCORE WITH
ROBERT HELPS

When Gunther Schuller and the American Symphony Orchestra and I were scheduled in 1978 to premiere Bob Helps's *Gossamer Noons*, on the poetry of James Purdy—a piece that was one of Bob's most important compositions—Bob had a breakdown. David Del Tredici, Idith Meshulam (his prize pupils), and I called and called his apartment in Brooklyn, but he would not answer. He just would not come out of his apartment. He missed the premiere and the recording of *Gossamer Noons* for CRI the next day. For so many years Bob was in a state of perpetual crisis, and as much as I loved singing with him more than any other pianist, I couldn't make peace with his erratic emotional life.

It would be almost two decades before he came back into my life substantially, but when he did, he seemed much better. He'd taken a permanent position as a professor of piano at the University of South Florida and, perhaps just as important, outlived his parents, with whom he'd had a difficult relationship for many years. Bob seemed liberated at last, finally able to be the warm, satisfied man, great pianist, composer, and teacher that he was for the last decades of his life until his death from cancer in 2001. Idith Meshulam and I became close friends due to our fondness and love for this man.

I've been lucky with my collaborators, with the music we made. Lucky indeed. Despite some conspicuous interruptions, I don't think that I had a more synchronistic relationship with anyone than I had with Bob Helps.

Figure 69. With Bob Helps at the recording session for *But Yesterday Is Not Today* for New World Records, 1977. Courtesy of Barbara Jaffe.

Back in 1977, I had joined Bob in San Francisco to appear at Chamber Music West, a summer festival. They wanted *Pierrot*. Bob and I also performed a full recital comprising Debussy's *Proses lyriques*, Berg's *Seven Early Songs* and Schumann's *Liederkreis*. We got terrific press. Heuwell Tircuit of the *San Francisco Chronicle* wrote:

> Beardslee has been cited as the high priestess of modern music—replete with a fat catalog of recordings. So her beautifully poised Berg was no surprise, albeit early Berg. (The songs sound less like Berg than slightly stoned Richard Strauss.) But the Schumann was definitive. Every little turn of emotion and phrase was colored to maximum effect, with never a hint of exaggeration. The polish of details—both in the singing and in the stylish piano partnership—was miraculous. I have not heard the equal on recordings from anyone. And here is the thing: it really is not all that much of a voice, as such. What came through was sterling musicianship, intelligence and total devotion. If those sound petulant tribute, you're wrong. The Schumann performance was one of the most memorable vocal achievements the city has heard in years—recital or operatic. Here is the woman who should be part of any complete recording of the Schumann songs, should any develop.[105]

And in the same paper, a week later, Robert Commanday wrote about our Debussy: "The beauty of Helps' performance was critical for it is in the piano that the finest poetry of the songs is heard. From Helps, this was delicately formed, lustrous in tone, sensuous and warm."[106]

Bob always made me outperform myself through his playing. He could play the piano with such color and subtle dynamics that he held the listener in his thrall. When Bob and I performed together, we were so attuned to each other that the result was always me at my best.

I spent that summer of the festival in San Francisco with my old friend Ellen Faber, her two young boys, and my son Baird. Ellen had decided she wanted to see the West Coast and enjoy the California climate, so I rented Harold Farberman's large house in Oakland. Harold was the conductor of the Oakland Symphony at the time. He'd worked in London for a time and trained Leon Botstein. (Harold now teaches at Bard College and is a friend.) There was a beautiful white dog, a ping-pong table for the boys, a piano, and a maid. Bob and I rehearsed in the grand living room. What more could you ask for!

Forward in time to 1987: I was sixty-two, and I knew beyond the shadow of a doubt that I was singing on borrowed time. And then Bob called me one day from Florida and proposed an all-Ravel program for the fiftieth anniversary of Ravel's death. I told Bob that I was retired, that I didn't want to start performing again. (At least I didn't think I did. Mind you, this was still before my calamitous falling-out with Richard Goode about the concert at the Metropolitan Museum of Art.) But as I've said before, I could never refuse Bob. I told him, "This is my last appearance before it becomes embarrassing."

Bob came up from Florida, and we rehearsed at David Del Tredici's New York apartment. David had been a piano student of Bob's at Princeton and they were close, lifelong friends. We mounted the Ravel program at New York's Alliance Française in December 1987. Virgil Thomson was in attendance that afternoon and later wrote a letter to Bob: "You and Bethany Beardslee are unbelievably a pleasure both separately and together. Once every 25 or 30 years a team works like that. Yours is the first I have encountered since Pierre Bernac and Francis Poulenc used to work together."[107] That kind of enthusiasm naturally shored up our confidence. Bob wanted to do the program again in Boston. Actually, we repeated the program five more times. Then, unstoppable, we created a second French program of Debussy, Ravel, and Duparc. We put that program on at the Longy School of Music in Boston and then in Colorado Springs. The reviews were magnificent and convinced me that I wasn't wrong to be performing: "Her performance showed the triumph of the highest musical intelligence and technique over the inevitable ravages of age on the human voice, no matter how well cared for."[108]

Then we were asked to do Ravel's *Histoires naturelles* at the inauguration of the Catherine Bach Miller Theater at Columbia—which is actually the old McMillin Academic Theatre all dressed up. For only the second time in our careers, I shared a program with Jan DeGaetani. She sang Ives, and I sang Ravel. It would be the last time I saw her. Jan died in 1989 at the very young age of fifty-six.

The composer Laura Kaminsky mounted the Midtown Masters series to celebrate the newly renovated Town Hall. She asked Bob and me to participate. It was a nostalgic event for me. I had heard so many wonderful recitalists there when I was at student: Lotte Lehmann, Jennie Tourel, Elisabeth Schumann, Uta Graf. We repeated our all-French program and I felt, astonishingly enough, as if I'd finally "arrived." There I was on the stage of Town Hall, a classical song recitalist, looking out on an audience of composers, friends who had followed my career for so many years. The critic Tim Page wrote: "The audience was made up of a Who's Who in 20th century music: One couldn't swing the proverbial cat without hitting a composer."[109]

I wasn't singing new music, but they were all there to hear me. Page's review was lovely and something to cherish this late in my career. He wrote: "It was and remains a good voice—healthy, flexible, expressive, with a silvery timbre and an especially warm middle range. But it is empathy and care that elevate her work to the status of high art. What soprano can phrase with her skill? One is captivated not only by the narrative of a song, but by its sheer phonic beauty as well."[110]

In the spring of 1990, at sixty-five years old, I sang my last professional concert with Bob at the University of Wisconsin in Madison. Although I would appear two more times after that, I consider that recital to have been my true farewell. It is where I should have stopped, and where for all intents and purposes I gave the farewell concert I wanted to, with the musician who over my whole career I best loved to make music with.

This was how I should have left the stage. Steve Groark wrote the next day that ours was "the finest vocal recital" he'd heard in Madison in twenty-two years. To my great pleasure, he commented, "While one assumes that Beardslee does not improvise, there was that feeling of discovery, of exploration, of adventure in her performances that provided an intensification of the revelatory nature of her art."[111]

CHAPTER FIFTY-FIVE

FAREWELL AND FAREWELL

My bitter mood has turned to peace;
My sundrenched window opens wide
On daytime thoughts of world I love,
To daydreams of a world beyond . . .
O scent of fabled yesteryear!

—*Pierrot lunaire*[112]

In 1977—*fifteen* years before I stopped singing—the critics were already subtly articulating my decline: "The years have been very kind to chamber singer Bethany Beardslee, who can still spin out those supernally expressive soprano notes in a set of Debussy songs, then grovel about in the mezzo speech-song of Schoenberg. She is a consummate artist."[113] In 1977, I was nowhere near retirement. But once the critics began commending me on how well I'd held up, it was hard not to see its specter at the edge of every successful performance.

On April 14, 1985, Richard Dyer did a long interview with me for the *Boston Globe* in anticipation of my farewell Boston appearance at a benefit concert for Monadnock. Dyer opened the piece by quoting Andrew Porter in the *New Yorker*: "Any thought of retirement seems premature. Her place in musical history and in musicians' heart is assured." Dyer's article is

Figure 70. Publicity photo, ca. 1984. Photograph by Elsa Kahler.

luxuriously long, and I realize now when I read it that it's also full of theatrical embellishments. Among other things, I lied about my age. I guess
everyone does that. I also named Louise Zemlinsky as my most important
voice teacher. "She gave me everything—she had a fantastic ear, and never
let anything go by." Poor Mr. Swanson—he must have turned over in his
grave. I guess that at sixty years old I still felt I needed to solidify my place
in the history of the Second Viennese School in America. Oh, well!

As the question of my vocal stamina was becoming a perennial concern, I explained "You can sing contemporary music for a very long time,
as long as you don't let yourself scream and bellow. If you sing good music,
it doesn't matter what period it's from. It is never a question of what period
you're singing—the question is whether it's a good score."[114]

Every concert I did in these late years took a tremendous amount out of
me. I cherished each one, and I feared each one. I knew that I ran the risk
of being called out for being past my prime. But opportunities kept coming up. Jacques and I did a final *Pierrot* together in New York in 1985. I
relearned all of the pitch elements for him, just to be on the safe side. The
ensemble was new, so we prepared extra carefully with sectional rehearsals.
It was for a memorial concert for dear old Roger Sessions, who had died
earlier that year at the age of eighty-eight. Roger had mentored so many
composers I'd worked with at Princeton. He was an uncompromising figure, and I remember how upsetting it was for Milton when he died.

In January 1989, I was able to do my beloved Berg *Seven Early Songs*
once again with the Princeton Chamber Symphony. Then Arthur Burrows,
a teacher at Bard, asked me to do Hugo Wolf's *Italienisches Liederbuch*.
Arthur had a beautiful voice but also terrible stage fright, and his voice
once cracked.

On Thursday May 3, 1990, I performed *Pierrot* with the New York New
Music Ensemble at Princeton. I carefully noted on the front of the program
in my files, "*Pierrot* my last!" The day after that concert, Daniel Webster
wrote in the *Philadelphia Inquirer*: "[She] made it seem that these 21 songs,
which so revolutionized music in 1912, were as lyrical and accessible as
Schubert's songs. The point of virtuosity is to make the impossible easy."[115]
I was now sixty-five years old. My voice had changed. It was heavier. With
a small, light voice like mine, I really had done the maximum with it. But
there was no way around it: My voice was tending to flat. I started missing the firing action in my body, of those singing muscles that you need to
support sound. My pitch was under. Both Gunther Schuller and Bob Helps
called me out at different times for being under the pitch while we were

recording three cycles of French songs for Gunther's recording company Gunmar Records.

That same year the New England Conservatory gave me an honorary doctorate. They also asked me to do a three-week residency where I coached and worked with the voice students. The conservatory had an excellent student orchestra, with which I performed Ravel's *Shéhérazade*, a piece I had always dreamed of singing. I used two tremendous resources left in my sixty-five-year-old voice: strong diction and wonderful French!

Arlene Zallman had joined up with a wonderful group of composers in Boston and Cambridge to form the Griffin Music Ensemble. The group had the support of AT&T and the Wang Center for the Performing Arts— which was nice backing. They asked me to sing Erik Satie's *Socrate* for the third concert of their 1990–91 season. Singing with me was a young soprano, Karol Bennett, whose lovely voice shared many qualities of my own as well as a wildly dramatic flair. Karol came up to Rhinecliff for some coaching and at that same time fell madly in love with Tony Brandt, another member of Griffin and a composer out of Harvard. As joyous as it all was and as happy as I was for Arlene, I was really starting to break down. My diary entry the next day:

April, 1991

Dear Diary.

I sang Socrate, I know I must stop singing before the public. I'm 65. So that's that.

End of entry.

B.

Farewell, farewell, farewell, and [*whoops!*] farewell. Almost two years later, in 1993, Jacques got in touch and wanted me to do a benefit for the Guild of Composers at Carnegie Recital Hall. He had two composition students whose works he wanted to get played, Susan Forrest Harding and Meir Serrouya. He was sure that if I sang people would come. I really didn't want to do it, but Jacques always managed to talk me into things. I was teaching at Vassar that spring and took advantage of the negotiation with Jacques to bring on one of my new colleagues from Vassar, the pianist Diane Walsh.

Figure 71. With my former Vassar student Tara Loughran, at the wedding of another former Vassar student, Catherine Viscardi, ca. 2008.

She played a piano piece by Nikos Skalkottas beautifully, as well as the five songs I had performed with Yehudi Wyner at an ISCM concert.

It turned out that I liked the Serrouya piece that Jacques wanted me to sing, even though it meant learning to sing and pronounce Hebrew lyrics—which was a first for me. And yet my reluctance didn't abate. I'd done my last performance in Wisconsin with Bob Helps. It was without doubt the moment to quit—while I was ahead. But I did the concert, and it didn't go well. Alex Ross reviewed it for the *New York Times*. He was kind, but I heard the tape, and I knew better. I was awful. It was time to stop singing.

I had retained an incredible stamina over the last part of my career, which was remarkable, given the kind of music that I was singing and the presuppositions that people made about how hard modern music was on the voice. It wasn't hard on mine. My voice endured and ultimately made it difficult for me to discern the moment when it was really done. In many ways I was interpretively stronger than ever and had a mature heaviness to my voice. Through my fifties and sixties, there were ways in which I sang better than I ever had.

When I first formally retired in 1985, I still had my full voice. The day after my 1985 Boston farewell concert, Richard Dyer wrote: "Beardslee closed her local career as she had begun it three decades ago, as one of the smartest and most musical singers in the business, one of the few intelligent enough to leave while everyone in the audience could still exclaim, 'Why so early?' If she were a 19th century diva, she would have at least another decade of farewell concerts ahead of her."[116] . . . Famous last words.

I spent a decade doing concerts in which the critics and I agreed that I wasn't done singing, and then I crossed over somewhere. Richard Goode and I canceled that concert in 1990 that I didn't want to cancel. I did concerts after that which were successes, as if to prove Richard had been wrong. Then I did a concert that was the one concert too many. How does an artist know how to stop when she's ahead? How do you know the moment before the moment too late? I put on a concert at Carnegie Recital Hall that I never should have done. I learned two new pieces at the last moment of my career and sang in Hebrew, which I'd never before done. But that was the concert after the moment in which I should have quit.

On May 20, 1997, the Composers Guild held a tribute concert for me. The program had music by Schoenberg, Ravel, and Babbitt. Judith Bettina sang *Philomel*; Christine Schadeberg sang *Pierrot lunaire* and the Ravel Mallarmé settings. The conductor that evening was Daniel Plante. Given all of the reviews I've quoted from in these pages, and the kindness that so many writers have shown me over the years, I'm struck by the fact that Daniel Plante's short written tribute essentially explains my career in precisely the way I would hope that it will be remembered.

> Tonight's concert is being held to honor one of our era's most important musicians. To say this is not to indulge in hyperbole but to define the proper place for a woman whose voice was an indispensable presence to the musical culture of the last half century and to whom generations of composers, fellow performers, and music lovers will always be grateful.
>
> For many of us Bethany Beardslee will always be considered the premiere vocal interpreter of her time of the music of Schoenberg, Berg, and Webern, achieving a stature in this literature that only a few have since been able to match. What is astonishing is that she achieved this status not at the end of a gradual process but rather right from the beginning of her career during the period when she and fellow Juilliard student Jacques Monod gave the world premiere of what is probably the wildest and certainly most forbidding example of contemporary vocal music, the *Five Canons*, op. 16 of Anton Webern.

Figure 72. Milton, me, and Christine Schadeberg at the Beardslee Tribute Concert, 1997.

Listening to these forty-five year-old performances once more, one is struck not only by the consummate technical mastery of her performance but also by the realization that she has led us to the work's heart, a heart that not many would have otherwise presumed to exist. Few of her fellow students who made up the audience for this performance could have known at the time, but it was undoubtedly from that moment, on May 8, 1951, that Bethany Beardslee's name would be indissolubly linked with the history of the music of our time.

In the years that followed, Miss Beardslee, often in collaboration with Jacques Monod or Robert Helps, became famous for her interpretations of *Pierrot Lunaire*, The *Book of the Hanging Gardens*, and almost the entire vocal music of the Viennese school. Such a commitment to our repertoire, however, attracted many composers to write for her voice, and in that she has been the most faithful and high-minded advocate that one could wish for. Indeed, it was for Bethany that the young Milton Babbitt wrote his 1951 song cycle "Du," beginning a collaboration that extended through two of his most celebrated and path breaking works of the early sixties, *Vision and Prayer* and *Philomel*, and continuing a decade later with *A Solo Requiem*. However, those who think of Miss Beardslee solely as the exponent and master of the most difficult 20th century music, misunderstand the nature of her art. One only has to hear her interpretations of Handel, Schubert, Schumann, or Debussy to realize that her artistic success derives not merely from technical gifts that allow her to perform Schoenberg or Babbitt, but from her understanding of the phrase, from her ability to shape, color, and inflect the sung word as to impart its meaning and emotion, and from a vocal timbre that is at once extraordinarily beautiful and individual.[117]

The last concert I ever gave was under the loggia of a tiny mountain town in eastern Tuscany: Strada in Casentino, where Arlene had a small hideaway that we had found together a few summers before. It was a gorgeous night in deep summer. Our audience was made up of the local townspeople, most of them elderly or the sons of elderly people who ran the shops—the hardware store where we bought gas canisters to heat water, the bakery where we got bread and wine every single day, the bar where we got our coffee and spent hours talking to Mirella, the owner.

The concert we organized was a ragtag program, built from the talent that we'd gathered in remote Italy that summer, rather than any particular musical vision. Arlene was just so enthusiastic about sharing music with the community around her new home. Many years after her divorce, she'd reignited an old romance with the saxophone player Victor Morosco—another Juilliard alum. Victor, Arlene, and I, along with Arlene's Wellesley College colleague the pianist and musicologist Charles Fisk, were all summering and visiting in the tiny house. Charles would go swimming every day in the Solano, the stony outlet of the Arno that ran through this part of the country. Victor would practice his saxophone down in the wine cellar of the old house, the massive stones that formed the foundation of the house somewhat muffling the noisiest part of his warmup. And Arlene would retreat to her sunny study on the second floor, where she had an electric piano on which she composed, listening to her music through headphones. I had grown used to hearing composers at work, the intermittent, aimless chords and simple tunes running across the upper keys. I'd listened to Godfrey for years, to Jacques before that, and over these last few decades, to Arlene working away. I could hear, through the ceiling, only the mute thump of her feet on the pedals as I sat in the musty den, reading Henry James for hours on end.

Arlene had built a program for saxophone, soprano, and piano that summer, and designed and photocopied the programs with the help of the municipal librarian. The concert on August 8 had a saxophone piece and piano pieces by Paul Creston; some Monteverdi madrigals in which Arlene had trained singers from a group of music students and music lovers who gathered weekly in Florence; a Chopin piece—Charles's particular area of expertise. Then Charles, Victor, and I put on a set of songs by Ludwig Spohr for voice, clarinet, and piano. Our versatile Victor played two more saxophone pieces, one of which was his own composition. Arlene was the official impresario, introducing each piece in her tentative Italian. She wore a gold lamé blouse. We were a team in our enthusiasms in those years. It was the last summer before she was diagnosed with cancer.

I sang an encore that night: "Sì, mi chiamano Mimì." It was my last official performance. What else could I have sung under the echoing stone loggia, under the stars in the Italian night sky? By the next morning, the folding chairs would be stored back in the library closet, the farmers market would have resumed its domination of the loggia and surrounding square, and Arlene and I would have been back out on one of our day trips, trying to track down and visit every last Luca della Robbia ceramic in all of Tuscany.

I made another diary entry after I returned. This one read:

Sep. 8, 1993

Diary—

Due to swimming my body feels better. Did a lot this summer. Also went to Italy and sang 3 times—Monteverdi, Debussy & Spohr. It's incredible how I keep singing.

FINE

APPENDIX A

Discography

LPs (33 1/3 rpm) are designated monaural or stereo. Some compact discs (CDs) are reissues of LPs.

1950

Weber, Ben. *Concert Aria after Solomon*, op. 29. Bethany Beardslee, soprano, with chamber orchestra, conducted by Frank Brieff. *Three Contemporaries*. American Recording Society ARS-10, 33 1/3 rpm (LP monaural).

1951

Berg, Alban. *Seven Early Songs*; two unedited songs on "Schliesse mir die Augen beide." Bethany Beardslee, soprano, with Jacques Monod, piano. Dial 15, 33 1/3 rpm (monaural).

Webern, Anton. Four Songs, op. 12. and the Piano Variations, Opus 27. Bethany Beardslee, soprano, with Jacques Monod, piano. *Webern: Concerto for Nine Instruments*. Dial Records 17, 33 1/3 rpm (LP monaural).

1958

Křenek, Ernst. *Sestina* for Voice and Instrumental Ensemble. Bethany Beardslee, soprano, with instrumental ensemble, conducted by the composer. Twentieth Century Composers Series. Epic Records LC3509, 33 1/3 rpm (LP monaural).

1959

Berg, Alban. Five Songs, op. 4 (*Altenberg Lieder*) *by Alban Berg*. Bethany
    Beardslee, soprano, with the Columbia Symphony Orchestra, conducted by
    Robert Craft. Columbia Masterworks ML5428, 33 1/3 rpm (LP, stereo).
New York Pro Musica. *Elizabethan and Jacobean Ayres, Madrigals and Dances*.
    Noah Greenberg, musical director. Decca "Gold Label" Series DL 9406, 33
    1/3 rpm (LP, monaural).
Stravinsky, Igor. *Threni: id est Lamentationes Jeremiae Prophetae*. Bethany
    Beardslee, soprano, with the Columbia Symphony Orchestra, conducted by
    the composer. Columbia Masterworks MS6065, 33 1/3 rpm (LP, stereo).

1960

New York Pro Musica. *Spanish Music of the Renaissance*. Noah Greenberg,
    musical director. Decca "Gold Label" Series DL9409, 33 1/3 rpm (LP, stereo).

1961

Babbitt, Milton. *Du* (song cycle). *Music of Mel Powell and Milton Babbitt*.
    Bethany Beardslee, soprano, with Robert Helps, piano. Son Nova 1
    (Contemporary Classics), 33 1/3 rpm (LP, stereo).
Berg, Alban. *Seven Early Songs; Der Wein. Music of Alban Berg*. Bethany
    Beardslee, soprano, with the Columbia Symphony Orchestra, conducted by
    Robert Craft. Columbia Masterworks M2L 271, 33 1/3 (LP, stereo).
Powell, Mel. *Haiku Settings. Music of Mel Powell and Milton Babbitt*. Bethany
    Beardslee, soprano, with Robert Helps, piano. Son Nova 1 (Contemporary
    Classics), 33 1/3 rpm. (LP, stereo).

1962

Schoenberg, Arnold. *Das Buch der hängenden Gärten*, op. 15. Bethany Beardslee,
    soprano, with Robert Helps, piano. Son Nova 2 (Contemporary Classics), 33
    1/3 rpm. (LP, stereo).

1963

Schoenberg, Arnold. *Pierrot lunaire*, op. 21. *The Music of Arnold Schoenberg*, Vol. 1. Bethany Beardslee, soprano, with the Columbia Chamber Ensemble, conducted by Robert Craft. Columbia Masterworks M2S 679, 33 1/3 rpm. (LP, stereo).

1967

An Eighteenth Century Vocal Recital. Music by Haydn, Pergolesi, and Storace. Bethany Beardslee, soprano, with the Musica Viva Ensemble, conducted by James Bolle. Monitor Collectors Series MCS(C) 2124, 33 1/3 rpm (LP, stereo).

1968

Shapey, Ralph. *Incantations for Soprano and Ten Instruments*. *Incantations/ Music for 13 Players*. Bethany Beardslee, soprano, with the Contemporary Chamber Players of the University of Chicago, conducted by the composer. Composers Recordings Inc. (CRI) SD 232, 33 1/3 rpm (LP, stereo). Reissue: CD690 (CRI American Master Series), 1996 (CD).

1969

Ashforth, Alden. *The Unquiet Heart*. *Three Song Cycles*. Bethany Beardslee, soprano, with the UCLA Chamber Ensemble, conducted by John Dare. Composers Recordings Inc. (CRI) SD 243, 33 1/3 rpm (LP, stereo).

Babbitt, Milton. *Philomel*. Bethany Beardslee, soprano, with recorded soprano and synthesized sounds by the composer. Acoustic Research Contemporary Music Project in collaboration with Deutsche Grammophon, AR 0654 083, 33 1/3 rpm (LP, stereo). Reissue: Bridge Records 9391, 2013 (CD).

Batstone, Philip. *A Mother Goose Primer*. *Three Song Cycles*. Bethany Beardslee, soprano, with Victoria Bond (Echo) and the UCLA Chamber Ensemble, conducted by John Dare. Composers Recordings Inc. (CRI) SD 243, 33 1/3 rpm (LP, stereo).

Lerdahl, Fred. *Wake*. Bethany Beardslee, Boston Symphony Chamber Players, conducted by David Epstein. Acoustic Research Contemporary Music Project in collaboration with Deutsche Grammophon, AR 0654 083, 33 1/3 rpm (LP, stereo). Reissue: Bridge Records 9391, 2013 (CD).

1971

Babbitt, Milton. *Vision and Prayer. Columbia-Princeton Electronic Music Center Tenth Anniversary Celebration.* Bethany Beardslee, soprano, with synthesized sound by the composer. Composers Recordings Inc. (CRI) SD 268, 33 1/3 rpm (LP, stereo).

1977

But Yesterday Is Not Today: The American Art Song 1927–1972. Bethany Beardslee, soprano, with Robert Helps, piano; Donald Gramm, bass-baritone, with Donald Massard, piano. New World Records NW 243, 33 1/3 rpm (LP, stereo). Reissue: New World Records 80243-2, 1996 (CD).

1978

Helps, Robert. *Gossamer Noons.* Bethany Beardslee, soprano, with the American Composers Orchestra, conducted by Gunther Schuller. Composers Recordings Inc., CRI SD 384, 33 1/3 rpm (LP, stereo).

1979

Perle, George. *Thirteen Dickinson Songs; Two Rilke Songs. American Contemporary Songs by George Perle.* Bethany Beardslee, soprano, with Morey Ritt, piano. Composers Recordings Inc., American Contemporary series, CRI 403, 33 1/3 rpm (LP, stereo).

1980

Babbit, Milton. *Philomel.* Bethany Beardslee, soprano, with recorded soprano and synthesized sounds by the composer. New World Records NW 307, compact disc. Reissue: New World Records 80466-2 CD, 1995 (CD).

Babbitt, Milton. *A Solo Requiem. Milton Babbitt, Mel Powell.* Bethany Beardslee, soprano, with Continuum (Cheryl Seltzer and Joel Sachs, piano). Nonesuch N-78006, 33 1/3 rpm (LP stereo).

Powell, Mel. *Haiku Settings.* Bethany Beardslee, soprano, with Cheryl Seltzer, piano. Nonesuch N-78006, 33 1/3 rpm (LP, stereo).

Powell, Mel. *Little Companion Pieces.* Bethany Beardslee, soprano, with the
Sequoia String Quartet. Nonesuch D-79005, 33 1/3 rpm (LP, stereo).
Schoenberg, Arnold. String Quartet no. 2. Bethany Beardslee, soprano, with the
Sequoia String Quartet. Nonesuch D-79005, 33 1/3 rpm (LP, stereo).

1982

Tribute to Soprano Bethany Beardslee. Music by Philip Batstone, George Perle,
Malcolm Peyton, and Godfrey Winham. Composers Recordings Inc., CRI
724. Recorded 1969, 1979, 1982. Reissue: Composers Recordings Inc., 724,
1997 (CD).

1989

French Music for Voice and Flute. Ravel, Caplet, Saint-Saëns, Ibert, Martin,
Roussel, Chaminade. Bethany Beardslee, soprano, with Eleanor Lawrence,
flute; Morey Ritt, piano; André Emelianoff, cello; and Jesse Levine, viola.
Musical Heritage Society MHS 512389M (CD).
Stories Airs and Verse: French Art Songs of Debussy and Ravel. Bethany Beardslee,
soprano, with Robert Helps, piano. GM Recordings, GM2029CD (CD).

Pierrot Records

Brahms, Johannes. *Brahms Lieder.* Bethany Beardslee, soprano, with Richard
Goode, piano. Pierrot Records (CD). Recorded 1996.
Scarlatti, Alessandro. *Su le sponde del Tebro* and *Cantata Pastorale per la Nascita
di Nostro Signore. A Christmas Concert.* Bethany Beardslee, soprano, with the
Monadnock Festival Orchestra, conducted by Jim Bolle. Pierrot Records PR
47815 (CD). Recorded 1966.
Schubert, Franz. *Schubert Lieder.* Bethany Beardslee, soprano, with Lois Shapiro,
fortepiano. Pierrot Records 3 (CD). Recorded 1995.
Schumann, Robert. *Bethany Beardslee Sings Schumann Lieder.* Bethany Beardslee,
soprano, with Lois Shapiro, piano. Pierrot Records (CD). Recorded 1996.
Winham, Godfrey. *Variations on a Theme by James Pierpont.* Alan Feinberg,
piano. Pierrot Records PR 47815 (CD). Recorded 1999.

A P P E N D I X B

P r e m i e r e s b y B e t h a n y B e a r d s l e e

(W) = World Premiere
(US) = North America, First Performance

Amy, Gilbert. *Cantata brève*, with an ensemble conducted by Samuel Baron. December 11, 1958. Rothschild Foundation, New York (US).

Ashforth, Alden. *Tanka Songs*, with David Del Tredici, piano. April 22, 1960. Clio Hall, Princeton University, Princeton, NJ (W).

———. *The Unquiet Heart*, with Robert Helps, piano. December 18, 1964. Oberlin Conservatory, Oberlin, OH; Instrumental version, conducted by John Dare. January 26, 1969. Royce Hall, UCLA, Los Angeles, CA (W).

Avni, Tzvi. *Collage*. October 9, 1980. University of Pennsylvania, Philadelphia, PA (US).

Babbitt, Milton. *Du*, with Jacques Monod, piano. May 8, 1952. Barnard College, New York (W).

———. *Four Canons*. March 24, 1976. McMillin Academic Theatre, New York (W).

———. *Philomel*. February 13, 1964. Amherst College, Amherst, MA (W).

———. *A Solo Requiem*, with Joel Sachs and Cheryl Seltzer, piano. February 10, 1979. Alice Tully Hall, New York (W).

———. *Sounds and Words*, with Robert Helps, piano. March 1, 1962. Chamber Music 61, Kaufman Concert Hall, New York (W).

———. *Three Theatrical Songs*, with Tom Lerner, piano, on the occasion of Babbitt's sixtieth birthday. March 24, 1976. McMillin Academic Theatre, New York (W).

———. *Vision and Prayer*. September 6, 1961. Grace Rainey Rogers Auditorium, Metropolitan Museum of Art, New York (W).

———. *The Widow's Lament in Springtime*, with Jacques Monod, piano. May 8, 1952. Barnard College, New York (W).

Batstone, Philip. *A Mother Goose Primer*, with the La Salle Quartet. February 27, 1968. University of Colorado Festival, Colorado Springs, CO (W).

Bauman, Alvin. *Four Songs of Emily Dickinson*, with Jacques Monod, piano. May 8, 1952. Barnard College, New York (W).

———. *The World Is Round*. April 28, 1952. Henry Street Playhouse, New York (W).

Berg, Alban. *Altenberg Lieder*, with orchestra conducted by Robert Craft. January 4, 1959. Fromm Music Foundation sponsored concert, Town Hall, New York (US).

———. "Hidden Text in the *Lyric Suite*," with the Columbia String Quartet and George Perle, lecturer. November 1979. State University of New York, Binghamton (W).

———. "An Leukon" (composed 1908). April 7, 1951. Juilliard School of Music, New York (US).

———. "Schliesse mir die Augen beide," with Jacques Monod, piano. Tonal and twelve-tone versions. All-Berg concert with *Seven Early Songs* and Four Songs, op. 2. December 18, 1950. Juilliard School of Music, New York (W).

Berger, Arthur. *Words for Music, Perhaps*. March 28, 1954. McMillin Academic Theatre, Columbia University, New York (W).

Boulez, Pierre. *Improvisation II sur Mallarmé*, ensemble conducted by Richard Dufallo. July 14, 1965. American-French Festival, Philharmonic Hall, Lincoln Center, New York (US).

———. *Le marteau sans maître*, ensemble conducted by Arthur Weissberg. April 2, 1962. Kaufmann Concert Hall (92nd Street Y), New York (US).

Brickle, Frank. *Varioso*, with computer synthesized tape. February 24, 1977. Guild of Composers, McMillin Academic Theatre, Columbia University, New York (W).

Citkowitz, Israel. *Five Songs from "Chamber Music,"* by James Joyce, with Robert Helps, piano. June 23, 1976. Gateway Arch, St. Louis, MO (W).

Cone, Edward T. "Epitaph," with Jacques Monod, piano. February 22, 1951. WNYC Radio, New York (W).

———. *Four Songs from "Mythical Story."* March 1, 1961. Chamber Music 61, Kaufman Concert Hall, New York (W).

———. *Philomela*. February 7, 1975. Buckley Recital Hall, Amherst College, Amherst, MA (W).

———. *Triptych*, with Lalan Parrott, piano (poetry by John Berryman). January 13, 1951. Proctor Hall, Princeton University (W).

Dallapiccola, Luigi. "Goethe Lieder." May 21, 1954. ISCM. McMillin Academic Theatre, Columbia University, New York (US).

Davies, Peter Maxwell. *Revelation and Fall* (on poetry of Georg Trakl), ensemble conducted by Richard Dufallo. July 10, 1968. Lincoln Center Festival, Philharmonic Hall, New York (US).

Delage, Maurice. *Quatre poèmes hindous*, with ensemble conducted by Tamara Brooks. April 14, 1978. Sanders Theatre, Cambridge, MA (US).

Eaton, John. *Holy Sonnets of John Donne*, with composer as pianist. March 16, 1957. Woodrow Wilson Hall, Princeton University, Princeton, NJ (W).

Edwards, George. *A Mirth but Open'd* (on poetry of George Herbert), with Christopher Oldfather, piano. 1987. Guild of Composers Concert, Christ and St. Stephens Church, New York (W).

El-Dabh, Halim. *Clytemnestra*. April 1, 1959. Martha Graham Dance Company, Adelphi Theatre, New York (W).

Escot, Pozzi. *Lamentus*, with ensemble conducted by Jacques Monod. October 26, 1965. Jordan Hall, New England Conservatory of Music, Boston, MA (W).

Fine, Vivian. *A Guide to the Life Expectancy of a Rose*, with Earl Rogers, tenor, and ensemble conducted by Jacques Monod. May 15, 1956. Rothschild Foundation, New York (W).

Harding, Susan Forrest. "Vision." May 23, 1993. Guild of Composers concert, Carnegie Recital Hall, New York (W).

Helps, Robert. *Gossamer Noons* (on poetry of James Purdy), with American Composers Orchestra, conducted by Gunther Schuller. May 23, 1978. Alice Tully Hall, Lincoln Center, New York (W).

———. *The Running Sun* (on poetry of James Purdy), with composer as pianist. November 13, 1972. Alice Tully Hall, Lincoln Center, New York (W).

———. *Two Songs* (on texts of Herman Melville), with composer as pianist. April 28, 1957. Drew University, Madison, NJ (W).

Holliger, Heinz. *Dörfliche Motive (Four Bagatelles for Soprano and Piano)*, with Heinz Holliger, piano. April 2, 1963. Carnegie Recital Hall, New York (Swiss Embassy concert) (US).

Huber, Klaus. *Auf die ruhige Nachtzeit*, with ensemble conducted by Gustav Meier. April 2, 1963. Carnegie Recital Hall, New York (Swiss Embassy concert) (US).

Huggler, John. *Sculptures*, with Boston Symphony, conducted by Erich Leinsdorf. November 12, 1964, Symphony Hall, Boston, MA (W).

———. *Seven Songs*, op. 74 (on texts by Edward Leavenworth), with Pro Arte Chamber Orchestra of Boston, conducted by Richard Pittman. 1980. Sanders Theatre, Harvard University.

Kahn, Erich Itor. *Marien Lieder*, with Russell Sherman, piano. May 12, 1959. Kaufmann Concert Hall, 92nd Street Y, New York (W).

———. *Music for Ten Instruments and Soprano*, with ensemble conducted by Jacques Monod. January 24, 1954. Carnegie Recital Hall, New York (W).

Kim, Earl. "Dead Calm," from *Exercises en Route* (on texts by Samuel Beckett), with ensemble conducted by John Harbison. April 29, 1963. McCosh Hall, Princeton University, Princeton, NJ (W).

———. "Gooseberries She Said," from *Exercises en Route* (on texts by Samuel Beckett), with ensemble conducted by the composer. November 25, 1968. Sanders Theatre, Cambridge, MA (W).

———. "They Are Far Out," from *Exercises en Route* (on texts by Samuel Beckett), with ensemble conducted by Arthur Weissberg. February 22, 1967. Rutgers University, New Brunswick, NJ (W).

Křenek, Ernst. *Die Nachtigall*, with Boston Symphony, conducted by Michael Tilson Thomas. July 19, 1970. Tanglewood, Lenox, MA (W).

———. *Sestina*. March 9, 1958. Fromm Music Foundation sponsored concert, New School, New York (US).

Leibowitz, René. *Four Songs*, op. 18. May 24, 1950. Juilliard School of Music, New York (W).

Lerdahl, Fred. *Wake* (on texts from *Finnegans Wake*, by James Joyce), with ensemble conducted by the composer. August 14, 1968. Marlboro Music Festival, Marlboro, VT (W).

Martirano, Salvatore. *Chansons Innocentes* (on poems of e. e. cummings), with Yehudi Wyner, piano. December 11, 1958. Rothschild Foundation, New York (W).

———. *Nina Nanna*, with Yehudi Wyner, piano. December 11, 1958. Rothschild Foundation, New York (W).

Monod, Jacques. *Four Songs for Clarinet and Voice*, with Meyer Kupferman, clarinet. May 19, 1951. Composers Forum, McMillin Academic Theatre, Columbia University, New York (W).

———. *Passacaille*, with ensemble conducted by the composer. April 1, 1951. McMillin Academic Theatre, Columbia University, New York (W).

Moss, Larry. *Ariel*, with New Haven Symphony Orchestra, conducted by Frank Brieff. March 2, 1971. Woolsey Hall, Yale University, New Haven, CT (W).

Nono, Luigi. *España en el corazón*. with Musica Viva Ensemble, conducted by James Bolle. April 9, 1958. Kaufmann Concert Hall, 92nd Street Y, New York (US).

Peel, John. *La Pythie* (on poetry of Paul Valéry), with ensemble Collage, conducted by Richard Pittman. March 5, 1979. Longy School of Music, Boston, MA (W).

Penderecki, Krzysztof. *St. Luke Passion* (soprano soloist), with the Minneapolis Symphony Orchestra, conducted by Stanisław Skrowaczewski. November 2, 1967. Orchestra Hall, Minneapolis, MN (US).

Perle, George. *Thirteen Dickinson Songs*, with Morey Ritt, piano. June 19, 1978. Westminster Choir College Art Song Festival, Princeton, NJ (W).

Peyton, Malcolm. *Four Shakespeare Sonnets*, with ensemble conducted by the composer. February 22, 1964. Grace Rainey Rogers Auditorium, Metropolitan Museum of Art, New York (W).

———. *Songs from Walt Whitman*, with composer at piano, Eric Rosinblith, violinist in fifth song. April 5, 1979. Jordan Hall, New England Conservatory, Boston, MA (W).

Phillipot, Michel. *Four Songs*, op. 2, with Jacques Monod, piano. May 8, 1952. Barnard College, Columbia University, New York (W).

Powell, Mel. *Haiku Settings*, with Robert Helps, piano. April 27, 1962. ISCM, New School, New York (W).

———. *Little Companion Pieces*, with Sequoia String Quartet. February 7, 1980. California Institute of the Arts, Santa Clarita, CA (W).

Randall, James K. *Improvisation on a Poem by e. e. cummings*, with Robert Helps, piano. April 29, 1963. McCosh Hall, Princeton University, Princeton, NJ (instrumental version recorded for CRI in 1973) (W).

Ruggles, Carl. *Toys*, with Vivian Fine, piano. September 29, 1968. Carl Ruggles Festival, Bennington College, Bennington, VT (W).

Sauget, Henri. *Les pénitents en maillots roses*, with Ben Jenkins, piano. May 12, 1950. Juilliard School of Music, New York (US).

Schonthal, Ruth. *Totengesänge*, with the composer as pianist. April 12, 1964. Carnegie Recital Hall, New York (W).

Schubart, Mark. *Yvan to Clare (Four Love Songs)* (to poetry of Yvan Goll), with the Lansing Symphony (orchestral song cycle). April 17, 1951. Sexton Auditorium, Lansing, MI (W).

Schwarz, Charles. *Three Songs for Soprano*, with Harriet Wingreen, piano. November 9, 1956. Town Hall, New York (W).

Seeger, Stanley. *La Femme à l'ombrelle*, with ensemble conducted by Jacques Monod. February 25, 1955. University of Illinois Contemporary Festival, Urbana, IL (W).

Serrouya, Meir. *Songs on Poetry of Uri Zvi Greenberg*. 1990 Guild of Composers concert, Carnegie Recital Hall, New York (W).

Shapey, Ralph. *Dimensions*. May 13, 1962. Fromm Music Foundation Concert at the New School, New York (W).

———. *Incantations for Soprano and Ten Instruments*. April 22, 1961. Composers Forum, Donnell Library Center, New York (W).

Shifrin, Seymour. "The Cat and the Moon" (on poetry by William Butler Yeats). February 22, 1954. WNYC Radio, Contemporary Music Festival, New York (W).

———. "No Second Troy" (on poetry by William Butler Yeats), with Jacques Monod, piano. February 22, 1954. WNYC Festival, New York (W).

Skalkottas, Nikos. *Five Selected Songs on Poetry of Hrissos Esperas*, with Yehudi Wyner, piano. May 20, 1973. ISCM Recital, Carnegie Recital Hall, New York (US).

Spies, Claudio. *Shirim le Hathunatham* (on texts by Yehudah HaLevi), with Da Capo Chamber Players. April 21, 1976. Carnegie Recital Hall, New York (W).

———. *Three Songs on Poems of May Swenson*, with Robert Helps, piano. May 20, 1973. ISCM Recital, Carnegie Recital Hall, New York (W).

———. *Verses from the Book of Ruth*, with women's chorus and Alan Broughton, piano. 1960. Swarthmore College, Swarthmore, PA (W).

Spinner, Leopold. *Five Songs*, op. 8, with Jacques Monod, piano. March 15, 1954. Bard College, Red Hook, NY (W).

Stravinsky, Igor. *Threni: id est Lamentationes Jeremiae Prophetae*, conducted by
Robert Craft. January 4, 1954. Town Hall, New York (US).

Sur, Donald. *The Sleepwalker's Ballad* (on poetry of Federico García Lorca),
with ensemble conducted by Charles Wuorinen. November 1972. Kresge
Auditorium, MIT, Cambridge, MA (W).

Vogel, Wladimir. *Arpiade*, with ensemble conducted by Samuel Baron. May 21,
1959. Swiss Music Concert, Donnell Library Center, New York (US).

Weber, Ben. *Concert Aria after Solomon*, op. 29, with ensemble conducted by
Frank Brieff. December 13, 1949. Alice M. Ditson Award Festival, McMillin
Academic Theatre, Columbia University, New York (W).

———. *Five Songs*, op. 15 (on poetry of Adelaide Crapsey), with Jacques Monod,
piano. November 19, 1950. Times Hall, New York (W).

———. *Four Songs for Voice and Cello*, with Seymour Barab, cello. February 21,
1954. McMillin Academic Theatre, Columbia University, New York (W).

Webern, Anton. *Drei Volkstexte*, op. 17. May 14, 1951, All-Webern program
conducted by Jacques Monod. Juilliard School of Music, New York (W).

———. *Five Canons*, op. 16. May 14, 1951. All-Webern program conducted by
Jacques Monod. Juilliard School of Music, New York (W).

———. *Three Songs*, op. 25 (on poetry by Hildegard Jone), with Jacques Monod,
piano. March 16, 1952. ISCM, McMillin Academic Theatre, Columbia
University, New York (W).

Wellesz, Egon. *The Leaden Echo and the Golden Echo*, op. 61 (on poetry of Gerard
Manley Hopkins), with ensemble conducted by Jacques Monod. April 13,
1955. ISCM, Kaufmann Concert Hall (92nd Street Y), New York (US).

Wilkinson, Marc. *Chants dédiés*, with ensemble conducted by Jacques Monod.
May 18, 1952. Barnard College, New York (W).

Winham, Godfrey. *The Habit of Perfection* (on poetry of Gerard Manley
Hopkins). May 20, 1958. Clio Hall, Princeton University, Princeton, NJ (W).

———. *To Prove My Love* (on three Shakespeare sonnets), with Robert Helps,
piano. March 1, 1961. Chamber Music 61, Kaufmann Concert Hall (92nd
Street Y), New York (W).

Winkler, David. *Three Shakespeare Sonnets*, with Robert Helps, piano. February
10, 1977. ISCM, Carnegie Recital Hall, New York (W).

Zallman, Arlene. "Now the Snow Lies on the Ground," with Yehudi Wyner,
piano. May 20, 1973. ISCM, Carnegie Recital Hall, New York (W).

———. "Per organo di Barberia," with Helen Harbison, cello. October 17, 1976.
Jewett Auditorium, Wellesley College, Wellesley, MA (W).

———. "Three Songs from Quasimodo," with Elinor Preble, flute; Helen
Harbison, cello; Charles Fisk, piano. October 17, 1976. Jewett Auditorium,
Wellesley College, Wellesley, MA (W).

N O T E S

1. Ehrhard Bahr, *Weimar on the Pacific: German Exile in Los Angeles and the Crisis of Modernism* (Berkeley: University of California Press, 2007).
2. David Denby, "Ten Perfect Orchestral Recordings," *New Yorker*, May 1, 2012.
3. Gunther Schuller, *Gunther Schuller: A Life in Pursuit of Music and Beauty* (Rochester, NY: University of Rochester Press, 2011), 419.
4. Ibid., 418–19.
5. Virgil Thomson, "Program of Contemporary Music: Small Stuff But Pleasant," *New York Herald Tribune*, January 16, 1951.
6. Schuller, *Gunther Schuller*, 103.
7. Ned Rorem, *Knowing When to Stop* (New York: Simon & Schuster, 1994), 185.
8. Roger Sessions, "Schoenberg in the United States," *Tempo* 9 (1944): 8–17. http://www.schoenberg.at/index.php/en/1944-roger-sessions-schoenberg-in-the-united-states.
9. Alan Rich, "The Music Critic as Sex Symbol," *New York*, March 31, 1969, 57.
10. Arthur Berger, "Songs by Webern," *New York Times*, March 16, 1952, 14.
11. Igor Stravinsky and Robert Craft, *Conversations with Igor Stravinsky* (London: Faber & Faber, 1959), 127.
12. Arnold Schoenberg, *Verklärte Nacht and Pierrot Lunaire* (New York: Dover Publications, 1994), 54–55.
13. Pierre Boulez, "Speaking, Playing, Singing," in *Orientations: Collected Writings*, ed. Jean-Jacques Nattiez, trans. Martin Cooper (Cambridge, MA: Harvard University Press, 1990), 330–35.
14. Robert G. Kopelson, "Jacques-Louis Monod and Chamber Ensemble at Sanders Last Night," *Harvard Crimson*, August 8, 1967, http://www.thecrimson.com/article/1967/8/8/jacques-louis-monod-and-chamber-ensemble-pevery/, accessed April 13, 2017.
15. Robert Craft and Igor Stravinsky, *Dialogues* (Berkeley: University of California Press, 1982), 105.

16. David H. Smyth, "Schoenberg and Dial Records: The Composer's Correspondence with Ross Russell," *Journal of the Arnold Schoenberg Institute* 12, no. 1 (June 1989): 68–90.

17. Kevin Bazzana, *Wondrous Strange: The Life and Art of Glenn Gould* (New York: Oxford University Press, 2004), 116.

18. Ross Parmenter, "Concert Is Given at Canadian Fete," *New York Times*, July 10, 1956.

19. Roger Dettmer, "The 12-Tone Boys at Fullerton Hall," *Chicago Tribune*, November 29, 1956.

20. Bruce Duffie, "Patron Paul Fromm: A Conversation with Bruce Duffie," April 9, 1986, posted 2009, www.bruceduffie.com/fromm.html.

21. David Gable, "Paul Fromm in American Musical Life," in *A Life for New Music: Selected Papers of Paul Fromm*, ed. David Gable and Christoph Wolff (Cambridge, MA: Harvard University Press, 1988), ix.

22. Duffie, "Patron Paul Fromm."

23. Ibid.

24. Originally quoted in Arthur Berger, "What Mozart Didn't Have: The Story of the Fromm Music Foundation," *High Fidelity* 9, no. 2 (1959): 43.

25. Howard Taubman, "Music: Twelve Tone; Works by Krenek and Ben Weber Offered," *New York Times*, March 10, 1958.

26. Donal J. Henahan in the *Chicago Daily News*, September 27, 1966.

27. Allen Hughes, "Singer, Pianist at Carnegie Hall," *New York Herald Tribune*, November 18, 1958.

28. Eric Salzman, "Bethany Beardslee Sings Schubert Work," *New York Times*, November 18, 1958.

29. Howard Taubman, "Modern Program Played at the Y.M.H.A.," *New York Times*, April 14, 1953.

30. Wallingford Riegger, "The Music of Vivian Fine," *American Composers Alliance Bulletin* 8, no. 1 (1958): 2–6.

31. John Martin, "'Clytemnestra' an Epic Full-Evening Work by a Modern Master," *New York Times*, April 6, 1958.

32. Martha Graham, *Blood Memory: An Autobiography* (New York: Doubleday), 2223–24.

33. Graham, *Blood Memory*, 3–4.

34. Stravinsky and Craft, *Conversations with Stravinsky*, 2.

35. Igor Stravinsky, interview by Jay S. Harrison, *New York Herald Tribune*, December 21, 1952, D5.

36. Claudio Spies, "Igor Stravinsky's *Threni*, Conducting Details," Moldenhauer Archives, Rosaleen Moldenhauer Memorial, Library of Congress, Washington, DC, posted 2000, http://hdl.loc.gov/loc.music/molden.2428152.bib.

37. Mark DeVoto, "Centenary of a Lesser-Known Scandal," *Boston Music Intelligencer*, March 27, 2013, http://www.classical-scene.com/2013/03/27/scandal/.

38. Jay S. Harrison, "Stravinsky's 'Threni' Has Premiere at Town Hall," *New York Herald Tribune*, January 5, 1959, 11.

39. Michael Steinberg, "An Exciting Musical Note," *Saskatoon Star-Phoenix*, August 3, 1959.

40. Christopher Fox, "Air from Another Planet," *Guardian*, January 16, 2009, www.theguardian.com/music/2009/jan/17/classical-music-schoenberg.

41. Michael Steinberg to author, December 10, 1961.

42. William Flanagan (signed W. F.), review of *The Music of Arnold Schoenberg*, vol. 1, *HiFi/ Stereo Review*, April 1963, 71–72.

43. Alfred Frankenstein (signed A. F.), review of *The Music of Arnold Schoenberg*, vol. 1, *High Fidelity Magazine*, March 1963, 81.

44. Allen Hughes, "Shapey's 'Incantations' in Debut at Finale of Composers Forum," *New York Times*, April 24, 1961.

45. Charles Rosen, *Arnold Schoenberg* (Chicago: University of Chicago Press, 1996), 6.

46. David Hamilton, "A Song Team for Schoenberg and Schubert," *High Fidelity*, March 1976, 73.

47. "Milton Babbitt on Electronic Music," YouTube video, 17:09, posted by Eric Chasalow on January 29, 2011, https://www.youtube.com/watch?v=UHNG9rexCsg, recorded 1997, from the Video Archive of Electroacoustic Music, Eric Chasalow and Barbara Cassidy, curators.

48. Ibid.

49. Milton Babbitt's quote taken from the program notes of the Colorado Springs concert, February 1968.

50. Eric Salzman, "Music: Three Distinguished Works; Babbitt, Kirchner and Carter Performed," *New York Times*, September 7, 1961.

51. Salzman, "Music: Three Distinguished Works."

52. Anonymous, "A Composer's Singer," *Newsweek*, September 18, 1961.

53. Howard Klein, "Two Singers Share Unusual Niche," *New York Times*, June 24, 1962.

54. Tad Wise, "When the Turnau Opera Players Reigned in Woodstock," *Woodstock Times*, September 16, 2012.

55. John Henken, "About the Piece: *Le marteau sans maître*," LA PHIL.com, http://www.laphil.com/philpedia/music/le-marteau-sans-maitre-pierre-boulez, accessed April 13, 2017.

56. Alan Rich, "Avant-Garde Work Is Performed and Explained: Pierre Boulez says 'Marteau Sans Maitre' Searches for Music's Link to Poetry," *New York Times*, May 25, 1963.

57. Rich, "Avant-Garde Work Is Performed and Explained."

58. Ned Rorem, *But Yesterday Is Not Today: The American Art Song 1927–1972*, New World Records 80243, 1977, 33 1/3 rpm, liner notes.

59. Milton Babbitt, composer's note on *Philomel*, 1964.

60. John Hollander, *Philomel*, reprinted in Hollander, "Notes on the Text of *Philomel*," *Perspectives of New Music* 6, no. 1 (Autumn–Winter 1967): 131–41.

61. Babbitt, composer's note on *Philomel*.

62. Hollander, "Notes on the Text of *Philomel*."

63. Eric Salzman, "Miss Beardslee Philomel Indeed," *New York Herald Tribune*, February 22, 1964.

64. Howard Klein, "Miss Beardslee Sings 'Philomel,'" *New York Times*, February 22, 1964.

65. Schuller, *Gunther Schuller*, 133.

66. Elliot Forbes, Lewis Lockwood, Donald Martino, and Bernard Rands, "Faculty of Arts and Sciences—Memorial Minute—Earl Kim," *Harvard Gazette*, May 25, 2000.

67. Mark Bauerlein and Ellen Grantham, eds., *National Endowment for the Arts: A History, 1965–2008* (Washington, DC: National Endowment for the Arts, 2009), https://www.arts.gov/sites/default/files/nea-history-1965-2008.pdf.

68. Harold C. Schonberg, "Leinsdorf Leads Boston Symphony in 2-Work Concert," *New York Times*, December 3, 1964.

69. Alan Rich, "The Boston's Composer," *New York Herald Tribune*, December 3, 1964.

70. Henry Raymont, "Marking Time: Cultural Program Abroad Is Modified to Win Congressional Support," *New York Times*, September 15, 1963.

71. Richard Killough at Columbia Records to Jay Hoffman, February 12, 1965, Beardslee personal archive.

72. Lukas Foss, program notes, Buffalo Philharmonic Orchestra, Sunday, Nov. 15–Tuesday, Nov. 17, 1964, Kleinhans Music Hall, Buffalo, NY.

73. Ivan Hewett, "Sir Peter Maxwell Davies Obituary," *Guardian*, March 14, 2016. https://www.theguardian.com/music/2016/mar/14/sir-peter-maxwell-davies-obituary.

74. Clark Mitze, "Modern Music Thins Symphony Audience," *St. Louis Globe-Democrat*, April 18, 1966.

75. Donal J. Henahan, "Another Martinon Success: *Lulu* Is Back in Town," *Chicago Daily News*, April 23, 1966.

76. Donal Henahan, "Rudolf Serkin, 88, Concert Pianist, Dies," *New York Times*, May 10, 1991.

77. Alan Rich, "The Music Critic as Sex Symbol."

78. Allan Kozinn, "Guardian of the Schoenberg Flame," *New York Times*, March 10, 1985.

79. Philip Batstone, notes on *A Mother Goose Suite*. *Tribute to Soprano Bethany Beardslee*, Anthology of Recorded Music NWCR724, 2007, compact disc, liner notes.

80. Leonard Rosenman, "Notes from a Sub-culture," *Perspectives of New Music* 7, no. 1 (1968): 122–35.

81. Alan Rich, "The Soft Sad Sounds of Modulo Z," *New York*, August 8, 1968, 51.

82. Harold C. Schonberg, "Music: Rarities by Bethany Beardslee," *New York Times*, February 24, 1970.
83. Schonberg, "Rarities by Bethany Beardslee."
84. Arnold Schoenberg, *Style and Idea: Selected Writings of Arnold Schoenberg*, ed. Leonard Stein, trans. Leo Black (Berkeley: University of California Press, 1975), 105.
85. Linda Winer, "A Night Rife with Gloom," *Chicago Tribune*, August 13, 1970.
86. Kenneth Sanson, "Phenomenal Soprano," *Chicago Today*, August 13, 1970.
87. Donal J. Henahan, "Music: Four Premieres," *New York Times*, November 15, 1972.
88. David Hamilton, "A Proper Attitude," *New Yorker*, May 20, 1974.
89 Allan Kozinn, "Milton Babbitt, a Composer Who Gloried in Complexity, Dies at 94," *New York Times*, January 29, 2011.
90. Eric Salzman, *New Music for Virtuosos*, New World Records, NW 209, 1977, 33 1/3 rpm, liner notes.
91. Benjamin Boretz, *The Music of Godfrey Winham*, Albany Records TROY1408, 2013, compact disc, liner notes.
92. George Perle, *Tribute to Bethany Beardslee, Soprano*, Anthology of Recorded Music NWCR724, 2007, compact disc, liner notes. Used by permission of Shirley Perle.
93. Richard Dyer, "Bethany Beardslee Triumphs," *Boston Globe*, April 14, 1978.
94. George Perle, "The Secret Programme of the Lyric Suite," *Musical Times* 118, no. 1614 (August 1977): 629–32.
95. Robert Croan, "Duo Dynamic at Frick," *Pittsburgh Post-Gazette*, December 15, 1981.
96. William C. Glackin, "A Spellbinding Singer," *Sacramento Bee*, March 3, 1982.
97. Croan, "Duo Dynamic at Frick."
98. Peter G. Davis, "Song-Bag Ladies," *New York*, January 9, 1984.
99. Bruce Duffie, "Pianist Richard Goode: A Conversation with Bruce Duffie," April 9, 1986, posted 2009, www.bruceduffie.com/goode.html.
100. Glackin, "A Spellbinding Singer."
101. Leighton Kerner, "The Cincinnati Kids," *Voice*, March 19, 1985.
102. John Rockwell, "Miss Beardslee Sings Brahms," *New York Times*, November 18, 1980.
103. Allen Hughes, "Concert: Miss Beardslee in Schoenberg 'Buch,'" *New York Times*, December 25, 1983.
104. Historic Piano Concerts, Inc., "Frederick Historic Piano Collection," http://www.frederickcollection.org/Graf1828.htm, accessed April 13, 2017.
105. Heuwell Tircuit, "A Sensitive Show of Chamber Music," *San Francisco Chronicle*, July 2, 1977.
106. Robert Commanday, "Schoenberg Work a High Point," *San Francisco Chronicle*, July 8, 1977.

107. Virgil Thomson to Robert Helps, December 6, 1987, Beardslee personal archive.
108. Gilbert R. Johns, "Beardslee's Voice Undaunted by Time," *Colorado Springs Gazette Telegraph*, October 17, 1988, Colorado Springs concert, program notes.
109. Tim Page, "A Soprano's Staying Power," *Newsday*, October 14, 1988.
110. Page, "A Soprano's Staying Power."
111. Steve Groark, "Beardslee Truly a Breed Apart," *Wisconsin State Journal*, April 2, 1990.
112. Translation from Robert Erich Wolf's liner notes to Arnold Schoenberg, *Pierrot Lunaire*, op. 21, and *The Book Of The Hanging Gardens*, op. 15, The Contemporary Chamber Ensemble, conducted by Arthur Weisberg, Elektra Nonesuch 9 79237-2, 1990, compact disc.
113. Paul Hertelendy, "Chamber Music Queen," *Oakland Tribune*, July 8, 1977.
114. Richard Dyer, "Farewell Not Goodbye for Beardslee," *Boston Globe*, April 14, 1985.
115. Daniel Webster, "Soprano Performs Schoenberg," *Philadelphia Inquirer*, May 5, 1990.
116. Richard Dyer, "Beardslee Bids a Joyful Farewell," *Boston Globe*, May 1, 1985.
117. Daniel Plante, "Tribute to Bethany Beardslee," May 20, 1997, Composers Guild program note. Used by permission of the author.

BIBLIOGRAPHY

Babbitt, Milton. Composer's note on *Philomel*. 1964. Courtesy AMP.
———. "Milton Babbitt on Electronic Music." YouTube video, 17:09. Posted by Eric Chasalow on January 29, 2011. https://www.youtube.com/ watch?v=UHNG9rexCsg. Recorded 1997. From the Video Archive of Electroacoustic Music, Eric Chasalow and Barbara Cassidy, curators.
Bahr, Ehrhard. *Weimar on the Pacific: German Exile in Los Angeles and the Crisis of Modernism*. Berkeley: University of California Press, 2007.
Batstone, Philip. Notes on *A Mother Goose Suite*. *Tribute to Soprano Bethany Beardslee*, Anthology of Recorded Music NWCR724, 2007, compact disc. Liner notes.
Bauerlein, Mark, and Ellen Grantham, eds. *National Endowment for the Arts: A History, 1965–2008*. Washington, DC: National Endowment for the Arts, 2009. Available online at https://www.arts.gov/sites/default/files/nea-history-1965-2008.pdf.
Bazzana, Kevin. *Wondrous Strange: The Life and Art of Glenn Gould*. New York: Oxford University Press, 2004.
Berger, Arthur. "Songs by Webern." *New York Herald Tribune*, March 16, 1952, 14.
———. "What Mozart Didn't Have: The Story of the Fromm Music Foundation." *High Fidelity*, 9, no. 2 (1959): 43.
Boretz, Benjamin. *The Music of Godfrey Winham*, Albany Records TROY1408, 2013, compact disc. Liner notes.
Boulez, Pierre. "Speaking, Playing, Singing." In *Orientations: Collected Writings*, edited by Jean-Jacques Nattiez, 330–35. Translated by Martin Cooper. Cambridge, MA: Harvard University Press, 1990.
Commanday, Robert. "Schoenberg Work a High Point." *San Francisco Chronicle*, July 8, 1977.
Craft, Robert, and Igor Stravinsky, *Dialogues*. Berkeley: University of California Press, 1982.
Croan, Robert. "Duo Dynamic at Frick." *Pittsburgh Post-Gazette*, December 15, 1981.

Davis, Peter G. "Song-Bag Ladies," *New York*, January 9, 1984.

Denby, David. "Ten Perfect Orchestral Recordings." *New Yorker*, May 1, 2012.

Dettmer, Roger. "The 12-Tone Boys at Fullerton Hall." *Chicago American*, November 29, 1956.

DeVoto, Mark. "Centenary of a Lesser-Known Scandal." *Boston Music Intelligencer*, March 27, 2013. http://www.classical-scene.com/2013/03/27/scandal/.

Duffie, Bruce. "Patron Paul Fromm: A Conversation with Bruce Duffie." April 9, 1986, posted 2009. www.bruceduffie.com/fromm.html.

———. "Pianist Richard Goode: A Conversation with Bruce Duffie." February 19, 1990, posted 2012. www.bruceduffie.com/goode.html.

Dyer, Richard. "Beardslee Bids a Joyful Farewell" *Boston Globe*, May 1, 1985.

———. "Bethany Beardslee Triumphs." *Boston Globe*, April 14, 1978.

———. "Farewell Not Goodbye for Beardslee." *Boston Globe*, April 14, 1985.

Flanagan, William. Review of *The Music of Arnold Schoenberg*, vol. 1. *HiFi/ Stereo Review*, April 1963.

Forbes, Elliot, Lewis Lockwood, Donald Martino, and Bernard Rands. "Faculty of Arts and Sciences—Memorial Minute—Earl Kim." *Harvard University Gazette Archives*, May 25, 2000.

Foss, Lukas. Program notes, Buffalo Philharmonic Orchestra, Sunday, November 15—Tuesday, Nov. 17, 1964. Kleinhans Music Hall, Buffalo, NY.

Fox, Christopher. "Air from Another Planet." *Guardian*, January 16, 2009. www.theguardian.com/music/2009/jan/17/classical-music-schoenberg.

Frankenstein, Alfred. Review of *The Music of Arnold Schoenberg*, vol. 1. *High Fidelity Magazine*, March 1963.

Gable, David. "Paul Fromm in American Musical Life." In *A Life for New Music: Selected Papers of Paul Fromm*, edited by David Gable and Christoph Wolff, 56. Cambridge, MA: Harvard University Press, 1988.

Glackin, William C. "A Spellbinding Singer." *Sacramento Bee*, March 3, 1982, B8.

Graham, Martha. *Blood Memory*. New York: Doubleday, 1991.

Groark, Steve. "Beardslee Truly a Breed Apart." *Wisconsin State Journal*, April 2, 1990.

Hamilton, David. "A Proper Attitude." *New Yorker*, May 20, 1974.

———. "A Song Team for Schoenberg and Schubert." *High Fidelity*, March 1976, 73.

Harrison, Jay S. "Stravinsky's 'Threni' Has Premiere at Town Hall." *New York Herald Tribune*, January 5, 1959, 11.

———. "Talk with Stravinsky: Composer Discusses His Music," *New York Herald Tribune*, December 21, 1952, D5.

Henahan, Donal J. "Another Martinon Success: *Lulu* Is Back in Town." *Chicago Daily News*, April 23, 1966.

———. "Music: Four Premieres." *New York Times*, November 15, 1972.

———. "Rudolf Serkin, 88, Concert Pianist, Dies." *New York Times*, May 10, 1991.

———. "The Ticking World of Lukas Foss." *Chicago Daily News*, September 27, 1966.

Henken, John. "About the Piece: *Le marteau sans maître*." LA PHIL.com. http://www.laphil.com/philpedia/music/le-marteau-sans-maitre-pierre-boulez, accessed April 13, 2017.

Hertelendy, Paul. "Chamber Music Queen." *Oakland Tribune*, July 8, 1977.

Hewett, Ivan. "Sir Peter Maxwell Davies Obituary." *Guardian*, March 14, 2016. https://www.theguardian.com/music/2016/mar/14/sir-peter-maxwell-davies-obituary.

Historic Piano Concerts, Inc. "Frederick Historic Piano Collection." http://www.frederickcollection.org/Graf1828.htm, accessed April 13, 2017.

Hollander, John. *Philomel*. Reprinted in Hollander, "Notes on the Text of *Philomel*." *Perspectives of New Music*, 6, no. 1 (Autumn–Winter 1967): 131–41.

Hughes, Allen. "Concert: Miss Beardslee in Schoenberg 'Buch.'" *New York Times*, December 25, 1983.

———. "Shapey's 'Incantations' in Debut at Finale of Composers Forum." *New York Times*, April 24, 1961.

———. "Singer, Pianist at Recital Hall." *New York Herald Tribune*, November 18, 1958.

Johns, Gilbert R. "Beardslee Voice Undaunted by Time." *Colorado Springs Gazette Telegraph*, October 17, 1988.

Kerner, Leighton. "The Cincinnati Kids." *Voice*, March 19, 1985.

Klein, Howard. "Miss Beardslee Sings 'Philomel.'" *New York Times*, February 22, 1964.

———. "Two Singers Share Unusual Niche." *New York Times*, June 24, 1962.

Kopelson, Robert G. "Jacques-Louis Monod and Chamber Ensemble at Sanders Last Night." *Harvard Crimson*, August 8, 1967. http://www.thecrimson.com/article/1967/8/8/jacques-louis-monod-and-chamber-ensemble-pevery/, accessed April 13, 2017.

Kozinn, Allan. "Guardian of the Schoenberg Flame." *New York Times*, March 10, 1985.

———. "Milton Babbitt, a Composer Who Gloried in Complexity, Dies at 94." *New York Times*, January 29, 2011.

Martin, John. "'Clytemnestra' an Epic Full-Evening Work by a Modern Master." *New York Times*, April 6, 1958.

Mitze, Clark. "Modern Music Thins Symphony Audience." *St. Louis Globe-Democrat*, April 18, 1966.

Newsweek. "A Composer's Singer." September 18, 1961.

Page, Tim. "A Soprano's Staying Power." *Newsday*, October 14, 1988.

Parmenter, Ross. "Concert Is Given at Canadian Fete." *New York Times*, July 10, 1956.

Perle, George. "The Secret Programme of the Lyric Suite." *Musical Times* 118, no. 1614 (August 1977): 629–32.

———. *Tribute to Bethany Beardslee, Soprano.* Anthology of Recorded Music NWCR724, 2007, compact disc. Liner notes.

Plante, Daniel. "Tribute to Bethany Beardslee." May 20, 1997. Composers Guild Concert program note.

Raymont, Henry. "Marking Time: Cultural Program Abroad Is Modified to Win Congressional Support." *New York Times*, September 15, 1963.

Rich, Alan. "Avant-Garde Work Is Performed and Explained: Pierre Boulez says 'Marteau Sans Maitre' Searches for Music's Link to Poetry." *New York Times*, May 25, 1963.

———. "The Boston's Composer." *New York Herald Tribune*, December 3, 1964.

———. "The Music Critic as Sex Symbol." *New York*, March 31, 1969, 57.

———. "The Soft Sad Sounds of Modulo Z." *New York*, August 8, 1968, 51.

Riegger, Wallingford. "The Music of Vivian Fine." *Bulletin of the American Composers Alliance* 8, no. 1 (1958): 2–6.

Rockwell, John. "Miss Beardslee Sings Brahms." *New York Times*, November 18, 1980.

Rorem, Ned. *But Yesterday Is Not Today: The American Art Song 1927–1972.* New World Records 80243, 1977, 33 1/3 rpm. Liner notes.

———. *Knowing When to Stop.* New York: Simon & Schuster, 1994.

Rosen, Charles. *Arnold Schoenberg.* Chicago: University of Chicago Press, 1996.

Rosenman, Leonard. "Notes from a Sub-culture." *Perspectives of New Music* 7, no. 1 (1968): 122–35.

Ross, Alex. "Bethany Beardslee-Winham." *New York Times*, May 29, 1993.

Salzman, Eric. "Bethany Beardslee Sings Schubert Work." *New York Times*, November 18, 1958.

———. "Miss Beardslee Philomel Indeed." *New York Herald Tribune*, February 22, 1964.

———. "Music: Three Distinguished Works; Babbitt, Kirchner and Carter Performed." *New York Times*, September 7, 1961.

———. *New Music for Virtuosos.* New World Records, NW 209, 1977, 33 1/3 rpm. Liner notes.

Sanson, Kenneth. "Phenomenal Soprano." *Chicago Today*, August 13, 1970.

Schoenberg, Arnold. *Arnold Schoenberg Letters.* Edited by Erwin Stein. Translated by Eithne Wilkins and Ernst Kaiser. London: Faber & Faber, 1964.

———. *Pierrot Lunaire*, op. 21, and *The Book Of The Hanging Gardens*, op. 15. The Contemporary Chamber Ensemble, conducted by Arthur Weisberg. Elektra Nonesuch 9 79237-2, 1990, compact disc. Liner notes.

————. *Style and Idea: Selected Writings of Arnold Schoenberg.* Edited by Leonard Stein. Translated by Leo Black. Berkeley: University of California Press, 1975.

————. *Verklärte Nacht and Pierrot Lunaire.* New York: Dover Publications, 1994.

Schonberg, Harold C. [signed HCS]. "Composers Forum Hears Modernists." *New York Times*, February 2, 1953.

————. [signed HCS]. "Concert Devoted to the Works of Webern Presented by New Music String Quartet." *New York Times*, December 29, 1952.

————. "Leinsdorf Leads Boston Symphony in 2-Work Concert." *New York Times*, December 3, 1964.

————. "Music: Rarities by Bethany Beardslee." *New York Times*, February 24, 1970.

Schuller, Gunther. *Gunther Schuller: A Life In Pursuit of Music and Beauty.* Rochester, NY: University of Rochester Press, 2011.

Sessions, Roger. "Schoenberg in the United States." *Tempo* 9 (1944): 8–17.

Smyth, David H. "Schoenberg and Dial Records: The Composer's Correspondence with Ross Russell." *Journal of the Arnold Schoenberg Institute* 12, no. 1 (June 1989): 68–90.

Spies, Claudio. "Igor Stravinsky's *Threni*, Conducting Details." Moldenhauer Archives, Rosaleen Moldenhauer Memorial, Library of Congress, Washington, DC. Posted 2000. http://hdl.loc.gov/loc.music/molden.2428152.bib.

Steinberg, Michael. "An Exciting Musical Note." *Saskatoon Star-Phoenix*, August 3, 1959.

Stravinsky, Igor, and Robert Craft. *Conversations with Igor Stravinsky.* London: Faber & Faber, 1958.

Taubman, Howard. "Modern Program Played at the Y.M.H.A." *New York Times*, April 14, 1953.

————. "Music: Twelve Tone; Works by Krenek and Ben Weber Offered." *New York Times*, April 14, 1953, 31.

Thomson, Virgil. "Program of Contemporary Music: Small Stuff But Pleasant." *New York Herald Tribune*, January 16, 1951.

Webster, Daniel. "Soprano Performs Schoenberg." *Philadelphia Inquirer*, May 5, 1990.

Winer, Linda. "A Night Rife with Gloom." *Chicago Tribune*, August 13, 1970.

Wise, Tad. "When the Turnau Opera Players Reigned in Woodstock." *Woodstock Times*, September 16, 2012.

Additional bibliographic note: The singers Barbara Winchester and Kay Dunlop have compiled *Vocal Chamber Music: A Performer's Guide*, second edition (New York: Routledge, 2008), which contains a comprehensive list of many pieces for voice and ensemble with all the source information needed. It is a useful and unique book, well worth owning for any professional singer.

INDEX

American soprano Bethany Beardslee rose to prominence in the postwar years when the modernist sensibilities of European artists and thinkers were flooding American shores and challenging classical music audiences. With her light lyric voice, her musical intuition, and her fearless dedication to new music, Beardslee became the go-to girl for twelve-tone music in New York City. She was the first American singer to build a repertoire performing the music of Arnold Schoenberg, Anton Webern, Alban Berg, Milton Babbitt, and Pierre Boulez, making a vibrant career singing difficult music.

I Sang the Unsingable is the autobiography of the acclaimed twentieth-century art-song soprano. In her memoir, Beardslee tells the story of how she made her way from inauspicious depression-era East Lansing to Carnegie Hall, and how her unique combination of musical gifts and training were alchemy for challenging mid-century music. This is Beardslee's own perspective on a formidable catalog of premieres, a forty-six-year career, and a deep and lifelong dedication to performing the work of the composers of our time.

Born in 1925 in Lansing, Michigan, Bethany Beardslee is an American soprano. She is noted for her collaborations with major twentieth-century composers.

Minna Zallman Proctor is a writer, critic, and translator. She is editor-in-chief of *The Literary Review* and the author of *Do You Hear What I Hear?* and *Landslide: True Stories*.

"This book is disarmingly candid, wise, and elegantly personal. A memoir of a great singer-musician of our time, someone who set the standard for astonishing performances of new music, it is engrossing, moving, and filled with brilliant observations about music, musicianship, and the power of new music. It offers a unique and revealing account of the art of performance and singing in the heyday of musical modernism during the second half of the twentieth century. Beardslee's advocacy of composers—from Babbitt and Berg to Schubert and Mozart—as well as of her unjustly neglected contemporaries is an inspiration."

—Leon Botstein, Bard College, and music director, the American Symphony Orchestra

"Bethany Beardslee is unique. Her fascinating memoir is an invaluable addition to the history of twentieth-century music."

—Ned Rorem, author and composer

"This elegant, candid memoir not only documents the life and work of a great singing artist but also gives revealing glimpses of a host of major cultural figures, from Igor Stravinsky and Martha Graham to Pierre Boulez and Milton Babbitt. Beardslee is herself a significant creative force: through her exacting devotion to composers' visions, she expanded the universe of musical possibility."
    —Alex Ross, music critic

"A thoroughly fascinating journey. One has the unique opportunity to navigate with Bethany through both her surprising educational experiences and her personal influences on her journey to become one of the premier performers and recording artists of contemporary classical music."
    —Lawrence Schoenberg, Belmont Music Publishers

"This book candidly reveals the thoughts and activities of a truly remarkable singer's life. Bethany Beardslee's extraordinary experiences in and among the vanguard of twentieth-century music in New York City and beyond are truly illuminating and inspiring, and have rightly earned her a prominent place in the history of music. Yet it is quite apparent that her motivation was never for stardom, but simply to prepare and sing everything that came her way with total commitment and love of the art of singing. Brava!"
    —Lucy Shelton, soprano